# Frommer's®

# London with Kids

## 2nd Edition

## by Rhonda Carrier

Here's what the critics say about Frommer's:

"Amazingly easy to use. Very portable, very complete."
—*Booklist*

"Detailed, accurate, and easy-to-read information for all price ranges."
—*Glamour Magazine*

"Hotel information is close to encyclopedic."
—*Des Moines Sunday Register*

"Frommer's Guides have a way of giving you a real feel for a place."
—*Knight Ridder Newspapers*

BICENTENNIAL
1807
WILEY
2007
BICENTENNIAL

Wiley Publishing, Inc.

## About the Author

**Rhonda Carrier** settled in London in the mid-1990s, after studying languages and literature at Cambridge and the Sorbonne in Paris. For many years she worked as a writer and editor for leading London guides and listings magazines, as well as publishing award-winning short fiction. She currently lives mainly in Manchester, where her husband, the writer Conrad Williams, lectures in creative writing.

Published by:

## Wiley Publishing, Inc.

111 River St.
Hoboken, NJ 07030-5774

ISBN: 978-0-470-16545-4

Editor: William Travis
Production Editor: Suzanna R. Thompson
Cartographer: Tim Lohnes
Photo Editor: Richard Fox
Anniversary Logo Design: Richard Pacifico

Production by Wiley Indianapolis Composition Services

Front cover photo: Young girl holding British flag on Westminster Bridge
Back cover photo: London Horse Guards

For information on our other products and services or to obtain technical support, please contact our Customer Care Department within the U.S. at 800/762-2974, outside the U.S. at 317/572-3993 or fax 317/572-4002.

Wiley also publishes its books in a variety of electronic formats. Some content that appears in print may not be available in electronic formats.

Manufactured in the United States of America

5   4   3   2   1

# Contents

# List of Maps

## Acknowledgments

A huge debt of love, gratitude, and admiration is due to Conrad, who has done the hardest work of bringing up the kids for the best part of 5 years, while somehow finding the energy to write wonderful novels by night. Extra special thanks also to Holly and Jarvis McGrath, for accompanying us on some of our more eccentric and far-flung odysseys during research for the first edition, and to Alan and Evan McGrath for being there.

I'd also like to express my fond gratitude to the following for their support, companionship, input, and feedback:

Fiona Dunscombe, Barbara Dordi, and all the other talented Lumineuse writers around France; Judy and Joe Reynolds; Rachel Furst, and Paul and Evie Smith; Adi and Charlotte Welch; Sophie, Stef, and Johanna Bureau; Kasha, Lola, and Rex Harmer; Nick, Kate, Charlie, and Bella Royle; Szilvi, Laurence, Leo, and Melody Davey; Tristan, Lisa, and Ava Rogers; Paula Grainger and Michael and Nate Marshall Smith; Ayesha, Viv, and Rohan Luthra; Esme Major and brood; Gemma Hirst; Liz Wyse; Pete Fiennes and Sarah Guy; Diana Tyler; and lastly Laura Smith for keeping the kids so well entertained during the deadline panic.

Dea Birkett (www.deabirkett.com) merits a special mention both for her "Kids in Museums" campaign and her online Travelling with Kids Forum. Forum members who have taken time to share their London feedback and tips are Sarah R., Adam Steath, Jen, Helen H., and Jo Glanvill. Frommer's readers have also made valuable feedback, including Daly Stoltzfus.

Thanks also to our parents David, Mary, Leo, and Grenville, and to my brother David and stepfather Tim, for support and faith over the years.

Additional thanks to my editor William Travis, and to the innumerable individuals at London attractions, hotels, restaurants, stores, entertainment venues, and PR companies who helped fill in the blanks.

—Rhonda Carrier

## An Invitation to the Reader

In researching this book, we discovered many wonderful places—hotels, restaurants, shops, and more. We're sure you'll find others. Please tell us about them, so we can share the information with your fellow travelers in upcoming editions. If you were disappointed with a recommendation, we'd love to know that, too. Please write to:

*Frommer's London with Kids,* 2nd Edition
Wiley Publishing, Inc. • 111 River St. • Hoboken, NJ 07030-5774

## An Additional Note

Please be advised that travel information is subject to change at any time—and this is especially true of prices. We therefore suggest that you write or call ahead for confirmation when making your travel plans. The authors, editors, and publisher cannot be held responsible for the experiences of readers while traveling. Your safety is important to us, however, so we encourage you to stay alert and be aware of your surroundings. Keep a close eye on cameras, purses, and wallets, all favorite targets of thieves and pickpockets.

## Frommer's Star Ratings, Icons & Abbreviations

Every hotel, restaurant, and attraction listing in this guide has been ranked for quality, value, service, amenities, and special features using a **star-rating system.** In country, state, and regional guides, we also rate towns and regions to help you narrow down your choices and budget your time accordingly. Hotels and restaurants are rated on a scale of zero (recommended) to three stars (exceptional). Attractions, shopping, nightlife, towns, and regions are rated according to the following scale: zero stars (recommended), one star (highly recommended), two stars (very highly recommended), and three stars (must-see).

In addition to the star-rating system, we also use **six feature icons** that point you to the great deals, in-the-know advice, and unique experiences that separate travelers from tourists. Throughout the book, look for:

| | |
|---|---|
| **Finds** | Special finds—those places only insiders know about |
| **Fun Fact** | Fun facts—details that make travelers more informed and their trips more fun |
| **Moments** | Special moments—those experiences that memories are made of |
| **Overrated** | Places or experiences not worth your time or money |
| **Tips** | Insider tips—great ways to save time and money |
| **Value** | Great values—where to get the best deals |

The following **abbreviations** are used for credit cards:

| | | | | | |
|---|---|---|---|---|---|
| AE | American Express | DISC | Discover | V | Visa |
| DC | Diners Club | MC | MasterCard | | |

## Frommers.com

Now that you have this guidebook to help you plan a great trip, visit our website at **www.frommers.com** for additional travel information on more than 3,600 destinations. We update features regularly to give you instant access to the most current trip-planning information available. At Frommers.com, you'll find scoops on the best airfares, lodging rates, and car rental bargains. You can even book your travel online through our reliable travel booking partners. Other popular features include:

- Online updates of our most popular guidebooks
- Vacation sweepstakes and contest giveaways
- Newsletters highlighting the hottest travel trends
- Online travel message boards with featured travel discussions

# How to Feel Like a London Family

London changes at lightning speed—a fact I've only fully appreciated since spending time away from it—and preparing this guide for a second edition has involved almost as much work as writing the original from scratch. That's not surprising given the city's place as a world leader in the spheres of fashion, art, music, food, architecture, politics, finance, and so much more, and it's also part of the reason why Britain's capital is one of the most exciting places on the globe, both to visit and to live in.

London's greatest selling points are its vast size and extraordinary diversity—more than 300 languages are spoken here, and by 2015 it is estimated that 40% of Londoners will be from ethnic minorities. Very few places on earth can rival this city's cultural depth and rich heritage—combined, they create a city that proves endlessly fascinating to both its inhabitants and visitors. Yet London inspires and maddens in equal measure. Ask Londoners how they feel about the city, and they will roll their eyes and unleash a litany of complaints about the traffic, the crowds, and the prices. These caveats prove doubly annoying when you have kids. In fact, many people up and leave the capital when they start a family. Their reasons are no doubt valid, but I would argue that London is actually one of the world's *greatest* cities for children.

My husband and I thought we knew London to its core, having regularly written and edited for local guides and listings publications. It had been part of our jobs to keep up, as best anyone can, with its changes, including the latest restaurant, shop, and hotel openings. But rediscovering London from a new point of view—that of our young sons—has been a revelation. I have been, quite literally, astounded by the range and variety of activities that are on offer here for kids of all ages. In fact, what you read between these pages is only a small sampler—the crème de la crème—of all there is to experience here as a parent or a child.

Perhaps the biggest revelation of all has been just how much fun you can have in this expensive city for free or for very little money. Sure, there are high-priced premium attractions, but for each of them you'll find a wealth of wonderful parks and urban farms, one-off museums and galleries with great free workshops, and neighborhood cafes welcoming hungry families on a budget, which brings me to my two main pieces of advice. The first is not to underestimate the power of the simple or everyday: When I first visited London on day trips with my intrepid grandmother Molly, riding the Tube truly awed me. How, I wondered, did anyone ever manage to navigate its tangle of colored lines? (Don't worry; it's actually a breeze.) Keep in mind that a simple bus ride on a classic red double-decker might be all it takes to set Junior's heart aflutter. The second is to accept the appeal of the tacky where youngsters are concerned: As a kid, I adored all the rampantly tourist stuff that now riles me, such as Madame Tussaud's.

Much of the skill of being a parent is about learning to stop being a control freak and to go with the flow. If that means occasional trips to a wax museum instead of an art museum, or burgers and fries in a loud themed restaurant over authentic Asian dishes in a Vietnamese canteen, so be it—there'll be other times to soak in art, and other dinners. Family holidays are about pleasing everyone, while recognizing that not everyone can be pleased at the same time. Luckily, London caters to all tastes, moods, and whims, so it's easy to get the balance just right.

## 1 Frommer's Favorite London Family Experiences

- **Seeing the Sights from the Top of a Double-Decker Bus:** Get an overview of some of London's top sights from one of its red public buses, and you'll score one of the city's best bargains. The iconic open-backed Routemaster has largely been phased out, but the newer buses are more spacious and comfortable, and bus travel has the advantage of giving you a feel for where places are in relation to one another, unlike the Tube. Best of all, kids under 16 now get free bus travel.

  One of the City's best routes is the **no. 15** between Paddington and the East End via Piccadilly Circus, Trafalgar Square, and Fleet Street. Attractions you will see include Selfridges department store, the National Gallery, The Savoy Hotel, St. Paul's Cathedral, the Monument, and the Tower of London. Traffic is the only downer when you travel by bus, but special lanes on many streets mean you never get snagged in the worst jams, and if you're not in a hurry you can sit back and let the sights, smells, and sounds wash over you. Bag a front seat on the top deck for prime views. See p. 57.

- **Kite-Flying on Parliament Hill:** The 98m (320-ft.) summit of Hampstead Heath, with its views of St. Paul's Cathedral and farther afield, is the city's top spot for flying kites; on windy weekends it's full of kids and parents flying one-liners. (For more ambitious stunts with fancier kites,

you're better off going down to the open area near the Lido.) See p. 143.

- **Going to the Dogs:** An afternoon or evening at **Walthamstow Stadium** is an East End ritual—you'll encounter genuine local characters as well as exciting greyhound racing. Continue the Cockney theme at **Manze's,** one of London's oldest traditional pie-and-mash shops (where you can also sample jellied eels), with its original tiled interior. See p. 260 and 140.

- **Munching the Morning Away at Borough Market:** Encourage kids' interest in real food by taking them on a snacking trip around this historic market under railroad arches, now a gourmet food market Thursday to Saturday. Around 70 stalls offer free tasting samples of delicious cheeses, breads, cakes, jams, and other goodies, many organic and all produced with love. Don't miss the candy at Burnt Sugar or the chorizo rolls at Spanish specialist Brindisa. See p. 233.

- **Tackling the Sights and Delights of Kensington:** There's no avoiding this neighborhood west of the center, with its trio of world-class and wonderfully child-friendly museums (the Victoria and Albert Museum, Natural History Museum, and Science Museum) and its green spaces—Kensington Gardens, containing the Diana Memorial Playground; and Hyde Park, where you can horseback ride, in-line skate, row on the winding Serpentine lake, and much, much more. You might do it justice in about a week. See chapters 6 and 8.

- **Talking to the Animals in Battersea Park:** If there was ever a zoo to win the hearts of kids, the **Battersea Park Children's Zoo** is it, with its Mouse House, Butterfly Garden, and farm area; its cafe with outdoor tables where you can listen to exotic birds sing as you eat; its wildlife-themed playground with toddlers' toys; and its wildlife gift shop. After touring the zoo, you can explore the rest of Battersea Park with its ducks and herons, boating lake, fountains, peace pagoda, playparks, toddlers' club, art gallery, and more. Nearby, Battersea Rise and Northcote Road make up a little haven of child-friendly eateries, including Crumpet and Le Bouchon Bordelais. See p. 189.
- **Enjoying a Traditional Afternoon Tea:** Most swank hotels in the city serve this highly civilized, very English ritual at premium prices (typically, upwards of £28/$56 a head). Smart dress is generally required for these venues. A relaxed alternative is Chelsea's Bluebird "gastrodome," where kids get their own "Tiny Tea" of baby bridge rolls, fairy cakes or jelly and ice cream, and blackcurrant tisane or lemon verbena. See p. 100 and p. 123.
- **Ambling by the River:** Inhale the salty tang of the tidal Thames on a walk along the cultural hotbed of the South Bank east from Westminster Bridge. As well as close encounters with bridges historic and modern, and fabulous views of St. Paul's and the Tower of London, you can break your walk at a stunning array of attractions, including the London Eye, the Tate Modern, and Shakespeare's Globe theater. You can also shop at the crafts outlets of Gabriel's Wharf or Oxo Tower, or "beachcomb" when the tide is low. Finish at Shad Thames, an atmospheric quarter of converted old spice warehouses. See p. 199.
- **Riding in a London Taxi:** This isn't a cheap way of getting around town, but even if you make public transport your mainstay, try at least one trip in a traditional black cab—though not at rush hour, when you'll notch up a heavy bill for the luxury of sitting in a queue of traffic. Once ensconced, you're more than likely to strike up a conversation with your "cabbie"— many like nothing better than the chance to share their worldviews with passengers. And before you get snooty, know that a study carried out in 2000 found that London taxi drivers' brains are larger than those of most of their peers, due to their having to remember up to 400 routes within a 9.5km (6-mile) radius of Charing Cross, as part of a competence test known as "The Knowledge." See p. 58.
- **Idling Away a Morning at Portobello Market:** Get browsing at London's most famous market, best known for its Saturday antiques stalls but also for its fruit and vegetables and—best of all—innovative fashion on Fridays. The street is also lined with vintage clothing stores, where you're guaranteed to find something original. Stop past the north end of the market, where it peters out into junk stalls, for an obligatory custard pastry at one of the Portuguese bakeries. See p. 233.

## 2 The Best Hotel Bets

London accommodations are never a bargain in comparison with their counterparts elsewhere, but the city's hoteliers and B&B proprietors have lived up to the

# Greater London Area

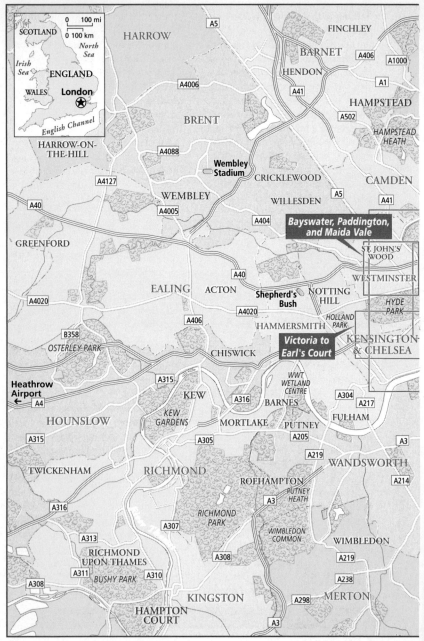

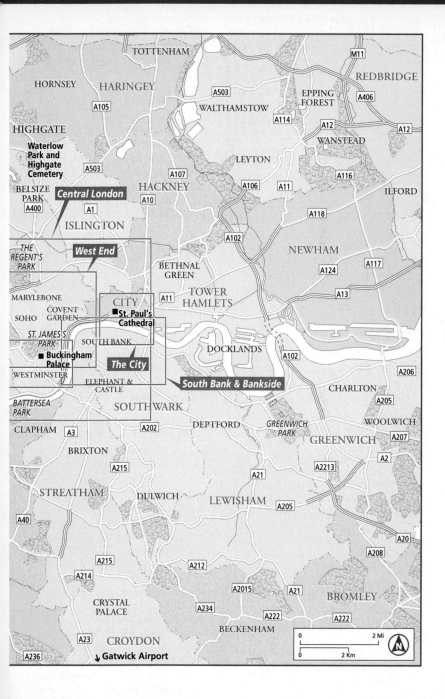

needs of visiting families over the past few years, and services and facilities for kids and their parents are improving all the time.

- **Most Family-Friendly:** Mayfair's **Athenaeum Apartments** 116 Piccadilly, W1; ☏ **020/7499-3464**) include a funky Family Apartment with mirrored Philippe Starck chairs, seats resembling giant computer keys, a kids' sleeping niche, and a games console that doubles as a coffee table. Like all the apartments here, it has a full kitchen and washing machine, and highchairs, potties, and strollers can be supplied free of charge. All junior guests, including those at the adjacent Athenaeum Hotel, get complimentary movies, gadgets, toiletries, and milk and cookies, and there are kids' menus throughout the hotel and on room service. See p. 67.

  The friendly but unobtrusive staff at **22 Jermyn Street** (22 Jermyn St., SW1; ☏ **020/7734-2353**), a family-run town house steps from Piccadilly Circus and St. James's Park, have thought of everything a parent might need, it seems. But if you have additional requirements, they'll go out of their way to procure them for you. Amenities include free kids' movies delivered to your room or suite with complimentary popcorn; wipe-clean drawing books, musical cassettes with singalong books; the owner's own lively newsletter highlighting kid-friendly sights and restaurants; and cozy bathrobes for all ages. Staff members will even babysit while you use the trendy health club and pool nearby, or try out the owner's eating recommendations. See p. 70.

- **Best Neighborhood Option: Europa House** (79a Randolph Ave., W9; ☏ **020/7724-5924**) is a collection of spacious serviced apartments in a safe residential area with wide, tree-lined

avenues leading down to the picturesque canals of Little Venice, where a barge hosts puppet shows and companies run narrow-boat trips to London Zoo. You'll find an array of family-friendly delis, cafes, and pubs; an organic grocer; and a small 24-hour supermarket nearby, yet the center of London is just a 15-minute bus ride away. Best of all is the 1.4-hectare (3½-acre) enclosed garden to which the apartments have access, with a playground where little ones can make friends with local kids. Inside, the apartments are stylish but practically furnished. See p. 83.

North of the center, **La Gaffe** (107–111 Heath St., NW3; ☏ **020/7435-8965**) is an Italian restaurant and guesthouse in an 18th-century shepherd's house in villagey Hampstead. The charming shops, teahouses, restaurants, and historic pubs of Hampstead High Street and Flask Walk are a few minutes' walk away, as are the wild spaces of Hampstead Heath, full of local families flying kites, swimming in the Lido, and generally running amok. See p. 97.

- **Best Views:** Deluxe rooms and suites on the river side of the **Four Seasons Canary Wharf** (46 Westferry Circus, E14; ☏ **020/7510-1999**), east of the center in Docklands, overlook a dramatic sweeping bend of the Thames and have views as far back as the London Eye. Order from the superior kids' room service menu, and then sit in your window and watch boats and ferries chug by. In the morning, swim in the adjoining infinity-edge pool, which seems to merge with the river outside.

  History doesn't come much more in your face than at the **Grange City** (8–14 Cooper's Row, EC3; ☏ **020/7863-3700**), where some rooms look out over the Tower of London and Tower Bridge, which are virtually next door. There's even a section of the old London wall running alongside the hotel's large piazza, where kids can expend some energy while you enjoy a drink. Family rooms feature two double beds and a small sitting area. See p. 92.

- **When Hipness Is Important:** *The* glam opening of 2007, the **Haymarket Hotel** (1 Suffolk Place, SW1; ℂ **020/7470-4000**) makes no concessions to minimalism with its contemporary English luxe decor. Accommodations include a couple of stunning one- and two-bedroom suites, plus a four-story town house with both a private entrance and access via the hotel. Kids get unrestricted use of the pool, which has its own bar and sound system, and there's a fashionable North Italian restaurant where the chef will adapt dishes for kids. See p. 77.

  **High Road House** (162–166 Chiswick High Rd., W4; ℂ **020/8742-1717**), a western outpost of the fashionable Soho House members' club, turns its club room with its squidgy sofas and low-level tables into a family playroom between 11am and 4pm, with games, toys, table football, a pool table, and a large screen showing cartoons, in addition to full waiter service (there are kids' menus throughout the building, including as part of room service). Guest rooms fall into two categories: Playpens and the Playroom, with one Playpen kitted out to be baby-friendly. Mainly white, with lots of wood, they feel a little like upmarket beach cabins, and have bath products from the group's trendy Cowshed range. See p. 85.

- **When Price Is No Object:** The **Mandarin Oriental** (66 Knightsbridge, SW1; ℂ **020/7235-2000**) has one of the world's best spas, as well as a Michelin-starred restaurant,

but junior guests aren't overlooked: They get a storybook about a monkey who helps out at the Mandarin, an album to record their stay, teddies, mini-bathrobes, toiletries, and little umbrellas. The interconnecting family rooms are enormous, and there's great kids' room service. See p. 79.

  **Brown's** (Albemarle St., W1; ℂ **020/7493-6020**) is a London classic combining traditional charm with beautiful contemporary decor. Service is second to none, and that includes a warm welcome extended to even the youngest guests, who get an age-specific toy (perhaps a personalized copy of *The Jungle Book,* which was written here), funky kids' bed linen, a teddy bear, bathrobes and slippers, bath ducks, an excellent room service menu, and even a "kids' menu" of facials, foot and hand treatments, or a back rub, all in the chic spa. The ongoing "Family Affair" package gives you a good saving on interconnecting deluxe rooms, which are vast. See p. 70.

- **When Price Is Your Main Object:** The family-run **Crescent** (49–50 Cartwright Gardens, WC1; ℂ **020/7387-1515**) is virtually unique in its moderate price range in that it offers baby-listening, highchairs, a guest lounge, and access to a garden square and four tennis courts. It's the best central option for those keeping an eye on their pennies. See p. 74.

  The **Citadines** "Apart'Hotel" (18/21 Northumberland Ave., WC2; ℂ **0800/376-3898**) just steps away from Trafalgar Square offers exceptional value for its location and facilities. As with other members of the chain, it allows you to choose between hotel services (including a breakfast room, babysitting, and a launderette) or self-cater, since the flats all have full kitchens. One-bedroom apartments sleep up to four, two-bedroom duplex apartments sleep up to six. See p. 78.

- **Best Pool:** It's a close call between the 20m (65-ft.) Thameside infinity-edge pool at **Four Seasons Canary Wharf** (p. 96), open to kids for 2 hours each morning; and the calm blue 18m (59-ft.) basement pool at **One Aldwych** (1 Aldwych, WC2; ✆ 020/7300-1000), where children are welcome all day and underwater classical music is played. See p. 75.

- **Best Hotel Restaurant for Kids:** The **Marriott West India Quay** (22 Hertsmere Rd., E14; ✆ 020/7093-1000), may be primarily a business hotel, at least during the week, but its Curve seafood restaurant has a surprisingly noncorporate feel—especially on sunny days when its French windows are thrown open onto the wharf and tables are set up outside. A charming waitstaff and a bank of smiling chefs happily show kids what they're doing behind their semi-open counter. Children get crayons and coloring books to occupy them as they wait for well-cooked, high-quality kids' dishes, but don't be surprised if they're tempted by what Mom and Dad are having—perhaps a whole fish from nearby Billingsgate Market. See p. 138.

- **Tops for Teens:** The flexible arrangements at **base2stay** (25 Courtfield Gardens, SW5; ✆ 020/7244-2255) make it particularly ideal for a family with older kids, who might, for instance, book themselves a standard double for Mom and Dad and a room with two bunk beds for the teens. There are also superior doubles that can fit up to three guests on an additional sofa/chairbed, and deluxe doubles that can fit up to four—you can pick and mix any of the above to form a two- or three-room unit to suit your needs All units have a mini-kitchen with microwave and fridge, allowing a degree of self-catering. See p. 82.

- **Tops for Toddlers:** The **Athenaeum Apartments** (p. 67) can't be beat for their amenities for babies and toddlers, including baby movies, toy boxes, highchairs, potties, strollers, and more.

## 3 The Best Dining Bets

British food, long a joke among visitors, has come of age over the last 15 years or so, and London is now one of the world's gastronomic capitals. Though people don't tend to expect much of the food in a restaurant that sets out its stall as a family-friendly venue, that, too, has changed, and there is now a host of places serving wonderful cuisine that keeps both you and the kids happy.

- **Best Family Dining: The Wallace** (Manchester Sq., W1; ✆ 020/7563-9505), a newcomer in the glass-roofed courtyard spot of the Wallace Collection, is the kind of place where there's something for everyone, and at fair prices given the quality and setting. Its vast menu of seasonal French dishes, served from breakfast through afternoon tea, plus at dinner on Fridays and Saturdays, includes excellent kids' main courses such as steamed lemon sole with fresh vegetables, and organic beef burger with Provençal tomato and olive oil crushed potatoes. Other kid-pleasers are pancakes with sugar, *tartines* (open sandwiches), *piperade* (scrambled egg) with goats' cheese, and Parisian-style afternoon teas of croque-monsieur, finger sandwiches, and pastries. See p. 109.

  **Carluccio's Caffè** (8 Market Place, W1; ✆ 020/7636-2228), and more than 20 other venues) is a bustling, great-value all-day Italian eatery with a bargain three-course kids' menu featuring homemade *grissini* (bread-sticks), breaded chicken breast with rosemary potatoes or pasta with a choice of sauces, real ice cream, and more. In summer, don't miss the fresh lemonade; in winter, warm up with a *cioccolata fiorentine*—a Florentine-style hot chocolate served in an espresso cup. See p. 109.

- **Most Kid-Friendly Service: Crumpet** (66 Northcote Rd., SW11; © 020/7924-1117) loves kids so much, it gives them a rear play area with a Wendy house and toys, and a large kids' menu (including home-cooked organic baby food, and "picnic teas"). Parents, meanwhile, benefit from a stroller park and the chance to buy little essentials such as a "messy pack" with a disposable bib and wipes, or diapers. Staff couldn't be friendlier or more patient with kids. This modern tearoom specializes in "proper tea," made with tea leaves and served with scones with jam and clotted cream, but you can also come for breakfast, cakes, or all-day soups, sandwiches, salads, and so on. See p. 133.
- **Best Kids' Menu:** Award-winning canteen-style Indian **Imli** (167–9 Wardour St., W1; © 020/7287-4243) provides a wonderful menu of gentle, lightly spiced kids' dishes free on weekends (noon–5pm), but it's a great value the rest of the time, too. They choose from starters of banana *dosa* (south Indian pancake) with chutney, *sev puri* (potato-filled wheat crisps with yogurt-date chutney and vermicelli), and *papdi chaat* (whole wheat crisps and bean sprouts with vermicelli and mint chutney), then mains of chicken in a smoked tomato fenugreek sauce with rice, seasonal vegetables in a cumin sauce with *pav* bread, or grilled chicken breast with cumin and turmeric mash. The feast is rounded off by chocolate and orange zest ice cream, fig and ginger ice cream, or cardamom rice pudding. See p. 116.

Otherwise, French restaurants **Le Cercle** (1 Wilbraham Place, SW1; © 020/7901-9999) and **Roussillon** (16 St Barnabas St., SW1; © 020/7730-5550) both offer tasting menus for budding gastronomes. See p. 120 and p. 122.

- **Best Neighborhood Hangout: Sam's Brasserie** (11 Barley Mow Passage, W4; © 020/8987-0555) in Chiswick is the kind of place every parent wishes was local to them. An all-day neighborhood brasserie and bar, it serves daily brunch from 9am, snacks, drinks, lunch, and dinner. Families come in force at weekends, when there are toys put out for kids, plus free face-painting on some Saturday mornings. The head chef has two young sons and knows how to make healthy but interesting food for kids, including shepherd's pie with broccoli and homemade fish fingers with pea mash, and at Sunday lunch half-portions of the roasts. See p. 130.
- **Best Outdoor Eating:** You get a real taste of the great outdoors at **Frizzante@CityFarm** (1A Goldsmith's Row, E2; © 020/7739-2266)—it's in the middle of a farmyard, complete with clucking chickens and a garden with a kids' play area. The homemade Italian cuisine includes all-day breakfast with eggs from those same chickens, great pizzas and pasta dishes, and superb cakes and puddings. See p. 135.
- **Best Park Cafe:** Along with a striking grass-roofed, glass-fronted building, the lovely views of the surrounding royal park and palaces from its decked terrace make **Inn the Park** (St. James's Park, SW1; © 020/7451-9999) very special. It offers

diners the choice of upscale cafe fare, including children's lunch sets, or seasonal British cuisine—or you can pre-order a wonderful picnic to take into the park itself. See p. 106.

- **Best Museum or Gallery Cafe:** The **National Dining Rooms & Bakery** (Trafalgar Sq., WC2; ✆ 020/7747-2525) in the National Gallery is open from breakfast through afternoon tea, for everything from coffee and pastries to three-course lunches; midweek, it serves early/pre-theater dinners. Foodie parents won't be disappointed, but neither will kids in search of familiar comfort food, from boiled eggs with toast "soldiers" to macaroni cheese. The bakery has lighter fare: breads, pies, tarts, cookies, pastries, soups, salads, "savory pots" (pâtés and the like) with toast, ice creams, fruit juices, and smoothies. See p. 116.

- **Best View: Babylon at The Roof Gardens** (99 Kensington High St., W8; ✆ 020/7368-3993) has one of London's most sensational locations— a lush rooftop garden with views of west and south London, with resident flamingos and ducks, a fishpond, and tropical trees and plants. The ambitious Modern European food is best sampled at Sunday lunch, when a magician does the rounds. The Young Diners' menu changes all the time but might feature roast tomato soup with chive cream, cheddar cheese soufflé, and sea bass with creamy mash. Summer sees alfresco barbecues and a shellfish bar. See p. 117.

- **Best Breakfast: Leon** (136 Brompton Rd., SW3; ✆ 020/7589-7330), one of a small chain of Mediterranean/North African cafes and takeaways, is especially useful at breakfast, offering everything from organic toast with Marmite, bacon sandwiches, or organic porridge with honey, seeds, or homemade blackcurrant compote, to full English breakfasts. Put an extra spring in your step with a blackcurrant "power smoothie" or a carrot, orange, and ginger juice. See p. 121.

- **Best Brunch: The Blue Elephant** (3–6 Fulham Broadway, SW6; ✆ 020/7385-6595) wows kids with its junglesque interior of trees, ponds, and waterfalls studded with statues and baroque ornaments; its imaginative Thai fare; and most of all its Sunday buffet brunches with displays of exotic fruit carved into spectacular shapes; as well as free face-painting and sugar-spinning demos. See p. 125.

- **Best Fish and Chips:** Trendy renovation work hasn't put off the East End taxi drivers who come to **Fish Central** (149–52 Central St., EC1; ✆ 020/7253-4970), but junior diners are made welcome by the cheery staff, kids' portions, and patio for fine weather. Little extras that single this place out from your average "chippy" include homemade bread, fresh veggies, and wonderful desserts, but you're best off sticking to the spanking-fresh battered cod or haddock with lip-smacking chips and mushy peas. See p. 140.

- **Best Pizza:** Families return again and again to **Italian Graffiti** (163–5 Wardour St., W1; ✆ 020/7439-4668) for its superb (and enormous) crisp-based pizzas cooked in a wood-fired oven. Adding to the ambience of this cozy family-run venue are its open fireplaces, its large windows from which you can observe the bustle of Soho, and the big-hearted staff, who might even whisk your kid away to show them how to make pizza. See p. 114.

- **Best Burgers:** Stealing the thunder of Ed's Easy Diner, the **Gourmet Burger Kitchen** mini-chain (Condor House, EC4; ✆ 020/7248-9199; and nearly

20 branches) consulted New Zealand celeb chef Peter Gordon when developing its award-winning, good-value burgers. These run the gamut from the classic to the exotic ("the Jamaican," with mango and ginger sauce; or "the Kiwiburger," with beet root, eggs, pineapple, cheese, and relish). Junior incarnations are available, and there are great fries and heavenly shakes. See p. 137.

- **Best Sausages: S&M Café** (268 Portobello Rd.; ℭ **020/8968-8898;** two other venues) serves sausage and mash (the "S&M" that make up its name) in a variety of guises, traditional or otherwise, including pork, lime, and sweet chile, and mushroom and tarragon. Lashings of gravy and creamy potatoes complete the picture. Stodgy, old-school puddings are available if you have room to spare. See p. 128.

- **Best Vegetarian Restaurant:** The award-winning **World Food Café** (14 Neal's Yard, WC2; ℭ **020/7379-0298**) serves everything from veggie or vegan Mexican platters and Middle Eastern *meze* to Indian thalis and West African stews in a lovely, light-filled space, against a world-music soundtrack. The welcome is friendly, the food colorful and appealing to junior palates—gorgeous desserts include mango kulfi ice cream with fruit. Buy the cookbook to relive the experience when you get home. See p. 113.

- **Best Fast Food: Hummus Bros** (88 Wardour St., W1; ℭ **020/7734-1311**) serves healthy fast food without additives or preservatives (with leftovers donated to charity). The basic ingredient is Middle Eastern/Greek chickpea-based spread hummus, freshly made and served with warm pita bread. Add hot or cold toppings from hard-boiled eggs, guacamole, or fava beans to chunky beef, and you have the perfect, nutritiously sound light lunch or dinner. There are also salads, soups, sides such as tabbouleh or barbecued aubergine, gorgeous desserts, and drinks for all seasons. See p. 115.

- **Best Asian Food: Tamarind** (20 Queen St., W1; ℭ **020/7629-3561**) serves Michelin-starred northwest Indian Moghul cuisine, including a special kids' menu on Sunday lunchtimes (free to under-10s accompanied by two or more adults). This three-course feast of exotic flavors includes pan-fried potato cakes with split lentils, ginger, toasted cumin and spinach stuffing, and tandoori-grilled chicken in a mild creamed tomato and honey sauce. Among standout adult dishes are lamb cutlets marinated with raw paw-paw, garlic, paprika, and peppercorns. See p. 103.

- **Best Ice Cream:** The London outpost of an award-winning family firm of Kent ice-cream makers, **Morelli's Gelato** (Harrods, SW1; ℭ **020/7893-8959**) churns out wonderful Italian ice cream in an extraordinary range of flavors, from traditional favorites to inventions such as French aniseed, plum cake, and even, in the festive season, Christmas pudding! See p. 122.

# 2

# Planning a Family Trip to London

Planning a family trip anywhere is a fine art. Overplan, and your vacation can start to resemble a military expedition—or worse, a school outing. Underplan, and you miss out on some great experiences because you're forced to make last-minute decisions without the full facts at your disposal. Tread a fine line and—most importantly—*get kids involved* in the upcoming adventure. Talk about what you'd all like to see and do, taking everyone's wishes and needs into account rather than making assumptions. Remember to maintain enough flexibility to allow room for the *unplanned*.

This chapter guides you through the practical quagmire, and gives you the information you'll need to make your trip as stress-free and easy as possible.

## 1 Visitor Information

The **British Tourist Board** has a walk-in information center and a couple of smaller offices in London (p. 44), an excellent website (see "Helpful Websites," below), and offices around the world. (See www.visitbritain.org for the location nearest you.)

For details of **magazine listings,** see p. 61. The best-known, *Time Out,* also publishes some of its information online at www.timeout.com/london. The *Evening Standard*'s website, www.thisislondon.co.uk, lists film, music, theater art, restaurant, and pub choices, plus ticket offers and promotions. For information on theater programs and tickets, see p. 247.

**HELPFUL WEBSITES** The most useful general website for visitor information in Britain is the official Tourist Board site, **www.visitbritain.com**, which lists accommodations, attractions, events, and transport options around the country. It also has "travel tools" such as a route planner, a currency converter, and a brochure-ordering facility. Its little sister, containing

more specific information about the city (customized according to where you are from), is **www.visitlondon.com**. Amazingly comprehensive, this has events listings, ticket-booking for shows, concerts, and hundreds of other events; hotel and B&B reservations (with a best-price guarantee); and even airline-ticket and package booking. Its 24-hour TV channel, **London TV** (SKY channel 244, or viewable on the website), showcases current highlights. Look out for its special offers, which may include 10% off the **London Pass** (p. 142).

The Tourist Board has its own kids' site, **http://kids.visitlondon.com**, with listings for young visitors and Londoners alike. From the main website, it's also possible to click through to a "Young London" section, for teens, students, and young adults. The Mayor's office, meanwhile, has information for kids and teens at **www.london.gov.uk/young-london**.

Another dedicated kids' site well worth a browse is **www.show.me.uk**, the offspring of the wonderful **www.24hour museum.org.uk**. "Show Me" lists thousands of U.K. museums and galleries (including information on their child-friendliness) but also clicks through to a London miniguide with tips from resident kids, news of the latest attractions, and related online games to play before or after your visit.

The former *Guardian* newspaper's kids' travel specialist has her own website, **www.deabirkett.com**, with a handy family travel forum for exchanging tips and views. You'll also find information about her Kids in Museums campaign to find the U.K.'s most family-friendly museum (an annual award). See also **www.takethe family.com**, a very professional family vacation guide with a London section that includes a hotel-booking facility, plus a "Talk the Family" info-swapping forum including online debates by Dea Birkett.

The very good **www.londonfreelist. com** has a kids' page with no-cost/low-cost events and activities; while **www. londonfamilies.co.uk**, **www.london treasures.com**, and **www.fun4families. org.uk** have suggestions for activities and outings. (The latter also has handy online beginner's guides to visiting art galleries, the theater, and so on.)

More general kids' sites include, **www. familiesonline.co.uk**, **www.childfriendly. net** (with handy user reviews), **www.arts andkids.org.uk**, and **www.kidzango. com**. Also check out **www.family-travel. co.uk**, a highly rated site with travel advice, news, a notice board, and subscription-based destination reports; **www.babygoes2.com**, with advice, info, tips, location reports and features, shopping resources, and a guide to recommended-by-parents villas and hotels worldwide, with or without childcare; **www.mumsnet.com**, with features, discussions, product reviews, weekend break recommendations, and a facility whereby you can meet other moms in your area; **www.all4kidsuk.com**, a family directory and parent resource site with area-based guides for everything from hotels to toddlers' music classes; and **www.young travellersclub.co.uk**.

For help finding your way around, see **www.streetmap.co.uk**; key in the street name, telephone area code, or postal code of the place for which you are looking, and a map of the area with the location circled will appear. Another useful tool is **www.streetsensation.co.uk**, which allows you to "explore" some of the main streets in zone 1, such as Marylebone High Street and Carnaby Street, through scroll-along photographs of their restaurants, pubs, and shops, backed up by listings information. It's not always 100% up-to-date, though, so do check if you're making a special trip.

For information on getting from the airports to central London, go to **www. baa.com**, which also has a guide and terminal maps for Heathrow, Gatwick, and Stansted airports, including flight arrival times, duty-free shops, and airport restaurant locations. For local transport within London, see **www.tfl.gov.uk**.

## 2 Entry Requirements & Customs

### ENTRY REQUIREMENTS

Citizens of the United States, Canada, Australia, New Zealand, and South Africa require passports to enter the United Kingdom, but do not require visas. Irish citizens and citizens of European Union countries need only identity cards. The maximum stay for non–European Union visitors is 6 months. Some Customs officials request proof that you have the means to leave the country (usually a round-trip ticket) and means of support while you're in Britain. (Someone in the U.K. will have to vouch that they are supporting you, or you may be asked to show documents that indicate that you have an income.) If you plan to fly on from the United Kingdom to a country that requires a visa, it's wise to secure the visa before you leave home.

Because of child custody and abduction concerns, applying for children's passports usually requires plenty of documentation. In some cases, the consent of both parents or legal guardians and an in-person appearance by the child(ren) are required during the application process. Consult these websites for complete details: http://travel.state.gov in the U.S., www.ppt.gc.ca in Canada, www.passports.gov.au in Australia, and www.passports.govt.nz in New Zealand.

## CUSTOMS
### WHAT YOU CAN BRING INTO LONDON

**For Non-E.U. Nationals 18 Plus**  You can bring in, duty-free, 200 cigarettes, 100 cigarillos, 50 cigars, or 250 grams of smoking tobacco. The amount allowed for each of these goods is doubled if you live outside Europe.

You can also bring in 2 liters of wine and either 1 liter of alcohol over 22 proof or 2 liters of wine under 22 proof. In addition, you can bring in 60cc (2 oz.) of perfume, a quarter liter (250ml) of eau de toilette, 500 grams (1 lb.) of coffee, 200 grams (½ lb.) of tea, and goods totaling £145 ($290). Customs officials tend to be lenient about general merchandise, realizing the limits are unrealistically low.

You can't bring your pet straight to England. Six months' quarantine is required before it can be allowed in. An illegally imported animal may be destroyed.

**For E.U. Citizens**  Visitors from fellow European Union countries can bring into Britain any amount of goods as long as the goods are intended for their personal use—not for resale.

Pets can now travel between the U.K. and other E.U. countries without quarantine, provided they adhere to certain conditions—see www.defra.gov.uk.

### WHAT YOU CAN TAKE HOME

**For U.S. Citizens**  Returning **U.S. citizens** who have been away for at least 48 hours are allowed to bring back, once every 30 days, $800 worth of merchandise duty-free. You'll pay a flat rate of duty on the next $1,000 worth of purchases. Any dollar amount beyond that is subject to duties at whatever rates apply. On mailed gifts, the duty-free limit is $200. Keep your receipts or purchases accessible to expedite the declaration process. ***Note:*** If you owe duty, you are required to pay on your arrival in the United States—either by cash, personal check, government or traveler's check, or money order (and, in some locations, a Visa or MasterCard).

To avoid paying duty on foreign-made personal items you owned before your trip, bring along a bill of sale, insurance policy, jeweler's appraisal, or receipts of purchase. Or register items that can be readily identified by a permanently affixed serial number or marking—think laptop computers, cameras, and CD players—with Customs before you leave. Take the items to the nearest Customs office or register them with Customs at the airport from which you're departing. You'll receive, at no cost, a Certificate of Registration, which allows duty-free entry for the life of the item.

With some exceptions, you cannot bring fresh fruits and vegetables into the United States. For specifics on what you can bring back, download the invaluable free pamphlet *Know Before You Go* online at **www.cbp.gov** (click on "Travel").

**For Canadian Citizens**  For a clear summary of **Canadian** rules, download the booklet *I Declare* from www.cbsa-asfc.gc.ca. Canada allows its citizens a C$750 exemption after an absence of 7 days, and you're allowed to bring back duty-free one carton of cigarettes, 1 can of tobacco, 40 imperial ounces of liquor, and 50 cigars. In addition, you're allowed to mail gifts to Canada valued at less than C$60 a day, provided they're unsolicited and don't contain alcohol or tobacco (write on the package "Unsolicited gift, under $60 value"). All valuables should be declared on the Y-38 form before departure from Canada, including serial numbers of valuables you already own, such as expensive foreign cameras.

**For Australian Citizens**    The duty-free allowance in **Australia** is A$900 or, for those under 18, A$450. Citizens can bring in 250 cigarettes or 250 grams of loose tobacco, and 2.25 liters of alcohol. If you're returning with valuables you already own, such as foreign-made cameras, you should file form B263. A helpful brochure available, *Know Before You Go*, is available on www.customs.gov.au.

**For New Zealand Citizens**    The duty-free allowance for **New Zealand** is NZ$700. Citizens over 17 can bring in 200 cigarettes, 50 cigars, or 250 grams of tobacco (or a mixture of all three if their combined weight doesn't exceed 250 grams); plus 4.5 liters of wine and beer, or 1.125 liters of liquor. New Zealand currency does not carry import or export restrictions. Fill out a Certificate of Export, listing the valuables you are taking out of the country; that way, you can bring them back without paying duty. For more info, see www.customs.govt.nz.

## 3 Money

### POUNDS & PENCE

Britain hasn't adopted the euro and is still using the pound (£), made up of 100 pence (written "p"). There are £1 and £2 coins, as well as coins of 50p, 20p, 10p, 5p, 2p, and 1p. Banknotes come in denominations of £5, £10, £20, and £50.

As a general guideline, the price conversions in this book have been computed at the rate of £1 = $2. Bear in mind, however, that exchange rates fluctuate daily.

### ATMs

ATMs are found all over London, usually outside banks but also in some larger stores. You'll usually get a better exchange rate using an ATM (currency exchange booths take a huge commission or give an unfavorable rate, or both), but your bank may charge a fee for using a foreign ATM. You may also need a different PIN to use at overseas ATMs; check in advance with your bank, and make sure you know your daily withdrawal limit.

The most popular ATM networks are **Cirrus/MasterCard/Maestro** (www.master card.com) and **VISA** (http://visa.com); check the back of your ATM card to see which your bank belongs to.

### TRAVELER'S CHECKS

Traveler's checks are becoming a thing of the past now that most cities and towns have 24-hour ATMs. But if you prefer the tried-and-true and don't mind showing an ID every time you cash a check, you can order checks at Amex (www. americanexpress.com) or Thomas Cook (www.thomascook.com) offices or major banks. Note that exchange rates are more favorable at your destination, and that it's helpful to exchange at least some money before going abroad in case you can't easily get to a bank (which gives better exchange rates than a hotel or shop). When you do change checks, note the rates and ask about commission fees; it can sometimes pay to shop around.

Keep a record of your traveler's checks' serial numbers separate from the checks so you're ensured a refund in an emergency.

### CREDIT CARDS

Most London stores and restaurants take credit cards, but sometimes there is a lower spending limit of £10 ($20) before you can use them. Credit cards are a safe

| What Things Cost in London | UK£ | US$ | Euro€ |
|---|---|---|---|
| Taxi Heathrow Airport—center | 40.00–70.00 | 80.00–140.00 | 58.00–100.00 |
| Heathrow Express train to center, adult | 14.50 | 28.00 | 20.10 |
| Heathrow Express to center, child 5 to 15 | 7.20 | 14.80 | 10.65 |
| Tube Heathrow—center, adult | 4.00 | 8.00 | 5.75 |
| Tube Heathrow—center, child 11 to 16 * | 2.00 | 4.00 | 2.85 |
| Tube Heathrow—center, child under-11 | free | free | free |
| Single Tube ride, adult (Zone 1) | 4.00 | 8.00 | 5.75 |
| Single Tube ride, child 11 to 16 (Zone 1) | 2.00 | 4.00 | 2.85 |
| Single Tube ride, child under-11 (Zone 1) | free | free | free |
| Single bus ride, adult | 2.00 | 4.00 | 2.85 |
| Single bus ride, child under 16 | free | free | free |
| West End movie ticket, adult | 9.00–12.50 | 18.00–25.00 | 13.00–18.00 |
| West End movie ticket, child | 9.00 | 18.00 | 13.00 |
| Local daytime phone call (per minute) | 0.02 | 0.04 | 0.03 |
| Margherita pizza at Pizza Express | 5.45 | 10.90 | 7.85 |
| 500ml still water at Pizza Express | 1.80 | 3.60 | 2.60 |
| 500ml still water at small supermarket | 0.45 | 0.90 | 0.64 |
| Packet of 20 small Pampers at Boots | 3.70 | 7.40 | 5.33 |
| 1 liter ready-mixed infant formula at Boots | 1.75 | 3.50 | 2.50 |

*\* Photocard needed. For Travelcard prices, see p. 57.*

way to carry money and also allow you to withdraw cash at any bank or at its ATM. (You pay interest on the advance the moment you receive the cash.) You now need a PIN both for purchasing with your card and for using an ATM, so if you don't have one, call your credit card company ahead of your trip—it usually takes 5 to 7 business days.

Many banks now assess a 1% to 3% "transaction fee" on **all** charges you incur abroad (whether you're using the local currency or U.S. dollars). But credit cards still may be the smart way to go when you factor in things such as exorbitant ATM fees and the higher exchange rates and service fees you pay with traveler's checks.

To report lost or stolen cards, see p. 61.

## 4 When to Go

A typical London-area forecast for a summer's day predicts "scattered clouds with sunny periods and showers, possibly heavy at times." Summer temperatures seldom rise above 78°F (25°C), nor do they drop below 35°F (2°C) in winter. London, as one of the mildest parts of the country, can be very pleasant in spring and fall. Yes, it rains, but you rarely get a true downpour. Rains are heaviest in November, when the city averages 6.5 centimeters (2½ in.).

For planning purposes, call ⓒ 0870/600-4242 for the latest forecast, or see www.bbc.co.uk/london/weather. The outlook is quite often wrong, but it's better than a total shot in the dark.

**London's Average Daytime Temperature & Rainfall**

|  | Jan | Feb | Mar | Apr | May | June | July | Aug | Sept | Oct | Nov | Dec |
|---|---|---|---|---|---|---|---|---|---|---|---|---|
| Temp. (°F) | 40 | 40 | 44 | 49 | 55 | 61 | 64 | 64 | 59 | 52 | 46 | 42 |
| Temp. (°C) | 4.4 | 4.4 | 6.7 | 9.4 | 12.8 | 16.1 | 17.8 | 17.8 | 15.0 | 11.1 | 7.8 | 5.6 |
| Rainfall (in.) | 2.1 | 1.6 | 1.5 | 1.5 | 1.8 | 1.8 | 2.2 | 2.3 | 1.9 | 2.2 | 2.5 | 1.9 |

# KIDS' FAVORITE LONDON EVENTS

British public holidays include New Year's Day (Jan 1), Good Friday and Easter Monday (late Mar or early Apr), May Day (1st Mon in May), spring and summer bank holidays (last Mon in May and Aug, respectively), and Christmas Day and Boxing Day (Dec 25–26). One or two extra days are added on as holidays if Christmas Day and/or Boxing Day fall on a weekend. For British school vacations, see p. 142.

London's hectic events calendar is continually evolving. I've listed my current favorites over the next few pages, but check ahead that an event is still running. Keep an eye out for new events in *Time Out* magazine or on **www.visitlondon.com** and, especially, **http://kids.visitlondon.com**.

Remember that in school vacations, many museums, galleries, and other venues host extra kids' activities—see their websites for details.

## January

**New Year's Day Parade.** This spectacular family procession winds through the heart of London (from Parliament Sq. to Green Park), complete with bands and dance troupes from around the world, clowns, stilt-walkers, dancing dragons, and vehicles of various guises. It sets out as Big Ben strikes noon and takes about 3 hours, passing lots of historical monuments on the way; get here an hour early to bag a good viewing spot, or book grandstand seating for £15 ($30) each. See www.londonparade.co.uk. January 1.

**London International Mime Festival.** A 2-week extravaganza of visual theater, this festival sometimes includes puppetry as well as mime, at a variety of venues. Not all shows are suitable for kids; download the brochure for details of shows for families (with kids 5+) and shows for parents with older kids (12+). See www.mimefest.co.uk. Second 2 weeks in January.

**Charles I Commemoration.** This march from the Buckingham Palace end of the Mall to the Banqueting House on Whitehall by cavaliers in 17th-century dress (members of the English Civil War Society) retraces the route that culminated in the public execution of Charles I in 1649. At noon a wreath is laid at the Banqueting House, and a short service is held before the march returns to its starting point. See www.english-civil-war-society.org. Last Sunday in January.

## February

**Chinese New Year.** Don't miss this riotous celebration, with lion and dragon dancers making their way among Chinatown restaurants, firecrackers, live music, and food stalls. A parade leaves the Strand at 11am and heads to Trafalgar Square for dragon and lion dances, art displays, and other entertainments. At 2pm and 5pm there are fireworks in Leicester Square, and celebrations and stage performances continue throughout the afternoon. See www.london.gov.uk. Late January or first half of February.

**Great Spitalfields Pancake Race.** Teams of four race up and down Dray Walk (at the Old Truman Brewery on Brick Lane, E1), all the while tossing pancakes to raise money for Save the Children. It starts at 12:30pm; to take part, you need to dress up and bring your own frying pan (contact the organizers in advance, via www.alter nativearts.co.uk). Proceeds go to a children's charity. Shrove Tuesday (last day before Lent).

## March

**St. Patrick's Day Parade.** This family parade showcases many of London's 400,000-strong Irish community. Participants congregate at Hyde Park Corner at 11am, leaving at noon and dispersing at Whitehall at about 3pm. En route, there are performances on a stage in Trafalgar Square, street theater, marching bands, a cultural village with songs, crafts, and a children's area called Nipperbout (for creative activities, face-painting, toddler play, and the like), a food market, and more. See www. london.gov.uk/stpatricksday. March 17 or 18.

**Oranges and Lemons Service.** This famous children's service at St. Clement Danes, the Strand, WC2, serves as a reminder of a nursery rhyme mentioning the "bells of St. Clements," though this church may not be the one in question. Pupils from a local school read the lesson, recite the rhyme, and sometimes play the tune on hand bells. After the service, all kids are given an orange and a lemon on their way out. Call ℭ **020/7242-8282.** Third week in March.

## April

**Oxford and Cambridge Boat Race.** This upstream battle between Oxford and Cambridge universities dates back to 1829. Covering 7km (4¼ miles) between Putney and Mortlake, the race starts just after 5pm and is best viewed from a riverside pub; see www.theboat race.org. (*Insider tip:* An equally exciting contest, the **Head of the River Race,** runs the same course in the opposite direction a week before the university race. It involves more than 400 vessels but draws fewer visitors, so it's a better option for those with tots.

See www.horr.co.uk.) Late March or early April.

**London Marathon.** About 40,000 competitors run this course from Greenwich Park to Buckingham Palace, watched by a half-million spectators. Bands and street performers line the route, giving the event a festival feel. Aim to reach your chosen vantage point at about 9am to get a good spot. Teams of British kids ages 11 to 17 can take part in the Mini London Marathon over the last 4.3km (2.7 miles) of the course. See www.london-marathon. co.uk. Mid- to late April.

**The Queen's Birthday.** Elizabeth II's actual birthday (she gets an "official" one, too, in June) is celebrated with gun salutes in Hyde Park at noon and at the Tower of London at 1pm. See www.royal.gov.uk. April 21.

## May

**Museums & Galleries Month.** Enjoy a month of free entry to national museums and galleries—most of them are free anyway, but throughout May host special events, workshops, and exhibitions, including family activities and night openings. See www.24hour museum.org.uk. All of May.

**Covent Garden May Fayre and Puppet Festival.** This gathering of puppeteers from around the country meets in the garden of St. Paul's Church on Bedford Street, WC2, close to where diarist Samuel Pepys made England's first recorded sighting of Mr. Punch in 1662. The day kicks off with a grand procession led by a brass band at 10:30am, followed by a church service with Mr. Punch in the pulpit, then Punch & Judy shows and puppet shows from noon to 5:30pm, when the event is rounded off by folk music, maypole dancing, clowns, and jugglers. See www.alternativearts.co.uk. Second Sunday in May.

**Royal Windsor Horse Show.** This is one of the country's biggest outdoor horse shows, hosting world-class competitions, including polo matches and stunning equestrian displays. It takes place in the private gardens and parkland of Windsor Castle, which are off-limits to the public the rest of the year, and are worth the trip out just to stroll or picnic in. However, there's also a funfair, a food and drink festival and food courts, and a 4×4 course. The Queen herself attends, and her husband the Duke of Edinburgh sometimes competes (at carriage driving—he is, after all, in his mid-80s now). See www.royal-windsor-horse-show.co.uk. Early or mid-May.

**Dulwich Festival.** This 10-day program of arts and cultural events for all ages in south London varies year by year in terms of its offerings but culminates in a "Green Fair" with stalls, demonstrations, activities, a funfair, performances by local groups, advice on green living, and, best of all, a teddy bears' picnic. You'll find more events especially for kids: perhaps a children's art exhibition, mind-reading, circus, or percussion workshops, and pond-dipping. See www.dulwichfestival.co.uk. Mid-May.

**June**

**Trooping the Colour.** On the Queen's official birthday (her actual birthday is Apr 21; see above), the monarch, seated in a carriage, inspects her regiments as they parade their colors. The procession on Horse Guards Parade begins at 11am. Applications for tickets for the seated stand around the Parade (write to Brigade Major, HQ Household Division, Horse Guards, Whitehall, London SW1A 6AX, enclosing a self-addressed envelope and International Reply Coupon) must be received in January or February, but those without tickets can watch the processions from The Mall. There are also gun salutes in Hyde Park and at the Tower of London. See www.royalgov.org.uk. Mid-June.

**Open Garden Squares Weekend.** This event opens up many of London's private garden squares and other gardens to the public for 2 days. Some of the gardens plan special activities for families, as denoted by the special symbol on the website—Russell Square, for instance, features music, Punch & Judy shows, and more. Other family-friendly participants might include Ham House (p. 186), Chiswick House (p. 200), the Brunel Museum gardens (p. 160), the Camden Arts Centre (p. 175), the Geffrye Museum gardens (p. 165), and Coram's Fields (p. 209). See www. opensquares.org. Early June.

**All England Lawn Tennis Championships.** This legendary tournament held at Wimbledon is a must for tennis fans young and not so young. See p. 259. Late June to early July.

**City of London Festival.** As well as classical concerts and art installations in venues such as St. Paul's Cathedral and the Barbican arts center (p. 243), this festival comprises many free outdoor events throughout the City—they might involve a procession with traditional bell ringers, a street show by Tanzanian acrobats, high-wire trapeze, juggling displays, street opera, performances by local kids, and even a motorized piano! See www.colf.org. Late June to early July.

**Greenwich+Docklands International Festival.** Come to this free program for mind-blowing, mainly outdoor performances, including aerial theater, acrobatics, bungee dance, giant puppetry, mirage effects, stilt walking, and more mind-boggling pieces. For 2007, many events take place in the open spaces of The O2 (p. 258). See www. festival.org. Late June to late July.

**Open Air Theatre.** Outdoor performances of Shakespeare, light opera/musicals, and kids' classics (the likes of Roald Dahl's *Fantastic Mr. Fox*) have taken place in The Regent's Park throughout the summer for 75 years now. Refer to p. 248 for more info. See www.openairtheatre.org. Late May to mid-Sept.

## July

**Crystal Palace Park Victorian Weekend.** These 2 days of activities celebrate the history of the famous Crystal Palace and surrounding park (p. 207), and include a Victorian and Edwardian funfair and amusements, brass bands, and guided walks. See www.crystalpalacefoundation.org.uk. Last weekend in June/first weekend in July.

**English Heritage Picnic Concerts.** You'll find you can picnic in stately grounds while enjoying music, from Motown to Vivaldi, and fireworks at this annual festival held at Marble Hill House. See www.picnicconcerts.com. From early July to late August.

**Soho Festival.** This annual fundraiser in the gardens of St. Anne's Church just off Shaftesbury Avenue boasts live music, food stalls, and a market selling vintage clothes and bric-a-brac. The spaghetti-eating competition and alpine horn blowing are the highlights (the waiters' race is now sadly defunct), but there's plenty of other family fun, which may include a puppeteer and face-painting. See www.thesohosociety.org.uk. Early July.

**Rise: London United Festival.** This free anti-racism, pro-diversity open-air music festival organized by the Mayor's office is usually held in north London's Finsbury Park. It has a main stage with big-name acts from the worlds of hip-hop, reggae, jazz, pop and indie, plus six other stages focusing on work from Cuba, India, Africa, and elsewhere.

Side attractions include a kids' play area, a funfair, food and drink stalls, and arts and crafts. See www.risefestival.org. Mid-July.

**Swan Upping.** This royal ritual, comprising the annual census (or "counting") of the swan population on parts of the Thames near Windsor (p. 262), dates back to the 12th century, when the monarch owned all mute swans—and ate many of them at royal feasts! They were counted to make sure they were not being stolen or killed by other people. The "swan uppers" row upriver for 5 days in skiffs flying flags and pennants. See www.thamesweb.co.uk/windsor. Third week in July (different departure points and times).

**The Proms.** Don't miss the annual Henry Wood Promenade Concerts at the Royal Albert Hall and their overspill into Hyde Park; the program includes family events. See p. 247. Mid-July to early September.

**Toddlerthon.** This toddlers' walk for charity (Great Ormond St. Children's Hospital in Bloomsbury) covers 150m (492 ft.) on Regent's Park athletics track, near London Zoo. See www.toddlerthon.co.uk/the-toddlerthon.asp. Last week in June.

## August

**National Playday.** This is a countrywide celebration of children's play, run by the Children's Society and the Children's Play Council and involving about 100,000 kids in a range of events in London and elsewhere. See www.playday.org.uk. Early August.

**Fruitstock.** The fantastic free music festival held at the Camden end of Regent's Park got a bit large and boisterous in 2006 and so was scaled-down into a ticket-only "village fête" in 2007, with a more homely vibe—Morris dancing, traditional fairground coconut shies and "welly wanging" (boot throwing), homemade cakes, a knitting tent, a farmers' market, arts and crafts, and fancy dress. The large stage has been replaced by small-scale performances by local theater groups, bands, and comedians. Though it's no longer free, proceeds do go to charity. Visit www.fruitstock.com. Early August.

**South East Marine Week.** With 2 weeks of special events celebrating the marine wildlife of London and its environs, Marine Week hosts coastal and inland activities ranging from arts and crafts and exhibitions of marine photographs to sailing with seals and rock-pool rambles. See www.southeast marine.org.uk. Early to mid-August.

**Kids Week.** Every August for the past decade, the West End has hosted an annual children's program of reduced-price theater tickets and special events (including workshops, behind-the-scenes tours, and even stage-fighting) for kids of all ages, even under-5s. Some hotels and restaurants welcome children for free in conjunction with it. Booking opens in July. See www.kidsweek.co.uk. Second half of August.

**Notting Hill Carnival.** This is one of Europe's biggest street festivals, with colorful floats, extravagantly dressed dancers, steel drums, calypso music, concerts, and Caribbean food. It starts around 10am, and the crowds—which can get tightly packed—are dispersed about 9:30pm. See www.rbkc.org.uk. Usually the last Sunday and Monday in August.

## September

**The Great River Race.** This colorful, madcap race from Richmond to Greenwich passes many historic landmarks and employs about 250 traditional boats, such as Hawaiian war canoes, Viking longboats, Chinese dragonboats, and naval whalers. Crews hail from all over the world. The best place to watch is between Battersea Bridge and Tower Bridge. See www. greatriverrace.co.uk. First or second week in September.

**Regent Street Festival.** This day of free family entertainment on the famous shopping street has a new theme every year, based on a chosen country's culture, music, and food, but it always includes dancing, concerts, food stalls, and in-store promotions. See www.regent-street.co.uk. Early September.

**Brick Lane Festival.** This lively street festival celebrates the ethnic diversity of this area of east London, with an outdoor world music stage, food stalls, outdoor theater, a film festival a street market, a funfair, and children's activities. See www.bricklanefestival.com. Second Sunday in September.

**The Mayor's Thames Festival.** During this glorious 2-day multicultural celebration of the river, which celebrated its 10th anniversary in 2007, the South Bank from Westminster Bridge to Tower Bridge is taken over by themed events and displays; street dancing and percussion boat rides; "beach" events on a stretch of shoreline; family crafts and activities; food and crafts stalls; a spectacular night procession, market, and carnival with outlandish floats and costumes; and a fireworks finale. See www.thames festival.org. Mid-September.

**Open House.** This 2-day event allows access to more than 600 architecturally significant buildings normally closed to the public. Free Archikids Explorers' Packs are basically activity-filled workbooks that help children 7 to 11 interrogate the buildings (they can join the Archikids online club, too). There are also family events involve building or modeling during the course of the weekend. See www.londonopenhouse.org. Usually third weekend in September.

**Horseman's Sunday.** At this eccentric event, which celebrates its 40th anniversary in 2008, more than 100 horses are blessed by a horseback vicar outside St. John's Church in Hyde Park Crescent, W2, before being trotted around the neighborhood, together with horse-drawn carriages. The event is in remembrance of an open-air service held in the 1060s to protest against the possible closure of local riding schools. Kids' games, activities, and entertainments are laid alongside music, raffles, and tombolas for adults. See www.stjohns-hydepark.com. Late September.

**Tree-Athlon.** This event to raise money to plant trees in urban spaces from London's East End to Peru consists of a 5km (3-mile) run in Battersea Park, followed by a tree "wish" and a seed planting. Registration is £18 ($36); the lower age limit is 14; under-18s need a parental consent form. For non-runners and younger kids there's an interactive tree trail walk taking in some of the park's loveliest trees, a tree ID competition, children's entertainers, face-painting, music, and refreshments. See www.tree-athlon.org/london_tree_athlon.php. Late September.

## October

**The Big Draw.** This festival consists of more than 1,000 children's free drawing events across the country; in London it involves most of the larger museums, as well as smaller venues such as the London Fire Brigade Museum (p. 167). See www.thebigdraw.org.uk. All month.

**The Baby Show London.** This huge 3-day parenting event, held at Earl's Court in west London (and again at ExCel in east London in late Feb/early Mar) gives you the chance to meet celebrity children's experts, buy toys and clothes, test strollers, and so on. There's a crèche if you want to leave your child for a while. Tickets cost £15 ($30) on the door, less if booked ahead. See www.thebabyshow.co.uk. Mid-October.

**Trafalgar Day Parade.** This annual parade by more than 600 sea cadets (naval trainees ages 12–18) from around the country commemorates Adm. Lord Nelson and his death at the Battle of Trafalgar. The event takes place in Trafalgar Square and includes music by cadet bands, the laying of a wreath, and a short service with hymns. See www.ms-sc.org. Sunday nearest October 21.

**Chocolate Week.** See p. 235. Late October.

**Opening of Parliament.** Here's your chance to see the Queen ride in one of her royal coaches from Buckingham Palace to the House of Lords, accompanied by the Household Cavalry. Inside (viewable only on TV), she ensconces herself on the throne and, after some eccentric behavior involving Black Rod (the senior official who summons the House of Commons) having a door slammed in his face, inaugurates the parliamentary year by reading an official speech drawn up by the government, stating its plans for the coming year. See www.parliament.uk. Late October to mid-November (plus shortly after a general election).

**Diwali on the Square.** The 5-day free Hindu and Sikh Festival of Lights celebrating the victory of good over evil is celebrated in Trafalgar Square with messages and prayers for peace, Bollywood and traditional dance performances, spectacular light and floating lantern displays, and free vegetarian food. Another good place to witness the celebrations is the gorgeous Shri Swaminarayan Mandir temple in north London (www.mandir.org), where rituals include the decorating of shrines, scattering of petals and rice grains, and fireworks. See www.london.gov.uk/mayor/diwali. October or November.

## November

**Guy Fawkes Night.** On the anniversary of the Gunpowder Plot (an attempt to blow up King James I and his Parliament, led by Guy Fawkes), huge bonfires are lit to burn effigies of Guy Fawkes. There are also spectacular fireworks displays, food stalls, and more. The best venues at which to see a show are Battersea Park, where the fireworks display is set to music and lights; Alexandra Park; and Ravenscourt Park. Check www.timeout.com/london for location listings. November 5 or the nearest Friday or Saturday night.

**London-to-Brighton Veteran Car Run.** The world's oldest motoring event, this car run involves about 500 pre-1905 vehicles on a 97km (60-mile) run from the southeast corner of Hyde Park to the Brighton seafront. Cars leave in pairs between 7 and 8:15am and drive at about 32kmph (20 mph) along Constitution Hill, Birdcage Walk, and Westminster Bridge into south London. Note that the day before the run, there's a concourse on Regent Street where up to 100 of the cars can be seen close up, plus driving demonstrations. See www.lbvcr.com. First Sunday in November.

**Lord Mayor's Procession & Show.** This is the journey by the Lord Mayor of the City of London, in his fairy-tale gilded state coach, from Mansion House to the Royal Courts of Justice to pledge allegiance to the Crown—just as Dick Whittington did in 1397, 1406, and 1419. (You can view the pledging by invitation only.) From the street (or grandstand seating costing £25/$50 but free to children on knees), you can watch the 5km (3-mile) procession being led by the enormous figures of Gog and Magog (the City's traditional guardians), accompanied by floats, bands, and tanks. The parade starts at 11am; get here much earlier to stake out a place. The show ends with a fireworks finale at 5pm (note that Blackfriars Bridge is reserved as a viewing spot for people with disabilities and those with small kids). See www.lordmayorshow.org. Second week in November.

**Christmas Lights.** The famous lights in Regent Street are switched on almost 2 months ahead of the big day, usually by a pop act that performs live in front of the crowd. A less commercialized event takes place on Marylebone High Street in mid-November, with more artistic lights, fireworks, and a street market. See www.regent-street.co.uk. Early November.

## December

**Christmas in Trafalgar Square.** A traditional Norwegian Christmas tree 25m (82 ft.) high, given by the people of Oslo every year since 1947 in gratitude for Britain's support of Norway in World War II, forms the backdrop to free carol concerts counting down the evenings to Christmas (they're free, but donations go to charity). The tree is lit in a ceremony in early December and remains in the square until "Twelfth Night" (Jan 6). See www.london.gov.uk. Early December until Christmas Eve (carols).

**Father Christmas at Harrods.** London's most magical Santa's grotto opens well ahead of the festive season (Harrods's Christmas World section actually opens in Aug!), but a visit is a must. Arrive early and expect queues of up to 2 hours, but don't worry—the cheery elves are on hand to keep things merry with singing, dancing, and free lollies and cookies. See www.harrods.com. From early November to Christmas Eve.

**Frost Fairs.** After a break of nearly 200 years, this famous fair returned to London in 2003. Come to the Bankside area (in front of Shakespeare's Globe) for 3 days of largely free fun: The program varies year to year but past attractions have included a lantern parade by local kids, a giant ice slide, husky dog sledding, a waterborne procession of Thames cutter boats, ice sculptures, adults' and kids' workshops in Mongolian yurts, entertainers, and a winter market with food, drink, and arts and crafts. Visit www.visitsouthwark.com. Mid- to late December.

**London International Horse Show.** This is one of Europe's top equine events, held in west London. As well as show jumping, there's dressage, dog agility performances, displays by mounted police, and a grand finale involving a procession with a Christmas theme—featuring Santa in his sleigh pulled by horses, and a singalong pantomime atmosphere. See www.olympiashowjumping.com. Mid- to late December.

**New Year's Eve.** The river is the place to head to welcome in the New Year, with a spectacular firework display launched from the London Eye (p. 142). It's visible from many other parts of London, too—Hampstead Heath is a good spot to watch from if you want to avoid the crowds. Alternatively, spend the evening at one of London's seasonal ice rinks (p. 214; the one at Somerset House is handy for the fireworks). Call ✆ **020/7983-4100.** December 31.

## 5 What to Pack

The British consider chilliness wholesome, and tend to keep room temperatures about 10° below the American comfort level, so bring sweaters year-round if you tend to get cold. Bring a light jacket, too, for cooler summer evenings.

Aside from common-sense advice about bringing hats, gloves, and scarves in winter, and sturdy, comfy shoes for walking, our best tip is to bring layers of clothing. Carry a jacket in your bag for those all-too-frequent days when you experience three seasons in 1 day. The only places you aren't allowed to be seen in normal casual attire are posh hotel restaurants and tea salons, where men will need smart shirts and trousers, and perhaps also sports jackets. Kids shouldn't wear jeans, sneakers, shorts, baseball caps, or other athletic gear.

Lastly, **travel light:** Take water, juice, and snacks to avoid having to pay high prices at convenience stores; wipes (and diapers if needed); and a handful of small toys to fill in long waits at restaurants or when stuck in traffic.

## 6 Health, Insurance & Safety

### TRAVEL INSURANCE AT A GLANCE

Check your existing insurance policies and credit card coverage before you buy travel insurance. You may already be covered for lost luggage, canceled tickets, or medical expenses. If your standard insurance doesn't cover travel and you decide that you'd like to purchase additional insurance, first ask your travel agent about a comprehensive package, which may be less expensive. The cost of travel insurance varies widely, depending on the cost and length of your trip, your age and overall health, and the type of trip you're taking.

For information in the U.S., contact one of the following popular insurers:

- **Access America** (© 800/729-6021; www.accessamerica.com)
- **Travel Guard International** (© 800/826-1300; www.travelguard.com)
- **Travelex Insurance Services** (© 800/228-9792; www.travelex-insurance.com)
- **Travel Insured International** (© 800/243-3174; www.travel insured.com)

For information in Great Britain, contact the following agency:

- **Columbus Direct** (© 0870/033-9988; www.columbus direct.com)

For information in Canada, contact:

- **Travel Guard International** (see U.S. contact information above).

**Trip-cancellation insurance** helps you get your money back if you have to back out of a trip, if you have to go home early (both of which are more likely if you're traveling with kids than not), or if your travel supplier goes bankrupt. Allowed reasons for cancellation can range from sickness to natural disasters to the State Department's declaration that your destination is unsafe for travel. In this unstable world, trip-cancellation insurance is a good buy if you're getting tickets well in advance—who knows what the state of the world, or of your airline, will be in 9 months? Insurance policy details vary, so read the fine print—and especially make sure that your airline is on the list of carriers covered in case of bankruptcy. For information, contact one of the insurers listed above.

Visitors from most other European countries are covered for **medical care** by the British National Health Service under the E.U. Reciprocal Medical Treatment arrangement, but you must get an EHIC card before departure (www.ehic.org.uk; it's also known as the CEAM in France).

Australian citizens also benefit from a reciprocal agreement between Britain and Medicare. See www.dh.gov.uk for guidance on health treatment for overseas visitors.

Most other non-E.U. nationals need **medical insurance** for all but emergency care. With the exception of certain HMOs and Medicare/Medicaid, your insurance should cover medical treatment—even hospital care—overseas. However, most out-of-country hospitals make you pay bills upfront and send a refund after you've returned home and filed the necessary paperwork. And in a worst-case scenario, there's the high cost of emergency evacuation. If you require additional medical insurance, try **MEDEX International** (© 800/732-5309; www.medexassist. com) or **Travel Assistance International** (© 800/821-2828; www.travelassistance. com).

## STAYING HEALTHY

There are no real health risks while you're traveling in England. For general advice on traveling with kids, read *Your Child Abroad: A Travel Health Guide,* by Dr. Jane Wilson-Howarth and Dr. Matthew Ellis (Bradt).

## WHAT TO DO IF YOU GET SICK AWAY FROM HOME

For information on emergency treatments, doctors, and drugstores, see p. 60. If you or your child has an illness impossible to explain quickly and that warrants swift and accurate treatment (such as epilepsy, diabetes, asthma, or a food allergy), invest in a **MedicAlert E-HealthKEY** (© 888/633-4298; www. medicalert.org). This alerts doctors to the carrier's condition and gives them access to their records through a PC or 24-hour response center. The company also has various "Kid Smart" services, including notifying designated family members should your child need emergency treatment in your absence. Alternatively, free membership in the **International**

**Association for Medical Assistance to Travellers** (www.iamat.org) gets you a Traveller Clinical Record providing physicians with your medical history, plus a directory of approved physicians (charging) in 125 countries.

Pack **prescription medications** in your carry-on luggage in their original containers with pharmacy labels; otherwise, they won't make it through airport security. Also bring along copies of prescriptions in case you or anyone in your family loses their medication or runs out, and carry the generic name of prescription medicines in case a local pharmacist is unfamiliar with the brand name. It's also a good idea to obtain a reference for a London pediatrician in case of a sudden illness. Failing that, your hotel's front desk should be able to put you in touch with a local doctor if any illnesses flare up during your London stay.

## 7  Words of Wisdom & Helpful Resources

Rule number one is to **hold hands with your child** and not let him or her out of your sight for a second, unless he or she is being supervised by someone you trust. If you have a stroller, fitting a Buggyboard (a board allowing kids to stand on the back of a stroller) is a good idea if you have an older child who can't manage huge walks but doesn't want to sit in their stroller all day, or if you have two kids. Be especially careful around **intersections**—London is full of aggressive drivers. Always cross at traffic lights or at "zebra crossings," although don't assume that just because it's the law, a driver will stop at the latter—wait until they have slowed down and are motionless before proceeding.

Avoid situations where your child could get swept away in a **crowd,** and with older kids agree on **a place to meet should you get parted**—at the information desk at a museum, for instance. Make sure they have your cellphone number and hotel address on them, with instructions to approach a member of the police force should they not be able to find you. And common sense dictates that kids should be made aware of the importance of **never divulging their names to a stranger,** and that their names should never be visible on their bags or clothing.

For more tips on safety, especially with regard to London neighborhoods, see p. 63.

### FOR SINGLE PARENTS

Online, **Single Parent Travel Network** (www.singleparenttravel.net) offers excellent advice, travel specials, and a free electronic newsletter. **Family Travel Forum** (www.familytravelforum.com) also hosts a single-parent travel bulletin board for tips from fellow travelers.

Within the U.K., the charity **One Parent Families** (the president of which is *Harry Potter* author J. K. Rowling) has travel tips on its website (www.oneparentfamilies.org.uk). Its free help line is ✆ 08000/185026. **Gingerbread** (www.gingerbread.org.uk), which has merged with One Parent Families, has downloadable fact sheets and a free advice line at ✆ 08000/184318.

Note that youth hostels (p. 90) offer good rates for single people traveling with kids.

### FOR GRANDPARENTS

Mention the fact that you're a senior when you make your travel reservations. Check with your airline (especially America West, Continental, and American) to see if they offer senior discounts; many hotels offer discounts for seniors, too. In most cities, people over the age of 60 qualify for reduced admission to theaters, museums, and other attractions, as well as for discounted fares on public transportation.

**Grand Travel** (✆ 800/247-7651; www.grandtrvl.com) deals exclusively with luxury holidays for grandparents and grandkids (mainly ages 7–17), including a combined London-and-Paris trip including two London shows, a ride on the London Eye, and accommodations at the Courthouse Hotel Kempinski (p. 76). **Elderhostel** (© **800/454-5768;** www. elderhostel.org), a not-for-profit travel organization, offers study programs for older adults (including art or theater in London), plus a broad range of intergenerational adventures (though none in the U.K. at present).

## FOR FAMILIES WITH SPECIAL NEEDS

In theory, all public buildings in Britain should have been wheelchair accessible since October 2004, but many architecturally valuable places have been exempted. That said, most museums and venues now have excellent access and facilities for those with disabilities, and many hotels now have specially adapted rooms. The Tube continues to be an embarrassment,

with very few stations with elevators; ask at a station for a map highlighting stations that do have step-free access from street to platform. New-style buses (as opposed to old-style Routemasters; see p. 56) have sliding ramps on the back doors.

Many travel agencies offer customized tours and itineraries for travelers with disabilities. **Flying Wheels Travel** (© **507/ 451-5005;** www.flyingwheelstravel.com) offers escorted tours and cruises that emphasize sports and private tours in minivans with lifts. London is among their destinations. **Accessible Journeys** (© **800/846-4537;** www.disabilitytravel. com) caters specifically to slow walkers, wheelchair travelers, and their families and friends.

**Holiday Care** (www.holidaycare.org.uk) offers holiday and travel information advice for travelers with disabilities, including discounts on accessible rooms at various London hotels for members. Its information line is © **0845/124-9971.**

## 8 The 21st-Century Traveler

## PLANNING YOUR TRIP ONLINE
### SURFING FOR AIRFARES

The "big three" online travel agencies, **Expedia.com, Travelocity.com,** and **Orbitz.com,** sell most of the air tickets bought on the Internet. (Canadian travelers should try Expedia.ca and Travelocity.ca; U.K. residents can go for Expedia.co.uk and Opodo.co.uk.) Each has different deals with the airlines and may offer different fares on the same flights, so shop around. Of the smaller travel agency websites, **SideStep** (www.sidestep.com) has gotten the best reviews from Frommer's authors. It's a browser add-on that purports to search more than 150 sites at once, but in reality only beats competitors' fares as often as other sites do.

Remember to check **airline websites;** you can often shave a few bucks from a fare by booking online directly through

the airline and avoiding a travel agency's transaction fee. For the websites of airlines that fly to and from London, go to "Getting There," below.

Great **last-minute deals,** which are not necessarily a viable option for those with kids, are available through free weekly e-mail services provided directly by the airlines. Sign up for weekly e-mail alerts at airline websites, or check sites that specialize in last-minute deals, such as **Smartertravel.com, Site59.com,** and **Lastminutetravel.com.** For listings of bargain sites and airlines around the world, go to **www.itravelnet.com**.

If you're willing to give up some control over your flight details (not a great idea with young kids), use an **"opaque" fare service** such as **Priceline** (www. priceline.com) or its smaller competitor **Hotwire** (www.hotwire.com). Both offer rock-bottom prices in exchange for travel on a "mystery airline" at a mysterious time of day, often with a mysterious change of planes en route. The mystery airlines are all major, well-known carriers, and the airlines' routing computers have gotten a lot better than they used to be. But your chances of getting a 6am or 11pm flight are pretty high, and you might find this too inconvenient with kids in tow. Hotwire tells you flight prices before you buy; Priceline usually has better deals than Hotwire, but you have to play their "name our price" game. If you're new at this, the helpful folks at **BiddingForTravel** (www.biddingfortravel.com) do a good job of demystifying Priceline's prices and strategies. Priceline also now offers non-opaque deals that allow you to pick exact flight options.

## SURFING FOR HOTELS

Shopping online for hotels is generally done one of two ways: by booking through the hotel's own website, or by booking through an independent agency (or a fare-service agency such Priceline). Internet hotel agencies continue to multiply in mind-boggling numbers, so shop around, as prices can vary considerably from site to site. Keep in mind that hotels at the top of a site's listing may be there for no other reason than that they paid money to get the placement.

Of the "big three" sites, **Expedia** offers a long list of special deals and "virtual tours" or photos of available rooms so you can see what you're paying for. **Travelocity** posts unvarnished customer reviews. Also reliable are **Hotels.com** and **Quikbook.com.** An excellent free program, **TravelAxe** (www.travelaxe.com), can search multiple hotel sites at once and conveniently lists the total price of the room, including the taxes and service charges. Another booking site, **Travelweb** (www.travelweb.com), is partly owned by the hotels it represents (including the Marriott and Hyatt chains) and is therefore plugged directly into the hotels' reservations systems—unlike independent online agencies, which have to fax or e-mail reservation requests to the hotel, a good portion of which get misplaced in the shuffle. It's a good idea to **get a confirmation number** and **make a printout** of any online booking transaction.

In the opaque fare service category, **Priceline** and **Hotwire** are even better for hotels than for airfares; with both, you're allowed to pick the neighborhood and quality level of your hotel before offering up your money. On the downside, many hotels stick Priceline guests in their least desirable rooms. Be sure to go to the BiddingForTravel website (see above) before bidding on a hotel room on Priceline; it features a fairly up-to-date list of hotels that Priceline uses in major cities. For both Priceline and Hotwire, you pay upfront, and the fee is nonrefundable. *Note:* Some hotels do not provide loyalty program credits or points or other frequent-stay amenities when you book a room through opaque online services.

## SURFING FOR CAR RENTALS

For booking car rentals online, the best deals are usually found at car-rental company websites, although all the major online travel agencies also offer car rental reservations services. Priceline and Hotwire work well for car rentals, too; the only "mystery" is which major rental company you get, and for most travelers the difference between Hertz, Avis, and Budget is negligible.

## INTERNET ACCESS AWAY FROM HOME
### WITHOUT YOUR OWN COMPUTER

There are very few London streets without at least one Internet cafe. One of the most ubiquitous is **easyInternet** (www.easyeverything.com), with 7 branches in the capital at press time, including Oxford Street and Trafalgar Square. Aside from formal cybercafes, most **public libraries** offer Internet access free or for a small charge. Avoid **hotel business centers** and **Internet kiosks** unless you're willing to pay exorbitant rates; on the other hand, some hotels may offer a terminal with free or low-cost access in their lobby.

To retrieve your e-mail, ask your **Internet Service Provider (ISP)** if it has a Web-based interface tied to your existing e-mail account. If your ISP doesn't have such an interface, you can use the free **mail2web** service (www.mail2web.com) to view and reply to your home e-mail. For more flexibility, you may want to open a free, Web-based e-mail account with **Yahoo! Mail** (http://mail.yahoo.com) or **Fastmail** (www.fastmail.fm). Your home ISP may be able to forward your e-mail to the Web-based account automatically.

If you need to access files on your office computer, check out **GoToMyPC** (www.gotomypc.com). The service provides a Web-based interface through which you can access and manipulate a distant PC from anywhere—even a cybercafe—provided your "target" PC is on and has an always-on connection to the Internet. The service offers top-quality security, but if you're worried about hackers, use your own laptop rather than a cybercafe computer to access the GoToMyPC system.

## WITH YOUR OWN COMPUTER

More and more hotels, cafes, and retailers are signing on as wireless (Wi-Fi; wireless fidelity) "hotspots" from which you can get high-speed connection without cable wires, networking hardware, or a phone line (see below). **Boingo** (www.boingo.com) and **Wayport** (www.wayport.com) have networks in airports and high-class hotel lobbies. IPass providers also give you access to a few hundred wireless hotel lobby setups. Best of all, you don't need to be staying at the Four Seasons to use

the hotel's network; just set yourself up on a nice couch in the lobby. The pricing policies can be byzantine, with a variety of monthly, per-connection, and per-minute plans, but in general you pay around $20 a month for unlimited access (with the possibility of extra charges at some premium locations).

There are also places that provide **free wireless networks** in cities around the world. To locate these free hotspots, go to **www.personaltelco.net/index.cgi/WirelessCommunities**.

If Wi-Fi is not available at your destination, most business-class hotels throughout the world offer dataports for laptop modems, and a few thousand hotels in the U.S. and Europe offer free high-speed Internet access using an Ethernet network cable. (You can bring your own cables, but at most hotels you can rent them for around $10; call your hotel in advance to see what your options are.)

In addition, major Internet Service Providers (ISPs) have **local access numbers** around the world, allowing you to go online by placing a local call. Check your ISP's website or call its toll-free number and ask how you can use your current account away from home, and how much it will cost.

Wherever you go, bring a **connection kit** of the right power and phone adapters, a spare phone cord, and a spare Ethernet network cable—or find out if your hotel supplies them.

## USING A CELLPHONE

The three letters that define much of the world's **wireless capabilities** are GSM (Global System for Mobiles), a big, seamless network that makes for easy cross-border cellphone use throughout Europe and dozens of other countries worldwide. In the U.S., T-Mobile, AT&T Wireless, and Cingular use this quasi-universal system. In Canada, Microcell and some Rogers customers are GSM, and all Europeans and most Australians use GSM.

If your cellphone is on a GSM system, and you have a world-capable multiband phone such as many Sony Ericsson, Motorola, or Samsung models, you can make and receive calls across much of the globe, including London. Just call your wireless operator and ask for "international roaming" to be activated on your account. Unfortunately, per-minute charges can be high—usually $1 to $1.50 in London.

That's why it's important to buy an "unlocked" world phone from the get-go. Having an unlocked phone allows you to install a cheap, prepaid, removable computer memory phone chip (called a **SIM card**) in your destination. (Show your phone to the salesperson; not all phones work on all networks.) You'll get a local phone number and much, much lower calling rates. Getting an already locked phone unlocked can be a complicated process, but it can be done; just call your cellular operator and say you'll be going abroad for several months and want to use the phone with a local provider.

For many, **renting** a phone is a good idea. (Even world-phone owners will have to rent new phones if they're traveling to non-GSM regions.) While you can rent a phone from any number of overseas sites, including airports and car rental agencies, we suggest renting the phone before you leave home. That way you can give loved ones and business associates your new number, make sure the phone works, and take the phone wherever you go—especially helpful for overseas trips through several countries. Alternatively, some upper-range hotels offer cellphone rental.

Phone rental isn't cheap. If you don't bring your own, you're better off buying a prepaid or pay-as-you-go phone in the U.K. Handsets start at about £50 ($100), and you recharge them by buying top-up cards (available from most newsagents and phone shops) in denominations of £10 ($20) and up. Major networks Orange (www.orange.co.uk), Vodafone (www.vodafone.co.uk), and O2 (www.O2.co.uk) have their own shops. Alternatively, there are branches of Carphone Warehouse (www.carphonewarehouse.com) all over London, including Waterloo Station, selling phones on various networks. Make sure you tell your provider that you need a model that can make and receive international calls.

Two good wireless rental companies are **InTouch USA** (© **800/872-7626;** www.intouchglobal.com) and **RoadPost** (© **888/290-1616;** www.roadpost.com). Give them your itinerary, and they'll tell you what wireless products you need. InTouch will also, for free, advise you on whether your existing phone will work overseas; call © **703/222-7161** between 9am and 4pm EST, or go to http://intouch global.com/travel.htm.

For trips of more than a few weeks spent in one country, **buying a phone** becomes economically attractive, as many nations have cheap, no-questions-asked prepaid phone systems. Once you arrive at your destination, stop by a local cellphone shop and get the cheapest package; you'll probably pay less than $100 for a phone and a starter calling card. Local calls may be as low as 10¢ per minute, and in many countries incoming calls are free.

## 9 Getting There

### BY PLANE
Heathrow is a bit closer to central London than Gatwick, but there is a fast train service from both airports to the West End (see "Getting into Town from the Airport," below). **High season** on most airlines' routes to London is usually from June to the beginning of September. **Shoulder season** is from April to May, early September to October, and December 15 to 24. **Low season** is from

November 1 to December 14, and from December 25 to March 31.

## FROM THE UNITED STATES & CANADA

Airlines that fly regularly between the U.S. and London include: **American Airlines** (② 800/433-7300; www.aa.com), **British Airways** (② 800-AIRWAYS; www.britishairways.com), **Continental Airlines** (② 800/231-0856; www.continental.com), **Delta Air Lines** (② 800/221-1212; www.delta.com), **Air India** (② 800/223-7776; www.airindia.com), **Northwest Airlines** (② 800/225-2525; www.nwa.com), **United Airlines** (② 800/538-2929; www.united.com), and **Virgin Atlantic Airways** (② 800/821-5438; www.virgin-atlantic.com).

**Air Canada** (② 888/247-2262; www.aircanada.com) flies daily to Heathrow from various Canadian cities.

## FROM AUSTRALIA

Qantas (② 13-13-13; www.qantas.com) and **British Airways** (② 1300/767177; www.britishairways.com) fly to London from Australia.

## FROM SOUTH AFRICA

South African Airways (② 0861/359722; www.flysaa.com), **British Airways** (② 011/441-8600; www.britishairways.com), and **Virgin Atlantic Airways** (② 011/340-3400; www.virgin-atlantic.com) fly to London from Johannesburg and/or Cape Town.

## GETTING INTO TOWN FROM THE AIRPORT

For information on Heathrow, Gatwick, and Stansted, including travel to and from these airports, and flight arrivals and departures, see www.baa.com.

## LONDON HEATHROW AIRPORT

Heathrow (② 0870/000-0123) is about 25km (15 miles) west of central London. As of this writing, Terminals 1 and 2 receive the intra-European flights of several European airlines. Terminal 3 receives most transatlantic flights on U.S.-based airlines, and Terminal 4 handles the long-haul and transatlantic operations of British Airways. In late March 2008, however, some operations, including British Airways, will move to the new Terminal 5, and a program of refurbishment or even rebuilding of the existing terminals will be rolled out that will utterly transform Heathrow by 2012.

Heathrow's two Underground (Tube) stations, servicing Terminals 1, 2, and 3, and Terminal 4, respectively, will be joined by a rail/Underground station at Terminal 5, which will be the terminus for the **Heathrow Express** (www.heathrowexpress.com). This takes you to Paddington Station in 15 to 20 minutes. Trips cost £15 ($30) each way in economy class, £7 ($14) for kids 5 to 15. You can pre-book tickets online, or get them at self-service machines at Heathrow. There's also the **Heathrow Connect** from Paddington, which costs about half the price because it stops at various points en route (it takes about 30 min., depending how many stops it makes). This will run from Terminal 4 after the opening of Terminal 5.

By Tube it takes up to an hour to get to central London, with tickets costing £4 ($8) for adults and £2 ($4) for kids 11 to 16 (less if you buy a Travelcard; see p. 56).

A taxi from Heathrow is likely to cost £40 to £70 ($80–$140).

## GATWICK AIRPORT

Gatwick (② 0870/000-2468) is 45km (28 miles) south of London. The fastest way to get to the center is aboard a **Gatwick Express train** (www.gatwickexpress.co.uk), taking you to Victoria Station in 30 minutes (35 min. on Sun). The one-way charge in standard class is £15 ($30) for adults, £7 ($14) for kids 6 to 16. A slower but cheaper alternative are **National Express coaches** (www.nationalexpress.com) from to Victoria coach station (next to Victoria train station), taking 1 hour 5 minutes or more. One-way tickets cost £7 ($14) for adults, about half that for kids 3 to 15.

Make sure you don't get on a coach that takes you via Brighton.

The airport's official taxi concessionaire, **Checker Cars** (© **0800/747737**), charges about £77 ($154) for journeys into central London, plus an extra £8 ($16) if you enter the Congestion Charge zone between 7am and 6pm.

## LONDON STANSTED AIRPORT
Stansted (© **0870/000-0303**), located some 65km (40 miles) northeast of London, mostly handles flights to and from the European Continent, mainly by budget airlines. The **Stansted Express train** (www.stanstedexpress.com) takes an average of 45 minutes to get to London's Liverpool Street Station, costing £15 ($30) for adults, £7 ($14) for kids one-way. There are a variety of coach options, the quickest being the Terravision Express Shuttles to Liverpool Street Station or Victoria, taking 55 minutes and 75 minutes respectively. Fares are £8 ($16) for adults, £4 ($8) for kids to both destinations.

A **taxi** to the West End by the official taxi company, **Checkercarz** (© **0800/ 747737**), is about £90 ($180).

## LONDON CITY AIRPORT   London City Airport (© **020/7646-0000**; www. londoncityairport.com), 5km (3 miles) east of the business community of Canary Wharf, and 16km (10 miles) from the West End, receives flights from a number of cities in western Europe and Scandinavia. It now has its own DLR station taking you to Bank station in 22 minutes; adult single fares are £4 ($8). Black cabs into the West End cost £30 ($60).

## GETTING THROUGH THE AIRPORT
Generally, you'll be fine if you arrive at the airport **1 hour** before a domestic flight and **2 hours** before an international flight; if you show up late, tell an airline employee and he or she will probably whisk you to the front of the line. Bring a current, government-issued photo ID such as a driver's license or passport. Keep your ID at the ready to show at check-in, the security checkpoint, and sometimes even the gate. Children under 18 do not need government-issued photo IDs for domestic flights but they do for international flights to most countries, including Britain.

The Transportation Security Administration (TSA) has phased out **gate check-in** at all U.S. airports. Passengers with e-tickets can still beat the ticket-counter lines by using **airport electronic kiosks** or **online check-in** from their home computer. Ask your airline which alternatives are available, and if you're using a kiosk, bring the credit card you used to book the ticket or your frequent-flier card. If you're checking bags or looking to snag an exit-row seat, you will be able to do so using most airlines' kiosks; again, call your airline for up-to-date information. **Curbside check-in** is also a good way to avoid lines, although a few airlines still ban curbside check-in; call before you go.

Security checkpoint lines are getting shorter, but some doozies remain. If you have trouble standing for long periods of time, tell an airline employee; the airline will provide a wheelchair. Speed up security by **not wearing metal objects** such as big belt buckles. If you've got metallic body parts, a note from your doctor can prevent a long chat with the security screeners. Keep in mind that only **ticketed passengers** are allowed past security.

Federalization has stabilized **what you can carry on** and **what you can't.** The general rule is that sharp things are out, nail clippers are okay, and food and beverages must be passed through the X-ray machine—but that security screeners can't make you drink from your coffee cup. Bring food in your carry-on rather than checking it, as explosive-detection machines used on checked luggage have been known to mistake food (especially chocolate, for some reason) for bombs. The TSA has issued a list of restricted items; check its website (**www.tsa.gov**) for details.

Airport screeners may decide that your checked luggage needs to be searched by hand. You can now purchase luggage locks that allow screeners to open and re-lock a checked bag if hand-searching is necessary. Look for Travel Sentry certified locks at luggage or travel shops and Brookstone stores (you can buy them online at www.brookstone.com). These locks, approved by the TSA, can be opened by luggage inspectors with a special code or key. For more information on the locks, visit www.travelsentry.org. If you use something other than TSA-approved locks, your lock will be cut off your suitcase if a TSA agent needs to hand-search your luggage.

## FLYING FOR LESS: TIPS FOR GETTING THE BEST AIRFARES

It's becoming more widely realized that passengers sharing the same airplane cabin rarely pay the same fare—travelers who need to purchase tickets at the last minute, change their itinerary at short notice, or fly one-way often get stuck paying the premium rate. Here are some ways to keep your airfares down.

- If you can book your ticket **long in advance, stay over Saturday night,** or **fly midweek** or **at less-trafficked hours,** you may pay a fraction of the full fare. If your schedule is flexible, say so, and ask if you can secure a cheaper fare by changing your flight plans.

- Keep an eye on local newspapers for **promotional specials** or **fare wars,** when airlines lower prices on their most popular routes. If you can travel in the off season, you may snag a bargain this way.

- Search the **Internet** for cheap fares: Try www.expedia.com, www.travelocity.com, or www.orbitz.com, which can include hotel deals with your fare. Sign up to receive **e-mail notification** when a cheap fare becomes available to your favorite destination. There are also facilities such as www.sidestep.com that compare offers on various sites. Note that even with the major airlines listed above, you can often shave a few bucks from a fare by booking directly through the airline (online).

- **Consolidators,** also known as bucket shops, are great sources for international tickets. Start by looking in Sunday newspaper travel sections; U.S. travelers should focus on the *New York Times, Los Angeles Times,* and *Miami Herald. Beware:* Bucket shop tickets are usually nonrefundable or rigged with stiff cancellation penalties, often as high as 50% to 75% of the ticket price. Several reliable consolidators are worldwide and available on the Internet. **STA Travel** (© 0800/ 781-4040; www.statravel.com), the world's leader in student travel, offers good fares for travelers of all ages. **Flights.com** (www.flights.com) started in Europe and has excellent fares worldwide, including to London.

- Join **frequent-flier clubs.** Accrue enough miles and you'll be rewarded with free flights and elite status. It's free, and you'll get the best choice of seats, faster response to phone inquiries, and prompter service if your luggage is stolen, if your flight is canceled or delayed, or if you want to change your seat. With more than 70 mileage awards programs on the market, consumers have never had more options, but the system has never been more complicated—what with major airlines folding, new budget carriers emerging, and alliances forming (allowing you to earn points on partner airlines). Investigate the program details of your favorite airlines before you sink points into any one.

## FLYING WITH KIDS

If you plan carefully, you can make it fun to fly with your kids.

- You'll save yourself a good bit of aggravation by **reserving a seat in the bulkhead row.** You'll have more legroom, your children will be able to spread out and play on the floor underfoot, and the airline might provide bassinets (ask in advance). You're also more likely to find sympathetic company in the bulkhead area, as families with children tend to be seated there.

- Be sure to **pack items for your kids in your carry-on luggage,** from pacifiers to diapers.

- **Have a long talk with your children** before you depart on your trip. If they've never flown before, explain to them what to expect. If they're old enough, you may even want to describe how flight works and how air travel is even safer than riding in a car. Explain to your kids the importance of good behavior in the air— how their own safety can depend upon them being quiet and staying in their seats during the trip.

- **Pay extra careful attention to the safety instructions** before takeoff. Consult the safety chart behind the seat in front of you and show it to your children. Be sure you know how to operate the oxygen masks, as you will be expected to secure yours first and then help your children with theirs. Be especially mindful of the location of emergency exits. Before takeoff, plot out an evacuation strategy for you and your children.

- Ask the flight attendant if the plane has any **special safety equipment for children.** Make a member of the crew aware of any medical problems your children have that could manifest during flight.

- **Be sure you've slept sufficiently** for your trip. If you fall asleep in the air and your child manages to break away, there are all sorts of sharp objects that could cause your child injury. Especially during mealtimes, it's dangerous for a child to be crawling or walking around the cabin unaccompanied by an adult.

- **Be sure your child's seat belt remains fastened properly,** and try to reserve the seat closest to the aisle for yourself. This will make it harder for your children to wander off—in case, for instance, you're taking the red-eye or a long flight and you do happen to nod off. You will also protect your child from jostling passersby and falling objects—in the rare but entirely possible instance that an overhead bin pops open.

   In the event of an accident, unrestrained children often don't make it—even when the parent does. Experience has shown that it's impossible for a parent to hold onto a child in the event of a crash, and children often die of impact injuries.

- **Try to sit near the lavatory,** though not so close that your children are jostled by the crowds that tend to gather there. Consolidate trips there as much as possible.

- **Accompany children to the lavatory.** They can be easily bumped and possibly injured as they make their way down tight aisles. It's especially dangerous for children to wander while flight attendants are blocking passage with their service carts. It's wise to encourage your kids to use the restroom as you see the attendants preparing to serve.

- Be sure to **bring clean, self-containing compact toys.** Leave electronic games at home. They can interfere with the aircraft navigational system, and their noisiness, however lulling to children's ears, will surely not win the favor of your adult neighbors. Magnetic checker sets, on the other hand, are a perfect distraction, and small coloring books and crayons also work well, as do card games such as Go Fish.

- Some airlines **serve children's meals first.** When you board, ask a flight attendant if this is possible, especially if your children are very young or seated toward the back of the plane. After all, if your kids have a happy flight experience, everyone else in the cabin is more likely to as well.

- You'll be grateful to yourself for packing **tidy snacks** such as rolled dried fruit, which are much less sticky and wet and more compact and packable than actual fruit. Blueberry or raisin bagels also make for a neat, healthy sweet and yield fewer crumbs than cookies or cakes. Ginger snaps, crisp and not as crumbly as softer cookies, will also help curb mild cases of motion sickness. And don't forget to stash a few resealable plastic bags in your purse. They'll prove invaluable for storing everything from half-eaten crackers and fruit to checker pieces and matchbox cars.

## BY CAR

If you plan to take a rented car across or under the English Channel, check with your rental company about license and insurance requirements before you leave.

## BY FERRIES FROM THE CONTINENT

There are many "drive-on, drive-off" car-ferry services across the Channel. The cheapest and most popular crossings are Dover to Boulogne, Calais, and Dunkerque. For details, see "Sailing to & from Europe," under "By Boat," below.

## BY SHUTTLE

Eurotunnel (© **08705/353535;** www. eurotunnel.com) carries motor vehicles through the Channel between Calais,

France, and Folkestone, U.K., in 35 minutes. You don't even need to book in advance, though you get better deals if you do, and if you travel during off-peak hours. Prices start at £49 ($98) per car one-way, but you'll generally pay much more than that. Note that if you miss your pre-booked train but arrive within 2 hours of it, you are allowed free onto the next available departure. This is a pain-free option for parents since passengers don't even need to get out of their cars.

The A20/M20 links London directly with the Channel ports of Folkestone and Dover (where you'll arrive by ferry; see p. 36).

## BY TRAIN
### FROM THE CONTINENT
**Eurostar** (© **0870/530-0003;** www.euro star.com) operates frequent express trains between its new station, London's St Pancras International (which has replaced Waterloo), and Calais, Brussels, Lille, Paris, Disneyland Paris, Avignon, and even the Alps, depending on the time of year. The London-Paris journey time has been shortened from 2 hours and 50 minutes to 2 hours and 15 minutes.

Fares vary according to how far ahead you book and the degree of flexibility you require regarding exchanges/refunds but can be as low as £59 ($118) per adult and £50 ($100) per child 4 to 11 for a return ticket in standard class.

### BRITRAIL TRAVEL PASSES
Low-cost flights between many cities now mean that flying can be cheaper than taking a train, as well as a quicker, though not an environmentally sound, alternative. If you do plan to get around a lot by train outside London, money-saving BritRail passes allow a child ages 5 to 15 to travel free when accompanied by one adult, with subsequent children traveling at a 50% discount. See www.britrail.net for details or to buy passes. You can also find out the times of British national

trains, and book tickets on www.thetrain line.com (note that it is frequently cheaper to buy two single journeys than a return).

## BY BUS

This is your cheapest but slowest and least comfortable means of getting to London from the Continent. If you must, **Eurolines** (© **0870/808080;** www. nationalexpress.com/eurolines) is a reputable operator running buses to and from Paris (from 6 hr., 15 min.); Amsterdam (from 9 hr., 15 min), and more, with "funfares" (pre-booked e-tickets) starting at just £13 ($26). Its Eurolines Plus option is a more luxurious service to Paris, with increased legroom, reclining seats, and individual headphones for music and video entertainment.

## BY BOAT
### CROSSING THE ATLANTIC

**Cunard Line** (© **800/7-CUNARD;** www.cunardline.com) runs regular luxurious transatlantic cruises on the mighty 13-deck *Queen Mary 2*. Kid-friendly amenities include a basketball court, planetarium, nursery and children's center, kids' entertainment (ages 3–6, 7–12,

and 13–17), and family pool. Fares vary according to the season and your cabin grade, with an average 6-day crossing with an ocean view costing about £1,250 ($2,500) per person.

### SAILING TO & FROM EUROPE

The shortest and cheapest sea route between the U.K. and the Continent is from Dover to Boulogne, Calais, or Dunkerque. Operators on these routes are **P&O Ferries** (© **08705/980333;** www. poferries.com), **Norfolkline** (© **0870/ 870-1020;** www.norfolk-line.com), and the Budget operator **Speedferries** (© **0870/220-0570;** www.speedferries. com). Ferries take from 50 minutes. A short stay (up to 5 days) round-trip from Dover to Calais with P&O costs from £50 ($100) for a car and passengers; longer stays are more expensive.

Note that www.ferrybookers.com, a useful one-stop shop for ferries and Eurotunnel (p. 35), often quotes better prices than the operators themselves. Click on "Route Info" for details of most routes between the U.K. and France, the Netherlands, Spain, and Ireland.

## 10 Show & Tell: Getting Kids Interested in London

Involving kids in planning your forthcoming adventure is the best way to get them interested. Use this book to show them what they can look forward to in London, whether it be the views over the city from the London Eye Ferris wheel or the "super-sensing" dinosaur at the Natural History Museum. Also, get them to browse **websites** such as http://kids.visit london.com and www.show.me.uk.

Depending on your kids' ages, rent **movies** such as *101 Dalmatians, Finding Neverland, The World is Not Enough, Bridget Jones's Diary* or its sequel, and any of the *Harry Potter* movies, all of which have scenes set in identifiable areas of London.

A good resource for kids ages 3 and up is *The Usborne London Sticker Book,* which has more than 100 color stickers of London sights to peel off and stick down by area, from a double-decker bus to London Bridge, plus a simple map. The same company produces the mini-paperback *Book of London,* a children's sightseeing guide with lots of photos, a map, and more than 100 recommended websites. It's suitable for kids about 6 and up.

Another good activity book, this time for those about 7 and up, is *Pop-Up London* (Tarquin), with six main London scenes to create, including St. Paul's Cathedral and the Tower of London, plus smaller pop-ups. Children 4 and over will enjoy the classic *This is London* by M. Sasek (Universe), a beautifully illustrated tour of London taking in sites as varied as the ravens at the Tower of London and the Billingsgate fish market. It was written in 1959 but the reprint includes updated London facts.

Young girls might enjoy *Katie in London* (Orchard), which describes how the eponymous heroine and her cousin are taken on a tour of London by a talking stone lion from Trafalgar Square. We meet her again in *Katie and the Dinosaurs,* when she visits the Natural History Museum and befriends a little dinosaur who can't find his way home. In a similar but decidedly more French vein, *Madeline in London* (Picture Puffin) tells of the madcap adventures of a Paris schoolgirl and her classmates in London. By the same publisher, *The Sandal* is the delightful tale of a little girl who leaves her shoe in the British Museum after seeing one that belonged to a Roman child.

Boys might prefer *Adam Sharp 02: London Calling* (Golden Books), in which an 8-year-old supersleuth tries to find out who stole Big Ben. In *The Runaway Ravens of the Royal Tower* (Red Fox), it's the famous birds from the Tower of London that have gone missing, together with a brave young traveler who tried to find them. The reader's job is to find them all via cryptic clues and rhymes.

Some well-known fictional Londoners include *Paddington Bear,* by Michael Bonds (Picture Lions); this is the charming tale of a stowaway Peruvian bear taken in by a couple who find him at Paddington Station. His adventures continue in *Paddington at the Palace,* where he is taken to see the Changing of the Guard. Another visitor to the royal household is Winnie the Pooh, in A. A. Milne's verse collection *When We Were Very Young* (Methuen), which includes the famous ditty, "They're changing guard at Buckingham Palace." Farther south of the palace, Wimbledon Common provides the setting for Elizabeth Beresford's *The Wombles* (Puffin) and its strange creatures.

For older readers, Peter Pan, the little boy who wouldn't grow up, appears as a baby in *Peter Pan in Kensington Gardens* and flies over the rooftops of Bloomsbury in the better-known *Peter Pan and Wendy.* You can get both in one volume (Penguin or Oxford World's Classics). For a Peter Pan–themed walk, see p. 195.

Also for older kids, *Tales from Shakespeare* (Orion) is an illustrated introduction to works by the Bard. Mid-teens with good reading skills might like to dip into Sir Arthur Conan Doyle's famous *The Adventures of Sherlock Holmes* (Penguin) or even some of Charles Dickens's masterful evocations of Victorian London, including *Oliver Twist, David Copperfield,* and *Great Expectations* (Penguin).

For history, try *The Story of London: From Roman River to Capital City* (A&C Black), featuring the people and events that have shaped the city, with cutaway drawings and buildings, cartoons, and quizzes. The same publisher produces the kid-oriented *Royal London Britannia: 100 Great Stories from British History* (Orion), which recounts lots of fascinating London lore, such as the story of the princes in the Tower.

*Dick Whittington* (Ladybird) tells the fairy tale based on the real-life 14th-century Lord Mayor of London, while *The Little Queen* (Hodder) is a beautifully illustrated biography of Queen Victoria for young children. A great historical audiobook for ages 10 and up is *The Fairytales of London Town* (Hodder), with stories, poems, and fairy tales both classic and modern.

Lastly, for arts-mad older kids, *Looking at Pictures* (A&C Black) is an introduction to art for young people, told through the National Gallery's collection.

# 3

# Suggested London Itineraries

These itineraries were devised with the aim of keeping walking and Tube- or taxi-riding to a minimum by keeping you relatively close to the city center, and by breaking outings down into neighborhoods where the main sights are within walking distance of one another. They seek to balance culture and education with fun and time outdoors.

## 1 The Best of London in 1 Day

Capturing London in 1 day (a virtually impossible task) means surveying the scene in the most efficient way possible—via the Thames, the city's artery. From there you can branch out to see some of London's finest and most famous sights on the culture-drenched South Bank and Bankside. Make sure to wear comfy shoes. This itinerary takes you on a boat trip (always a child-pleaser), a big wheel (ditto), and back in time into London's fascinating history. *Start: Tube to Westminster or Waterloo Station, then short walk to the London Eye. Boat tours leave from Waterloo Pier directly below the Eye.*

### ✈❶ London Eye ✿✿✿
The world's biggest observation wheel allows you a glorious overview of one of the world's greatest cities. This is the best way to get an idea of London's sprawl, and also a means of seeing some of its most famous monuments in a single glance, including Buckingham Palace and Westminster Abbey. See p. 142.

### ❷ Riverboat Cruise ✿✿
Jump on a riverboat at Waterloo Pier just below the Eye (or cross to Westminster Millennium Pier, Savoy Pier, or Embankment Pier). The Catamaran cruisers have hop-on, hop-off day tickets that include a ride on the Eye. Seagulls accompany you as you travel the 6.5km (4 miles) to historic Greenwich the way Henry VIII did, reminding you how close to the sea you are. En route enjoy in-yer-face views of such London icons as the Tate Modern, St. Paul's, and the Tower of London. See p. 148.

### ✈ ❸ BOROUGH MARKET ✿✿✿
Disembark at Bankside on the return leg of your cruise and backtrack east up the river by foot. You may be hungry by now, and if it's Thursday, Friday, or Saturday you're in luck—this atmospheric fruit-and-veg market dating to Roman times hosts a gourmet food market where you can taste and buy treats galore. If it's not on, nearby **fish!** (𝄜 020/7407-3803) is a great seafood choice.

### ✈❹ Tate Modern ✿✿✿
By Bankside Pier on the way back from Greenwich lies Britain's best collection of international modern art, which excites as much by its setting—a looming former power station—as its content. The old turbine hall hosts temporary installations that kids love to explore, while the Surrealist collection, one of the world's finest, has playful works that intrigue younger

visitors. The new Learning Zone has games and interactives; the new Family Zone has books, quizzes, and games to introduce ages 5 and up to modern art, plus an activity pack. Kids also love the junior Multimedia Guide, a hand-held computer with videos, music, and games. See p. 179.

### ⑤ Millennium Footbridge ✪✪

Stroll over the silver spine of this pedestrian bridge leading from the Tate Modern to St. Paul's and the historical heart of London. It no longer has the famous wobble that closed it down upon opening in 2000, but kids love it.

### ⑥ St. Paul's Cathedral ✪✪

Built to replace a Norman cathedral that burned down in the Great Fire (itself believed to have occupied the site of two previous Saxon cathedrals, a Christian church, and before that a Roman temple), St. Paul's is most famous for its Whispering Gallery. Here, an acoustic anomaly allows you to hear someone whisper at the walls way across the other side—a source of endless amusement to kids. A steep 378-step climb to the Stone Gallery of this Christopher Wren-designed structure rewards you with panoramic views. Other highlights are the crypt, with the tombs of Lord Nelson and the Duke of Wellington; and "Great Paul," England's biggest bell (hear it daily at 1pm). See p. 155.

### ⑦ Museum of London ✪✪✪

Trace the city's compelling 250,000-year history since prehistoric times in an appropriate setting overlooking its Roman and medieval walls. Yet another wave of expansion will make some areas off-limits until 2009, but there's still plenty to see, including a special display, "London's Burning," featuring lots of interactive exhibits that bring the terrible Great Fire to terrifying life. See p. 169.

## 2 The Best of London in 2 Days

Use your second day in London to explore at least parts of "Museumland," otherwise known as South Kensington. When cultural overload threatens, take refuge in world-famous department store Harrods, and then head for the green expanse of Kensington Gardens, home to London's best children's playground. *Start: Tube to South Kensington, then a 2-minute walk.*

### ① Natural History Museum ✪✪✪

Overwhelming in scope, Britain's three-building "storehouse" of plants, minerals, and fossils makes itself accessible to families with its Discovery Guides, inspiring kids to explore volcanoes and earthquakes, dinosaur teeth, the source of the earth's energy, and a whole lot besides. Under-7s also get Explore Backpacks covering everything from oceans to monsters. Highlights are Investigate, a science lab for 7- to 15-year-olds; the animatronic *T. Rex;* The Power Within, where you experience what an earthquake feels like; the Wildlife Garden, a haven for sheep, foxes, pheasants, and more; and the Darwin Centre, where ages 8 and up can watch museum scientists engaged in cutting-edge research and look at some of the 22 million preserved specimens on 27km (17 miles) of shelves, some collected by Charles Darwin himself. See p. 148.

### ② Science Museum ✪✪✪

Also gargantuan, this five-floor museum of science and industry has touch-screen terminals with itineraries for families, teens, and those with special interests. Hands-on galleries include the Launch Pad, where you experiment with natural forces; the Challenge of Materials, with a glass bridge responding to visitors in its

# Suggested London Itineraries

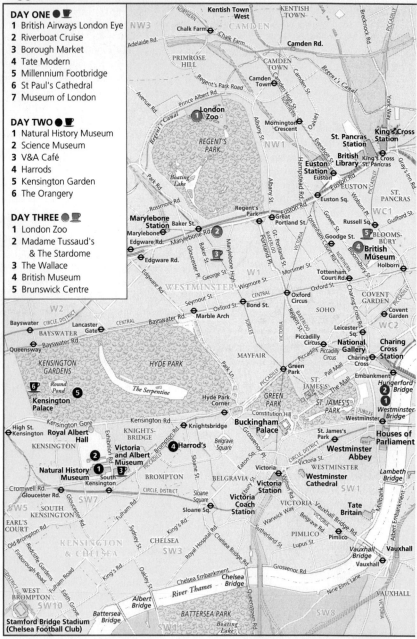

**DAY ONE** ●☕🍺
1. British Airways London Eye
2. Riverboat Cruise
3. Borough Market
4. Tate Modern
5. Millennium Footbridge
6. St Paul's Cathedral
7. Museum of London

**DAY TWO** ●☕🍺
1. Natural History Museum
2. Science Museum
3. V&A Café
4. Harrods
5. Kensington Garden
6. The Orangery

**DAY THREE** ●☕🍺
1. London Zoo
2. Madame Tussaud's & The Stardome
3. The Wallace
4. British Museum
5. Brunswick Centre

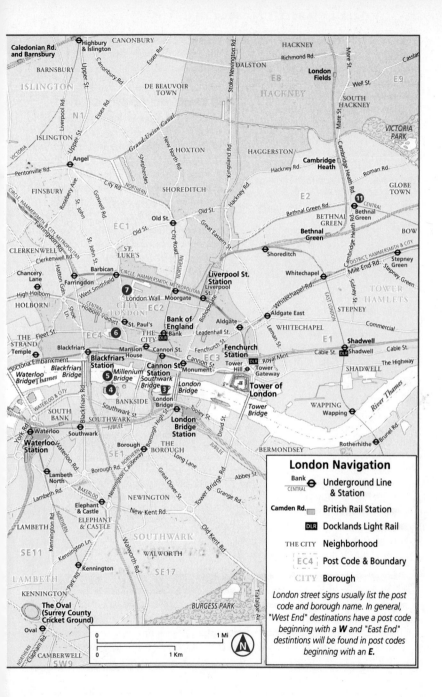

changes in light and sound; and Who Am I?, where you can morph your face to make it look older or younger. For thrills, the SimEx Simulator lets you feel a dinosaur's breath on your neck or the impact of an explosion in space, and the Motionride Simulator puts you in the cockpit of a Harrier Jump Jet. Even tots get their own interactive spaces, and the museum has one of two IMAX movie theaters in London, which show nature-based 2-D and 3-D films on screens as tall as four double-decker buses. See p. 150.

---

**V&A CAFÉ**

You probably won't have the time or energy to explore the wonderful Victoria and Albert Museum today, but take advantage of its historic cafe (✆ **0870/906-3883**) with its half-price meals for under-10s—it occupies the V&A's three original refreshment rooms, which were the world's first-ever museum restaurants.

---

**❹ Harrods**

For better or worse, a trip to London wouldn't be complete without a visit to the "Palace in Knightsbridge" with its 330-plus departments. The Toy Kingdom will make your head spin, but among the stratospherically priced frivolities are a good choice of "real" toys and books. There's also designer kidswear, chi-chi nursery furniture, a children's theater, and a kids' hair salon. On your way back down to reality, stop in at the second-floor pet shop to see cats, birds, and exotic beasties; don't miss the lavish food hall and a fresh ice cream at Morelli's Gelato. See p. 223 and p. 122.

**❺ Kensington Gardens**

Once part of neighboring Hyde Park, this is home to Kensington Palace, final home of Princess Diana, who's remembered in the innovative Diana Memorial Playground with its loose Peter Pan theme—a previous playground on the site was funded by the book's author, J. M. Barrie. Designed for kids up to 12, it's based around an almost life-size pirate ship and has tepees, a beach cove, and much more. Just outside it, don't miss the Elfin Oak, a gnarled tree stump carved with elves, fairies, and small creatures. On the nearby Round Pond you can sail model boats, and a short walk away is a statue of Peter Pan. If it's summer, cross into Hyde Park and take a boat out on the Serpentine. See p. 203.

---

**THE ORANGERY**

Designed for Queen Anne in 1704, this elegant building with its Corinthian columns and woodcarvings, set beside Kensington Palace, is an atmospheric settings for afternoon tea—a good alternative if you're exhausted by your day and want to head home for an early night. It's open all day (to 5pm in winter and 6pm in summer) for cakes and light lunches, too, and has a kids' menu. See p. 186.

*Buckingham Palace*

---

## 3 The Best of London in 3 Days

Use your third day to see the new attractions at the conservation-conscious London Zoo, then stroll down through Regent's Park for an altogether tackier experience at Madame Tussaud's legendary waxworks museum. After lunch, eschew celebrity culture in favor of that of ancient civilizations at the mighty British Museum. *Start: Tube to Camden Town or Regent's Park, then a short walk; alternatively, you can arrive by canalboat (p. 181).*

## ❶ London Zoo (K)

London Zoo's efforts to improve conditions and breeding rates included, in 2007, the addition of a £5.3-million ($10.6-million) Gorilla Kingdom with a moated island, a "day gym," "bedrooms," and a paddling pool. Another new feature is the Clore Rainforest Lookout, with up-close views of South American monkeys and birds, sloths, iguanas, agoutis, and more. Other high points are the reptile handling sessions, the kids' zoo with its "touch paddock" and advice sessions on looking after pets, and the BUGS biodiversity exhibition, where you can watch white-coated men growing trays of Polynesian snails and the like. Adults appreciate the zoo's famous architecture. See p. 190.

## ❷ Madame Tussaud's & The Stardome (K)

Cheesy as hell but much-loved by kids, this world-famous attraction, set up in 1835, strives to keep up with the times—new attractions include Kate Moss, with whom you can pose for a photo shoot, and the *Black Pearl* from *Pirates of the Caribbean,* which you can clamber aboard to help Johnny Depp search for the Dead Man's Chest. The place is perhaps still best known for its long-standing Chamber of Horrors, with re-creations of infamous murder scenes; other exhibits include Chamber–Live!, with actors posing as serial killers (strictly for ages 12 and up). If you cling to the hope of gleaning something cultural from a visit, head for Spirit of London, a "time taxi" ride through the city's history. The old Planetarium has ceded place to the Stardome, with a 360-degree show by the creators of *Wallace & Gromit*—it's still about space,

but now takes a quirky look at fame through the eyes of aliens. See p. 167.

> **3️⃣ THE WALLACE** (K)(★)(K)
> Among the gaggle of child-friendly eateries on and around Marylebone High Street leading south from near Madame Tussaud's, this French brasserie in the courtyard of a museum off the beaten track is open for breakfast through afternoon tea, and offers an excellent kids' menu. See p. 109.

## ❹ British Museum (K)(★)(★)

Guided and audio tours help you to break down this "cabinet of curiosities," with its 4km (2½ miles) of galleries, into manageable chunks. These include Family Audio Tours on the themes "Bodies," "Boardgames," and "Beasts," and family trail sheets; there are also activity backpacks, art materials to borrow, and books to consult in the Hamlyn Children's Library. Among the most famous exhibits are the **Rosetta Stone,** the discovery of which led to the deciphering of hieroglyphics; the **Egyptian royal tombs,** with their mummies; and **Lindow Man,** a body superbly well-preserved in peat. See p. 157.

> **5️⃣ BRUNSWICK CENTRE**
> If you don't choose to linger in the British Museum's glass-roofed Great Court with its kid-friendly cafes, head to this regenerated 1960s housing development with its central piazza full of good places for a family dinner, including branches of Carluccio's Caffè, Giraffe, Strada, and Square Pie. See p. 110.

# 4

# Getting to Know London

When choosing a site for the British Airways London Eye, an observation wheel built to herald the new millennium, planners decreed the center of London to be Jubilee Gardens on the South Bank. But while it's true that the southern bank of the Thames has become the city's cultural heart over the last decade or so, in many ways London life turns its back on its river. Practically speaking, Trafalgar Square is the city's hub—it's to the statue of Charles I here that British mileposts measure distances to London, and the piazza, now partly pedestrianized, has become the venue for all kinds of cultural celebrations, as well as being home to the National Gallery, storehouse of many of the country's most precious artworks.

Dozens of communities radiate out from Trafalgar Square; each has its own personality, and they are often described as "villages." In fact, if you feel daunted by London's vastness and the almost preposterous choices of things to do, it's a good idea to pick a neighborhood or two and explore them in greater depth, rather than try to cover everything. Marylebone, Little Venice, and Hampstead are particularly great areas for families, so you might want to use these as starting points.

This chapter provides you with a brief orientation to the city's neighborhoods and tells you how to get around London by public transport or on foot. In addition, the "Fast Facts" section, later in this chapter, helps you find everything for traveling families, from babysitters to late-night pharmacies to medical support.

## 1 Orientation

### VISITOR INFORMATION

The **London Tourist Board** (© 08701/566366; www.visitlondon.com) runs the walk-in **Britain & London Visitor Center** at 1 Lower Regent St., SW1 (Tube: Piccadilly Circus), which has booking services for hotels, trains, major attractions, and theater tickets, plus a Transport Desk for Tubes and buses within the city; you can also get a London Pass (p. 142) here. It also offers currency exchange and VAT refunds, and has a shop selling books and souvenirs, and public Internet access. It's open Monday 9:30am to 6:30pm, Tuesday to Friday 9am to 6:30pm, and Saturday and Sunday 10am to 4pm (June–Sept Sat 10am–5pm); staff members speak at least eight languages. There are additional Tourist Information centers at Greenwich (next to the *Cutty Sark*) and within the Vinopolis wine attraction at Southwark on the South Bank, plus there's a small kiosk in the arrivals hall at Waterloo Station.

### PUBLICATIONS

*Time Out* magazine (£2.50/$5) comes out every Tuesday and is available at all newsstands and newsagents. As well as comprehensive listings of exhibitions, movies, sports events, theater arts, restaurants, and more, it has a special "Kids' London" section.

On a smaller scale, the London Saturday editions of *The Guardian* and *The Independent* newspapers (£1.40/$2.80) each come with a free local listings supplement, called *The Guide* and *The Information* respectively; each has children/family events listings. *Where London* is a monthly magazine of listings available free in many upper-range hotel rooms, or costing £4 ($8) from retailers (see www.wheremagazine. com for subscriptions, at £40/$80 within the U.K., £48/$96 the rest of Europe, and £58/$116 the rest of the world). *INLondon* is a similar if more upmarket option resembling a glossy magazine, costing £7 ($14) where sold.

## CITY LAYOUT
### AN OVERVIEW OF LONDON

**Central London** is roughly bounded by Park Lane to the west, Marylebone Road/ Euston Road to the north, Gray's Inn Road to the east, and Victoria Street to the south. When suburbanites talk about going "up west," they mean the **West End,** another hazy concept that, although roughly synonymous with "Central London," implies they have in mind Oxford Street shopping, Soho nightlife, Chinatown's restaurants, the theaters of Covent Garden and the Strand, the cinemas of Leicester Square, or the hotels of Mayfair. Indeed, given that most hotels, restaurants, and major attractions are in this area, it's probably where you'll spend most of your time. On the other hand, many families choose to live outside the center because of high property prices and lack of space, so bear in mind that you'll find a great deal of kids' facilities and community activities in some of the "villages" outside the center.

**West of the Center,** the upscale neighborhoods of Belgravia, Knightsbridge, and South Kensington have some major stores and attractions, which have brought in their wake a good choice of hotels and eateries. Chelsea, to the south of here, is a family magnet, particularly along the King's Road. Earl's Court is more down at the heel but is fertile hunting ground for budget accommodations, as are Paddington and Bayswater to the north of Hyde Park; the latter are on the up because of the redevelopment of the canalside. Neighboring Maida Vale, Notting Hill, Holland Park, and Chiswick are popular areas with London's wealthier families and hence have good amenities for visitors with kids.

**South of the Thames,** the South Bank and the riverbank area—stretching east as far as Tower Bridge—is subject to ongoing regeneration and is one of the city's cultural hot spots. Hotels and restaurants are burgeoning here, but the rest of south London is patchy, with truly deprived areas as well as real gems worth traveling out of the center for. Back across the river from the South Bank, **the City** with a capital "C" is one of the world's great financial centers, but it's not all glass skyscrapers and sharp suits—this is where London began (it's the original square mile that the Romans called *Londinium*) and it retains much of its historical, architectural, and social interest. Bordering it to the north, Clerkenwell is one of London's most fashionable and vibrant areas, and a surefire hit with teens.

To the east of the City, the sprawling **East End** is another area that, though largely deprived, has a great deal of character and many sights that bear witness to its fascinating history. The business-dominated area of the regenerated Docklands has some surprisingly kid-friendly attractions, restaurants, and accommodations to rival those of the West End.

**North London** properly begins at Islington, a family area full of great stores and restaurants. Farther afield are more bases for young families, including Stoke Newington,

# Central London

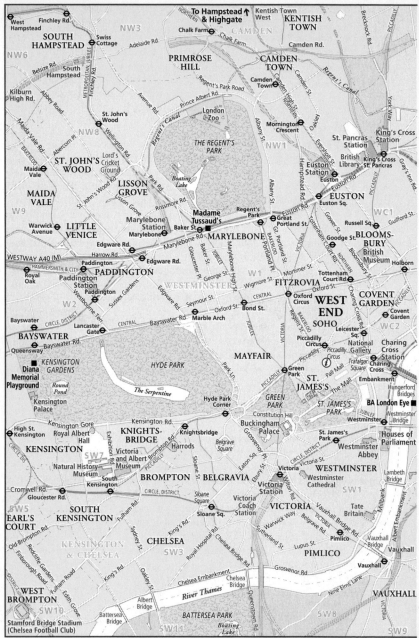

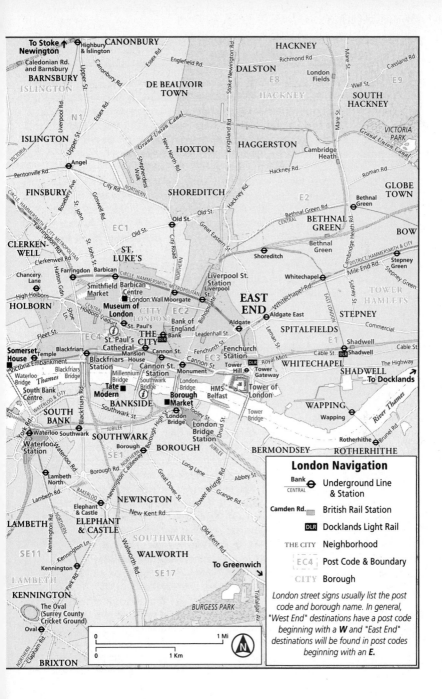

**London Navigation**

| | |
|---|---|
| Bank / CENTRAL ⊖ | Underground Line & Station |
| Camden Rd. ▭ | British Rail Station |
| DLR | Docklands Light Rail |
| THE CITY | Neighborhood |
| EC4 | Post Code & Boundary |
| CITY | Borough |

*London street signs usually list the post code and borough name. In general, "West End" destinations have a post code beginning with a **W** and "East End" destinations will be found in post codes beginning with an **E**.*

## The Flow of Time: London's River

Thirty million years ago, before Britain was an island, the Thames was a mere tributary of the Rhine. By A.D. 50 it had changed course; it gave Britain its capital after the invading Romans established *Londinium* as a port at the highest point of the tide. (It now reaches farther inland due to rising sea levels and the fact that Britain is tilting—the Environment Agency says the east coast of Britain is sinking into the sea at a rate of 15 centimeters every century.)

The Romans consolidated the river as an international port (trade with the Continent had started in the Bronze Age), constructing mills, wharves, and bridges. London Bridge was the first crossing, lined with houses and shops; it has been replaced several times—most recently in the 1960s when the previous one was taken apart and shipped to Lake Havasu, Arizona. There are now 14 bridges in central London, the most recent being the Golden Jubilee footbridges built in 2002.

About 100km (60 miles) from the sea, the Thames becomes tidal, flowing "the wrong way" toward its source twice a day as the sea pushes up the estuary. As the tide falls, the foreshore (riverbed) is revealed, and in the mud and shingle you can discover fascinating clues to London's past, including clay tobacco pipes and pottery fragments (see p. 193 for organized "beachcombing" walks).

The Thames was most splendid under the Tudors and Stuarts, when the river-loving monarchs lived in lovely waterside palaces at Hampton Court, Kew, Richmond, Whitehall, and Greenwich, using the waters as a "royal highway." Fittingly, the Thames saw many monarchs' final journeys in the form of stately funeral processions, including that of Elizabeth I in 1605, and that of Henry VIII in 1547. It's said that during the overnight stop at Syon House (p. 188), his coffin came apart and dogs licked his remains.

Today you can travel the same waters, albeit less regally, on passenger ferries or tourist vessels from Westminster—upriver to Hampton Court via Richmond and Kew, or downriver to the glittering stainless-steel Thames Barrier via Greenwich (p. 148). Alternatively, you can walk all or part of the Thames Path from the river's source at Thames Head down to the Thames Barrier, or wander along the South Bank with its riverside attractions, restaurants, pubs, and shopping malls. (A walk along the Embankment on the other side can be frustrating for little kids because of its high walls.)

When you're here, try to picture in your mind's eye the Lord Mayor's processions that took place from the 15th century to the middle of the 19th, in barges covered with gold leaf, some rowed with silver oars. In the 17th and 18th centuries, Frost Fairs (p. 24) were held on the river during winter freezes, complete with fairground amusements and stalls, performing animals, and ox roasts. Today, The Mayor's Thames Festival (p. 21) is a spectacular family-oriented celebration of the river, including the transformation of part of the shore on the South Bank into a temporary urban beach. The river also hosts a variety of annual regattas, including the famous Oxford and Cambridge Boat Race (p. 18).

and green and lovely Hampstead and Highgate. A little south toward the center, movie stars and musicians bring up their broods on hip Primrose Hill.

## FINDING YOUR WAY AROUND

It's not easy finding an address in London, as the city's streets—both names and house numbers—follow no pattern whatsoever. London is checkered with squares, mews, closes, and terraces that jut into, cross, overlap, or otherwise interrupt whatever street you're trying to follow. And house numbers run in odds and evens, clockwise and counterclockwise, when they exist at all—many establishments don't have numbers, though the building right next door does. If you have trouble finding a place, ask someone.

Throughout this book, street addresses are followed by their postal areas, such as SW1 and EC1. The original post office was at St. Martin-le-Grand in the City, so the postal districts are related to where they lie geographically from there. Victoria is SW1, since it's the first area southwest of St. Martin-le-Grand; Liverpool Street is east central of St. Martin-le-Grand, so its postal area is EC1.

If you plan to explore in any depth, you'll need the *London A to Z*, an indispensable map book with a street index, which most Londoners carry around with them. It's available at bookstores and newsstands in various sizes and prices, depending on the exact areas it covers.

## THE NEIGHBORHOODS IN BRIEF

### Central London Neighborhoods

**St. James's & Mayfair** Though it adjoins the hellish Piccadilly Circus, St. James's, which basks in its royal associations (it's home to **Buckingham Palace** and **Clarence House,** for instance, the official residences of the Queen and her eldest son respectively), has a very "gentlemen's club" feel, with its luxurious shops selling suits and its old-fashioned barber's shops. It's not child-unfriendly, though: The world-renowned department store **Fortnum & Mason** has a good food hall, restaurant, and children's section. At 22 Jermyn St. is an outstanding, if expensive, hotel (there's also a good moderate option, the Sanctuary House Hotel).

North of St. James's, bounded by Piccadilly, Park Lane, Oxford Street, and Regent Street, **Mayfair** is renowned for its hotels—the grandest in London—and its designer clothes shops, art galleries, and glitzy auction houses. Many of them lie along New and Old Bond streets. Attractions tend to be low-key—**Handel House Museum** is an example. West toward Park Lane, **Shepherd Market** is an unexpected and rather quaint little village of inns, restaurants, cafes, small shops, and galleries. A few minutes' walk away, **Grosvenor Square** (pronounced "*grov-nor*") is nicknamed "Little America" because it's home to the American Embassy, statues of Roosevelt and Eisenhower, and a memorial garden to those who died in the terrorist attacks of September 11, 2001.

**Marylebone, Regent's Park & Fitzrovia Marylebone** is a fashionable district extending north from Oxford Street to Regent's Park, and west from the largely Middle Eastern Edgware Road to stately Portland Place. Though it's a largely residential area popular with well-off young families and poodle-loving old ladies alike, you're almost certain to come here to visit **Madame Tussaud's** waxworks. Its hub is **Marylebone High Street,** with an unbeatable selection of kid-friendly stores and eateries, and a great Sunday farmers' market. This leads south past the impressive **Wallace Collection** to indispensable department stores such as **Selfridges** and **John Lewis.** Marylebone is a prime area for central accommodations to suit all pockets, from five-star hotels to town-house B&Bs.

At Marylebone's northern extreme lies the lovely **Regent's Park,** home to an open-air theater, the London Zoo, and more. To its east, **Fitzrovia,** once a magnet for literary bohemians, is a smaller, more laid-back version of Soho, with its terraced restaurants, cafes, and bars, many around **Charlotte Street.**

**Bloomsbury & Holborn** Bloomsbury, bounded roughly by Euston Road to the north, Tottenham Court Road to the west, Gray's Inn Road to the east, and High Holborn to the south, is best known as the erstwhile home of "the Bloomsbury Set" of writers and artists, which included Virginia Woolf and her sister Vanessa Bell. It's still a liberal-thinking, academic area where you'll find the **University of London** and other colleges, many **bookstores,** and the **British Museum,** a repository of treasures from around the globe. **Coram's Fields** is one of the city's best playgrounds, and the neighboring **Foundling Museum** an engrossing testament to a tragic past. This is also one of your best bets for moderately priced hotels and B&Bs in the center, while the **Brunswick Centre** with its array of family-friendly eateries has improved the area's reputation as a culinary no-man's land.

**Holborn** (pronounced "*ho*-burn"), south of Bloomsbury and east of Covent Garden, lacks major attractions, though **Sir John Soane's Museum** and **Dickens Museum** are atmospheric spots for those with older kids. In fact, the entire history-laden district remains charmingly Dickensian in spirit—the

Victorian author featured the two Inns of Court (where law students perform their apprenticeships and barristers' chambers are located) in some of his novels. Though not traditionally a hotel area, it does have some good options within walking distance of the heart of the action.

**Covent Garden & the Strand**   Covent Garden, based around a glorious restored flower, fruit, and vegetable market building, is touristy in parts, trendy in others, but generally great fun. As well as must-see attractions such as the **London Transport Museum** and **Somerset House,** it's the starting point for London's **Theaterland,** which takes up much of **the Strand** and extends along Shaftesbury Avenue as far as Piccadilly Circus. There are also some first-rate hotels on the Strand or just off it, and a vast choice of restaurants in the district (just be wary of tourist traps).

**Trafalgar Square**   The Strand leads to London's biggest piazza, which lacks outdoor cafe terraces at which to linger but does impress, with its magnificent lion sculptures (which older kids love clambering on), its soaring 56m (185-ft.) column from which Admiral Nelson gazes down, its fountains, and the Fourth Plinth (p. 51). Though the tradition of pigeon feeding here has thankfully been banned, visitors still flock here to get a sense of just *being* in London, as well as to visit the precious artworks of the mighty **National Gallery,** or get creative in the **London Brass Rubbing Centre.** Trafalgar Square, long a focal point for New Year's revelry, now hosts celebrations of the city's ethnic diversity, too. Not surprisingly, it's a little too noisy to make it a great place to stay with kids.

**Soho & Chinatown**   Soho, a cosmopolitan nightclubber's paradise, is

## The Fourth Plinth

It's confused people for years—that empty plinth at the northwest corner of Trafalgar Square. Why is there no statue on it? The fact is, the plinth, built in 1841, was intended to host an equestrian statue, but funds ran out and for more than a century and a half it was unused. Now, however, it displays temporary works by contemporary artists (each for 12–18 months)—in April 2007 it became home to Thomas Shütte's translucent yellow, red, and blue perspex *Hotel for the Birds*. Let's hope the pigeons find the accommodations to their taste, and that it makes up for the fact that pigeon-feeding in Trafalgar Square has now been outlawed.

bordered by Regent Street to the west, Oxford Street to the north, Charing Cross Road to the east, and Shaftesbury Avenue to the south. Though much of its notorious sex industry has been edged out by fashionable restaurants and boutiques, Soho is also the heart of London's expanding gay scene and may be a little too lively for younger kids, and there is only one really family-friendly place to stay, the Courthouse Hotel Kempinski. Teens, though, love Carnaby Street, a key local universe in the Swinging '60s that became a tourist trap but is newly hip again, with exciting fashion stores. Hamleys, the world-famous toy store, is on the Soho side of Regent Street.

Between Shaftesbury Avenue and Leicester Square is London's **Chinatown,** centered on Gerrard Street. It's small but authentic, and packed with good restaurants.

**Piccadilly Circus & Leicester Square** Piccadilly Circus, with its giant neon billboard and its statue of Eros, is a postcard cliché, a place tourists seem to descend on when they're not sure what else to do. Largely soulless in spite of some impressive architecture, it draws idle youth with its giant Funland arcade and massive themed restaurants. Nearly as tawdry, but free of traffic and fumes, is **Leicester Square,** largely taken up

by multiscreen cinemas set in old entertainment palaces, plus various nightclubs. Accommodations are overpriced and noisy—with the exception of the fabulous new Haymarket Hotel.

### West London

**South Kensington** There's no avoiding this area south of Kensington Gardens if you're with kids—it houses three major museums, all of them extremely child-friendly (the **Natural History Museum, Science Museum,** and **Victoria and Albert Museum**). **Kensington Gardens** to the north also has London's very best playpark, the **Diana Memorial Playground. Hyde Park,** with its wonderful boating lake, is a few minutes' walk away. To the west, shoppers come out in full force on **Kensington High Street,** a great spot for eating *en famille.* You're likely to spend a lot of time here, so you might want to make it your base; if so, the area offers moderately priced hotels, B&Bs, and self-catering apartments, plus a youth hostel.

**Knightsbridge, Brompton & Belgravia** Neighboring Knightsbridge is a top residential, hotel, and shopping district south of Hyde Park. Its best-known attraction is **Harrods,** "the Notre Dame of department stores;" don't miss its extravagant Toy Kingdom. Chi-chi kids' clothing boutiques and other luxury stores abound in Knightsbridge and adjoining Brompton and Belgravia, as do deluxe hotels and apartments; budget options are nonexistent.

**Westminster, Victoria & Pimlico** Westminster, a triangular area south of Buckingham Palace and St. James's Park, bordered by the Thames to the east, has been the seat of the British government since Edward the Confessor. As well as visiting grand historic landmarks such as **Houses of Parliament, Big Ben,** and **Westminster Abbey,** you can inspect **Churchill's Cabinet War Rooms** and walk down **Downing Street** to see **no. 10,** home to Britain's prime minister.

If you're looking for accommodations, **Victoria** just to the south of Westminster has lots of moderately priced and cheap hotels and B&Bs because of the train station, though the area can be noisy. (Be aware, too, that many of the hotels along Belgrave Road are occupied by welfare recipients.) Adjacent **Pimlico,** home to the wonderful **Tate Britain,** is a little less frenetic, and the area as a whole is a good base for those planning day trips to Windsor and Legoland.

**Chelsea** This stylish Thames-side district stretching west of Pimlico has always been a favorite of writers and artists, including Oscar Wilde and Henry James; more recent residents have included Mick Jagger, Margaret Thatcher, and a host of "Sloane Rangers" (the 1980s name for posh local gals, derived from Sloane Sq.). **King's Road,** which was at the forefront of fashion both in the Swinging '60s (Mary Quant launched the miniskirt here) and at the birth of punk, is now "yummy mummy" central, with expensive strollers vying for sidewalk space. On the upside, kids' boutiques, toy stores, and family-oriented restaurants are more densely packed here than anywhere else in London. The few hotels tend to be upmarket, but be warned that transport is an issue (there's a dearth of Tube stops west of Sloane Sq.).

**West Brompton & Earl's Court** North of Chelsea, things shift progressively downmarket as you move through **West Brompton,** focused around flower-filled Brompton Cemetery, and into **Earl's Court,** which attracts a youthful crowd (often gay) to its pubs, wine bars, and coffeehouses. You'll only want to stray here for its B&Bs and budget hotels (some of them very good) within a 15-minute Tube ride of Piccadilly.

**Bayswater, Paddington, Little Venice & Maida Vale Bayswater** and **Paddington,** north of Kensington Gardens and Hyde Park, are rather shabby "in between" areas with lots of budget B&Bs. That said, there are some excellent accommodations choices with easy transport links to the West End, and parts of Paddington have seen regeneration of late, especially around the "basin" area of canals. **Hyde Park** is also handily nearby.

The new canal walkways connect Paddington to delightful **Little Venice** with its floating cafes on boats, its puppet barge, and its family-friendly pubs and restaurants. Little Venice segues into villagey **Maida Vale,** a great family base with surprisingly easy transport links into central London.

**Notting Hill** West of Bayswater, Notting Hill has long been popular with wealthy young families for its elegant houses set on quiet, leafy streets. Its restaurants, clubs, and bars are some of the trendiest in town. **Portobello Road** is the setting of a famous, funky street market, and plenty of hip kids' boutiques dot the area. Truly kid-friendly hotel options are nonexistent, however.

**Holland Park, Shepherd's Bush & Farther West** Holland Park immediately west of Notting Hill is an even more exclusive residential neighborhood, popular with families for its lovely eponymous park. Adjoining it, Shepherd's Bush is a rapidly gentrifying but still scruffy area, home to BBC Television Studios, which you can tour.

**Chiswick,** southwest of Shepherd's Bush, is little known to visitors but has lots of attractions and good family restaurants, plus an outstanding new hotel, High Road House. This part of London gateway to the western outer reaches of the city, worth venturing out to for historical landmarks such as **Hampton Court Palace, Syon House,** and **Osterley House,** as well as green areas such as **Bushy Park** and **Brent Lodge Park.**

## South of the River

**The South Bank to Rotherhithe** Across Waterloo Bridge from the Strand, this area is home to the **South Bank Arts Centre,** western Europe's largest. Recent large-scale regeneration is complete, but it's a constantly changing area where you'll always find something going on, whether it's world-class concerts and shows, ad hoc riverside entertainment, or free foyer events and exhibitions. But it's not all art on the South Bank. Thrills and kid-oriented attractions, from the **BA London Eye** to the **London Aquarium,** mean it has something for the entire family.

The South Bank turns into the exciting **Bankside** area, home to the wonderful **Tate Modern** and numerous other attractions worth exploring, from the HMS *Belfast* to a reconstruction of **Shakespeare's Globe** theater. The hotel scene is blossoming in these districts, and you'll find some interesting family-friendly options, including budget chains, offering better rates than more central venues, as well as good places to eat.

Adjoining Bankside, **Borough** and **Bermondsey** are historically rich and colorful areas that, although somewhat off the beaten track, boast ancient inns and markets, including wonderful **Borough Market;** intriguing old wharves and spice warehouses; and small-scale, offbeat attractions, notably the **Fashion & Textile Museum** and **Old Operating Theatre, Museum, and Herb Garret.**

**Rotherhithe** to the east of here is a little-known and -explored area that nevertheless boasts the city's most child-friendly youth hostel and great venues for kids, including **Southwark Park,** an organic city farm, and the **Brunel Museum.**

The remainder of south London is a mosaic of quite deprived (but often culturally rich) districts such as **Brixton,** and family enclaves such as **Clapham** and **Balham.** If you don't mind being a 30-minute Tube ride from the West End, you can find some quirky B&Bs and self-catering options here.

One place worth traveling out for in its own right is **Greenwich** to the southeast. Though its palace, Henry VIII's favorite, is long gone, visitors still come for nautical attractions such as the 1869 sea clipper, *Cutty Sark,* and the **National Maritime Museum,** as well as its lovely park, its historical **Royal Observatory** (home to Greenwich Mean Time, the basis of standard time throughout the world), and its market. From here it's not far to spellbinding **Eltham Palace** or the unusual attractions of **Woolwich**—the **Old Station Museum, Royal Artillery Museum,** and stunning **Thames Barrier.**

Other southern venues worth a train ride out of the center include **Dulwich Picture Gallery, Horniman Museum, Crystal Palace Park** with its dinosaur park and the National Sports Centre, and **Croydon Airport Visitor Centre.**

Over to the southwest, **Battersea** is home to a great park complete with children's zoo, plus a flourishing eating scene clustered around Battersea Rise, about 10 minutes from the park. Just to the west are **Wimbledon, Barnes, Richmond, Kew,** and **Twickenham,** famous primarily for their green spaces—**Wimbledon Common,** the **WWT Wetland Centre, Richmond Park,** and the **Royal Botanic Gardens.** Wimbledon is also known for its tennis; if you're not here for those glorious 2 weeks in summer, **Wimbledon Lawn Tennis Museum** will have to suffice.

### The City & Around

**The City** The City was where the Roman conquerors first settled, and despite the Great Fire of 1666, the bombs of 1940, and the IRA bombs of the 1990s, it retains some of its medieval character amid the modern tower blocks. Landmarks include Sir Christopher Wren's masterpiece, **St. Paul's Cathedral,** along with **The Monument** (to the Great Fire), and the **Tower of London,** shrouded in legend and gore. The City's 2,000 years of history unfold at the **Museum of London,** while the **Barbican Centre** is a hotbed of culture for all ages.

You'll most likely venture here during the day, although there are some surprisingly family-friendly places to stay. Be warned, though, that things can go deathly quiet on weekends—and that includes restaurants and cafes. Trendy but atmospheric **Smithfield Market** (into which trucks still rumble through the night, unloading beef carcasses), on the border of the City and Clerkenwell, is your best bet for dining.

**Clerkenwell** itself, home to London's oldest church, St. Bartholomew-the-Great, has been reinvented by the moneyed and fashionable in the last decade, and hot restaurants, clubs, and art galleries continue to spring up.

**The East End** One of London's poorest regions, the East End extends east from the City walls, encompassing **Spitalfields, Whitechapel, Bethnal Green,** and other districts. That doesn't mean it's not worth visiting—you'll find, among other attractions, the wonderful **Museum of Childhood** at Bethnal Green, the **Discover** interactive play center, eclectic **Spitalfields Market,** the explosive **Royal Gunpowder Mills,** good parks, the wild space of **Epping Forest,** and lots of excellent ethnic cuisine (the area has seen successive waves of immigration).

There's a dearth of hotels here, though, except in the **Docklands** district, a business area with old Thameside warehouses converted into chic lofts, entertainment complexes, shops, restaurants, and museums, including the fascinating **Museum in Docklands.** The area is only a 20-minute ferry ride from Westminster Pier, and you can enjoy the relative quiet and first-rate river or dock views from plush hotels offering good weekend rates for families.

### North London

**Islington** Families move here for the spacious houses set on tranquil squares, and though there are few "sights" as such, there are good parks, plus an unbeatable range of offbeat shops and kid-friendly pubs, cafes, and restaurants. It also has well-priced accommodations from which it's no great schlep to the center.

**Hampstead** This desirable residential district (Sigmund Freud and D. H. Lawrence lived here, and John Le

## The Wild Life of the Thames

Whichever way you travel the Thames, take time to wonder at the fact that this river was once so full of fish that London's apprentices became tired of eating salmon. That said, a campaign in the 1960s—after the river was declared biologically dead in 1957—made this one of the world's cleanest urban rivers. Despite its muddy appearance (caused by silt being stirred up on the bottom), it supports an estimated 122 fish species and many invertebrates, as well as birds such as herons and cormorants. Several species of seal have also been seen, as well as dolphins and porpoises, and even sea horses (known for their sensitivity to dirty water), American crayfish (which have bred after being dumped by a restaurant), and Chinese mitten crabs (escapees from ships in the 1930s).

Sometimes whales have even been known to stray along the Thames, probably as a result of noise pollution making them lose their bearings. In January 2006, news broadcasts around the globe were dominated by the attempt (ultimately unsuccessful) to save a northern bottlenose dolphin that became beached on the shore near Battersea Park. For more information about the whale (whose skeleton is now held in the research center at the Natural History Museum; see p. 148) and about how to contribute to whale conservation, see www.thameswhale.info.

Carré still does) is popular with Londoners on a family day out, for its splendid **heath** and its high street with chic shops and appealing restaurants, pubs, and tearooms. Though it has few hotels, there are a couple of homely guesthouses. As a whole, the area is just 20 minutes by Tube from Piccadilly Circus.

**Highgate** This is another choice residential area. Moody **Highgate Cemetery,** London's most famous burial ground and the final resting place of Karl Marx and other famous figures, is best experienced without children, but **Waterlow Park,** with its centerpiece **Lauderdale House,** is one of London's most child-friendly gems. The wild expanses of **Highgate Wood** are not far away.

**The Best of the Rest** Other family enclaves to explore are Hippyish **Stoke Newington,** with a good park, a nature reserve in an atmospheric old cemetery, and a high street filled with organic stores, cafes, and secondhand bookshops. Ultra-hip **Primrose Hill** is home to movie stars, supermodels, and their brats. At sedate **St. John's Wood,** you can enjoy a stately game of cricket on a long summer's day at the world-famous **Lord's.**

## 2 Getting Around

### BY PUBLIC TRANSPORTATION

The London Underground and the city's buses operate on the same system of six fare zones. The fare zones radiate in rings from central Zone 1, which is where most visitors spend the majority of their time. Zone 1 covers the area from Liverpool Street in the east to Notting Hill in the west, and from Waterloo in the south to Baker Street,

Euston, and King's Cross in the north. To travel beyond Zone 1, you need a multi-zone ticket. Note that all single one-way, round-trip, and 1-day pass tickets are valid only on the day of purchase.

Tube, bus, river, and road maps are usually available at all Underground stations, or download them from the excellent **Transport for London (TfL)** website: www.tfl.gov.uk. The website's free Journeyplanner service can help you work out your most direct route. **TfL Information Centers** offering maps, advice, and entry tickets to certain major attractions can be found at major Tube stations (Piccadilly Circus; Liverpool St.; and Heathrow Airport Terminal 123); national rail stations (Euston and Victoria); and bus and coach stations (Victoria and West Croydon; the latter is closed on weekends); there's also one in Camden Town Hall opposite King's Cross/St Pancras Station (also closed weekends). Most are open from at least 9am to 5pm, usually much longer. A 24-hour public-transportation information service is also available at ℰ **020/7222-1234.**

**TRAVEL DISCOUNTS**     Travel within London is fearsomely expensive, particularly if you buy one ticket at a time. If you plan to use public transport a lot, **Travelcards** offer unlimited use of buses; Underground, including the Docklands Light Railway (DLR; p. 180); trains except the Heathrow Express; and trams in Greater London. The card can be for a day, 3 days, a week, a month, or a year (up to 4 months for kids), and it offers a third off scheduled riverboat service tickets as well. You can get peak and off-peak versions on 1-day cards; the latter can be used after 9:30am Monday to Friday, and all day weekends and public holidays. They're available from Tube stations, TfL Information Centers, Oyster Ticket Stops, and train stations. For all but 1-day and weekend cards, you need a passport-size photo. You can also get **bus passes.** The **Oyster Card** is a travel smartcard that can store your Travelcard, bus pass, or prepay tickets (which cost less than a normal single fare); you can renew any of these online or by phone, or at the places you can buy Travelcards. As a guide to savings, an annual single adult Tube fare in Zone 1 is reduced from £4 ($8) to £1.50 ($3) by using an Oyster Card. Tube stations and TfL Information Centers accept American Express, Diners Club, MasterCard, and Visa. For the **London Pass,** which includes unlimited free transport in addition to access to more than 70 London attractions, see p. 142.

Thankfully, in view of the overall frequent hikes in prices, **children under 11** travel free on the Tube and DLR if accompanied by a ticket holder (one adult can take up to four nonpaying children). Under-16s travel free on buses and trams; for reductions on the Tube or DLR (including child-rate Travelcards), they need an Oyster photocard (for which you have to present a European ID card or your passport).

## BY TUBE

The Underground, or Tube, decrepit though it is, is the fastest and easiest way to get around, given the state of London's traffic. With kids it can be a nightmare, however—there are very rarely elevators for those with strollers or little children, staff can mysteriously evaporate into thin air when you need assistance, and escalators are often at a standstill, meaning you'll be subjected to long, steep descents by foot as irate commuters barge past you. If you do have a stroller, especially a cumbersome double stroller, give yourself a head start by picking up a Tube map that marks out the 50 or so stations with access for travelers with limited mobility (as in, step-free access from the street and lifts to the platforms). This may help you plan your journey to some degree. You are not supposed to bring unfolded strollers into the Underground 7:30 to 9:30am and 4 to 7pm but I've never seen this rule enforced.

## Travelcard Prices

At press time, the following prices were in effect for cards for Zones 1 through 2 (notice that you can get cards that exclude Zone 1 and hence are cheaper). Prices traditionally increase each February.

**1-Day Travelcards**

Peak times: £6.60 ($13) adults; £3.30 ($6.60) kids over 10. Off peak: £5.10 ($10) adults, with up to four kids over 10 paying £1 ($2) each.

**3-Day Travelcards**

£16 ($33) adults; £8.20 ($16) kids. No off-peak rates available.

**7-Day Travelcards**

£23 ($46) adults; £12 ($24) kids over 10. No off-peak rates available.

**Monthly-Day Travelcards**

£89 ($178) adults; £45 ($90) kids over 10. No off-peak rates available.

---

Tube stations are clearly marked with a red circle and blue crossbar bearing the word UNDERGROUND). The color-coded route map may look complicated but is actually quite user-friendly once you've got the hang of it. You can transfer as many times as you like, as long as you stay in the Underground and have a ticket covering the zones in which you have traveled. Some of the ticket machines take credit cards and/or notes; others take exact change only. You can also pay at the ticket offices, but there are often queues. The flat fare for one trip within Zone 1 or between Zone 1 and any other zone is a massive £4 ($8), £2 ($4) for kids over 10 (photocards needed), but money-saving options are available (see "Travel Discounts" on p. 56).

When you've bought your ticket or pass, slide it into the slot at the automated gate (if you have a stroller, there's a special staffed gate), and pick it up as it comes through on the other side; Oyster Cards are swiped over the circular yellow devices. Hold onto tickets or Travelcards—they must be presented when you exit the station at your destination or you'll be fined. Tube hours (about 5:15am–11:45pm, an hour later on Sat) may come as a bit of a shock to those used to later subway hours.

### BY BUS

The bus system is slightly cheaper than the Underground and gives you better views of the city, though congested streets mean your trip will inevitably be slower. If you have a stroller, it's often easier to get on a bus than to fight your way down to a Tube train; specially designated bays in the middle of the bus are for strollers (make sure you put the brake on), but if someone is already aboard with an unfolded stroller, the driver is supposed to ask you to fold yours (more often than not, they don't). The new single-level "bendy buses" and low-floor double-deckers are easier to board and have more space to park strollers than the classic Routemasters, now almost entirely phased out.

A bus journey in London costs £2 ($4) for adults; kids under 16 go free (ages 14 and 15 need a photocard). You can bring this down by using a Travelcard, bus pass, or Oyster Card (p. 56); an adult 1-day bus pass costs £3.50 ($7). In central London, before boarding at the stop, you have to purchase tickets at the machines (exact change only), although these have been known to swallow cash without coughing up a ticket. If this happens to you, or the machine is out of order, you don't have any option but to climb aboard, tell the driver, and hope he or she believes you.

Transport for London's Information Centers (listed on p. 56) and some Tube stations have bus maps, or you can download one from the TfL website. Avoid taking a night bus with kids; they get horribly crowded and can be rowdy.

## BY TAXI

**Black cabs** are comfortable and well designed, and some of the drivers are true local characters who'd like nothing better than to offer visitors their own, often eccentric, takes on London life. You can hail a taxi in the street (available if the yellow taxi sign on the roof is lit), go to a cabstand (at major rail, Tube, and bus stations), ask your hotel porter to flag you one, or call for one (② 0871/871-8710), which incurs a £2 ($4) surcharge.

Like passengers in all other cars, cab riders are required to wear **seat belts.** (Your driver won't enforce this rule, though by law it's his or her responsibility and the driver risks a big fine if you don't buckle up.) The law regarding **child passengers** is the same for cabs as for cars, which is that in the rear, a child under 3 must use an appropriate child restraint *if available,* while anyone 3 and up must wear an adult seat belt if a child restraint is not available. (This rule is enforced even though most kids under 8 aren't tall enough to use standard seat belts safely; if this bothers you, you'll have to carry your own booster seat around with you.) If you are carrying a tiny baby in a car seat, you will be able to strap your baby in as you do in your car; if you have a single stroller, you can push it right into the taxi and put the brake on. (With a double-stroller, you might have to collapse it, get in, and then unfold it again, or hold your baby or toddler on your knee.)

**Fares** within Greater London depend on the time of day, the distance traveled, and the taxi's speed, and are displayed on the meter. There is a £2.20 ($4.40) minimum fare. For an average journey lasting 15 to 30 minutes and covering 6.5km (4 miles), expect to pay about £11 to £15 ($22–$30) on weekdays; you'll pay a bit more at night, on weekends, and during holiday seasons. Though there are no longer extra charges for luggage, you'll pay a £2 ($4) surcharge if you come from Heathrow into Greater London, and a whopping £4 ($8) per journey around Christmas and New Year. Despite these high prices, drivers expect a tip of 10% to 15% of the fare. You'll also have to pay an extra 10% to 15% if you have the audacity to want to pay by debit or credit card.

**Minicabs** are meterless, sometimes unlicensed, cars—you negotiate the fare in advance—so they're cheaper but riskier (sexual assaults are regular if not common). Always pre-book a car through a licensed operator (call ② 020/7222-1234, or use the search facility on www.tfl.gov.uk); if you are at all unsure, ask to see the operator's or driver's Public Carriage Office license. Additionally, check that the driver already knows your name and destination before you get in, sit in the back, and carry a mobile phone.

## BY CAR

Driving is a major headache in London: Traffic is hellish, parking is difficult and extremely expensive, and the Congestion Charge, covering the center, adds an extra daily cost. If you do arrive by car, park it and forget about it. (Call your hotel ahead of your trip and inquire if it has a garage and what the charges are, or ask for the name and address of a garage nearby.)

## BY BICYCLE

I don't recommend cycling with kids in London's heavy traffic. For cycling in parks, see p. 211.

## 3 Planning Your Outings

Getting from A to B with kids in tow often requires planning on a military scale. Factoring sightseeing, bathroom breaks, and snack stops into your plans and remaining flexible enough to cope with the unexpected—whether it be blisters or a national strike—is an epic feat. My advice is to make a plan, with a list of sights you intend to see, details of how you will get between them, and suggestions for pit stops, but don't beat yourself up if it doesn't go according to plan.

### FINDING A RESTROOM/PUBLIC TOILET

Anyone who's gotten beyond the diaper stage needs to know where the nearest restroom is at all times, though you can help yourself by ensuring that everyone goes before leaving the hotel or apartment, and on the way out of restaurants and museums. Luckily, most attractions, big or small, have child-friendly facilities these days, whether it's a fold-down diaper-changing board or toilet stalls big enough for more than one family member.

If you're out and about, there are restrooms at parks and rail stations, many automatically sterilized after use. Some of the latter may charge anything from 20p (40¢) to £1 ($2). Many high-street stores and venues, including some branches of Starbucks and Woolworths, refuse to let anyone use their toilets "for insurance reasons." Department stores (p. 222) are an exception (most have several restrooms and baby-changing, and one or two even have a baby-feeding room). Large branches of bookstore chains such as Borders and Waterstone's can be useful, although sometimes you'll need to ask a member of staff to unlock the door for you. Otherwise, major hotel lobbies and restaurants will normally take pity on you if your child really is getting to bursting point. McDonald's is a handy standby.

### NURSING MOMS & INFANTS

No one will bat an eyelid if you breastfeed in public in London, whether it be in a restaurant or on public transport. (My second son was fed on buses, riverboats, and Tube trains while we gallivanted around the city for the first edition of this guide, as well as in parks and playgrounds.) Should modesty prevail, **John Lewis** department store (p. 224) has a special feeding room in its parents' facility.

---

### FAST FACTS: London

**Area Codes** See "Telephone Tips" on the inside front cover of this book.

**Baby Equipment** If you're staying with friends or in a budget apartment that can't provide you with baby equipment as an upscale hotel will, contact **Chelsea Baby Hire** (© 020/8789-9673; www.chelseababyhire.com), which has strollers, stair gates, cribs, foldout beds, highchairs (including portable versions), car seats, and more. (For baby products outlets, see p. 238).

**Babysitters** All expensive and some moderate hotels will arrange a sitter for you; usually this will be from a reputable outside agency rather than one of their staff members. Many of them use **Sitters** (© 0800/389-0038; www.sitters.co.uk) or **Rockabye Babysitter** (© 020/7624-0060) both of whom you can also contact directly. Those using a sitter for a booking at a hotel or temporary address should expect to pay about £60 ($120) for a minimum 4-hour booking, which includes a booking fee and taxi home for the sitter; those in permanent residence in London can pay an annual membership fee. Temporary nannies can also be arranged. For male nannies (who will do everything from play football with your kids to take them to museums), contact **My Big Buddy** (© 0780/977-7884; www.mybigbuddy.com).

*Business Hours*   The major high-street **banks** are generally open Monday to Friday 9:30am to 3:30pm, though some of the bigger branches stay open until 5:30pm, and a few are open on Saturday morning. Most have 24-hour ATMs outside, though some close for a few hours at night. **Restaurants** in London tend to stay open all day from late morning on, or earlier if they serve breakfast; fewer and fewer open only for set lunch and dinner hours. **Stores** generally open at 9am or 10am and close at 5:30pm or 6pm, or 7pm or 8pm on Wednesday or Thursday. On Sunday, many shops open for 6 hours (the maximum), from 10am to 4pm or 11am to 5pm. Many malls stay open until at least 8pm, and many supermarkets and superstores stay open from 8am until 10pm or 11pm Monday to Saturday, plus Sunday as above. Many large supermarkets (generally out of the center) are now open 24 hours except Sunday. Some shops open on public holidays, but banks are closed. Almost all shops are closed on Christmas Day (Dec 25), and some are closed on New Year's Day (Jan 1).

*Climate*   See "When to Go," in chapter 2.

*Currency*   See "Money," in chapter 2.

*Dentists*   For dental emergencies, call **UCL Eastman Dental Institute** (© 020/7915-1000; Tube: King's Cross or Chancery Lane).

*Doctors*   Call © **999** in a medical emergency. Some hotels have physicians on call; many of them use **Doctorcall,** who you can also contact direct (© 020/7291-6666); it charges a £115 ($230) callout fee 7am to 10pm; any medicines prescribed will be on top of this. If you're worried about any aspect of your health or your child's, you can get free advice by calling **NHS Direct** at © 0845-4647 24 hours a day; they will tell you if you need to see a medical practitioner and provide you with contact details, but you have to pay for the latter unless your country has reciprocal arrangements with the U.K. (p. 24).

*Drugstores*   Every police station has a copy of the names of late-hour chemists (dial 0 and ask the operator for the local police). One of the most central late-opening stores is **Bliss Pharmacy,** 5 Marble Arch, W1 (© 020/7723-6116; Tube: Marble Arch), open daily from 9am to midnight. See also **Boots the Chemist** (p. 235).

*Electricity*   The British current is 240 volts, AC, so you'll need a converter or transformer for U.S.-made electrical appliances, as well as an adapter that allows the plug to match British outlets. Some (but not all) hotels supply them for guests. If you've forgotten one, you can buy a transformer/adapter at most branches of **Boots the Chemist** (p. 235).

*Embassies & High Commissions*   See www.fco.gov.uk for the contact details of all embassies and high commissions. The **U.S. Embassy** is at 24 Grosvenor Sq., W1 (© 020/7499-9000; www.usembassy.org.uk; Tube: Bond St.). The **Canadian High**

**Commission** is also in Grosvenor Square, at MacDonald House at no. 1 (© 020/7258-6600; www.international.gc.ca). The **Australian High Commission** is at Australia House, Strand, WC2 (© 020/7379-4334; www.australia.org.uk; Tube: Charing Cross or Aldwych). The **New Zealand High Commission** is at New Zealand House, 80 Haymarket, SW1 (© 020/7930-8422; www.nzembassy.com; Tube: Charing Cross or Piccadilly Circus). The **French Embassy** is at 58 Knightsbridge, SW1 (© 020/7073-1000; www.ambafrance-uk.org; Tube: Knightsbridge). The **German Embassy** is at 23 Belgrave Sq., SW1 (© 020/7824-1300; www.london.diplo.de; Tube: Hyde Park Corner). The **Italian Embassy** is at 14 Three Kings Yard, Davies St., W1 (© 020/7312-2200; www.amblondra.esteri.it; Tube: Bond St). The **Irish Embassy** is at 17 Grosvenor Place, SW1 (© 020/7235-2171; Tube: Hyde Park Corner).

*Emergencies* For police, fire, or an ambulance, dial © **999.**

*Holidays* See "When to Go," in chapter 3.

*Hospitals* The **University College Hospital,** is recommended by GPs as having the casualty department, or emergency room, to which they would bring their own children in an emergency. Its new location is 235 Euston Rd., N1 (© **0845/155-500;** Tube: Euston Sq. or Warren St.) Many other London hospitals also have accident and emergency departments.

*Legal Aid* In every case in which legal aid is required by a foreign national within Britain, the British Tourist Authority advises visitors to contact their embassy.

*Mail* A 10-gram airmail letter or a postcard to North America or Australia costs 54p ($1.05), with mail generally taking about a week. A 10-gram airmail letter or a postcard to continental Europe costs 48p (96¢); mail generally takes about 5 days. See "Post Offices," below, for locations.

*Maps* See "Finding Your Way Around," under "Orientation," earlier in this chapter.

*Money & Credit Cards* See also "Money," in chapter 2. The main American Express office is at 30–31 Haymarket, SW1 (© 020/7484-9640; Tube: Piccadilly Circus). It's open Monday to Saturday from 9am to 6pm, Sunday 10am to 5pm.

For **lost or stolen credit cards,** file a report at the nearest police station; then call the relevant company. For **Amex,** call © **0800/587-6023;** for **Visa,** call your issuing bank or © **0800/891725;** for **MasterCard** call © **0800/964767;** for **Diners Club** call © **08700/190-0011.**

If you need emergency cash over the weekend when banks and some American Express offices are closed, you can have money wired to you via **Western Union** (© **0800/833833;** www.westernunion.com).

*Newspapers & Magazines* The serious British dailies are *The Guardian, The Independent, The Times,* and *The Daily Telegraph;* all have online versions. On Sunday, the Guardian's sibling, *The Observer,* is strong on culture. *Metro* is a free daily London newspaper available at Tube stations, with news, features, reviews, and events; it's published by the same group as the *Evening Standard,* another local that is sold at all newsagents, at newsstands, and from vendors posted near Tube stations and the like. For events listings, the weekly *Time Out* magazine (published each Tues) is unrivaled, although *The Independent* and *The Guardian* on Saturday have listings pullouts (p. 45).

Copies of the *International Herald Tribune, USA Today, Le Monde, Die Tageszeitung,* and most major international newspapers and magazines, are sold at many newsagents and newsstands, especially around the main transport terminals and tourist centers.

*Police*   In an emergency, dial ℂ **999** (free).

*Post Offices*   To find a post office close to you, call ℂ **08457/223344** and give them your postal code (p. 13); or check out www.postoffice.co.uk. London's main post office is just off Trafalgar Square at 24–28 William IV St., WC2 (ℂ **020/ 7484-9307**; Tube: Charing Cross). It's open Monday and Wednesday to Friday 8:30am to 6:30pm, Tuesday 9:15am to 6:30pm, Saturday 9am to 5:30pm. Standard branches are open Monday to Friday from 9/9:30am to 5:30pm; some larger ones, such as the one on Baker Street, are also open Saturday 9am to 12:30pm. Some smaller ones may close for an hour at lunchtime.

*Pubs*   No alcohol can be served to anyone under 18. Children under 16 are allowed in certain rooms in some pubs when accompanied by a parent or guardian. A sign above the door will state the individual pub's policy on admission.

*Radio*   **BBC Greater London Radio** (94.9) is one of the best stations to listen to while you're in the capital. Between midday and 3pm Monday to Friday, Robert Elms presents a lively magazine show including fascinating facts and oddities about London, and featuring guests from the fields of arts, entertainment, media, and politics. **LBC** (97.3) is another local station with news and London-based chat, while **KISS FM** (100, 101, and 105–108) is a capital-based dance music station.

Countrywide 24-hour radio channels include **BBC Radio 1** (98.8 within Greater London), with new music, live studio sessions, concerts, and festival broadcasts; **BBC Radio 3** (91.3), with classical music, jazz, world music, drama, and arts discussions; **BBC Radio Five Live** (909), with live news and sports; **Virgin Radio** (105.8) for classic and current rock 'n' roll; and **XFM** (104.9) for the best guitar music, alternative dance, and hip-hop. Classical buffs listen to **Classic FM** (100–102), which is an active participant in Kids Week (p. 21) and has produced child-oriented CDs such as *Classic FM Mozart For Babies*. **Jazz FM** (102.2) is the place for jazz, blues, and big-band music.

Especially for kids, **BBC7,** one of the BBC's digital radio networks (available on digital radio, on TV sets, and via the Internet), has "Big Toe" stories from best-selling children's authors every morning at 7am, plus, from 2 to 5pm daily, stories, songs, quizzes, and games on CBeebies, the radio version of the BBC children's channel (note that you can listen to the stories at any time on the website). **Capital Disney** is a dedicated digital kids' channel with music from big acts and up-and-comers, news and reviews, famous guests, games, competitions, DVD and game reviews, and features for and by children; you can listen online at www.capitaldisney.co.uk. **Capital FM** (95.8) itself is a pop and rock station.

*Safety* Pockets of luxury rub shoulders with deprived areas even in London's center, so stay cautious and alert at all times, and if you feel in the slightest degree uneasy, leave the area at once.

The usual common-sense tips apply: Don't leave money or valuables on display on your person, and be especially wary of **pickpockets** in confined public spaces such as the Tube. At an **ATM,** don't allow yourself to be distracted by anyone while making your transaction. **Muggings** occur anywhere, even on seemingly innocuous residential streets, so don't walk alone **after dark,** especially in unlit open spaces such as parks (most are locked, anyway). You may also want to avoid the **Tube** late at night, when people start to spill out of pubs.

Homelessness is a big problem in London, as in many major urban centers. Many **derelicts** sit by ATMs, hoping for handouts; few are threatening, but steer clear of any obviously under the influence of drink or drugs. A particular area to steer clear of in this respect is the top of **Charing Cross Road** around the Centrepoint building. **King's Cross,** though slowly being regenerated as a result of the Eurostar station relocating here, is another seedy and rough area to avoid. You'll probably also want to steer clear of **Soho** and **Piccadilly Circus** late at night, when there's lots of drunken leering and swaggering.

There has been an upswing in the police presence on the streets and in public parks in recent years, partly in response to the terrorist attacks of July 2005, but also in a bid to crack down on "antisocial behavior." Not wishing to be a scaremonger, I must stress that there is a disturbing number of mentally ill individuals on the city's streets (the result of a misguided "Care in the Community" campaign to close down mental institutions), and you need to be on your guard. Report any incidents to the nearest police station if you can. The most central station is **West End Central Police Station** at 27 Saville Row, W1 (&#9742; **020/ 7437-1212**); the website www.met.police.uk lists the others borough by borough. All stations are open 24 hours a day. Alternatively, report a crime on the **Crimestoppers line,** &#9742; **0800/555111.** The confidential **Anti-Terrorism Hot Line** is &#9742; **0800/789321.**

*Taxes* There is a 17.5% national **value-added tax (VAT)** added to all hotel and restaurant bills, which is included in the price of many items you purchase; see p. 221 for refund protocol.

Airport departure taxes, which are always subject to change but are about £20 ($40) for flights within Britain and the European Union; and £80 ($160) for flights to the U.S. and other countries, are usually included in air tickets, but check in advance.

*Taxis* See "Getting Around," earlier in this chapter.

*Telephone* See "Telephone Tips" on the inside front cover of this book for more information on dialing to, from, and within London.

**Toll-free numbers:** Numbers beginning with 0800 are toll-free within the U.K. except from mobile phones, but calling a 1-800 number in the U.S. from England costs the same as an overseas call.

There are three types of **public pay phones:** those taking only coins, those accepting only phone cards, and those taking both phone cards and credit cards. **Phone cards** are available in three values: £5 ($10), £10 ($20), and £20

($40), and are reusable until the total value has expired (or you can get rechargeable ones). Those sold at post offices give you free calls on Saturday between noon and midnight to selected countries.

See "The 21st-Century Traveler" in chapter 2 for information on using a cell-phone.

*Time Zone* Most of the year, Britain is 5 hours ahead of the time observed on the East Coast of the United States, though because the U.S. and Britain observe daylight saving time at slightly different times of year (Britain puts its clocks forward by an hour the last Sun in Mar, and back by an hour on the last Sun of Oct), there's a brief period (about a week) in the spring when London is 6 hours ahead of New York. Most European Union countries are an hour ahead of the U.K.

*Tipping* In **restaurants,** service charges of 15% to 20% are usually added to the bill. Sometimes this is clearly marked; if in doubt, ask. If it isn't included, it's customary to add 15% to the bill unless service was lousy (or even if service was included—pay for catering staff is terrible here). **Hotels** often add a service charge of 10% to 15% to most bills. In smaller B&Bs, the tip isn't likely to be included, so tip people who performed special services, such as for the person who served you breakfast. Or you can ask that 10% or 15% be added to the bill and divided among the staff. Tip chambermaids £1.50 ($3) per day (more if you've made their job extra-difficult). It's standard to tip taxi drivers 10% to 15% of the fare. Barbers and hairdressers expect 10% to 15%. Tour guides expect about £4 ($8), although it's not mandatory. Theater ushers don't expect tips.

*Transit Information* See "Getting Around," earlier in this chapter.

*Water* London's water is safe to drink. Tap water is free in restaurants, so be sure to ask for it if you don't want to pay for bottled water.

*Weather* Call ℂ **0870/600-4242** for current weather information, or see www.bbc.co.uk/london/weather.

# 5

# Family-Friendly Accommodations

First the bad news: London is an expensive and overcrowded city, so hotel rooms here can seem small and overpriced in comparison with their equivalents elsewhere. It's especially difficult to find acceptable options at the budget end of the scale. Very cheap rooms here tend to be a tight fit for two, and won't accommodate a rollaway or sometimes even a crib. For that reason, it's important that you are crystal-clear about your needs when making a booking, and that if you need a triple or "family" room, you ask for it.

The good news is that, since the turn of the century, the number of hotel rooms in London has increased massively—the last 4-yearly Visit London census, in 2006, recorded a 20% rise in the number of hotel rooms since 2002 alone, to almost 85,000. That number is set to rise still more in the run-up to the 2012 Olympics, especially in the eastern areas of the city. And with increasing competition, standards seem to be rising—this, however, is sometimes only a superficial improvement on the level of decor.

The majority of these extra rooms are in no-frills **chain hotels,** it's true, but don't overlook these as a family option—they may not be the most stylish or charming, but they do offer decent, clean accommodations in great central locations or in farther-flung but quieter districts. And you'll know what to expect

rather than just hoping for the best. I've reviewed some chain hotels where the locations merited checking out. Otherwise, see "The Chain Gang" on p. 75 for suggestions.

An increasingly popular alternative to hotels for families with young kids or teens is **serviced apartments,** which offer space, flexibility (to eat out or cook a meal), and relative value for the money. (Prices can end up as little as £50/$100 per person per night for five-star options.) A good-value, chain name in this field is the Europe-wide Citadines Apart'hotels (p. 75 and p. 78). For more self-catering apartments, see the suggestions throughout this chapter, or check out www.london 4rent.com, which specializes in high-end properties but includes cheaper options, or www.apartment-hotels.com, a specialist in affordable family accommodations.

Of course, if you're willing and able to fork over the money, London's historic **grand hotels** can't be beat for cachet and atmosphere; some are snooty, it's true, but others are surprisingly welcoming toward young guests, and these are the ones focused on in this guide. At the other end of the luxury spectrum, some of London's **designer boutique hotels** have realized that style need not preclude a child-friendly attitude. It's worth bearing in mind that top-end hotels are especially keen to accommodate families when business travelers go home, and they often offer special weekend rates.

This is particularly true of hotels in the Docklands area, which are good bargains at weekends.

Down the scale somewhat, **B&Bs** can be great places to stay with kids, each offering a true "home away from home" in a foreign city, and more personal touches than any hotel can provide. Those outside the center often offer excellent rates, increased space, and proximity to some of London's natural areas, such as Hampstead Heath. You do get breakfast—often a fully cooked English version that will set everyone up for an entire day of sightseeing. (**Hotel breakfasts**—as opposed to those at B&Bs—tend to be enormously expensive; you're better off seeking out a local cafe.)

**The London Bed & Breakfast Agency Ltd.** (© **020/7586-276;** www.londonbb. com), **London B&B** (© **800/872-2632** in the U.S.; www.londonbandb.com), and **Uptown Reservations** (© **020/7937-2001;** www.uptownres.co.uk), are all reputable agencies that can arrange B&B accommodations in private homes, plus some self-catering apartments; family rooms cost about £145 ($290).

Lastly, real budget accommodations come in the form of London's **youth hostels,** which often offer family rooms (p. 90).

**RESERVATION SERVICES**   Various websites offer hotel and apartment discounts. Three of my favorites are www. londonnights.com, www.londontown. com, and www.smoothhound.co.uk. In my experience, though, rooms booked on the Internet don't always come up to scratch—they can be tiny, for instance, or in inferior parts of the hotel (the hotels themselves are usually uninspiring chains, too). It's therefore essential that you clarify, when booking, that your accommodations should be large enough. Note also that booking through such websites can be time-consuming and frustrating, as the hotels you choose may not have the

special offers available on the type of room you need.

**A NOTE ABOUT PRICES**   The price categories provided below divide up as follows: **Very Expensive** means a family of four pays more than £250 ($500) per night, **Expensive** means a bill of £175 to £250 ($350–$500), **Moderate** means £100 to £175 ($200–$350), and **Inexpensive** less than £100 ($200). Unless otherwise stated, published prices are **rack rates.** Many of them, particularly in the case of expensive hotels, don't include the government-imposed **VAT** (value-added tax) of 17.5%, so check when booking, as this can add a hefty slab to your bill. Always ask for a **better rate,** particularly at the first-class and deluxe hotels (B&Bs generally charge a fixed rate), and check the hotels' websites for **special online rates.**

**RESERVE IN ADVANCE**   It's common sense that those with children in tow should **always book accommodations in advance,** especially during the peak season (roughly Apr–Oct). Many hotels and B&Bs still offer **nonsmoking rooms,** but double-check when you book. All very expensive and some lower-category hotels offer **babysitting** services, but because these are generally outsourced from reputable agencies, they require 24 hours' notice. If you need a **crib** or **highchair,** reserve one in advance, too, as most hotels have limited numbers.

For a description of London **neighborhoods** (including those likely to have accommodations suitable for families), see p. 49.

If you've a late flight in or an early flight out, you might need to stay near an **airport.** Websites www.airporthotels4 less.co.uk and www.holidayextras.co.uk offer good discounts, especially on three-bed and family rooms. Otherwise, **Hilton London Heathrow Airport** (© **020/ 8759-7755;** www.hilton.co.uk) is pricey but has a pool to keep little ones occupied; it's also actually part of Terminal 4 and has a glass wall facing the runways. Six minutes by car from Gatwick, the **Copthorne Hotel London Gatwick** (© **01342/348800;** www.millennium hotels.co.uk) has a pool, squash courts, and large grounds. Gatwick's South Terminal is also home to the first **Yotel** (© **020/710-8010;** www.yotel.com), with cabin-style rooms that can be rented for periods of 4 hours and up. A 12-hour stay in a Premium cabin with a double bed that can fold up into a couch, a shower, free Internet access, and 24-hour room service costs £82 ($164); children

can share with you, with cribs provided by advance request. A second Yotel was scheduled to open at Heathrow as this guide went to press.

At Stansted Airport, the **Radisson SAS** (© **01279/661012;** www.stansted. radissonsas.com), linked to the airport via a walkway, boasts great runway views and a pool and spa. Rates range from moderate to expensive, depending on when you stay and whether you get an online deal.

Alternatively, see the airports' websites for accommodations suggestions, including discounts.

## 1 Central London

### ST. JAMES'S & MAYFAIR
**VERY EXPENSIVE**

There's a **Four Seasons** hotel (p. 96) on Park Lane.

**The Athenaeum Apartments** ✰✰✰   The Athenaeum, a hotel with a mixture of chintzy and more soberly modern guest rooms, has a secret—four Edwardian town houses converted into apartments around the corner from the main building, containing some of London's best choices for family stays. These are decorated in a variety of styles to suit all tastes, but those with kids should try to snag the Family Apartment— a pop art spectacular with mirrored Philippe Starck chairs, seats resembling giant computer keys, a kids' sleeping niche off the living room, and a games console that doubles as a coffee table (with nostalgia-inducing games such as Space Invaders). It comes supplied with funky building blocks and a welcome bag with a sticker book, teddy bear, and bath duck. Practical as well as appealing, all apartments come with full kitchens, washing machines, and highchairs on request. Potties and strollers can be supplied free of charge. Guests can fend for themselves or avail themselves of the hotel's many services—there's even a grocery shopping service, though there are small supermarkets close by if you prefer to handle the shopping, and the kitchen can provide hampers (baskets) for picnics. (Hyde Park is also mere steps away.)

Alternatively, you can stay in interconnecting rooms in the hotel, which overlook Green Park and the river. All junior guests can register for the complimentary kids' film library, which includes everything from *Baby Einstein* to *Pirates of the Caribbean;* age-specific toy boxes are also provided, plus Xboxes, PlayStations, and iPod docking stations for older kids by request. Bathroom goodies include a mini toothbrush, tear-free toiletries, and kids' bathrobes and fluffy slippers; milk and cookies are provided at turndown.

There are further swanky one- and two-bedroom contemporary apartments at The Athenaeum's sister property, **23 Greengarden House,** a 15-minute walk away in Marylebone; guests there (over-12s) can use the hotel's spa.

116 Piccadilly, W1J 7BJ. © 020/7499-3464. Fax 020/7493-1860. www.athenaeumhotel.com. 33 units. From £150 ($300) double room in hotel; from £380 ($720) apt. Rollaway beds £35 ($70); cribs free. Rates include continental or English breakfast. AE, DC, MC, V. Tube: Green Park. **Amenities:** Restaurant; bar; spa; business services; hair salon;

# Where to Stay in Central London

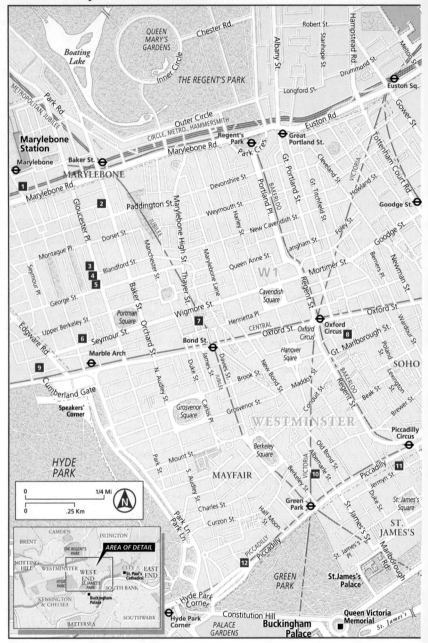

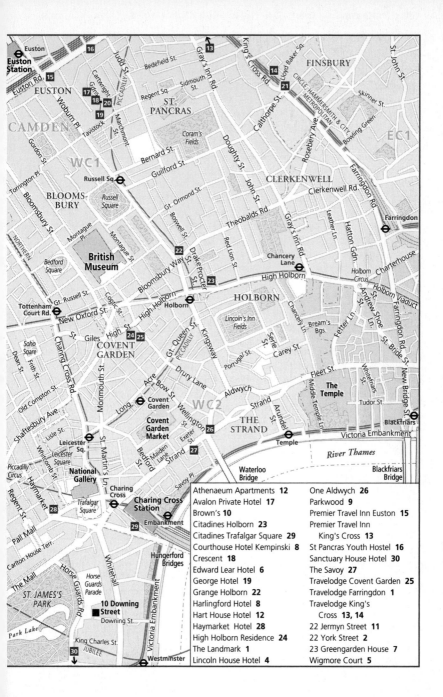

| Athenaeum Apartments **12** | One Aldwych **26** |
| Avalon Private Hotel **17** | Parkwood **9** |
| Brown's **10** | Premier Travel Inn Euston **15** |
| Citadines Holborn **23** | Premier Travel Inn |
| Citadines Trafalgar Square **29** | King's Cross **13** |
| Courthouse Hotel Kempinski **8** | St Pancras Youth Hostel **16** |
| Crescent **18** | Sanctuary House Hotel **30** |
| Edward Lear Hotel **6** | The Savoy **27** |
| George Hotel **19** | Travelodge Covent Garden **25** |
| Grange Holborn **22** | Travelodge Farringdon **1** |
| Harlingford Hotel **8** | Travelodge King's |
| Hart House Hotel **12** | Cross **13, 14** |
| Haymarket Hotel **28** | 22 Jermyn Street **11** |
| High Holborn Residence **24** | 22 York Street **2** |
| The Landmark **1** | 23 Greengarden House **7** |
| Lincoln House Hotel **4** | Wigmore Court **5** |

24-hr. room service; massage; babysitting; laundry service; same-day dry cleaning; free CD loan. *In room:* A/C, TV/DVD/CD player w/pay movies, dataport, minibar, hair dryer, trouser press, iron, safe.

**Brown's** ★★★    If style matters to you, Brown's will be one of your top choices in London. This classic hotel, created in 1837 and occupying 11 Georgian town houses, retains much of its traditional charm (especially in its wood-paneled bar, English tearoom, and Grill restaurant), but a recent transformation has endowed it with a beautifully restrained contemporary look. It's a risky mixture, but it works very well. Yet it's not a case of style over substance at Brown's: Service here is second to none, and that includes a warm welcome extended to even the youngest guests. As part of the ongoing "It's a Family Affair" offer, children booking a deluxe room for a Friday, Saturday, Sunday, or bank-holiday Monday night net their parents another deluxe room, interconnecting or adjacent, for free. Prices for this offer start at £480 ($960) per night, including continental breakfast, or you can upgrade to a classic or deluxe suite (comprising interconnecting executive rooms). Deluxe rooms are vast, and the interconnecting ones are linked via doors within the walk-in wardrobes, creating a sort of secret passageway between rooms that my sons found a hoot. Alternatively, you can fit one rollaway in deluxe rooms through junior suites, and two rollaways in all other suites.

Children get an age-specific gift on arrival—perhaps an animal-themed helium balloon or a personalized copy of *The Jungle Book,* which was actually written here, as Rudyard Kipling was among the hotel's illustrious guests (a DVD of it is also available from the library). Under-3s eat and drink for free, and those 3 to 12 pay half-price on any menu in the hotel. If I had to find fault with Brown's it would be with the bathtubs—they look gorgeous but are just too big for an adult to have a comfortable soak without sliding down into the water! On the other hand, the turndown staff bring you a free nightly bath gift from the spa, and the kids' bathroom is provided with a nonslip mat, mini bathrobes and slippers, ample supplies of kids' toiletries, bath ducks, and a temperature tester. If that's not relaxing enough, the chic spa even offers a "kids' menu" of facials, foot and hand treatments, or a back rub.

Albemarle St., W1S 4BP. ⓒ 020/7493-6020. Fax 020/7493-9381. www.roccofortehotels.com. 136 units. From £310 ($620) double; from £800 ($1,600) suite. Rollaway beds £50 ($100); cribs free. AE, DC, MC, V. Tube: Green Park. **Amenities:** Restaurant; bar; tearoom; spa and gym; concierge; business services; 24-hr. room service; massage; babysitting; same-day laundry and dry cleaning. *In room:* A/C, DVD w/pay movies and music, dataport, minibar, hair dryer, safe.

**22 Jermyn Street** ★★★    There's nothing, it seems, that the discreet, knowledgeable staff at this town-house hotel—run by the same family for nearly a century and reinvented as an upscale boutique hotel in 1990—haven't thought of when it comes to their junior guests, whether it's candies and musical cassettes with singalong books, or practicalities such as safety features, baby thermometers, baby baths, changing mats, and bottle warmers. They'll even bring you diapers should you run out, and staff will babysit, or provide agency staff if you prefer. The owner produces a wonderfully personal range of newsletters detailing the city's best sights, shows, shops, and restaurants, one of them especially for kids. My one caveat is that the hotel is subject to round-the-clock noise since it's close to Piccadilly Circus.

Families generally pay to have a comfy queen-size sofa bed set up in one of the two-room suites, although there are also five double rooms. There's no dining room, but the good and varied room service menu features kid-friendly fare, all of which is available in smaller portions, although with sufficient notice the kitchen tries to provide any dish you care to order. Alternatively, there's a "high tea" of finger sandwiches and scones. Entertainment includes a 14-channel satellite TV, an extensive complimentary video library (with free popcorn, salted and sweet), GameBoys, and books to read or draw in and then wipe clean. After soaking in the deep tubs, little ones can wrap up in a child-size bathrobe, available for all ages.

*Insider tip:* If you're heading out for a walk in nearby St. James's Park (p. 206), ask the kitchen for bread or croissants for the ducks, geese, and pelicans.

22 Jermyn St., SW1Y 6HL. ✆ 020/7734-2353. Fax 020/7734-0750. www.22jermyn.com. 18 units. £220 ($440) double; from £310 ($620) suite; £450 ($900) 2-bedroom suite with sofa bed. Cots free. AE, DC, MC, V. Tube: Piccadilly Circus. **Amenities:** Access (over-18s) to nearby health club with swimming pool £15 ($30); concierge; business services; 24-hr. room service; physical therapy and massage; babysitting; same-day laundry and dry cleaning. *In room:* TV/VCR w/pay movies, dataport, minibar, safe.

## MODERATE

**Sanctuary House Hotel**   This small hotel, set above a pub famous for its award-winning traditional beers, may not sound like the most family-friendly option, but its weekend rate, inclusive of continental breakfast, is a superb bargain in this part of town. The rooms are a bit chintzy and they're not huge, but each can accommodate one rollaway bed and one crib (you have to supply your own bedding for the latter). The adult beds (king-size four-posters in the superior rooms) are extremely comfortable, and the small bathrooms have both a tub and shower. Rooms are on the first to fifth floors (there's an elevator), away from the bustle of the ground-floor Ale & Pie House (owned by the Fuller's brewery), which offers old-style British dishes such as Welsh lamb (most available in half-portions), and has highchairs and a nonsmoking section. Note, however, kids aren't allowed in on Thursday and Friday nights, when the pub gets too busy (it's tiny). There is a further good-value Fuller's pub-hotel on the South Bank, The Mad Hatter, with interconnecting rooms for families; and another, The Fox & Goose, with a patio garden, at Ealing, 15km (10 miles) from Heathrow airport.

33 Tothill St., SW1H 9LA. ✆ 020/7799-4044. Fax 020/7799-3657. www.fullershotels.com. 34 units. £110–£195 ($220–$390) double. Children under 12 stay free in parent's room. Rollaway beds free; cribs free. Rates include continental breakfast Fri–Sun. AE, MC, V. Tube: St. James's Park. **Amenities:** Restaurant/bar. *In room:* A/C, TV, dataport, beverage-maker, iron (on request), trouser press.

# MARYLEBONE, REGENT'S PARK & FITZROVIA
## VERY EXPENSIVE

**The Landmark** 🐾   The *pièce de résistance* of this impressive Victorian railway hotel (it's actually joined to Marylebone Station by an ornate walkway) is its 15m (49-ft.) semi-ozone pool and whirlpool, given a sparkling fresh look as part of its incorporation into the hotel's new state-of-the-art spa. It's a shame, though, that the hotel has added a £10 ($20) per day surcharge (£7/$14 for over-2s) for guest use of this facility. Another highlight is the eight-story atrium through the middle of the building—home to the Winter Garden, a stunning setting for afternoon teas and Sunday jazz brunches. For all young kids, a whole range of amenities, from pacifiers, diapers, and toiletries to baby-walkers, are available.

The traditionally decorated guest rooms are some of the biggest in the capital; their large windows make them seem airier still. This is especially noticeable in the marble bathrooms with their deep tubs, walk-in showers, twin sinks, and separate toilet. Family rooms, which cost £299 ($599) per night as part of the Family Escapes deal (including cookies for the kids, and breakfast), have extra space still and two queen-size beds

## In the Swim

A splash in the pool is a great way of burning off energy or relaxing before or after a hard day's sightseeing. My favorite pool is at the **Four Seasons Canary Wharf** (p. 96), which has an infinity edge that can almost make you believe you're swimming in the Thames, which it overlooks. It's actually part of the adjoining health club, but kids get their own session from 9 to 11am every morning. There's unrestricted access to the funky 18m (59-ft.) basement pool at the ultra-fashionable new **Haymarket Hotel** (p. 77), which has its own sound system and poolside bar, while **One Aldwych** (p. 75) has a smallish but swanky basement pool with underwater classical music. **The Landmark** (p. 71) has a larger one that's been refurbished as part of its plush new spa

At 25m (82 ft.), the **Grange City** (p. 92) has the biggest pool of the hotels reviewed in this guide; **The Rembrandt's** is smaller and very toddler-friendly, with Aquababes classes, and there's a tiny pool in the spa of the **Courthouse Hotel Kempinski** (p. 76). If you're on a budget, the sparkling-clean pool at **Crown Moran** (p. 98), set beneath a lovely atrium, is exceptional given the rates.

next to each other. They're available for up to two adults and two kids under 13. For a little more parental privacy, you'll need interconnecting rooms. When booking, be sure to state whether you want a room facing the main road, the internal atrium, or the station. The latter rooms are quieter, but double glazing throughout means that all rooms are peaceful (though there's the occasional shudder from Tube trains passing right beneath). Make sure to investigate the website offers thoroughly before booking: Reductions on weekend rates can be up to 70%.

*Insider tip:* Marylebone Station has an excellent little community of shops for everyday needs, including a newsagent, a Marks & Spencer Simply Food store for breakfast and snack fare, a great bagel stand, and a specialist cheese outlet.

222 Marylebone Rd., NW1 6JQ. (© 020/7631-8000. Fax 020/7632-8080. www.landmarklondon.co.uk. 299 units. £455–£535 ($910–$1,070) double; from £625 ($1,250) suite. Children under 14 stay free in parent's room. Rollaway beds £60 ($120); cribs free. AE, DC, MC, V. Tube: Marylebone. **Amenities:** 3 restaurants; 2 bars; spa; gym; concierge; business services and IT center; 24-hr. room service; massage; babysitting; laundry service; same-day dry cleaning. *In room:* A/C, TV w/pay movies, VCR/DVD players on request, PlayStations, dataport, minibar, hair dryer, safe.

## EXPENSIVE

**22 York St.** ✻✻    The sheer homeliness of this wonderful little Georgian townhouse B&B comes as something of a shock given its location just a couple of minutes from the roar of Baker Street. Guest rooms really couldn't be more appealing, with their gorgeous rug-strewn wooden floors, French antique furniture, and soft quilts. In the delightful breakfast room, guests congregate around a long curved table to enjoy a specially selected continental breakfast and to exchange sightseeing tips (a highchair can be provided). A pleasant lounge offers satellite TV, along with complimentary tea and coffee. Of the 20 rooms, 2 are triples (one double and one single bed), and 3 are family rooms (one double and two single beds). There's no elevator, and the owner is keen that parents take into account the stone staircases and other hard surfaces.

22 York St., W1U 6PX. © 020/7224-2990. Fax 020/7224-1990. www.22yorkstreet.co.uk. 20 units. £120 ($240) double; £165 ($330) triple; £200 ($400) quadruple. Cribs free. Rates include continental breakfast. AE, MC, V. Tube: Baker St. **Amenities:** Babysitting. *In room:* TV, dataport, hair dryer.

## MODERATE

If the following is full, similar places worth a try are **Hart House Hotel** (© 020/7935-2288; www.harthouse.co.uk) and the **Minotel Wigmore Court Hotel** (© 020/7935-0928; www.wigmore-court-hotel.co.uk), both on the same road as the Lincoln House. What the latter lacks in friendliness (at least in my experience), it makes up for with its self-catering kitchen and laundry facilities.

**Lincoln House Hotel**    One of the virtues of this welcoming B&B is that all rooms, with the exception of the budget singles, have minifridges—handy for families for storing milk, snacks, and so on (don't worry—they're silent fridges that won't keep you awake). A flask is also provided, to fill from the chilled water machine in the corridor. Rooms, which include triples and quads (the latter have a double bed, a single, and a pullout) aren't enormous but are by no means tiny by London standards, and there are clever features such as beds designed for storing luggage underneath. Many guests also find the French-style built-in plastic shower cubicles a tad on the cozy side, but in my experience they're clean and adequate (perhaps I'm just more accustomed to them from traveling in France a lot).

Breakfasts offer a more than customary choice: In addition to the continental breakfast included in the room rate, you can get a full English or more unusual Greek-influenced options. It's an extra £3.50 ($7) if you do deviate from the standard continental option, but free to kids under 15. Look out for discounts of up to 30% on the website, which can reduce the price of a family room to less than £100 ($200).

33 Gloucester Place, W1U 8HY. © 020/7486-7630. Fax 020/7486-0166. www.lincoln-house-hotel.co.uk. 23 units. £89–£115 ($178–$230) double; £129 ($258) triple; £139 ($278) quad. MC, V. Tube: Marble Arch. *In room:* Wi-Fi, minifridges.

## INEXPENSIVE

**Edward Lear Hotel** 🏔 *Value*    For the price, this long-popular budget choice in the former town house of Victorian artist and limerick writer Edward Lear (whose illustrated works punctuate the walls) is outstanding—the very low rates include a full English breakfast (with free seconds if you're not full), plus a guest lounge with free Internet access. Rooms (doubles with shared facilities, shower, or bathtub; triples with shared facilities or showers; and quads with shower or bathtub) aren't huge or particularly inspiring, and the area can be hectic (ask for one of the back rooms if this bothers you), but the price is right and the staff is friendly. Cribs can be provided, and there are highchairs in the breakfast room.

The **Parkwood** (© 020/7402-2241; www.parkwoodhotel.com), across the Edgware Road in Bayswater and just a few steps from Hyde Park, is a similar spot run by the same people, with fresh new decor and statues of Laurel and Hardy. They also run the **George Hotel** (© 020/7837-8777; www.georgehotel.com), set in Bloomsbury and offering access to the same tennis courts as the other hotels on Cartwright Gardens (p. 216).

28–30 Seymour St., W1H 5WD. © 020/7402-5401. Fax 020/7706-3766. www.edlear.com. 31 units, 12 with bathroom. £60–£99 ($120–$198) double; £65–£99 ($130–$198) triple; £81–£125 ($162–$250) family room. Children under 2 stay free in parent's room. Cribs free. Rates include English breakfast. MC, V. Tube: Marble Arch. **Amenities:** Free Internet access in guest lounge. *In room:* TV, beverage-maker.

## BLOOMSBURY & HOLBORN

With the regeneration of the Brunswick Centre with its piazza full of family-friendly eateries (p. 110), this neighborhood is more attractive than ever to families—particularly if you're arriving by Eurostar at its new St Pancras terminal.

### EXPENSIVE

**The Grange Holborn** is a very similar proposition to its sister hotel the **Grange City** near the Tower of London (p. 92).

### MODERATE

**Crescent** ⭑   The warmth of this excellent little family-run B&B is attested to by its many loyal fans, who return again and again for its comfortable rooms and little touches that make it virtually unique in this price range—baby-listening according to staff availability, highchairs in the breakfast room, cribs, and, best of all, for kids needing to burn off excess energy, access to a private garden square and to four tennis courts (staff can loan out rackets and balls). The Crescent celebrated its 50th birthday in 2006, and some staff members are proud to welcome the grandchildren of those who first stayed here in their own youth. Rooms are fairly plain but clean and pleasant (some can smell a bit musty); all but some of the singles are en suite. There's no elevator, but ground-floor rooms are available. The English breakfasts are robust enough to keep you going all day, and there's a pleasant quiet lounge for hot drinks and snacks.

In the same price range and offering access to the same tennis courts, the **Harlingford Hotel** at no. 61–63 (© **020/7387-1551;** www.harlingfordhotel.com) has a more contemporary decor.

49–50 Cartwright Gardens, WC1H 9EL. © 020/7387-1515. Fax 020/7383-2054. www.crescenthoteloflondon.com. 27 units. £97 ($194) double; £110 ($220) triple; £120 ($240) family room. Cribs free. Rates include English breakfast. MC, V. Tube: Euston or Russell Sq. **Amenities:** Tennis courts; guest lounge. *In room:* TV, beverage-maker, hair dryer, iron, safe.

### INEXPENSIVE

As well as good B&Bs, this is an area with plentiful chains, including **Premier Travel Inn** (p. 75).

**Avalon Private Hotel**   Don't come to the Avalon expecting luxury, and you won't be disappointed. But for the price, this is a more-than-acceptable option, with full English breakfast included in the rates, and an early check-in time (rooms are guaranteed to be ready by noon). It also offers access to the same garden square and tennis courts as the Crescent and the Harlingford (see above), and has a pleasant guest lounge overlooking the square, with free Internet access and filled with guidebooks and maps so you can plot your adventures. Top-floor rooms, often filled with students, are reached via steep stairs, but bedrooms on the lower levels have easier access. The triples have either three single beds or a double and a single, while "quads" have a double bed and either two or three singles. A handful of units have tiny shower rooms; all units have basins. Reserve online and you'll net yourself a decent saving.

46–47 Cartwright Gardens, WC1H 9EL. © 020/7387-2366. Fax 020/7387-5810. www.avalonhotel.co.uk. 27 units. £63–£80 ($126–$160) double; £74–£90 ($148–$180) triple; £84–£99 ($168–$198) quad. Rates include English breakfast. AE, DC, MC, V. Tube: Euston or Russell Sq. **Amenities:** Tennis courts; guest lounge w/free Internet access. *In room:* TV, beverage-maker, safe.

**High Holborn Residence** *Finds Value*   Make like a student at one of the venerable London School of Economics' residence halls, which offers B&B accommodations to

## The Chain Gang

Though the bulk of their clients are business travelers, some of the big hotel chains offer superb family rates if you don't mind absence of character and an impersonal feel. **Premier Travel Inn** (© 0870/242-8000; www.premier travelinn.com) has more than 480 budget hostelries around the country, including around 15 in the capital at the time of writing, among them in County Hall, Tower Bridge, Southwark, Putney Bridge, Kew, Wimbledon, Hammersmith, Kensington, King's Cross, Euston (Bloomsbury), Hampstead, and Wembley. Prices vary slightly from inn to inn, with the best rates at those outside the center (some charge differently for weekdays and week-ends, too). But family rooms for up to five (with pullout sofa bed, plus a free cot where needed) are always the same rate as doubles, and kids under 16 get free breakfasts (continental or cooked). They also get a Kid Pack, and there are "Great Days Out" offers on tickets to nearby attractions, includ-ing free entry for kids. For **Travelodge,** which is similar, see p. 76. For **Holi-day Inn,** where kids stay and eat free, see p. 96.

Better still, because they offer self-catering amenities in conjunction with free standard hotel services (such as use of a breakfast lounge, a laundry, and babysitting services), **Citadines** Apart'hotels (© 0800/376-3898 within U.K.; www.citadines.com) consist of moderately priced, basic studios and apartments. In London, you'll find them in the City (Barbican), South Kens-ington, Holborn, and Trafalgar Square (p. 78).

individuals and families during summer vacation (mid-Aug to late Sept). One of six halls in a number of decent locations, this is handy for the shops and theaters of Covent Garden, the museums of Bloomsbury, and the varied entertainments of the South Bank. Most rooms are en suite triples with telephones, but some of the twin-bedded doubles have shared bathrooms. As you'd expect, given the context, the decor and furnishings tend toward the functional, but rooms are clean, bright, and airy. Linen and towels are provided (and changed every 3 days). Guests can make use of the bar, TV lounge, game room with pool table, self-catering kitchenette, and launderette.

178 High Holborn, WC1V 7AA. © 020/7955-7575. Fax 020/7955-7676. www.lse.ac.uk/collections/vacations. 494 units. £49–£70 ($98–$140) twin; £80 ($160) triple. Rates include buffet-style continental breakfast. MC, V. Tube: Hol-born. **Amenities:** Bar; kitchenette; game room; launderette; TV lounge.

## COVENT GARDEN & THE STRAND
### VERY EXPENSIVE

Note that **The Savoy** on the Strand, reviewed in the first edition of this guide, was about to close for a massive (and much-needed) 2-year renovation at the time of this writing, with reopening scheduled for 2009.

**One Aldwych** ⟨⟨⟨  This stunning conversion of a former newspaper HQ is adult in feel, with simple but chic guest rooms with contemporary furnishings, crisp white linens, and luxurious bathrooms with all-natural toiletries and funky mini-TVs on stalks. But don't let this put you off—One Aldwych more than welcomes kids through its impressive doors, offering a children's DVD, CD, and games library, a book (sometimes

London-themed), complimentary teddy bears; milk and cookies, milkshake, or fruit cocktail, depending on age; slippers and bathrobes for ages 7 and under; and bottle warmers on request. Wooden cots and very comfy rollaways (with bed rails if required) can be placed in rooms from the deluxe double category and up, or some of the standard (smallest) doubles interconnect. But best of all are the executive suites with two or three bedrooms, some with kitchenettes, some with dining rooms, and some with private gyms. Some rooms have fabulous views over Waterloo Bridge and the National Theatre. See the website for special weekend rates and packages.

Kids won't be able to resist the divine 18m (59-ft.) basement pool, complete with underwater music (if you can't hear it, ask to staff to switch it on). Eats-wise, kids' portions and highchairs are available in the two modern European restaurants (Axis and the more informal mezzanine-level Indigo), while the room-service menu has a well-thought-out children's section available until 11pm. *Insider tip:* If you don't want to pay for a full breakfast, the Cinnamon Bar, part of the hotel but with a separate entrance, serves delectable cookies, muffins, fruit salad, yogurt with berry compote, smoothies, and juices, plus great espressos for flagging parents.

1 Aldwych, WC2B 4RH. © 020/7300-1000. Fax 020/7300-1001. www.onealdwych.com. 105 units. £360–£435 ($720–$870) double; from £575 ($1,150) suite. Rollaway beds £65 ($130), free for under-16s; cribs free. AE, DC, MC, V. Tube: Covent Garden or Temple (closed Sun). **Amenities:** 2 restaurants; 2 bars; indoor pool; gym; treatment rooms; sauna and steam room; concierge; 24-hr. room service; massage; babysitting; laundry service; same-day dry cleaning; movie-screening room. *In room:* A/C, TV/VCR w/pay movies, CD player, fax, free Wi-Fi Internet access, minibar, hair dryer, safe.

## INEXPENSIVE

**Travelodge** *Value* A very well-located branch of the nationwide budget chain (see "The Chain Gang" on p. 75), this Travelodge is an especially good choice if you want to catch some shows—it's on the fringes of Theaterland. Rooms are functional, some with shower only, but perfectly adequate given the price, and family rooms (with a double, a sofa, and a pullout) cost no more than a double. There's a bar-cafe serving light snacks and pizzas, in addition to continental and English breakfasts (free to children under 10), though with so many great eating options nearby, it's hard to imagine why you'd stay in, unless you get totally worn out from the equally great neighborhood shopping. Be aware that there's no left-luggage facility. Travelodge is fast expanding: At the time of writing, there are central branches in Marylebone, King's Cross (two), and Farringdon, and others at Battersea, Kew Bridge, Wimbledon, Wembley, Park Royal, City Road (near Old Street), Liverpool Street, Docklands, and City Airport, although not all of them offer family rooms.

*Insider tip:* Family rooms can cost as little as £26 ($52) when booked well ahead at the Saver rate—an incredible bargain for central London. Note that you can also cancel a Travelodge room up to noon on the day of arrival, without paying a penny (although not rooms booked at the Saver rate).

10 Drury Lane, WC2B 5RE. © 0870/191-1745. Fax 020/7831-1548. www.travelodge.co.uk. 153 units. £95 ($190) double or family room. Cots free. 24-hr. parking (no reservations) £15 ($30). AE, DC, MC, V. Tube: Covent Garden. **Amenities:** Bar-cafe. *In room:* TV, beverage-maker, Wi-Fi (fee), hair dryer (on request).

## TRAFALGAR SQUARE, PICCADILLY & SOHO
### VERY EXPENSIVE
**Courthouse Hotel Kempinski** *Finds* Another rare offering in the hotel wasteland of Soho, the Courthouse Kempinski is in the heart of the action (virtually opposite

Carnaby St.) yet remains blissfully free of traffic noise. Inside a former magistrates' court, it retains many of the building's original features—including the Victorian prison cells, now converted into little booths in the bar—with rather *recherché* modern design. The result isn't entirely successful, at least to my eye, but your kids might, as mine did, like such playful touches as the two armchairs fashioned like giant seashells. You may be more interested in the building's history—Charles Dickens reported, Napoleon bore witness, and Mick Jagger defended himself here.

Families tend to stay in interconnecting doubles and twins, but kids up to 12 can stay in a parent's room or suite free of charge. Junior guests get a welcome gift, kids' toiletries, robes and slippers, and complimentary snacks and bedtime drinks. Breakfast is free for under-5s, and half price for kids ages 6 to 12. The room service menu has a kids' section—it's a better-than-average choice, but standards, both in the quality of food and the standard of service, aren't what you might reasonably expect at this price level. With the choices in surrounding Soho, you're best advised to head out (there's also an on-site brasserie serving light Italian bites, fish, and salad, and a Thai/Indian fusion restaurant). What might keep you here is the small basement pool; it's part of Sanook Spa, and you need to pre-book a time slot to use it, which means that you'll probably have it to yourselves.

19–21 Great Marlborough St., W1F 7HL. ℭ 020/7297-5555. Fax 020/7297-5566. www.courthouse-hotel.com. 116 units. £270–£390 ($540–$780) double; from £550 ($1,100) suite. Rollaway beds £45 ($90) but free to kids under 12; cribs free. AE, DC, MC, V. Tube: Oxford Circus. **Amenities:** 2 restaurants; bar; roof terrace; indoor pool; spa; concierge; 24-hr. room service; babysitting; laundry; dry cleaning; ironing service. *In room:* A/C, TV w/pay movies and games, CD player, minibar, dataport, Internet access via TV, hair dryer, safe.

## Haymarket Hotel ℛ

*The* glam opening of 2007, the Haymarket is a surprise opening in an area with a paucity of accommodations options of any kind. Those familiar with the other Firmdale hotels in London won't be surprised by the decor—contemporary English luxe with no concessions to minimalism—but they will be impressed by the breathtaking sumptuousness of it all, and by the sculpture and other modern artworks. As well as the double rooms with their splendid granite, glass and oak bathrooms complete with double basins and TVs—it's possible to add a rollaway and/or a crib to these rooms—there are also a couple of stunning one- and two-bedroom suites, plus a four-story town house with both a private entrance and access via the hotel, three to five bedrooms, and a kitchen/diner. All guests can enjoy use of the 18m (59-ft.) swimming pool, which has its own sound system and bar; there's also a gym and a treatment room. The hotel's colorful, vast Brumus restaurant and bar serves seasonal North Italian dishes that will please kids and adults alike—they may enjoy the starters of child-friendly pasta dishes (the likes of ravioli with spinach, ricotta and sage butter, potato gnocchi with rocket pesto and goat's cheese, and orecchiette with spicy pork sausage and broccoli, averaging about £9/$18) while you tuck into a more substantial saltimbocca (veal with Marsala wine, baked artichokes, and shallots) or grilled leg of lamb, with aubergine, rosemary, and anchovy sauce. Dishes both here and on room service can be adapted for kids, too.

1 Suffolk Place. SW1Y 4BP. ℭ 020/7470-4000. Fax 020/7470-4004. www.firmdale.com. 51 units. £245–£310 ($490–$620) double; from £385 ($770) suite; from £2,250 ($4,500) 2-bedroom suite; £3,500–£4,500/week ($7,000–$9,000) town house, but call for quote. Rollaway beds £40 ($80); cots free. AE, MC, V. Tube: Piccadilly Circus. **Amenities:** Restaurant; bar; indoor pool w/bar; drawing room/conservatory; gym; treatment room; concierge; 24-hr. room service; babysitting; dry-cleaning service. *In room:* Cable TV, DVD/CD player w/library hire, A/C, Wi-Fi, minibar, safe, massage (on request), personal trainer (on request).

## MODERATE

**Citadines** *Value*   This "Apart'Hotel" (see p. 75 for others) has a marvelous location just steps away from Trafalgar Square, the National Gallery, and the London Brass Rubbing Centre (p. 50), and is also very handy for both Covent Garden and St. James's Park. For the prime setting, what it offers, in terms of prices and facilities, is exceptional. As with other members of the chain, it allows you to choose between hotel services (including a 24-hr. reception, a breakfast room, and a launderette) or self-cater according to your whim or budget, since the flats all have full kitchens complete with dishwasher, oven, microwave, and fridge. You're provided with linen and towel, which are changed once a week, when the apartment is cleaned—for an extra charge you can have it done more frequently. You can also get someone to shop for you, for a fee.

18/21 Northumberland Ave., WC2N 5EA. © 0800/376-3898. www.citadines.com. 187 units. £174 ($348) 4-person apt; £225 ($450) 6-person apt. Cribs free. Parking available for a fee. AE, MC, V. Tube: Charing Cross. **Amenities:** Breakfast room; business center; babysitting; Wi-Fi; cleaning service; laundry; dry cleaning. *In room:* Kitchen, cable TV, CD player, hair dryer, safe, iron.

## 2 West of the Center

### KENSINGTON & SOUTH KENSINGTON
#### VERY EXPENSIVE

**The Cheval Group** (www.chevalgroup.com) has three long-stay luxury apartment complexes in this area: **Gloucester Park** and **Hyde Park Gate** (both minimum 3 months) and **Thorney Court** (minimum 22 days).

**The Rembrandt**   For its location right opposite the V&A (p. 173), this popular hotel is competitively priced, if unexciting, and has the benefit of a 15m (49-ft.) pool in the basement health club—although it does seem a bit rich that guests must pay an extra £7.50 ($15) a day for the use of this facility when clients of the Cheval Apartments up the road (p. 79) get free access. That said, be sure to look at the different options when booking online, as you might find the same rates offered on the same room both with and without complimentary health club access (if booking by phone or e-mail, push for health club access to be included, as it will save you a tidy sum if four of you use the facility every day). The pool is a child-friendly one (lane swimmers will be better off at the nearby Chelsea Leisure Centre) where those with tots might like to join in on Aquababes sessions, and the fitness classes offered in the club include a "teen circuit" for ages 12 to 16. Guest rooms vary in quality but most have been upgraded of late to a contemporary style, so make sure you ask for one of these, and all now have air-conditioning and, most usefully, fridges. You can get interconnecting rooms, which put The Rembrandt at the lower end of our "Very Expensive" category (at least if you book standard doubles and twins), or there are some triples to which a rollaway can be added for a charge. The big, bright breakfast room/restaurant has also been brought up-to-date visually but remains traditional in its offering two carveries (roast) a day, at dinner and lunch, as well as other hot and cold dishes. It includes a kids' menu.

11 Thurloe Place, SW7 2RS. © 020/7589-8100. Fax 020/7225-3476. www.sarova.co.uk. 195 units. £125–£190 ($250–$380) double. Rollaway beds £45 ($90). Most rates include English breakfast. AE, V. Tube: South Kensington. **Amenities:** Restaurant; bar; health club (fee); Wi-Fi (fee); concierge. *In room:* TV w/pay movies, fridge, minibar (in some), iron, safe, Jacuzzi (in some).

## MODERATE

There's a **Citadines Apart'hotel** (p. 78) here, plus **Baden-Powell House** (p. 91), a scouting center offering hostel-style family rooms.

## KNIGHTSBRIDGE, BROMPTON & BELGRAVIA
### VERY EXPENSIVE

**Mandarin Oriental Hyde Park** ⚡    For parents seeking serious luxury and pampering, the Mandarin Oriental should be top of the list: Its superlative spa was voted the "World's Best Urban Spa" by *Condé Nast Traveler*. You'll need to arrange a sitter or take the kids off each other's hands for several hours, though: The spa works by a system of "time rituals," with a minimum booking of 1 hour and 50 minutes. Treatments, decided by you and your therapist during the "ritual," are based on traditional Eastern techniques. Expect to pay £200 ($400) for a "Holistic Time" package, then £100 ($200) for each additional 50 minutes. For a suitably decadent post-spa meal, head for Foliage, the hotel's ground-floor restaurant looking out onto Hyde Park. Here you're encouraged to created your own "tasting menu" from a multitude of smallish dishes, or even to hand yourself over to the chef's whim by ordering the six-course *menu surprise* of the best of the day's offerings. Whatever you decide, you're guaranteed to surprise your taste buds.

You might think that junior guests are overlooked amid all this luxury, but that's far from the case: They get a *Momo in London* storybook, about a monkey who helps out at the Mandarin (suited to kids about 6 and up), an album in which to paste photos and other mementos of their stay, teddies, and little umbrellas to take out in case the weather lets them down when exploring Hyde Park. The interconnecting family rooms are vast; stipulate if you want views of the park as opposed to Harvey Nichols department store or the inner courtyard. The style throughout is Victorian inspired but feels light rather than old-fashioned, and not at all chintzy. Kids get great room-service breakfast and meals, including the likes of squashy tomato soup, pasta of their choice with a sauce of their choice, and corn on the cob. Alternatively, there's a less formal all-day restaurant, The Park, where you can also enjoy afternoon tea. It's just a pity there's no swimming pool here. Not that my 4-year-old seemed to mind—he said he'd like to stay at the Mandarin "for 100 days" (a speedy parental calculation estimated the price of such a vacation to be roughly £80,000/$160,000—dream on, boy!).

66 Knightsbridge, SW1A 7LA. (℗ **020/7235-2000.** Fax 020/7235-2001. www.mandarinoriental.com. 198 units. £415–£475 ($830–$950) double; from £675 ($1,350) suite. Rollaway beds £75 ($150); cribs free. AE, MC, V. Tube: Knightsbridge. **Amenities:** 2 restaurants; bar; concierge; spa; 24-hr. room service; babysitting; same-day laundry and dry cleaning. *In room:* A/C, TV w/pay movies, DVD (by request) and CD players w/library, Internet access, minibar, safe, hair dryer.

### EXPENSIVE

The Cheval Group (www.chevalgroup.com) has two luxury serviced apartment/house complexes in this area, both with a minimum stay of 7 days: **the Cheval Apartments** giving access to the health club at The Rembrandt (p. 78), and **Phoenix House** with a private entrance to Le Cercle restaurant.

## VICTORIA & PIMLICO
### VERY EXPENSIVE

**51 Buckingham Gate** ⚡⚡    You're neighbor to none other than Her Majesty the Queen when you stay in one of these spacious studio suites and apartments (up to

# Where to Stay from Victoria to Earl's Court

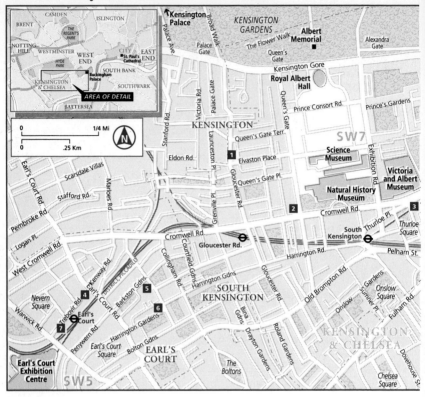

four-bedroom), which go out of their way to welcome families—as well as short stays; they offer extended stays that are useful for those relocating. The apartments, which occupy three town houses, have contemporary interiors, plus full kitchens (ready stocked with coffee, tea, and milk), with washing machine/dryer by request. Other practical needs you may have are anticipated—just holler, and staff will bring you a bottle warmer, baby duvet, crib bumper, or waffle blanket. Older kids get complimentary crayons and coloring books, use of PlayStations, DVD loan from reception (the TV shows the Cartoon Network), free juice and cookies, and their own dishes on the room-service menu should you not be feeling up to cooking or going out (you can also get breakfasts featuring organic ingredients in the "library"). Those up to 7 get an "Oddies" welcome pack with books and socks, those up to 10 get bathrobes and slippers, and all get skin-friendly Burt's Bees products. There's even a little courtyard garden in which to take the air. Nannies/babysitters can be arranged, perhaps while you visit the gym, sauna, steam rooms and spa, which is the only one in England to offer organic Sodashi treatments, including a special pregnancy massage. Look out for family promotions such as 1 night in a two-bedroom apartment, breakfast, and a London Duck Tour (p. 194) for £475 ($950). Make sure to specify that you want twin beds and a double in your two-bedroom apartment, or you may get two queen-size beds. The twice-daily maid service will help you keep them tidy. Rates seem higher but are

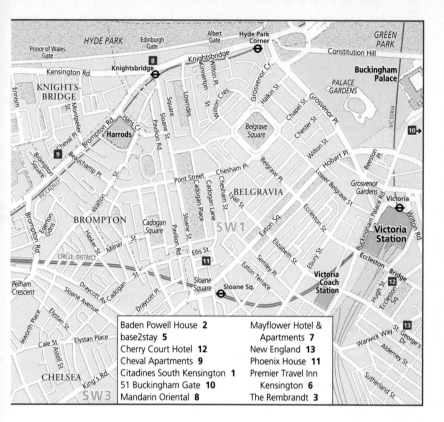

| | |
|---|---|
| Baden Powell House **2** | Mayflower Hotel & Apartments **7** |
| base2stay **5** | New England **13** |
| Cherry Court Hotel **12** | Phoenix House **11** |
| Cheval Apartments **9** | Premier Travel Inn |
| Citadines South Kensington **1** | Kensington **6** |
| 51 Buckingham Gate **10** | The Rembrandt **3** |
| Mandarin Oriental **8** | |

cheaper than interconnecting rooms in five-star hotels, and the kitchens save you money on eating out.

51 Buckingham Gate, London, SW1E 6AF. © 020/7769-7766. Fax 020/7233-5014. www.51-buckinghamgate.co.uk. 86 units. £290–£535 ($580–$1,070) 1-bedroom apt; £425–£610 ($850–$1,220) 2-bedroom apt. Rollaway beds free; cribs free. AE, MC, V. Tube: Victoria. **Amenities:** Spa; steam rooms; butler service (by request); concierge; business center; 24-hr. room service; nanny/babysitting service. *In room:* A/C, TV w/DVD/CD player w/DVD loan, fax, printer, kitchen (w/washing machine/dryer by request), Internet access.

## MODERATE

**New England** 🐾   The number of repeat customers speaks for itself at this long-established family-run B&B in a lovely stucco-fronted Georgian corner house with an elevator (unusual for this category). It's on a long street leading from behind Victoria Station toward the river. All rooms are bright and clean, with en suite bathrooms with power showers. Triples normally have three single beds, quads two large doubles; beds are handcrafted and very comfortable. Though cots or highchairs aren't provided, many people with babies do stay here, and staff members are happy to store milk in the kitchen. *Insider tip:* It's cheapest to book online, but you'll need to call the reception desk for up-to-date news on last-minute offers year-round (using the code noted on the website).

20 St. George's Dr., SW1V 4BN. 📞 020/7834-1595. Fax 020/7834-9000. www.newenglandhotel.com. 25 units. £99–£119 ($198–$238) double/twin; £139–£149 ($278–$298) triple; £149–£159 ($298–$318) quad. Rates include continental breakfast. MC, V. Tube: Victoria. *In room:* TV, dataport, hair dryer.

## INEXPENSIVE

**Cherry Court Hotel** (*Value*)   A bargain base for hard-core sightseers who don't intend to spend much time in their hotel, this friendly cheapie has been run by the Patel family for more than a quarter of a century. It's set in a Victorian terraced house in a side street that's surprisingly tranquil given its location close to the transport hub of Victoria Station, and even has an outside patio area at the rear. The rooms, though small and basic (what did you expect at these prices?) are impressively clean and, incredibly for this price, have air-conditioning and en suite showers and toilets, though the latter are tiny, too—and water pressure can be bad at busy times. For those with kids, there are triples, a quadruple, and a basement "family room" for five, all with double and single beds. The Patels go out of their way to provide visitors with information on the environs, and offer free Internet access in the reception area. There's no dining room, but a perfectly adequate basket of fresh fruit together with biscuits, a cereal bar, and a carton of juice is brought to your room each day.

23 Hugh St., SW1V 1QH. 📞 020/7828-2840. Fax 020/7828-0393. www.cherrycourthotel.co.uk. 12 units. £60 ($120) double; £85 ($170) triple; £100 ($200) quad; £120 ($240) family room for 5. AE, MC, V. Credit card payments incur a 5% surcharge. Tube: Victoria. **Amenities:** Patio garden. *In room:* A/C, TV, dataport, beverage-maker.

## WEST BROMPTON & EARL'S COURT
### EXPENSIVE

**base2stay** (★★ *Value*)   base2stay's prices nudge it over into our "Expensive" category, but it's a newish—and unusual option—worth mentioning for its flexibility, which makes it a sound option for those with older kids in particular. The idea was to synthesize elements of boutique and budget hotels to create a kind of serviced apartments at sensible prices, so all units have a minikitchen with microwave and fridge for self-catering (alternatively, you can get "base breakfast boxes" for £4.50/$9 each, and staff don't mind if you order in—in fact, there's a useful directory listing takeout options). A family with older kids might, for instance, book themselves one standard double for Mom and Dad and a room with two bunk beds for the children, or there are superior doubles that can fit up to three guests on an additional sofa/chairbed, and deluxe doubles that can fit up to four. Or you can pick and mix any of the above to form a two- or three-room unit to suit your needs. Rooms are muted and stylish (TVs are flatscreen, for instance) given the prices, which get better the longer you stay, and are kept extremely clean. Stipulate if you want a bathtub; some rooms have showers only.

25 Courtfield Gardens, SW5 0PG. 📞 020/7244-2255, or 800/511-9821toll-free from the U.S. and Canada. Fax 0845/262-8001. www.base2stay.com. £95–£119 ($190–$238) double; £149 ($298) room for up to 3; £189 ($378) room for up to 4. Cots free. AE, MC, V. Tube: Earl's Court. **Amenities:** Breakfast boxes. *In room:* A/C, TV w/pay movies, Internet access, minikitchen, hair dryer, iron (on request).

## MODERATE

**Mayflower Hotel & Apartments** (★ *Value*)   A rare star on a street of dispiriting B&Bs, the Mayflower comes with en suite rooms that stand out from the crowd with their chunky wooden furniture and colorful but tasteful bedspreads and cushions—some are almost designer in feel. The bathrooms, though diminutive and shower-only, are exceptional at this price. Rooms include some appealing triples and quads—see the website for the best rates (included in the ranges given below, and putting this squarely in the "moderate category")—but families may prefer the nearby one- and two-bed serviced apartments.

26–28 Trebovir Rd., SW5 9NJ. ✆ **020/7370-0991.** Fax 020/7370-0994. www.mayflowerhotel.co.uk. 48 rooms, 35 apts. £92–£165 ($184–$330) double; £115–£165 ($230–$330) triple; £140–£190 ($280–$380) quad; £145–£230 ($290–$460) standard 1-bed apt; £139–£279 ($278–$558) luxury 2-bed apt. Cribs free. Children under 2 stay free in parent's room. Rates include continental breakfast (at hotel). AE, MC, V. Tube: Earl's Court. **Amenities:** Laundry service; same-day dry cleaning. *In room:* A/C, TV, CD player, Wi-Fi, beverage-maker, hair dryer, trouser press, safe.

### INEXPENSIVE

**Rushmore Hotel**    This family-run little town-house B&B can't be beat on price. Guest rooms, though relatively small, are generally clean and even quite charming for this category, with original features—just steer clear of the attic room, as there's no elevator, poor water pressure, and low ceilings. The conservatory dining room, with its limestone floor, terra-cotta urns filled with cacti, and wrought-iron furniture, is a lovely place to enjoy an indifferent continental breakfast, and there's a small lounge for guests' use.

11 Trebovir Rd., SW5 9LS. ✆ **020/7370-3839.** Fax 020/7370-0274. www.rushmore-hotel.co.uk. 22 units. £79–£89 ($158–$178) double; £99–£129 ($198–$258) triple/quad. Cribs free. Rates include continental breakfast. AE, DC, MC, V. Tube: Earl's Court. **Amenities:** Laundry service; guest lounge; Wi-Fi. *In room:* TV, beverage-maker, hair dryer.

## BAYSWATER, PADDINGTON & MAIDA VALE
### EXPENSIVE TO VERY EXPENSIVE

**Europa House** 🐾🐾🐾    These are the top serviced apartments in London for those visiting with kids, mostly because of the delightful 1.4-hectare (3.5-acre) private garden they overlook—it's enclosed, so you can be assured it's safe. A little playpark at the garden's center offers your children the chance to get to know local youngsters. Staff members have handy items you can borrow to make the best of good weather, such as a picnic rug and a little play tent. What you lose in terms of distance from the city center is made up for in countless other ways: the ample space within the apartments, the brilliant range of nearby facilities (a 24-hr. supermarket and an organic grocery; restaurants, and pubs), and the 10-minute proximity of Little Venice, with its floating cafes, puppet barge (p. 251), and boat trips to London Zoo (p. 190).

The largely modern decor proves that style can be achieved on a budget; you wouldn't guess, unless you check the labels, that much of the gear is from IKEA. Little extras to make parents' lives easier include highchairs; kids' bowls, cups, cutlery, and bibs; a couple of funky toys; changing mats; toilet steps; and socket covers. You'll be comfiest in one of the 10 one- and two-bedroom apartments, though if you've a small child in a cot, the one-bedroom flat will be plenty big enough. The kitchens are well-appointed and you get "welcome packs" of groceries. The marble bathrooms are roomy (there are two in the two-bedders). The deluxe apartments are a bit swankier (bamboo flooring, more luxurious fabrics, and so on). My only quibbles are the lack of bathrobes and fancy toiletries, which it's not unreasonable to expect at these prices. Otherwise, it's gold stars all around.

79a Randolph Ave., W9 1DW. ✆ **020/7724-5924.** Fax 020/7724-2937. www.westminsterapartments.co.uk. 13 units. £165 ($330) 1-bed apt; £244–£262 ($488–$524) 2-bed apt. Cribs free. Parking available. AE, DC, MC, V. Tube: Maida Vale. **Amenities:** Babysitting; garden w/play area; laundry service; dry cleaning. *In room:* A/C (in deluxe apts), TV/VCR w/free video loan, CD player, Wi-Fi, kitchen, hair dryer, safe.

### MODERATE

There's a **Marriott** (www.marriott.com) in Maida Vale with a pool and an Italian restaurant specializing in pizzas. As well as rooms with two double beds, it has some one- to three-bedroom suites with full kitchens; rates range from inexpensive to expensive.

**Garden Court Hotel**  This popular, family-oriented hotel has been run by the same clan for more than half a century, and their devotion to their art comes through in the details, making this an attractive option despite a rate hike in recent years. A refurbishment of the listed 1870 town houses in 2004 means there's now an elevator taking you to the bright, clean, and comfortable rooms. The lounge, with its leather armchairs, is a calm place to enjoy complimentary tea, coffee, and hot chocolate, though fine weather will have you spoiled for choice between the hotel's pretty paved garden or the leafy Victorian garden square on which it is set. Singles to triples come either en suite or with shared facilities; the three family rooms (one double and two single beds) are en suite. Check exactly what you're getting when you book, as the terms "triple" and "family room" seem to be used interchangeably at times. Note that not all rooms can fit the travel cot provided, so this needs to be discussed in advance, too. A wide-ranging buffet breakfast is perfect for grazing or for picky kids. The hotel is near Whiteleys mall (p. 240), which has kids' activities, including Gymboree sessions, and a cinema.

30–31 Kensington Gardens Sq., W2 4BG. ℂ 020/7229-2553. Fax 020/7727-2749. www.gardencourthotel.co.uk. 40 units. £75–£115 ($150–$230) double; £150 ($300) triple; £170 ($340) family room. Cribs free. Rates include continental breakfast. MC, V. Tube: Bayswater. **Amenities:** Garden; lounge w/Internet access. *In room:* TV, hair dryer.

**The Pavilion**  A boho, raucous little joint sure to hit the spot with rebellious teens—as long as you're not counting on getting them to bed early—The Pavilion caters to flocks of rock 'n' roll and fashion hipsters who come for the atmosphere rather than the ultra-low prices. Transformed from an ordinary B&B by a former model and his sister, it has a number of quirkily themed rooms, including the Honky Tonk Afro Room (inspired by *Starsky & Hutch*), the Enter the Dragon Asian Room, and the Hippyish Flower Power Room. Although they're on the small side, the rooms (all en suite, with good showers) do include a *trompe l'oeil*–themed family room for two adults and two kids. Don't be surprised if a photo shoot is in progress during your stay, or if you bump into Leonardo DiCaprio or a member of Duran Duran on the stairs.

34–36 Sussex Gardens, W2 1UL. ℂ 020/7262-0905. Fax 020/7262-1324. www.pavilionhoteluk.com. 30 units. £100 ($200) double/twin; £120 ($240) triple; £130 ($260) family room. Rates include continental breakfast. AE, DC, MC, V. Tube: Edgware Rd. **Amenities:** Laundry service; same-day dry cleaning; drinks on room service. *In room:* TV.

## INEXPENSIVE

For the **Parkwood Hotel,** see p. 73.

**Oxford Hotel** *(Value)*  If your budget isn't elastic enough to get you into some of the excellent moderately priced accommodations in this area, this is a good budget alternative, with staff who genuinely seem to do their best not to compromise despite the rates. Set on a side street leading right down to the wide green spaces of Hyde Park, it's a few minutes' walk from Paddington Station, into which high-speed trains whiz from Heathrow airport. The street is quiet enough by day but can get rowdier at night, especially in summer when restaurants put tables outside and drinkers spill out of pubs. The interior stairs can be a little creaky, too (there's no elevator). The rooms are clean if uninspiring, and—remarkably at this price—have en suite toilets and shower rooms (tiny ones, admittedly), plus microwave ovens. Some are triples and some are four-person family rooms, which are more generously proportioned than you might imagine. Breakfasts are not a high point—you're better off finding a local cafe.

13 Craven Terrace, W2 3QD. ℂ 020/7402-6860. Fax 020/7262-7574. www.oxfordhotellondon.co.uk. 21 units. £66 ($132) double; £76 ($152) triple; £84 ($168) family room for 4. Rates include continental breakfast. AE, DC, MC, V.

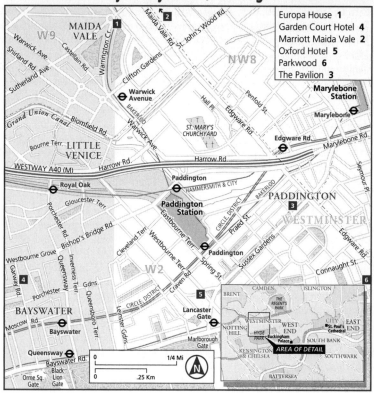

Tube: Lancaster Gate or Paddington. **Amenities:** Concierge; laundry service; dry cleaning. *In room:* TV, microwave, beverage-maker, hair dryer.

## FARTHER WEST

### VERY EXPENSIVE

**High Road House** ★★ *Finds*    A western outpost of the fashionable Soho House members' club in—yes, you've guessed it—Soho (both London and NYC), this hotel, open since mid-2006, also functions as a private dining room and club, with members getting preferential rates on rooms, but hotel guests are also accorded temporary access to the restaurant and club (booking is essential to eat). Guest rooms fall into two categories: the small Playpens, with showers, and then one larger Playroom, which has a free-standing claw-foot bathtub beside the bed. One of the Playpens is specially kitted out to be baby-friendly. A family of four with small children can be squeezed—and I mean squeezed—into a Playpen, where staff will set up a crib or child-size bed and also install a second foldable bed. For those with older kids, adjacent (but not interconnecting) rooms can be arranged. Mainly white, with lots of wood, they feel a little like upmarket beach cabins.

Kids' menus are available throughout the building, including as part of room service. The all-day European brasserie is the most congenial place to eat with kids, though the kids' menu is only served until 7pm. Food ranges from "small plates" (the likes of "devils on horseback"—bacon-wrapped prunes on toast—and hummus on flatbread) to more lavish dishes such as pan-fried scallops. Best of all, the club room with its squidgy sofas and low-level tables functions as a playroom for families between 11am and 4pm, with games, toys, table football, a pool table, and a large screen showing cartoons, in addition to full waiter service (there's an informal dining area). Kids love sprawling on the large but cozy mattress area here. Beware though, that it might get booked up for a private event. On Mondays it's given over to the Classic Scream movie showing for parents with babies (the group also runs the Electric Cinema on the Portobello Rd.; p. 257).

162–166 Chiswick High Rd., W4 1PR. ✆ 020/8742-1717. www.highroadhouse.co.uk. 14 units. £140 ($280) playpen double; £160 ($320) playroom double. Rollaway/folding beds free; cribs free. AE, MC, V. Tube: Turnham Green. **Amenities:** 2 restaurants; bar; club room; room service; Wi-Fi. *In room:* TV/DVD player, minibar, beverage-maker, safe, hair dryer.

## MODERATE

**Fish Court & Georgian House** ★    It's virtually impossible to feel the weight of English history more fully than at these historic rental properties overseen by the Landmark Trust, an architectural rescue and preservation charity (www.landmarktrust.org.uk)—they're on the grounds of Hampton Court Palace itself (p. 184) which, together with most of the courtyards, guests are free to wander at any time. (The atmospheric public rooms are accessible during normal opening hours.) Fish Court, an old pastry chef's dwelling on the first and attic floors of the service wing, sleeps up to six people in one double-bedded room, one twin-bedded room, and two rooms with one single bed apiece. Each unit has two bathrooms with a tub, plus a kitchen, a dining room, and a large living room. The Georgian House, in a former palace kitchen, sleeps up to eight over three floors (ground to second), in a double bedroom, two twin-bed rooms, and two single rooms, and also has two bathrooms and a private walled garden.

Both properties are furnished with simple, comfortably worn furniture, and have modern bathrooms and kitchens. Georgian House has a dishwasher, but neither has a washing machine, alas. They don't have TVs, either; instead you get jigsaw puzzles, large-scale maps denoting local footpaths, and a logbook to write down your experiences. Each property has a history album telling of the building's past and its restoration. Linen and towels are provided, except for the cribs. Rental periods range from a weekend to 3 weeks; off-peak rates can put both options in the moderate category, especially midweek in winter, while high-summer prices nudge them into the very expensive bracket. Central London is 35 minutes away by train, making this a great base between Heathrow and the center.

Hampton Court Palace, E. Molesey, Surrey, KT8. ✆ 01628/825925. Fax 01628/825925. www.landmarktrust.co.uk. 2 units. Fish Court from £637 ($1,274) for 4-night midweek stay in winter, to £2,248 ($4,496) for 1 week in high summer; Georgian House from £698 ($1,396) for 4-night midweek stay in winter, to £2,798 ($5,596) for 1 week in high summer. Cribs free. DC, MC, V. Train: Hampton Court. **Amenities:** Access to grounds; housekeeper. *In room:* Kitchen, games, maps.

## 3 South of the River

### SOUTH BANK TO ROTHERHITHE

#### EXPENSIVE

**London Bridge Hotel**    This fairly luxurious hotel on the buzzing south bank of the Thames is in a perfect spot for river strolls, checking out shows at the nearby kids' Unicorn Theatre (p. 251), and lazy mornings spent tasting the delights of the nearby

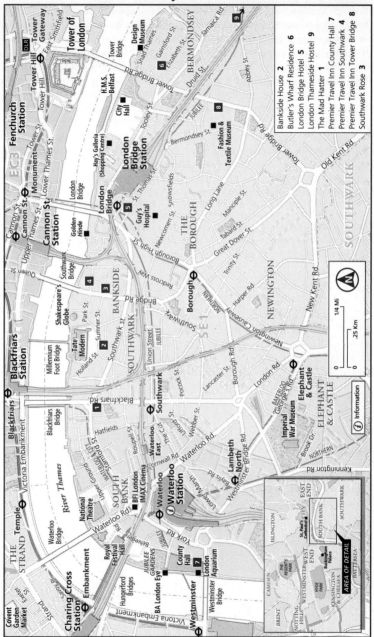

Bankside House **2**
Butler's Wharf Residence **6**
London Bridge Hotel **5**
London Thameside Hostel **9**
The Mad Hatter **1**
Premier Travel Inn County Hall **7**
Premier Travel Inn Southwark **4**
Premier Travel Inn Tower Bridge **8**
Southwark Rose **3**

Borough farmers' market (p. 233). Although this historically fascinating area can be hectic, double-glazing on the windows keeps out street noise. Families are most comfortably accommodated in the large deluxe rooms, which have a king-size bed and sofa bed, but if you're on a budget and don't mind being a bit more squashed, cots and roll-away beds can be placed in about 10 of the standard doubles. All guest rooms have been refurbished in a pleasant if unoriginal style since the first edition of this guide.

Up a notch, there are also three serviced apartments situated next to the hotel and sharing its facilities, each with a double room and a twin room, a large sofa bed, two bathrooms, and a kitchen. (Note that there's no elevator here.) Highchairs are available in the colonial Malaysian restaurant, where children's portions can be arranged (the same goes for room service), while a more adult-friendly restaurant serves modern Mediterranean cuisine, as well as breakfast.

8–18 London Bridge St., SE1 9SG. © 020/7855-2200. Fax 020/7855-2233. www.londonbridgehotel.com. 138 units. £99–£209 ($198–$418) double; £330 ($660) apt sleeping up to 6 (less if by week or month). Children under 12 stay free when sharing parent's room; 12 and over stay free but pay for breakfast. Rollaway beds free; cribs free. Rates include free continental or English breakfast for adults at weekends (children pay £7/$14 supplement for breakfast). AE, DC, MC, V. Tube: London Bridge. **Amenities:** Restaurant; bar; free access to nearby health club; 24-hr. room service; babysitting; laundry service; dry cleaning. *In room:* A/C, TV w/pay movies, dataport, minibar, beverage-maker, hair dryer, trouser press, safe.

**Southwark Rose** ⟨★⟩   This funky modern hotel has a prime location on a quiet street a few steps from the river and the Tate Modern. Combining boutique-style decor (leather fittings and bright splashes of color against a neutral background) with functionality, it's useful for its spacious, spotless family suites (a double in one room, a double sofa bed in the other) with good (though shower-only) bathrooms and kitchenettes. Doubles are on the small side but have room for a crib. Breakfast (a continental buffet) offers lots of choices, and prices in the attractive top-floor restaurant, which serves child-friendly modern and traditional food, including prawn cocktail and potato skins with sweet chile sauce and cheddar cheese, are good by London standards. The modern artwork in the lobby can be borderline risqué.

43–47 Southwark Bridge Rd., SE1 9HH. © 020/7015-1480. Fax 020/7015-1481. www.southwarkrosehotel.co.uk. 84 units. £170 ($340) double; £215 ($430) suite for up to 4. Cribs free. MC, V. Tube: London Bridge. **Amenities:** Restaurant; bar; gym; sauna; business lounge; laundry and dry-cleaning service. *In room:* A/C, TV, dataport, beverage-maker, hair dryer, iron, safe.

## MODERATE

**The Mad Hatter,** 3–7 Stamford St., SE1 (© 020/7401-9222), on the South Bank, is sister hotel to the Sanctuary House Hotel in St. James's (p. 71). Weekend rates make it an exceptional value. For the **London Thameside Hostel,** see p. 90.

## INEXPENSIVE

There's a **Premier Travel Inn** (p. 75) in a plum location on the riverfront within County Hall itself, and another at Southwark.

**Bankside House**   This superbly sited (and enormous) London School of Economics residence hall offers summer accommodations to visitors (late June to mid-Sept) within the shadow of the glorious Tate Modern. All of the basic but bright and airy rooms, bar a few singles, are en suite, and room-only rates here are a fabulous bargain, especially given that they include English or continental breakfast. There are no self-catering facilities—the one drawback to this venue—but there are washing machines, tea- and coffee-making facilities, a bar, and a game room. Larger families should note that there's another LSE property, **Butler's Wharf Residence,** in the fascinating former spice warehouse area west of here past Tower Bridge, with mainly five- and six-bed flats, rentable by the night or week, at rock-bottom prices.

24 Sumner St., SE1 9JA. © 020/7955-7575. Fax 020/7955-7676. www.lse.ac.uk/collections/vacations. 833 units. £61 ($122) twin; £86 ($172) triple; £95 ($190) quad. MC, V. Tube: Southwark. **Amenities:** Dining room; bar; game room; laundry facilities. *In room:* Hand basin.

## STREATHAM & BALHAM
### MODERATE
**Ambleside Family B&B**    Far from the madding crowd, this welcoming Swedish/English family-run B&B is in a splendid 1880s red-brick dwelling in a calm, leafy conservation area about a half-hour's Tube ride from central London. For families (up to five people), there's a large room with two comfy sofas, a "double" bed (linked twins), a sleeping loft with two singles, masses of cupboard space, and a balcony; for safety reasons it's unsuitable for infants and very young kids; or there's a "triple"—a double with a bed added for an adult or child. The decor is flowery without being intrusive. Communal areas include a plush dining room, a study (there's free broadband Internet access for guests), and a lovely garden with a patio area. The friendly owners will meet you at the station. The continental breakfast is good but the serving hours (8–9am) are rather restrictive.

34 Ambleside Ave., SW16 1QP. © 020/8769-2742. Fax 020/8677-3023. www.bednbrek.com. 3 units. £65 ($130) double; £85 ($190) triple; £105 ($210) family room with 4 occupants; £125 ($250) family room with 5 occupants. Rates include continental breakfast. AE, MC, V. Tube: Tooting Bec. **Amenities:** Free Internet access; study; garden. *In room:* TV, video (in family room), beverage-maker (in family room), hair dryer, iron (by request).

**The Coach House** *(Value)*    If you're looking for charming lodgings and don't mind being somewhat removed from the action, this ivy-clad former Victorian coach house converted into self-contained accommodations for up to five may well be for you. The main bedroom, boasting rustic oak beams and French windows looking onto the garden, has an en suite bathroom, and one double and one single bed. The second room has twin beds and its own bathroom and shower room. Ask in advance if you need a crib and highchair. The Coach House does have its own kitchen, but while the owners don't mind if you make snacks and heat ready-made meals, they discourage full-scale cooking. Luckily, there are fashionable restaurants aplenty in this family suburb (p. 131), and central London is 30 minutes away by Tube. Breakfasts (organic if required, for a small surcharge) are served in the main house, when the hostess happily shares her local knowledge with guests. The lack of a washing machine is a pain, although there's a launderette just a few minutes' walk away. Note that there's normally a minimum 3- or 5-night stay depending on the time of year.

2 Tunley Rd., SW17 7QJ. © 020/8772-1939. Fax 020/8181-6152. www.chslondon.com/ch. 1 unit. £120–£150 ($240–$300) for 3; £155–£175 ($310–$350) for 4; £175 ($350) for 5. Cribs free. Rates include English or continental breakfast. AE, MC, V. Tube: Balham. *In room:* Kitchen, TV, radio, Wi-Fi Internet access, hair dryer.

## RICHMOND & KEW
### EXPENSIVE
**The Victoria**    This highly regarded and very child-friendly gastropub close to Richmond Park (p. 205), boasts a handful of simple but stylish en suite double bedrooms, two of which can be turned into twins and two of which have space for a travel cot or camp bed. The beautifully firm queen-size beds are dressed with 100% Egyptian

## Putting the Youth in Youth Hostels

Yes, there are downsides to staying in a hostel. You might share the venue with a noisy school party; you normally have to share bathrooms; and sometimes you have to vacate it at certain times of day while they clean. But youth hostels are a much-underrated and under-utilized budget option for families—if you don't mind going back to basics. The family rooms (for those with children over 3) don't exactly scream glamour, but the two bunk beds are comfy enough (bed linen and duvets are provided but no towels), and there's always a washbasin. Cribs and highchairs are available in hostels welcoming under-3s, and most also offer cooked meals, with special menus for children under 10. Best of all, self-catering kitchens, present in all but a few hostels, allow you to save money on eating out (little kids rapidly tire of having to sit around in restaurants anyway). There are also laundry facilities in most, and some even have gardens where youngsters can let off steam.

If you're traveling with over-3s, it's worth asking a particular hostel not designated for families about staying there, since some may have bunk-bed rooms that can be booked by families for private use. And some hostels now have en suite rooms, often with single or double beds, if you want a little more privacy. Single parents aren't forgotten either—a discount is available when booking a family bunk-bed room.

All hostels have family games and activities, from board games to kite-making. Most also have a game room with the likes of pool, table tennis, and arcade games—perfect for when you return from sightseeing and want to relax while the kids make friends. Membership, at £23 ($46) for two-parent families and £16 ($32) for single parents, with under-18s free, is worth buying if you are planning multiple stays; without it you pay a supplement. It can be arranged at the time of booking, or visit www.yha.org.uk for info.

Britain's Youth Hostels Association has more than 200 hostels country-wide. A hundred are deemed suitable for children and seventy for kids under 3. Three of these are in London—including the **London Thameside**

cotton bed linen, and the showers are excellent. The out-of-the-ordinary breakfasts usually include home-baked muffins and handmade *pannetone* (Italian fruitcake), while coffee, organic juices, and baked goods are available all morning and afternoon. In the restaurant, the weekend lunch menu always features some simple dishes suitable for children, such as chicken club sandwiches with fries, with kid-size portions available and highchairs provided. The location, on a residential street, is peaceful—rooms are in a separate building across from the gastropub, so they avoid noise. Best of all is the large walled garden on the grounds, with tables outdoors in summer and a children's play area.

10 W. Temple Sheen, SW14 7RT. ✆ 020/8876-4238. Fax 020/8878-3464. www.thevictoria.net. 7 units. £109 ($218) double. Rollaway beds £10 ($20); cribs £10 ($20). Rates include continental breakfast. AE, MC, V. Train: Richmond. **Amenities:** Restaurant; bar; garden. *In room:* TV, flatscreen PC w/free broadband Internet access.

**Hostel** (formerly Rotherhithe Youth Hostel), in a surprising but not unpleasant location well away from the center of town on the way to historic Greenwich. This hostel is particularly child-friendly: As well as highchairs, baby bathtubs, monitors, strollers, and travel cribs (for which you need to bring linen), it offers a kids' library, a toy box, more than 30 board games, giant-size games, a blackboard, a PlayStation, a TV lounge, and a secure little brick-paved garden. All young visitors receive a free activity pack, discounted attraction tickets, self-guided local tour books and pamphlets, and rainy-day activities such as hostel treasure trails and quizzes. Bikes for adults and kids can be rented for £10 ($20) per day. Breakfast and dinner (with kids' menus) can be provided, as can picnic lunches, though there's a kitchen for self-catering. Local attractions include Southwark Park, the city's oldest municipal park; the organic Surrey Docks farm with its child-friendly cafe; the Brunel Museum (p. 160); and the historic Mayflower pub where the Pilgrims moored prior to their history-changing voyage (kids are welcome in the restaurant). Street parking in this area is free and unrestricted.

The other London hostels are **St Pancras Hostel** at 79–81 Euston Rd., Bloomsbury, convenient for transport links; and **St Paul's Hostel**, at 36 Carter Lane in the City, virtually opposite St. Paul's in an old choirboy school. Current prices—from about £107 ($214) for a room for four—technically tip them into our "Moderate" category, but remember that breakfast is included in this rate, and that you often get self-catering facilities. For a true budget hostel on the outskirts of London, trying the one at **Epping Forest** (p. 210), which also welcomes under-3s and has family rooms for about £56 ($112). Contact details for all of the above are **0870/770-6044**; www.yha. org.uk.

Note that **Baden-Powell House** (© **020/7590-6910**; www.scouts.org.uk) right beside the National History Museum in South Kensington is now a Scout Activity Centre but still offers family rooms to visitors, for around the same price as youth hostels.

## MODERATE

**The Bush Houseboat** ✪ *(Finds)*    An interesting, stylish and peaceful option perhaps best suited to those with older kids, this newly renovated houseboat is moored opposite the riverbank at Kew Gardens. It's so tranquil a spot, you'll have difficulty believing you're only 15 minutes from Westminster (by boat from Kew Pier; there are also boats in the opposite direction to Hampton Court and Richmond). In fact, the danger is that feeding the swans and geese or relaxing with one of the books or board games provided will often seem preferable to heading into the fray of central London. Accommodations consist of two double bedrooms (one with twin beds) and one single bedroom (the latter with a low ceiling); if you need a cot you'll have to bring your own, but towels and linen are provided. Then there's an open-plan living area with a lounge and a large kitchen with a breakfast bar, a dishwasher, and a washing machine.

The lounge has a wood-burning stove to keep things cozy when the wind bites, while there's a deck on while to soak up rays when the sun shines. River views are available from all rooms, although the best vista is from the dining room up in the panoramic wheelhouse. Note that there's a minimum 3-night stay, and a 10% reduction for 3 or more guests staying a week or longer.

Thames, near Kew Bridge, TW8 OEW. © 020/8892-7241. www.bushhouseboat.co.uk. 1 unit. £100 ($200) for 3 people; £120 ($240) for 4 people; £120 ($240) for 5 people. Parking available. No credit cards. Tube: Gunnersbury. *In room:* Kitchen, TV, VCR, books, board games.

## 4 East London

This is not really an area for budget accommodations, but if you feel like a day or two out of "the Smoke," heard far northeast to **Epping Forest,** where there's a **campsite** also featuring some log cabins and cottages and located beside a pub with a kids' playground (www.theelmscampsite.co.uk), plus a **youth hostel** (p. 90).

## CLERKENWELL
### MODERATE
**Francis Rowley Court**   A useful option for a single parent traveling with kids, this City University flat, available year-round, comprises three single rooms, each with a TV set, plus a lounge, a fully equipped kitchen, and a bathroom with a shower. Linen and towels are provided, as is a small hospitality pack. The best thing about this flat is its location in the heart of trendy Clerkenwell, just minutes from the Barbican and the hip Smithfield meat-market area. Be warned that the place gets booked up quickly, so reserve well ahead.

16 Briset St., EC1M 5HD. © 020/7040-8037. Fax 020/7040-8592. www.city.ac.uk/ems. 1 unit. £102 ($204) for all 3 rooms. DC, MC, V. Tube: Farringdon. **Amenities:** Kitchen. *In room:* TV, no phone.

### INEXPENSIVE
**Rosebery Hall**   This London School of Economics university hall offers rooms during the summer vacation (usually mid-June to late Sept), as well as—quite unusually for this type of accommodations—at Christmas (mid-Dec to early Jan). Though it inevitably attracts young backpackers, it's also popular with families on a budget. As with the other residences, the rooms are basic but well maintained and comfortable; here there are singles, twins, and triples, with all but some of the twins sharing bathroom facilities. The shared shower rooms are clean and spruce, and don't get overcrowded; and there are washbasins in all rooms. Other communal amenities include kitchenettes, beverage-making facilities, washing machines, a bar, and a game room; there are phones in all rooms. The modern building is on the fringes of fashionable Clerkenwell, a few minutes' walk from all the shops and restaurants of Islington's cosmopolitan Upper Street. If these don't tempt you, you can have breakfast on the patio outside. For other LSE residences, see p. 74 and p. 88.

90 Rosebery Ave., EC1R 4TY. © 020/7955-7575. Fax 020/7955-7676. www.lse.ac.uk/collections/vacations. 435 units. £50–£60 ($100–$120) twin; £62 ($124) triple. Rates include English or continental breakfast. MC, V. Tube: Angel. **Amenities:** Bar; kitchenette; beverage-makers; game room; launderette; TV lounge.

## SMITHFIELD & THE CITY
### EXPENSIVE
**Grange City**   History doesn't come much more in your face than at this hotel, one of two five-star properties owned by the growing Grange group (the other is in Holborn)—it has stunning views over the Tower of London and Tower Bridge virtually next door

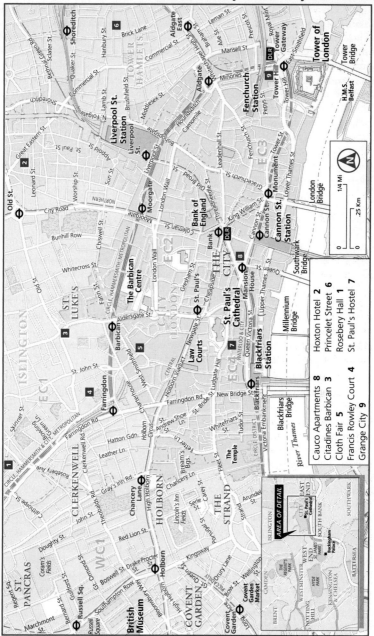

Hoxton Hotel **2**
Princelet Street **6**
Rosebery Hall **1**
St. Paul's Hostel **7**

Cauco Apartments **8**
Citadines Barbican **3**
Cloth Fair **5**
Francis Rowley Court **4**
Grange City **9**

(make sure you request a room on the south side to enjoy these), and there's even a section of the old London wall running alongside the hotel's piazza, a large space where the kids can expend some energy while you enjoy a drink (panels fill in some of the Wall's history). Another feature that makes this popular with families is the attractive 25m (59-ft.) pool, open to kids 10am to 4pm Monday to Friday and all day at weekends. Family rooms feature two double beds and a small sitting area—they're perfectly comfortable if not huge. There are also suites and penthouses to which you can add rollaways. The decor, as throughout the hotel, is both bland and a bit pretentious—this is not a place for lovers of contemporary chic. I can't vouch for the hotel's Japanese restaurant or French brasserie, but room service is of decent quality and features a variety of cuisines, from traditional British to Indian, if not a huge choice of dishes. The kids' menu is colorful, with dishes named after superheroes and cartoon characters, including Bugs Bunny's Garden (buttered winter vegetables with rice) and Superman's homemade mini cheeseburgers with fries; kids' mains cost about £6 ($12).
*Insider tip:* You can get great online bargains on certain nights booked well in advance—I've seen a family room going for as little as £140 ($280) including continental breakfast.

8–14 Cooper's Row, EC3N 2BQ. (C) **020/7863-3700.** Fax 020/7863-3701. www.grangehotels.com. 307 units. £185–£205 ($370–$410) double; £255 ($510) family room for 4; from £514 ($1,028) suite. Rollaway beds £45 ($90) or £25 ($50) for under-12s; cots £25 ($50). AE. MC, V. Tube: Tower Hill. **Amenities:** 2 restaurants; bar; indoor pool; golf facility; gym; spa; sauna; steam room; concierge; business center; 24-hr. room service; babysitting; dry cleaning and laundry service. *In room:* A/C, satellite TV w/pay movies, CD player, Internet access, beverage-making facilities, minibar, hair dryer, trouser press, safe.

## MODERATE

There's a **Citadines Apart'hotel** (p. 75) close to the Barbican arts center, and a child-friendly **youth hostel** (p. 90) close to St. Paul's.

**Calico Apartments** *Finds*   It's worth considering these luxury serviced apartments as an alternative to the Cheval Group's other properties in and around South Kensington (p. 78)—their less touristy location brings the price down into our "Moderate" category for some of the two-bed apartments, yet St. Paul's Cathedral, the Monument, the Tower of London, and the Museum of London are all within walking distance, and the Tate Modern is a couple of minutes' stroll away over the sparkling Millennium Bridge. You're also on the same street as a Tube station on the District and Circle lines, meaning central London is just 10 minutes away. The apartments are modern and quite stylish, with full kitchens, equipped with a welcome pack on your arrival. You get daily maid service during the week, and linen is changed once weekly, towels twice (more often by request and for an extra fee). Cots and highchairs are provided for free; a rollaway can be set up for a daily charge in some of the units. (Note that some of the two-beds have a double and a single, not a twin room). There's a minimum stay of 7 nights. You might like to arrange a sitter to take advantage of the complimentary day membership of the private London Capital Club or a nearby health club.

42 Bow Lane, EC4M 9DT. (C) **020/7489-2500.** Fax 020/7236-1166. www.chevalgroup.com. 45 units. £775–£1,100 ($1,550–$2,200) per week 1-bed apt; £1,400–£1,575 ($2,800–$3,150) per week 2-bedroom apt. Rollaway beds £20 ($40); cribs free. AE. MC, V. Tube: Mansion House. **Amenities:** Complimentary health club membership; dry cleaning and laundry service. *In room:* Maid service Mon–Fri, kitchen, CD player, Wi-Fi (£30/$60 per week).

**Cloth Fair**   Another Landmark Trust rental property (p. 86), Cloth Fair is in a Georgian house overlooking the yard of one of the rare churches that survived the Great Fire of London. Sleeping up to four in one double room and two single-bedded rooms over two floors (first and second), it also provides a crib for babies. (You need to bring your own linens.) There are two bathrooms, one with a tub, the other with a tub and shower; and a modern kitchen, unfortunately without a washing machine. Situated in the hip Smithfield meat-market district with its great bars, cafes, and restaurants, it's handy for the Barbican arts complex (p. 243) and the Museum of London (p. 169); it's also only a 15-minute walk or so from Covent Garden to the west. High-summer prices nudge it into the expensive category.

45 Cloth Fair, EC1. (C) **01628/825925.** Fax 01628/825925 www.landmarktrust.co.uk. 1 unit. From £606 ($1,212) for 4-night midweek stay in winter to £1,341 ($2,682) for 1 week in high summer. Cribs free. DC, MC, V. Tube: Barbican. **Amenities:** Housekeeper. *In room:* Kitchen and kitchen equipment.

## SHOREDITCH
### EXPENSIVE

**The Hoxton** ⚘   What makes this "urban lodge" worth mentioning, above all, are its periodic online sales, when you can bag a room—if you're quick enough on your keyboard—for £1 ($2), £29 ($58), or £59 ($118). You need to sign up on the mailing list to receive advance warnings of these offers. Opened in 2006, the place bills itself as a "business hotel," but I've found it surprisingly child-friendly—my kids loved the life-size paper reindeer in the lobby when we stayed in the run-up to Christmas, and there were several other families around. We were also allocated interconnecting rooms, which we hadn't expected to find here—in fact, 11 doubles and twins can connect, and these can be booked in advance. One rollaway or crib can also fit into a double or twin, which aren't huge. The decor is quite stylish given that the place claims to be a budget option (it isn't, unless you snare one of the hot deals), and you get a free breakfast bag of juice, yogurt and muesli, and a banana courtesy of Pret à Manger. Negatives, quite minor and in no way serious enough to prevent us returning should we get one of the discounted rooms, were the poor reception on the wall-mounted flatscreen TVs—there's no point in installing a snazzy TV if you can't get a picture—the lack of tubs in bathrooms with plenty of room for one (there are large wetrooms instead), and the offhand service in the bar and restaurant (actually operated by a separate company). The latter serves everything from sausage sandwiches to steaks and French brasserie–style dishes.

81 Great Eastern St., EC2A 3HU. (C) **020/7550-1000.** Fax 020/7550-1090. www.hoxtonhotels.com. £99 ($198). Rollaway beds £15 ($30); cribs free. Rates include breakfast bag. MC, V. Tube: Old St. **Amenities:** Restaurant; bar; reduced admission to local health club, £5 ($10) per day. *In room:* TV, free Wi-Fi.

### MODERATE

**Princelet Street** ⚘   This Landmark Trust rental property (p. 86) occupies a restored Huguenot silk weavers' house in the historically fascinating Spitalfields area just east of the City. Though a crib is provided (without linen), this is a better bet for those with older kids, as the four-story layout means lots of stairs for you to heft a baby up and down. Accommodating six, it has one double room and two twin-bedded rooms, two bathrooms and a shower room, a sitting room, a dining room, and a study. The well-stocked kitchen has both a dishwasher and a washing machine. There's no TV but an enclosed paved garden and plenty to keep you entertained nearby—the house is on the doorstep of trendy Spitalfields Market, which sells everything from books and records to clothes, crafts, and organic food (p. 236). It's is also just off Brick Lane with its vibrant ethnic festivals (p. 21), Indian restaurants, and Sunday junk market; but it's far enough away to lay claim to a quiet street. The Museum of Childhood

(p. 146) is within easy reach, too. Beware, if you have your own car: Parking is difficult in the area.

13 Princelet St., E1. 📞 **01628/825925.** Fax 01628/825925. www.landmarktrust.co.uk. 1 unit. From £604 ($1,208) for 4-night midweek stay in winter to £1,373 ($2,746) for 1 week in high summer. Cribs free. DC, MC, V. Tube: Aldgate E. **Amenities:** Garden; housekeeper. *In room:* Kitchen and kitchen equipment.

## DOCKLANDS
### VERY EXPENSIVE
**Four Seasons Canary Wharf** ⟡⟡⟡    This is the kind of place where the doorman addresses you by name, and where your kids are greeted with cookies and sweets laid out on a blackboard with a personal welcome message. But practicalities aren't forgotten either, whether it be diaper bins in the bathroom or child-size hangers in the vast wardrobes. Other complimentary baby and children's amenities include toiletries and baby products, bathrobes and slippers, activity bags, balloons, and chocolates, DVDs, and childproofing equipment if required. Basically, if it's not there and you need it, just call down and the peerless staff will go out of their way to get it to you post-haste. But the best reason to make this eastern outpost of the Four Seasons your base is that rates almost halve at weekends. Take advantage of that to come and enjoy the awesome views from the deluxe doubles on the river side of the hotel, from which you can see as far as the London Eye.

Families are generally accommodated in suites or interconnecting doubles, although very comfortable rollaways and superior metal cribs with colorful bed linen (no tacky travel cots here!) are available free of charge in standard rooms. Kids 6 months and up can enjoy use of the truly stunning adjoining Holmes Place 20m (66-ft.) infinity-edge pool overlooking the Thames between 9 and 11am each morning. At breakfast, they can tuck into such treats as "Monkey Madness" banana pancakes with maple syrup, and at lunch and dinner, they'll be served the likes of "Scuba Diver's" organic fish croquette. Children's room service is offered until 11pm.

While it seems like a fair trek from the heart of town, the Four Seasons is just 20 minutes by stress-free ferry ride from the heart of London (the boat docks at Canary Wharf Pier in front of the hotel). The central Four Seasons in Mayfair is more traditional in decor, with views over Hyde Park. In summer and most school vacations this location has a teen concierge to help older kids with their visits.

46 Westferry Circus, E14 8RS. 📞 **020/7510-1999.** Fax 020/7510-1998. www.fourseasons.com/canarywharf. 142 units. £310–£360 ($620–$720) double; from £650 ($1,300) suite. Children under 18 can share parent's room for free. Rollaway beds free; cribs free. AE, DC, MC, V. Tube: Canary Wharf. **Amenities:** Restaurant; bar; indoor pool; indoor tennis court; fitness center; access to spa; concierge; business services; 24-hr. room service; massage; babysitting; laundry service; same-day dry cleaning. *In room:* A/C, TV/DVD w/pay movies, PlayStation (pay by hour); dataport, minibar, hair dryer, safe.

## 5 North London

## CAMDEN & ISLINGTON
### MODERATE
**Holiday Inn** ⟡ *Value*    Rates at this member of the long-standing global chain can be at the very bottom end of this category, for a room with two double (queen-size) beds booked on certain dates at least 7 days in advance, making it exceptional value given its location just minutes' from London Zoo and The Regent's Park, as well as from the grungey delights of Camden High Street and its famous market (p. 233). The views aren't bad either—it overlooks the Camden Lock Canal—and the decor is modern

and surprisingly stylish. If you fancy a little more privacy, there are interconnecting rooms, too; suites are a step up, with larger beds, bathrobes, and turndown service. All rooms have tubs. As at all Holiday Inns, kids under 12 eat free—there's an all-day lounge bar for snacks and light meals, plus a restaurant serving British and Continental fare.

30 Jamestown Rd., NW1 7BY. © 020/7485-4343. www.ichotels.group.com. 130 units. About £100–£199 ($200–$398) double with 1 or 2 queen-size beds, but rates vary considerably. Cribs free. AE, MC, V. Tube: Camden Town. **Amenities:** Restaurant; lounge bar; gym; Wi-Fi, concierge; business center; 24-hr. room service; dry-cleaning and laundry service. *In room:* A/C, satellite TV w/pay movies, radio, beverage-making facilities, minibar, hair dryer, iron/trouser press, safe.

### INEXPENSIVE

**Kandara Guesthouse**    A cozy and child-friendly B&B in a tranquil conservation area about 10 minutes' walk of Islington Green and 15 minutes from Highbury Fields (p. 208), the Kandara Guesthouse has been run by the same family for more than half a century. Rooms are relatively plain but light and appealing, and the shared shower-rooms/toilets (there's generally one between two guest rooms, plus a couple of extra WCs) are pleasant and well maintained. Rooms include triples with either one double and one single bed, or three single beds; and family rooms with one double and two single beds. It's advisable to book cribs and highchairs ahead. The cooked breakfasts, vegetarian and otherwise, use top-rate ingredients and are worth an early awakening.

68 Ockendon Rd., N1 3NW. © 020/7226-5721. Fax 020/7226-3379. www.kandara.co.uk. 11 units. £59–£73 ($118–$146) double; £70–£82 ($140–$164) triple; £75–£88 ($150–$176) family room. Cribs free. Rates include English breakfast. AE, MC, V. Tube: Highbury or Islington. *In room:* TV, beverage-maker.

## HAMPSTEAD
### MODERATE

**Hampstead Village Guesthouse**    The very antithesis of the chain hotel experience, this child-welcoming and informal B&B in a Victorian house close to Hampstead Heath is popular with families for its self-contained studio flat, which comprises a very large room with its own corner kitchenette, shower, and toilet. It normally has a double bed and two singles, but there's room for another single if needed. Facilities for tots include highchairs, cots, and toys. The decor throughout is homey in a "lived-in" bohemian way, mixing antique and handmade furniture (including comfy beds), books, and knickknacks. When the weather permits, you can enjoy a tranquil and leisurely cooked breakfast (optional; £7/$14) in the garden. The B&B is a bit difficult to find, so get clear directions to avoid wandering around with cranky kids.

2 Kemplay Rd., NW3 1SY. © 020/7435-8679. Fax 020/7794-0254. www.hampsteadguesthouse.com. 9 units. £75–£90 ($150–$180) double; £145–£170 ($290–$340) studio according to occupancy. Rollaway beds free; cribs free. AE, MC, V. (5% surcharge on credit cards.) Tube: Hampstead. *In room:* TV, small fridge, beverage-maker, hair dryer, iron, hot-water bottle.

**La Gaffe** *(Value*    This Hampstead institution oozes quaintness, combining an Italian restaurant, a wine bar, and accommodations in an 18th-century shepherd's house. Bedrooms are cozy though a little chintzy, some with four-poster beds; all are en suite and comfortable for those worn out from romps on the Heath nearby. The compact family room is an especially good value, since along with a four-poster bed, a shower room, an attached single room, and a washing machine, it has just about enough space for another fold-out single bed. There's a charming patio for warm weather and a conservatory for less clement times. The Italian restaurant serves up generous and reasonably priced helpings of classics such as gnocchi in a tomato and mushroom sauce.

107–111 Heath St., NW3 6SS. (℃) 020/7435-8965. Fax 020/7794-7592. www.lagaffe.co.uk. 18 units. £95–£125 ($190–$250) double; £125 ($250) family room for up to 4. Rollaway beds free; cribs free. Rates include continental breakfast. AE, MC, V. Tube: Hampstead. **Amenities:** Restaurant; bar. *In room:* TV, beverage-maker, hair dryer, iron and trouser press by request.

## CRICKLEWOOD
### MODERATE

**Crown Moran Hotel** ★★ *Value*    This is an unexpected burst of genuine Irish hospitality 20 minutes north of the center—this is a largely Irish area, and the hotel is part of a minichain with properties in Dublin and Cork. Formerly one of London's oldest and most colorful pubs, it was converted into a hotel complex in 2003 and, true to the spirit of Irish conviviality, the older building houses five bars ranging from quiet lounges to happening spots with live music and DJs. All offer casual dining and snacks throughout the day (the daily specials are a very good value); or you can eat more formally in the King Sitric restaurant, which offers a fusion of modern Irish and international cuisine, such as traditional smoked salmon with Irish soda bread and capers. The Sunday lunches (when a play area is set up) and weekend brunches are popular with local families, and there are kids' menus and highchairs. But you may not have any space left after your scrumptious full Irish breakfast (including bacon, sausages, traditional black-and-white pudding, egg, and toast), which is included in the room rate (full English is also available).

Accommodations-wise, cots can be set up free in the standard doubles. If you have one older child you can book one of the 15 family rooms with one double and one single bed, otherwise you'll need to go for interconnecting rooms. The impeccably clean rooms, which are in an ultra-modern annex, are large and stylishly appointed for the price, with exceptional bathrooms with big tubs and luxurious toiletries. And I haven't even mentioned the 12m (39-ft.) pool, sauna, steam room, and gym yet. If you're still dubious about the area (it's not a looker, granted—think industrial Brooklyn), take a peek at the map to see how close you are to the northern end of lovely Hampstead Heath. Buses run from right outside direct to Marble Arch, and there are two Tube stations nearby. If you have a car, there's good-value parking at the hotel, and you're outside the congestion zone.

*Insider tip:* Look out for special rates on the website, which make this wonderful place even more of a bargain—I've seen a family room for as little as £109 ($218), or even £80 ($160) per night when booked for 2 nights.

142–52 Cricklewood Broadway, NW2 3ED. (℃) 020/8452-4175. Fax 020/8452-0952. www.crownmoranhotel.co.uk. 116 units. £125–£190 ($250–$380) double; £145–£210 ($290–$420) family room for 3. Cribs free. Rates include full Irish breakfast. AE, DC, MC, V. Tube: Kilburn. **Amenities:** Restaurant; cafe; 5 bars; pool; health club; concierge; travel desk; currency exchange; business facilities; 24-hr. room service; babysitting/baby-listening; laundry; dry cleaning. *In room:* A/C, satellite TV, voice mail, Internet access, beverage-maker, trouser press, iron, safe.

# 6

# Family-Friendly Dining

London has gone from culinary laughingstock to one of the world's food capitals in a relatively short space of time. Part of its appeal is its cosmopolitanism—you can enjoy about every cuisine under the sun here, from Moroccan to Vietnamese. However, "Modern British" has also made its mark (classic fare souped up with flavors and techniques from around the world), and traditional British cooking—such as bangers and mash, shepherd's pie, apple crumble, and custard—has made a comeback. The attendant stuffiness has gone out of the restaurant scene, including dress codes, and the emphasis now is on healthful food, variety, and flexibility in a relaxing environment.

All of this is great news for families, but it means that the competition for space in this chapter was fierce—all the more so when you know that more than 250 new restaurants opened in London in 2006 alone! As a result, many places you'd expect to see here might not be reviewed. You don't need to be told about such global chains as **Planet Hollywood, TGI Friday's,** and **Hard Rock Cafe**—suffice it to say that I've been there and I won't be going back in a hurry. Just because a company sets out to woo kids doesn't mean there aren't better places to go.

Don't assume that a place offering a **kids' menu** is the best option: Children quickly get bored of choosing among chicken nuggets, pasta, and pizza. It's possible to order imaginatively from adult menus, either by selecting from the starters and sides, or by consulting the

staff on dishes that can be provided in child-size portions. Children also love the social aspect of sharing a lot of smaller dishes with their parents: Restaurants serving Lebanese *meze* and Spanish tapas are ideal for this sort of family dining.

This guide focuses on places where you can get good food and a genuine welcome without breaking the bank, though London is a very expensive city when it comes to dining out—eating outside the center, in "villagey" areas, can save you money. Venues classified as **"Inexpensive"** are those in which a family of four can conceivably eat and drink for less than £35 ($70), but these are in short supply. At restaurants classified as **"Moderate,"** a meal should cost you £35 to £60 ($70–$120), and this is the category on which this guide focuses. Anything upwards of that is **"Expensive."** If these figures make your vacation seem impractical, consider staying someplace with self-catering facilities, whether it be an apartment or a youth hostel. Or take packed lunches or picnics out with you (p. 106) as often as possible.

Other good ways to save money are to **breakfast** in a cafe rather than at your hotel, and to take advantage of early-evening **pre-theater menus,** or of **"lunch" deals,** which often go on until 5 or 6pm. You probably want to feed the kids early anyway, and you can always order room service snacks after they've hit the sack.

**Afternoon teas** are an alternative for those who want to eat early, serving kiddy-pleasing fare such as finger sandwiches, scones, and cakes (leaving parents to enjoy a civilized dinner after the children are asleep). Yet these are not a money-saving option, with an average cream tea costing upwards of £28 ($56) at a posh hotel, such as **The Ritz** (150 Piccadilly, W1; ℂ 020/7499-1818), **Claridge's** (Brook St., W1; ℂ 020/7629-8860), and the **Dorchester** (Park Lane, W1; ℂ 020/7629-8888), which is one of the last places in London serving old-fashioned "high teas" (substantial meals, served from 4:45pm, that can replace dinner; dishes include poached salmon and spinach tart). Note that you have to book about 6 weeks ahead for The Ritz, even though there are five sittings daily.

**Pubs** are often good places to find relatively inexpensive, home-cooked food. Many **"gastropubs"** (converted pubs serving upscale food, often Modern British) welcome families, although you'll pay more in such establishments. Some pubs don't allow children at all, but many have certification allowing kids in between specific hours (usually not after 9:30pm), when accompanied by an adult. The best way to find out is to ask; www.pubs.com also offers guidance on family-friendly pubs in London.

If in doubt, head for an **Italian** restaurant. Whether it be a family-run trattoria or an Italian-inspired chain such as Pizza Express (p. 115), they generally ensure a warm welcome and convivial atmosphere; simple, child-pleasing food; and fair prices.

**HOURS**   It's a rare London restaurant or cafe that closes for Sunday these days (though you'll find some fish specialists closed on Mon); Christmas is the only time when a number of places close. Many now serve food throughout the day, without a break between lunch and dinner, especially when they pride themselves on catering to families. Hours of service are listed in the descriptions below.

**RESERVATIONS**   Most places, except pubs, cafes, and fast-food joints, prefer or require reservations, and you nearly always get a better table if you book ahead. For famous or very trendy places, you might need to reserve weeks in advance, but even if you haven't, it's worth trying to get in if you are in the area.

**TAXES & TIPPING**   All restaurants and cafes are required to display the prices of their food and drink in a place visible from outside. Charges for service, as well as any minimums or cover charges, must also be made clear. For advice on tipping, see p. 64.

## 1 Restaurants by Cuisine

### AFTERNOON TEA
Café in the Crypt ⭐ (Trafalgar Sq., $, p. 117)

Café 2, Tate Modern ⭐⭐ (South Bank, $$, p. 132)

Crumpet ⭐⭐ (Clapham, $, p. 133).

The Original Maids of Honour ⭐ (Kew, $, p. 134)

The Refectory@Southwark Cathedral ⭐ (Southwark, $, p. 131)

### AMERICAN
Big Easy (Chelsea, $$, p. 123)

Rainforest Café ⭐ (Piccadilly Circus, $$$, p. 114)

Smollensky's Bar & Grill ⭐⭐ (The Strand, $$$, p. 112)

Texas Embassy Cantina (Trafalgar Sq., $$, p. 116)

### BELGIAN
Belgo Centraal (Covent Garden, $, p. 113)

## BREAKFAST

Acorn House ⚜ (Clerkenwell, $$, p. 136)

Bluebird ⚜ (Chelsea, $$$, p. 123)

The Brewhouse (Hampstead, $, p. 106)

Carluccio's Caffè ⚜⚜ (Fitzrovia, $, p. 109)

Crumpet ⚜⚜ (Clapham, $, p. 133).

The Fountain ⚜ (St. James's, $$$, p. 103)

Frizzante@CityFarm ⚜⚜⚜ (Hackney, $, p. 135)

Giraffe ⚜ (Kensington, $$, p. 120)

Kalendar ⚜ (Hampstead, $–$$, p. 141)

Leon ⚜ (Knightsbridge, $, p. 121)

Le Petit Chez Gérard (Covent Garden, $$, p. 113)

Natural Cafe ⚜⚜⚜ (Westbourne Grove, $, p. 126)

The Place Below ⚜⚜ (The City, $, p. 137)

Queen's Park Cafe (Queen's Park, $, p. 106)

Smiths of Smithfield ⚜ (Clerkenwell, $$, p. 136)

The Wallace ⚜⚜⚜ (Marylebone, $$, p. 109)

## BRITISH (MODERN)

Acorn House ⚜ (Clerkenwell, $$, p. 136)

Boxwood Café ⚜ (Belgravia, $$$, p. 120)

The Engineer ⚜ (Camden Town, $$, p. 139)

Inn the Park (St. James's, $$$, p. 106)

Julie's Restaurant ⚜⚜ (Holland Park, $$$, p. 129)

National Dining Rooms & Bakery ⚜⚜⚜ (Trafalgar Sq., $$–$$$, p. 116)

## BRITISH (TRADITIONAL)

The Fountain ⚜ (St. James's, $$$, p. 103).

M Manze (South Bank, $, p. 140)

Manze's (Walthamstow, $, p. 140)

Meals ⚜⚜ (Bloomsbury, $$, p. 110)

The Narrow ⚜⚜ (Limehouse & Docklands, $$, p. 138)

Porter's English Restaurant (Covent Garden, $$$, p. 112)

S&M Café ⚜⚜ (Ladbroke Grove, $, p. 128)

Spaniard's Inn ⚜ (Hampstead, $$, p. 141)

## BURGERS

Ed's Easy Diner ⚜⚜ (Piccadilly Circus, $, p. 114)

Gourmet Burger Kitchen ⚜⚜ (The City, $, p. 137)

## CHINESE

Royal China ⚜⚜ (Limehouse & Docklands, $$, p. 138)

## CREPES

My Old Dutch Pancake House ⚜ (Bloomsbury, $, p. 110)

## FRENCH

Chez Kristof ⚜ (Hammersmith, $$$, p. 129)

Le Bouchon Bordelais ⚜⚜ (Clapham, $$$, p. 132)

Le Cercle ⚜ (Brompton, $$$, p. 120)

Le Petit Chez Gérard (Covent Garden, $, p. 113)

Roussillon ⚜ (Pimlico, $$$, p. 122)

The Wallace ⚜⚜⚜ (Marylebone, $$, p. 109)

## GERMAN

Stein's (Richmond, $$, p. 134)

## GLOBAL

Balans West (Earl's Court, $$, p. 125)

The Blue Kangaroo ⚜⚜ (Fulham, $$, p. 126)

Giraffe ⚜ (Kensington, $$, p. 120)

The Living Room (St. James's, $$, p. 106)

The Naked Turtle (Richmond, $$$, p. 133)

## INDIAN

Imli ⚜⚜⚜ (Soho, $, p. 116)

La Porte des Indes (Marylebone, $$$, p. 125)

**PORTUGUESE**

Lisboa Patisserie (Ladbroke Grove, $, p. 128)

**SEAFOOD**

Curve ✦ (Limehouse & Docklands, $$$, p. 138)

fish! ✦✦ (South Bank, $$, p. 131)

Fish Central (Clerkenwell, $$, p. 140)

Fishworks ✦✦ (Marylebone, $$$, p. 108)

Geales (Notting Hill, $$, p. 140)

Mr Fish (Westbourne Grove, $, p. 140)

**THAI**

The Blue Elephant ✦✦✦ (Fulham, $$$, p. 125)

**VEGETARIAN**

The Place Below ✦✦ (The City, $, p. 137)

World Food Café ✦ (Covent Garden, $, p. 113)

**VIETNAMESE**

Green Papaya (Hackney, $, p. 135)

## 2 Central London

### ST. JAMES'S & MAYFAIR

#### EXPENSIVE

One of the area's most child-friendly eateries is **Inn the Park** within St. James's Park (p. 106).

**The Fountain** ✦ BRITISH (TRADITIONAL)    One of several restaurants at the swish Fortnum & Mason department store (p. 223), The Fountain was scheduled to reopen after refurbishment at the time of this writing, although its murals, showing the imaginary travels of Mr. Fortnum and Mr. Mason to source edible goodies, remain intact. It's long been famous for its ice-cream sundaes (from about £6/$12) served during afternoon tea, but you might be equally happy with an original shake (flavors include toffee, praline, and black cherry), a Valrhona chocolate ice cream, or bread-and-butter pudding. For those without a sweet tooth, there are some traditional lunch and pre-theater mains, including salmon, fish and chips, Welsh rarebit, and pies, which you can spice up with one of Fortnum's own relishes or mustards. Another highlight is the full English breakfasts, which include dry-cured English bacon and exclusive Old English sausages.

18 Piccadilly, W1. ✆ 020/7734-8040. Highchairs. Reservations recommended. Main courses £10–£16 ($20–$32). AE, MC, V. Mon–Sat 8:30am–7pm; Sun noon–5pm. Tube: Green Park.

**Tamarind** ✦✦ INDIAN    The northwest Indian Moghul cuisine served at this basement restaurant has garnered it a Michelin star. And although it's a sophisticated environment for fine dining, kids are welcome on Sunday lunchtimes, when they can enjoy a new menu specially concocted for them (and free to under-10s when accompanied by two or more adults). It's a true three-course feast of exotic flavors: Starters include melon, plums, kumquats, and salad leaves in a pine-nut and honey dressing, or pan-fried potato cakes with split lentils, ginger, toasted cumin, and spinach stuffing; mains feature battered filets of tilapia fish or tandoori-grilled chicken in a mild creamed tomato and honey sauce, with seasonal vegetables or steamed rice; and for dessert, try the homemade vanilla ice cream with seasonal fruit. Adults might like to treat themselves to the good-value Sunday-lunch tasting menu; otherwise, standout adult dishes include a cold salad of spicy minced prawns with peppers, pomegranate, and coriander, and lamb cutlets marinated with raw paw-paw, garlic, paprika, and crushed peppercorns. Vegetarian menus are available, too.

20 Queen St., W1. ✆ 020/7629-3561. Highchairs. Reservations recommended. Main courses £11–£26 ($22–$52); kids' Sunday lunch menu £13 ($26). AE, MC, V. Mon–Fri noon–2:45pm and 6–11:30pm; Sat 6–11:30pm; Sun noon–2:45pm and 6:30–10:30pm. Tube: Green Park Station.

# Where to Dine in Central London & Clerkenwell

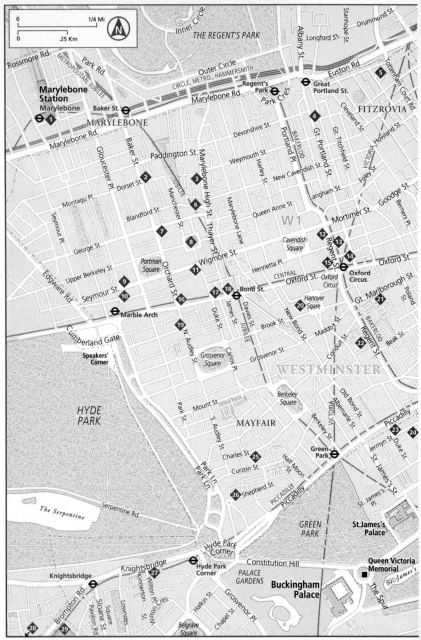

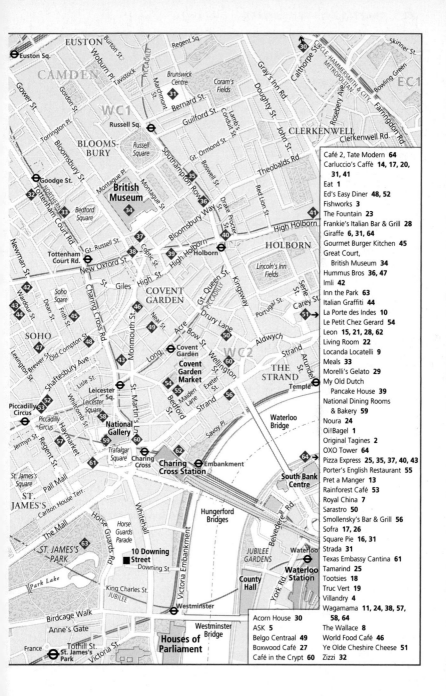

Café 2, Tate Modern **64**
Carluccio's Caffè **14, 17, 20, 31, 41**
Eat **1**
Ed's Easy Diner **48, 52**
Fishworks **3**
The Fountain **23**
Frankie's Italian Bar & Grill **28**
Giraffe **6, 31, 64**
Gourmet Burger Kitchen **45**
Great Court, British Museum **34**
Hummus Bros **36, 47**
Imli **42**
Inn the Park **63**
Italian Graffiti **44**
La Porte des Indes **10**
Le Petit Chez Gerard **54**
Leon **15, 21, 28, 62**
Living Room **22**
Locanda Locatelli **9**
Meals **33**
Morelli's Gelato **29**
My Old Dutch Pancake House **39**
National Dining Rooms & Bakery **59**
Noura **24**
Oi!Bagel **1**
Original Tagines **2**
OXO Tower **64**
Pizza Express **25, 35, 37, 40, 43**
Porter's English Restaurant **55**
Pret a Manger **13**
Rainforest Café **53**
Royal China **7**
Sarastro **50**
Smollensky's Bar & Grill **56**
Sofra **17, 26**
Square Pie **16, 31**
Strada **31**
Texas Embassy Cantina **61**
Tamarind **25**
Tootsies **18**
Truc Vert **19**
Villandry **4**
Wagamama **11, 24, 38, 57, 58, 64**
The Wallace **8**
World Food Café **46**
Ye Olde Cheshire Cheese **51**
Zizzi **32**

Acorn House **30**
ASK **5**
Belgo Centraal **49**
Boxwood Café **27**
Café in the Crypt **60**

## Park Life: From Restaurants to Picnics

London's parks are graced with wonderful and family-friendly restaurants and cafes, all with terraces so you can take advantage of fine weather. The cream of the crop is **Inn the Park** 🖈🖈🖈 (© **020/7451-9999**), a striking grass-roofed building in St. James's Park (p. 206), affording views of Duck Island and the surrounding palaces from its decked veranda. Its posh restaurant area offers modern British food—the likes of smoked eel and bacon salad with a poached egg, and grilled wild halibut with samphire butter (mains are £15–£23/$30–$46)—and a very good children's menu with roast chicken with broccoli, organic fishcake with spinach, and pork and leek sausages with mash, then chocolate tart with butterscotch ice cream, or ice cream by itself (kids' mains are all £7.50/$15). Or come for breakfast (everything from home-made crumpet with blackberry butter to full English), lunches from the self-service counter, afternoon or high tea, or just a warming glass of some of the best hot chocolate in town. Alternatively, the cafe makes up picnic baskets in summer, for picnics in the park, costing from £15 ($30) for adults, and £7.50 ($15) per child; the latter get finger sandwiches, organic crisps, fruit salad, homemade jaffa cake, and a strawberry smoothie, and a plush rug is loaned.

In west London, the cafe in the pavilion in the center of **Queen's Park** (© **020/8960-6946**; p. 206) is a real haven for parents, with a kids' menu of simple dishes such as rarebit for £3.50 ($7); treats such as Portuguese custard tarts and mugs of hot chocolate with whipped cream, marshmallows, and sprinkles; and plenty of space for them to run around. For moms and dads, the breakfast menu runs from homemade muesli with yogurt and honey to full English, and there are daily specials for lunch. Come during the week to take full advantage of the light and airy space, although at lunchtimes it still gets chaotic (and muddy if it's raining).

In north London, on Hampstead Heath, the charming **Brewhouse** in an old stable block adjoining historic Kenwood House (p. 143) is a gorgeous if often hectic spot for self-service cooked breakfasts, lunches, cakes (don't miss the lavender and orange sponge), and afternoon teas, especially when the sun lights up its huge terraced garden. It's open daily March through September 9am to 6pm, October 9am to dusk, and November through February 9am to 4pm.

## MODERATE

**The Living Room** GLOBAL    A central all-day spot, The Living Room occupies a former post-office building that famously appeared on the album cover of Bowie's *Ziggy Stardust and the Spiders from Mars*. It's a relaxed venue combining a restaurant, lounge, and bar over two floors, with a theatrical open kitchen and live music most evenings. Though there's a changing under-10s menu with the likes of tomato and mozzarella bruschetta, potato wedges with dips, roast chicken, mash, and broccoli, they might be tempted by the "Small Plates," bearing such fare as vegetable tempura or hummus with warm pita bread and paprika. Alternatively, sandwiches are served

If you're intent on really being in the great outdoors, some of best places to shop for exciting picnic fare are **department-store food halls.** Two of the most famous are Harrods and the newly enlarged Fortnum & Mason (p. 223). Nonmessy ideas for alfresco eating are great bread, cheeses, dips, chunky Spanish-style omelets, cakes, and bottles of concentrate (elderflower is lovely for summer). A cooler box is essential; you may already have one for car journeys, but if you don't want to invest in one, most supermarkets sell cooler bags that will see you through a picnic or two. Many hotels will also provide hampers for you with a little advance notice.

If you're heading to **Hyde Park,** try **Selfridges'** food hall (p. 224) or, 2 minutes' walk away, **Truc Vert** (42 N. Audley St., W1; ✆ **020/7491-9988**), a deli and brasserie selling top-notch charcuterie and farmhouse cheeses, plus superior picnic fare—sandwiches on artisanal bread, a daily quiche, and chocolate-orange brownies.

Farther east and handy for **Regent's Park, Villandry** (170 Great Portland St., W1; ✆ **020/7631-3131**) is another gourmet food store with a restaurant and bar tacked onto it. Most of the ready-prepared items at the take-away counter come directly from its own kitchen, while everything in the bakery is produced with organic flour, from the walnut bread, cheese straws, and spinach rolls to the almond croissants and to-die-for moist chocolate cake. If you're in too much of a hurry to browse, call ahead for a picnic hamper. Note that the restaurant sometimes hosts special events, such as an Easter egg–making class held while parents enjoy brunch.

Less obvious places to picnic in London are **Thames Barrier Park** east of the City (p. 155), and **Postman's Park** close to St. Paul's Cathedral and the Museum of London (p. 199). For the latter, consider a veggie takeout from **The Place Below** (p. 137). Note that indoor picnic venues are available at some large museums, including the Science Museum (p. 150) and the Natural History Museum (p. 148). **Carluccio's** (p. 109) has branches all over town, including in Smithfield Market, and provides a choice of picnic boxes costing from £30 ($60) for two, plus a great-value £10 ($20) kids' one with breadsticks, Milanese salami, breaded chicken breast, pasta salad with tomatoes, tuna mayonnaise, carrot and celery sticks, a chocolate bear, and fresh orange juice.

up to 7pm. The main menu features a motley crew of dishes from around the globe: You might enjoy clam chowder with sea asparagus and saffron potatoes, "Home Comforts" such as sausage and mash, steak-and-ale pie, or cheeseburger, or grownup fare such as sea bass with fennel purée and Morecambe Bay shrimps. This is a good place for weekend brunches; note also the good-value fixed-price daily lunch and pre-theater menus. There's a second London branch in Islington, though the menu differs.

3–9 Heddon St., W1. ✆ **08701/662225.** Highchairs. Main courses £9.50–£22 ($19–$44); kids' menu £6–£7 ($12–$14) for 2 or 3 courses. AE, MC, V. Mon–Sat 10am–1am; Sun 11am–midnight. Tube: Piccadilly Circus.

## INEXPENSIVE

**Sofra** 🎭 *Value* MIDDLE EASTERN    This Middle Eastern chain downsized after an over-energetic expansion but still offers one of central London's best bargains in the form of exceptionally well-priced set lunches (to 6pm). From just £8.95 ($18) you get two courses that might include a spinach and feta cheese börek (pastry) or falafel from among a choice of about 10 starters, and lamb tagine with vegetables, almonds, and dried fruit, served with couscous, or penne with dolcelatte cheese, from among 15 or so mains. You'll probably spend a bit more once you see the extensive desserts menu, which features rose or tahini ice cream, organic apricots stuffed with cream, and rose-water rice pudding. This branch is in a delightful, villagey part of Mayfair known as Shepherds Market, but inside it's rather cramped. There are three more Sofras, in Marylebone, St. John's Wood, and Covent Garden, plus the very central sibling **Özer** (5 Langham Place, W1).

18 Shepherd St., W1. ⓒ 020/7493-3320. Highchairs. Main courses £6.95–£20 ($14–$40). AE, MC, V. Daily noon–midnight. Tube: Green Park.

# MARYLEBONE, REGENT'S PARK & FITZROVIA
## EXPENSIVE

For **La Porte des Indes** with its family brunches, see its sister restaurant The Blue Elephant (p. 125).

**Fishworks** 🎭🎭 SEAFOOD    Dramatic expansion of this award-winning fish restaurant/fishmonger chain since the last edition of this guide (from three to nine London branches) hasn't impinged on quality. In bright, modern surrounds you can choose from a well-judged menu of classic seafood dishes, or splurge on the freshest oysters, a monster shellfish platter, or a whole fish from the shop counters up front (for non-fish-heads there's also the odd pasta, veggie, or steak offering). Kids can get a half-portion of anything on the menu for half-price, or choose from their own menu of fishcakes or—highly recommended and totally unlike the frozen stuff—fish fingers, or alternatively a bowl of mussels or plate of spaghetti with tomato sauce. Fries aren't generally part of the deal; instead there are superior side orders such as fennel, mint, lemon, and chile salad, or roasted tomatoes with pesto. *Insider tip:* If you're trying to keep the bill down and don't want to order starters, ask for the appetizer of fresh-made *taramasalata* (a dip of fish roe, olive oil, garlic, and bread crumbs). It comes with a couple of extra dips and enough bread to keep everybody munching while waiting for your mains, and is a bargain at £2.25 ($4.50). The other branches are in Islington, Primrose Hill, West-bourne Grove, Chiswick, Fulham Road, Battersea, Parson's Green, and Richmond.

89 Marylebone High St., W1. ⓒ 020/7935-9796. Highchairs. Reservations recommended. Main courses £12–£9.95 ($24–$20); kids' dishes £3.95 ($7.90) or half price from rest of menu. AE, MC, V. Mon–Sat noon–2:30pm and 6–10:30pm; Sun noon–2:30pm. Tube: Baker St.

**Locanda Locatelli** 🎭🎭 ITALIAN    You can count on a typical Italian welcome here (and the most stylish highchairs in town, clad in beige leather so as not to jar with the rest of the sleek decor)—its owner, celeb chef Giorgio Locatelli, once fumed to the press about the sniffy attitude of many British restaurateurs toward kids, and before this restaurant opened, staff received training in keeping junior diners happy. Food-wise, you're as far from nuggets and pizza as possible. There's no kids' menu as such, but the kitchen will rustle up kid-friendly goodies such as homemade spaghetti with tuna balls, and desserts like chocolate and banana beignets—Locatelli himself has been known to take junior diners into the kitchens to help make their own, and there are a few toys to keep them distracted. The sublime adult fare changes seasonally but might include the likes of calf's feet with pepper, potato, onion, and capers; roast rabbit leg with Parma ham, polenta, and radicchio; and Sicilian risotto cake with pistachio ice cream. All this said, if you've got a fidgety kid, this place may not be for you—service can be slow.

8 Seymour St., W1. ℂ 020/7935-9088. Highchairs. Reservations required (several weeks ahead). Main courses £20–£29 ($40–$58). AE, MC, V. Mon–Sat noon–3pm and 7–11pm; Sun noon–3:30pm and 7–10pm. Tube: Marble Arch.

## MODERATE

There's a branch of the child-friendly chain **Giraffe** (p. 120) just off Marylebone High Street, on Blandford Street, and a branch of the **Royal China** (p. 138) on Baker Street.

**Original Tagines** ⭐ MOROCCAN    This cozy little restaurant on a quiet road off Baker Street lures you in with its tempting aromas and warm North African decor. You'll be glad you succumbed: The food is divine, from traditional starters such as hummus, and *b'stilla* pastries (filled with pigeon, lemon-flavored eggs, and almonds), to full-blown dishes like couscous Imperial loaded with lamb, chicken, *merguez* (spicy North African sausage), and vegetables. Many of the *tagines* (stews) are cooked with fruit—lamb with caramelized pear, for instance, or chicken with prunes and almonds—and go down very well with kids, who can get smaller portions. Best of all, though, are the divine desserts—don't leave without at least sharing a bowl or two of the rice pudding with orangeflower water. *Insider tip:* The set lunches are a good bargain.

7a Dorset St., W1. ℂ 020/7935-1545. Highchairs. Reservations recommended. Main courses £9.50–£12 ($19–$24). MC, V. Mon–Fri noon–3pm and 6–11pm; Sat–Sun 6–11pm. Tube: Baker St.

**The Wallace** ⭐⭐⭐ *Finds* FRENCH    This newcomer tucked away within the museum's glass-roofed Sculpture Garden of the Wallace Collection (p. 174) is an elegant brasserie with tables shaded by camelia trees and silk-fringed parasols. It has a huge selection, including an excellent kids' menu of main courses: escalope of organic chicken breast *viennoise,* steamed lemon sole with fresh vegetables, and simple penne pasta with tomato sauce. But there's plenty more to please on the all-day menu, whether its brunchy fare such as pancakes with sugar or snacky dishes such as quiche, *tartines* (open sandwiches). Lunch and dinner dishes are for more adventurous palates: Think *steak tartare* with truffle, ox tongue with a piquant sauce, or civet of wild rabbit with sweet potato. The seafood counter has a tempting array, including oysters, and to finish up there are classic French desserts such as *poire Belle Hélène* (vanilla ice cream with poached pear and mascarpone) and *oeufs à la neige aux pralines* (a floating island of meringue in custard sauce with pralines). In short, it's the kind of place where everyone will find something they like, and at fair prices given the quality and setting.

The Wallace Collection, Manchester Sq., W1. ℂ **020/7563-9505.** Highchairs. Reservations recommended. Main courses £6–£45 ($12–$90); kids' main courses £7.50 ($15). AE, MC, V. Sun–Thurs 10am–5pm; Fri–Sat 10am–11pm. Tube: Bond St.

## INEXPENSIVE

There's a **Wagamama** (p. 123) behind Selfridges department store.

**Carluccio's Caffè** ⭐⭐ *Value* ITALIAN    If you don't like bustle, don't come to one of Carluccio's hectic all-day eateries. You'll miss out, though—despite being a rapidly growing chain (there are about 30 branches total, most of them in London), Carluccio's is a breath of fresh Italian air, and never compromises on the quality of its food, although the friendliness and efficiency of the waitstaff differs wildly. This most central branch, in a quiet square just a few steps from Oxford Circus, is useful if you're shopping in the West End. All the authentic regional dishes offered in the bright, modern space are on the smallish side, making them ideal for hungry kids (prices are in keeping with the size), but smaller portions of many dishes are available. There's also a wonderful, great-value "Per I Piccoli" menu starting with *grissini* and a soft drink; progressing to breaded chicken breast with rosemary potatoes, or pasta with a choice of sauces; and finishing with a tub of ice cream. This paper menu has things to color, and quizzes. Highlights of the main menu are the rich wild mushroom soup studded with pancetta, and homemade spinach and ricotta ravioli with butter and sage. *Insider tip:* Come for an early lunch to avoid the office hordes (you can't book during the day).

Other more or less central branches include the Brunswick Centre in Bloomsbury, Smithfield, Islington, Bond Street (in Fenwick's department store), St Christopher's Place (just off Oxford St., near Selfridges), Westbourne Grove, and South Kensington. See p. 106 for details of Carluccio's wonderful **picnic boxes.**

8 Market Place, W1. © 020/7636-2228. www.carluccios.com. Highchairs. Reservations for evening tables only. Main courses £4.95–£13 ($9.90–$26); kids' menu £4.95 ($9.90). AE, MC, V. Mon–Fri 7:30am–11pm; Sat 10am–11pm; Sun 10am–10pm. Tube: Oxford Circus.

## BLOOMSBURY & HOLBORN

Formerly a bit of a wasteland for family-friendly eateries, this area has been transformed by the revamp of the **Brunswick Centre,** a neglected 1960s housing development that has been transformed into an airy piazza with plenty of outdoor seating and a host of good places to eat *en famille,* including branches of **Carluccio's** (p. 109), **Giraffe** (p. 120), **Strada** (p. 115), and **Square Pie** (p. 111). Other options include branches of **Pizza Express** (p. 115) on Coptic Street, High Holborn, and Southampton Row; **ASK** (p. 115) on Southampton Row; and a **Wagamama** (p. 123) on Streatham Street. The British Museum also has a variety of good eating options in its atmospheric **Great Court** (p. 159).

### MODERATE

**Meals** 🏵🏵 BRITISH (TRADITIONAL)    Set within a chic home-furnishings store, this new restaurant/cafe has a quirky Arts and Crafts decor designed to conjure up subtle memories of Hansel and Gretel in the forest. Families head here mainly at weekends, when there's a fantastic all-day brunch menu featuring the likes of toasted crumpets with cream cheese and smoked salmon, pancakes with bananas, walnuts, and honey, Cumberland sausage with fried egg, bubble-and-squeak, and corned beef hash with eggs and HP sauce (a common zesty, brown sauce)—comfort food is definitely the buzzword here. But all week long it's a popular spot for breakfast, lunch, and light bites: The all-day menu lists everything from homemade muffins with preserves, granola, and fairy cakes to toasted country breads, soups, and quiches. The daily-changing lunch menu is more "grown up": Dishes might include crab and chile cakes with mint and coriander yogurt, or courgette fritters with vine tomato sauce, or a classic fish pie. There are also good afternoon teas at a bargain £13 ($26).

Heals, 196 Tottenham Court Rd., W1. © 020/7580-2522. Highchairs. Main courses £5.50–£18 ($11–$36). AE, MC, V. Mon–Wed 10am–6pm; Thurs 10am–8pm; Fri 10am–6:30pm; Sat 9:30am–6:30pm; Sun noon–6pm. Tube: Goodge St.

### INEXPENSIVE

**My Old Dutch Pancake House** 🏵 CREPES    This clean, airy space has been filling diners with its wide range of genuine Dutch pancakes—slightly thicker than crepes

## Food on the Go: Sandwiches & Snack Stops

There'll be days when you don't have the time, money, or inclination to sit down for a full lunch, especially if you're dining out in the evening. One of the best sandwich chains is **Pret a Manger** (298 Regent St.; ℂ 020/7932/ 5219), with scores of branches selling its handmade, no-additives sandwiches, plus sushi, salads, soups, hot wraps, pastries, and desserts. High points are the classic tuna and the carrot cake. Also first class are the juices and smoothies. A similar but slightly less ubiquitous place is the simply named **Eat** (319 Regent St.; ℂ 020/7636-8309), with great handmade sandwiches (including wheat-free options), pies, soups, salads, and desserts.

Bagel aficionados can get a fix at **Oi!Bagel** (ℂ 020/7723-7321), which has branches at Marylebone Station, W1; in the West One Shopping Centre on Oxford Street, W1; and elsewhere. Their fresh handmade bagels come in a variety of guises, from breakfast specials (including melted cheese and Marmite, and sausage) to gourmet (goat's cheese and pepper, or Thai chile chicken), and there's soups, too. If you're in the East End, it's worth seeking out the almost legendary (and much cheaper) **Brick Lane Beigel Bake** (159 Brick Lane, E1; ℂ 020/7729-0616), open round-the-clock and producing more than 7,000 bagels a night, which you can enjoy filled with smoked salmon, salt beef, chopped liver, and more. Prices range from just 20p to £1.60 (40¢–$3.20). Other breads and cakes are sold here, too.

For something more hearty, **Square Pie** (ℂ 020/8533-7555) sells traditional and modern pies at Selfridges' food hall (p. 224), the Brunswick Centre (p. 110), Spitalfields Market, Canary Wharf, and Heathrow Airport. Choose from classics such as steak and mushroom, or more adventurous takes such as jerk chicken with okra and sweet potato. They come in two sizes for larger and smaller appetites, and there are also sausage rolls, veggie rolls, pies without pastry (stews), side-order salads, sweet pies such as cherry and apple, and shakes. Prices start at about £4.90 ($9.80) for a small takeout pie with gravy, great mash, and mushy or garden peas. It's also worth knowing about the family-size "Take Me Home and Bake Me" pie.

but still light in texture, and huge in diameter—for years now. Savory options run the gamut from the highly recommended Amsterdammer with smoked bacon, apple slices, and maple syrup, to chili con carne, chicken curry, or smoked salmon with mushrooms or dill. All are served on enormous traditional blue and white tableware. You can also get salads; oddities such as *bitterballen* (a traditional starter of bread crumbs, onions, cheese, and garlic, served with sour cream), sweet pancakes, and waffles. This is definitely a sharing kind of place; portions are huge so three pancakes should be enough for four unless you're ravenous. Parents should try the fruit-flavored beers, kids the smoothies or shakes, one of them made with real Belgian chocolate. There are other branches on the King's Road in Chelsea and in Ealing, W5.

132 High Holborn, WC1. ℂ 020/7242-5200. Highchairs. Main courses £5.95–£9.95 ($12–$20). AE, MC, V. Mon–Sat 11am–11pm; Sun 11am–10pm. Tube: Holborn.

## COVENT GARDEN & THE STRAND

Many restaurants in this theater district exist purely to sell substandard fare to unwary tourists, but there are also some very fine choices, many offering good-value pre-theater menus, including the restaurants at hotel One Aldwych (p. 75).

### EXPENSIVE

**Porter's English Restaurant** BRITISH (TRADITIONAL)   This is a long-standing family favorite for its old-fashioned, and calorie-laden, English food—think steak-and-kidney-pudding, deviled chicken and mushroom pie, traditional roasts, and the kind of stodgy desserts you imagine are served up at British boarding schools. Under-12s get a menu of hearty fare such as sausage, mash, and beans, or roast beef and potatoes with Yorkshire pudding and peas, plus desserts such as trifle, or syrup sponge pud and custard. They also get their own cocktails, including a nonalcoholic piña colada. Decor-wise, you may have expected a little more class given that it's owned by the Earl of Bradford. Still, kids are entertained by such tacky touches as the old porter's cart dangling from the ceiling. Note the deals combining dinner with a trip on the London Eye (p. 142) or entry to other attractions, or West End shows such as *The Lion King* (p. 253).

17 Henrietta St., WC2. ⓒ 020/7836-6466. www.porters.uk.com. Highchairs. Reservations recommended. Main courses £9.95–£19 ($20–$38); kids' main courses £6 ($12). AE, DC, MC, V. Mon–Sat noon–11:30pm; Sun noon–10:30pm. Tube: Covent Garden.

**Smollensky's Bar & Grill** 🎡🎡 AMERICAN   Famous for its Family Days (most Sat–Sun noon–3pm) featuring the likes of clowning, magic, a Punch & Judy show, goodie bags, disco dancing, face-painting, and use of a PlayStation, Smollensky's has lost its American-diner decor in favor of something more contemporary—bare brick walls and warm colors are now the order of the day. Parents sit back and enjoy the surprisingly good food—the obligatory steak, burgers, ribs, and jambalaya, but also excellent pasta dishes (hot smoked salmon, lemon oil, and rosemary is a highlight)—and a fine array of cocktails while the kids are kept well entertained. They also get their own menu: For under-7s there are burger or chicken or fish goujons with fries, or penne pasta; for "mini adults" there's jambalaya with basmati rice, sirloin steak with grilled tomatoes, flat mushroom, and fries, or lemon and thyme chicken breasts with fries. Desserts range from gingerbread man with ice cream to tots to rich chocolate mousse or fresh fruit for "mini adults" and there's a good choice of shakes, juices, and kids' cocktails. The other branches, at Tower Bridge (with great views) and Canary Wharf, aren't so kiddy-oriented.

105 The Strand, WC2. ⓒ 020/7497-2101. www.smollenskys.com. Highchairs. Reservations recommended. Main courses £7.55–£30 ($15–$60); kids' main courses £3.95–£8.50 ($7.90–$17). AE, DC, MC, V. Daily noon–11:30pm. Tube: Covent Garden.

### MODERATE

**Sarastro** MEDITERRANEAN   This flamboyant place, which bills itself as "the show after the show," is a great spot for a celebration—it's laid out like an opera house, with rich draperies, theatrical knickknacks, and even a number of gilded opera boxes in which diners can sit. It's trashy, but enjoyably so. Families are best off coming for the Sunday "opera cabarets," which kick off at 1:30pm. For £20 ($40) per person, half that for kids, you watch performances by young talent and students from leading opera houses, including the Royal Opera and English National Opera nearby, while enjoying a three-course menu that includes Turkish/Greek hors d'oeuvres such as cheese *börek* (pastries), mains such as Anatolian-style lamb, and a Turkish dessert or fresh fruit.

126 Drury Lane, WC2. ℂ 020/7836-0101. Reservations recommended. Main courses £7.50–£16 ($15–$32). AE, DC, MC, V. Daily noon–midnight. Tube: Covent Garden.

## INEXPENSIVE

**Belgo Centraal** BELGIAN    The novelty has worn off for many, but Belgo is still a fun place to bring kids, who find it entertaining that its waiters dress in monks' habits (a reference to the Trappist-brewed beers served here). The descent to the basement in the clanking industrial lift is a thrill, and the beer hall atmosphere jolly. Where parents are concerned, the main draw is that two kids ages 12 or under eat free from the Mini Belgo menu for each adult who orders a main course from the a la carte menu. This Mini menu changes from time to time but includes the likes of roast chicken with tarragon sauce and fries, and wild boar sausage with Belgian mash and a forest fruit sauce. For adults, the mainstay is mussels and *frites,* served traditionally or in a variety of more exotic sauces (from Thai to Portuguese), but there are other Belgian dishes for those who aren't fans of sea critters, including roast chicken in a mustard and leek sauce, and wild boar and Chimay beer sausages with mash and a berry *jus,* plus non-Belgian dishes, including steaks and "surf 'n' turf." There's another branch, Belgo Noord, in Camden, plus the sister Bierodrome bars on nearby Kingsway (WC2), in Islington, and in Clapham in south London—all are welcoming to kids and offer the "Kids Eat Free" deal as part of their menu.

50 Earlham St., WC2. ℂ 020/7813-2233. Highchairs. Main courses £8.25–£18 ($17–$36); kids' menu free with adult main course. AE, DC, MC, V. Mon–Thurs noon–11pm; Fri–Sat noon–11:30pm; Sun noon–10:30pm. Tube: Covent Garden.

**Le Petit Chez Gérard** *Finds* FRENCH    This new cafe—a little sister to the Chez Gérard brasseries purveying very good *steak frites* to Francophiles and homesick French expats—is worth knowing about for its menu of snackier but authentic Gallic dishes, from pastries and breakfast baguettes, both served all day, to more substantial baguettes served with fries and salad, well-executed burgers, a "terrace menu" of sophisticated salads or croque-monsieur, and classic desserts such as bitter chocolate mousse, lemon tart, and ice creams and sorbets. It's useful if you don't want a huge evening meal—prices aren't horrific given the touristy location, and the courtyard tables are great for people-watching.

The Market, Covent Garden Piazza, WC2. ℂ 020/7836-0633. Main courses £6.50–£11 ($13–$22). AE, MC, V. Mon–Sat 10am–9:30pm; Sun 10am–8pm. Tube: Covent Garden.

**World Food Café** VEGETARIAN    This lovely, light-filled, friendly, and award-winning cafe serves inexpensive veggie and vegan snacks and lunches from around the globe to a world-music soundtrack. You'll find everything from Mexican platters and Middle Eastern *meze* to Indian thalis and West African stews. The owner is a travel writer and photographer, and many of the recipes have been picked up during his perambulations; they're good enough to have spawned a cookbook. There's no kids' menu, but most of the food is colorful and appealing to junior palates—and there are snack plates (falafels, tortillas, oat pancakes . . .), gorgeous desserts (try the mango kulfi ice cream with fruit), and fruit *lassis.* Kids love watching the activity in the semi-open kitchen or peering down into the hippie haven of Neal's Yard below. Come off peak, though, as it can get very busy.

14 Neal's Yard, WC2. ℂ 020/7379-0298. Highchairs. Main courses £5.50–£9 ($11–$18). MC, V. Mon–Sat noon–5pm. Tube: Covent Garden.

## PICCADILLY CIRCUS & LEICESTER SQUARE
### EXPENSIVE

**Rainforest Café** ⚘ AMERICAN    It's your parental duty to bring your offspring to this jungle-themed extravaganza at some juncture, but if you enter into the spirit of things, it can be fun—unless if you have a child of a nervous disposition, in which case stay away (many have to be whisked out in a hurry). Most kids, though, love the animatronic, growling wildlife and quickly get used to the rather disconcerting tropical storms that rumble over your heads as you sample gimmicky-sounding but reasonable fare such as Congo Pasta (fettuccine with olive, tomatoes, spinach, Parmesan, and basil) and Major Mojo Bones (sticky barbecue ribs). The kids' menu is a whole lot more expensive than most, but choice is wide, and several options are organic (certain allergies can also be catered to). Desserts tend to be of the immensely gooey variety. *Insider tip:* Avoid weekends, when reservations ("priority seating requests"—a guarantee of getting a table within 5–10 min. of an allocated slot) aren't taken and you can expect to queue for up to 2 hours.

20–24 Shaftesbury Ave., W1. ℭ 020/7434-3111. Highchairs. Reservations recommended Sun–Fri. Main courses £11–£18 ($22–$36). Kids' menu (main course and dessert) £10 ($20). AE, DC, MC, V. Mon–Thurs noon–10pm; Fri noon–8pm; Sat 11:30am–8pm; Sun 11:30am–10pm. Tube: Leicester Sq.

### INEXPENSIVE

There are branches of **Wagamama** (p. 123) just off Leicester Square and just off Haymarket.

**Ed's Easy Diner** ⚘⚘ BURGERS    Now that the large North London branch of this popular retro American diner (based on Los Angeles' Apple Pan Diner) has closed, this Piccadilly Circus incarnation (plus the one in Covent Garden, at Great Newport St.) is probably the most child-friendly—avoid the one in Soho (on Old Compton St.), which is hardly big enough to swing a cat. It's all very corny on the surface—a jukebox plays rock 'n' roll, hokey signs cover the walls, and the decor is heavily themed—but the burgers are top-notch, as are trimmings such as onion rings and shakes (the banana and peanut butter malt should be on anyone's "last meal" list). You can also get hot dogs, chili, salads, and the wickedest of "alco-shakes" (dark rum and chocolate, or Baileys liqueur, with optional Oreo cookies). The under-13s Junior Bites menu of burgers (veggie included), hot dogs, or chicken filets, served with fries or green salad, can be supplemented by Mini Moo shake or a sundae, or there are sodas and juices. There are further branches in Chelsea (on King's Rd.) and the Bluewater mall (p. 240).

Trocadero, 19 Rupert St., W1. ℭ 020/7287-1951. Highchairs. Main courses £4.65–£7.75 ($9.30–$16); kids' main courses £4.20 ($8.40). AE, MC, V. Sun–Tues noon–10pm; Wed noon–10:30pm; Thurs noon–11pm; Fri–Sat noon–midnight. Tube: Piccadilly Circus.

## SOHO & CHINATOWN
### MODERATE

**Italian Graffiti** ⚘ ITALIAN    People return again and again to this cozy family-run venue for its superb (and vast) crisp-based pizzas, cooked in a wood-fired oven, although the homemade fish soup is also a big draw. Adding to the ambience are the open fireplaces, in which fires flicker when the weather is inclement; the large windows from which you can observe the bustle of Soho; and the big-hearted staff, who sometimes whisk kids away as honored guests to show them how to make pizza. Portions are enormous (a starter would suffice as a main course for an adult, never mind a child), so be conservative when you order or you won't have time for traditional desserts such as the highly recommended tiramisu.

## The Chain Gang

With more than 300 branches around the country, **Pizza Express** ⭐, 29 Wardour St., W1 (ⓒ **020/7437-7215**; www.pizzaexpress.com), has obviously been getting it mostly right over the past 40 years, though no one disputes that you'll get better, more Italian pizzas elsewhere. What you come here for is familiarity and consistency—everyone has their favorites among the 20-plus classic and Roman-style pizzas, the handful of pasta dishes and salads, and the desserts, ranging from rich chocolate numbers to light Sicilian lemon sorbet. Staff are definitely more on the ball in some branches than others, but kids are kept out of mischief with a "Piccolo Pack" of games and activities (you may have to ask for this). Unusually for a big chain, branches are individual in feel, often because they're in an interesting old building that's retained some of its original features. Many are currently undergoing a makeover in line with an overall move back to the company's designer roots (note that the Chiswick branch has pieces by eminent pop artist Peter Blake).

Other Italian-inspired chains worth knowing are **ASK** (48 Grafton Way, W1; ⓒ **020/7388-8108**; www.askcentral.co.uk), with more than 20 branches in London, and its slightly more upmarket sibling **Zizzi** (33–41 Charlotte St., W1; ⓒ **020/7436-9440**; www.zizzi.co.uk), with 14 branches. There's also **Strada** (Royal Festival Hall, SE1; ⓒ **020/7401-9126**; www.strada.co.uk), with 30 branches at the time of writing.

A non-Italian family-oriented chain is **Tootsies** (35 James St., W1; ⓒ **020/ 7486-1611**; www.tootsiesrestaurants.co.uk; with eight other London branches), which was undergoing an image and menu overhaul at the time of writing but will continue to focus on burgers and organic kids' pasta dishes. Let's hope the revamp (which includes the creation of two sister restaurants, Dexters, in south London), includes a improvement in the level of service. For noodle chain **Wagamama,** the globally inspired **Giraffe,** and bustling Italian **Carluccio's Caffè,** see p. 123, 120, and 109.

163–5 Wardour St., W1. ⓒ **020/7439-4668.** Highchairs. Reservations recommended. Main courses £7–£15 ($14–$30). AE, DC, MC, V. Mon–Fri noon–3pm and 5:30–11:30pm; Sat noon–11:30pm. Tube: Oxford Circus.

### INEXPENSIVE

**Hummus Bros** ⭐ *Value* LUNCH & SNACKS    Perhaps an unlikely success story, this cafe and take-away serves fast food approached from a new angle—a healthy one, with a credo of no additives or preservatives (and the donation of leftovers to charity). The basic ingredient is Middle Eastern/Greek chickpea-based spread hummus, freshly made and served with warm pita bread. Add to that a choice of hot or cold toppings, from hard-boiled eggs, guacamole, or fava beans to chunky beef, and you have the perfect, nutritiously sound light lunch or dinner. There are also salads, soups, sides such as tabbouleh or barbecued aubergine, gorgeous desserts (don't miss the milk-based malabi with date honey), and drinks for all seasons, from fresh mint and ginger lemonade to hot spiced apple juice with cinnamon, nutmeg, and cloves. There's a second branch in Holborn, at Southampton Row, but it's closed weekends.

88 Wardour St., W1. ℂ 020/7734-1311. Main courses £2.50–£6 ($5–$12). MC, V. Mon–Wed 11am–10pm; Thurs–Fri 11am–11pm; Sat noon–11pm; Sun noon–10pm. Tube: Piccadilly Circus.

**Imli** 𝒢𝒢𝒢 *Value* INDIAN   You want to broaden your kids' horizons? Then head for this award-winning canteen-style restaurant, which launched to great critical acclaim in 2005 (it's a little sister to Tamarind; p. 103). It offers tapas dishes based on modern Asian street food, designed to be shared by friends and families—you're recommended to order three dishes each, which will be brought to your table when they are ready, rather than as starters or mains; alternatively, group tasting menus are proposed to parties of six or more. A wonderful menu of gentle, lightly spiced children's dishes is offered free at weekends from noon to 5pm with each adult eating from the regular lunch menu, but it's great value the rest of the time, too. Adult fare ranges from the adventurous (mushroom, ginger, and coconut kabobs, and raspberry and black salt sorbet) to the familiar (*matar paneer*—peas with Indian cheese), and the drinks are out of this world. Take-away is available.

167–9 Wardour St., W1. ℂ 020/7287-4243. Highchairs. Tapas dishes £2.95–7.65 ($5.90–$15); kids' menu £4.95 ($9.90) (free Sat–Sun noon–5pm with 1 adult lunch). MC, V. Daily noon–11pm. Tube Tottenham Court Rd.

# TRAFALGAR SQUARE
## EXPENSIVE
**National Dining Rooms & Bakery** 𝒢𝒢𝒢 BRITISH (MODERN)   This new venue within the mighty National Gallery (p. 176) is a versatile proposition that allows the flexibility many families need when dining together. Foodie parents won't be disappointed by the likes of fresh crab with chilled tomato soup and tarragon for starters, mackerel filets with rhubarb, sorrel, and Roseval potatoes as a main, or by the extensive selection of British cheeses. Children get a more manageable selection of familiar comfort food: crudités, boiled eggs with toast soldiers, macaroni cheese, fish and chips, crispy chicken drumsticks with broccoli, and grilled beef burger with fries. Desserts range from the reassuring (warm treacle tart with clotted cream) to the inventive (caramelized raspberry custard), but it's the sundaes that are the real attraction. The bakery, lacking the stupendous Trafalgar Square views of the restaurant, has lighter fare: As well as breads, pies, tarts, cookies, and pastries, you can enjoy soups, salads, "savory pots" (pâtés and the like) with toast, ice creams, fruit juices, and smoothies. Sunday lunch here is a feast of daring takes on traditional themes; afternoon tea, at £12 ($24), a real bargain when compared with swank hotels.

Sainsbury Wing, National Gallery, Trafalgar Sq., WC2. ℂ 020/7747-2525. Highchairs. Lunch £25 ($50) for 2 courses, £30 ($60) for 3 courses; kids' dishes £2.50–6.50 ($5–$13). AE, DC, MC, V. Thurs–Tues 10am–5pm; Wed 10am–8:30pm. Tube: Charing Cross.

## MODERATE
**Texas Embassy Cantina** AMERICAN   This loud, cheerful joint appeals to family groups—parents can survey the mayhem over the rims of some of the best margaritas in London, while kids get crayons to keep them occupied while they wait for taco dinners, hot dogs, or more from a pleasingly varied children's menu. Adult fare can vary in quality but the fajitas are normally a safe bet. The adult dessert menu, featuring the likes of *sopapillas* (Mexican pastries made with cinnamon and honey), chocolate peanut-butter-cup pie, and Key lime pie, is far more interesting than the kids' (ice cream, with or without apple pie). The waitstaff is friendly, if not always up to the mark when it comes to speaking English—you might find yourself explaining something more than once.

1 Cockspur St., SW1. ✆ **020/7925-0077.** Highchairs. Main courses £7.50–£17 ($15–$34); kids' main courses £4.75 ($9.50). AE, DC, MC, V. Mon–Wed noon–11pm; Thurs–Sat noon–midnight; Sun noon–10:30pm. Tube: Charing Cross.

## INEXPENSIVE

**Café in the Crypt** ★ *Value* AFTERNOON TEA/LUNCH & SNACKS   This award-winning and atmospheric cafe in—as the name suggests—a church crypt, complete with centuries-old stone pillars, brick vaulted ceilings, and gravestones set into the floor, was scheduled to reopen at the time of writing, after an overhaul as part of the restoration of the building. Gothic and perhaps even a little spooky in feel, it's strangely relaxing, too—you'd never guess you're seconds away from the bustle of Trafalgar Square, with classical music soothing away potential traffic noise. Full meals (including good-value English breakfasts), snacks, and afternoon cream teas are available from a self-service counter, with most dishes prepared daily on-site. You can also get picnics to take out, and there are kids' lunchboxes including a mini brass-rubbing kit with instructions, which might lure them into trying out the on-site brass-rubbing center (p. 50).

St. Martin-in-the-Fields, Trafalgar Sq., WC2. ✆ **020/7766-1158.** Highchairs. Main courses £5.95–£7.50 ($12–$15); kids' lunchboxes £3.95 ($7.90). MC, V. Mon–Wed 8am–8pm; Thurs–Sat 8am–10:30pm; Sun noon–8pm. Tube: Charing Cross.

## 3 West London

### KENSINGTON & SOUTH KENSINGTON

The "Big Three" **museums**—the Victoria & Albert (p. 173), Natural History Museum (p. 148), and Science Museum (p. 150)—contain some of the most family-friendly cafes and restaurants in this area, as well as designated picnic areas. You can also get great afternoon teas in the gorgeous **Orangery** restaurant behind Kensington Palace, or snacks at **Café Boardwalk,** by the Diana Memorial Playground (p. 209). A picnic in Kensington Gardens is another option.

### EXPENSIVE

**Babylon at The Roof Gardens** ★★ MODERN EUROPEAN   Owned by none other than Virgin tycoon Richard Branson, this restaurant brought back to life a long-standing venue with one of London's most sensational locations—a lush rooftop garden with views of west and south London, above the old Barkers' department store (the building now also houses the new Whole Foods Market; p. 237). You can stroll around the amazing gardens with their resident flamingos and ducks, a fishpond, and tropical trees and plants before or after your meal. The reincarnation of the spot sees a luxurious but restrained new decor—some tables are in leather booths—in which to enjoy generally excellent, ambitious food such as risotto fritter of smoked bacon as a starter, and saddle of wild English rabbit with bubble-and-squeak as a main. Families tend to come for Sunday lunch, when a children's entertainer is laid on, performing magic from table to table. This prix-fixe menu goes beyond the traditional: You might enjoy a brunchy main such as eggs Benedict, Florentine, or Royale, or a new twist on the roast in the form of rump of Welsh lamb with roast garlic, fondant potato, girolles, and green beans in a red wine *jus*. Kids under 13 get their own Young Diners' menu, which changes all the time but might feature roast tomato soup with chive cream, cheddar cheese soufflé, and line-caught sea bass with creamy mash. Alternatively, the summer months see alfresco barbecues and a shellfish bar. If you're on a budget, look out for the good-value lunch menus.

7th Floor, 99 Kensington High St., W8. ✆ **020/7368-3993.** Highchairs. Reservations recommended. Main courses £16–£27 ($31–$53); Young Diners menu £6 ($12) 2 courses, £8 ($16) 3 courses. AE, DC, MC, V. Mon–Sat noon–3pm and 7–11pm; Sun noon–3pm. Tube: High St. Kensington.

# Where to Dine from Belgravia to Earl's Court

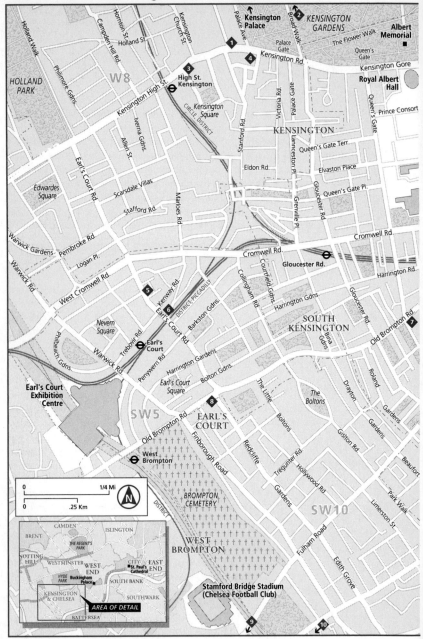

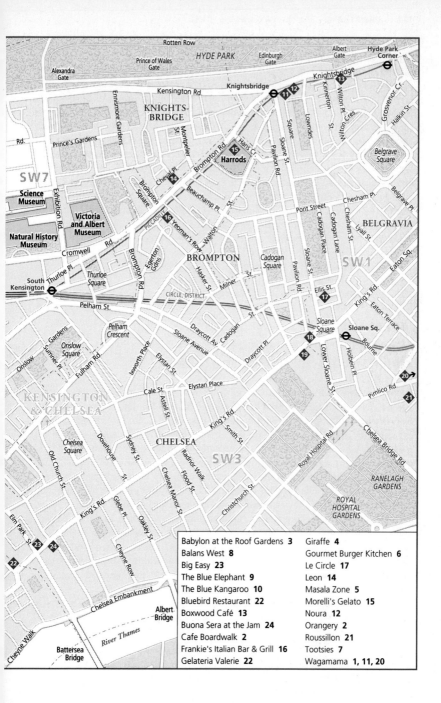

| | |
|---|---|
| Babylon at the Roof Gardens **3** | Giraffe **4** |
| Balans West **8** | Gourmet Burger Kitchen **6** |
| Big Easy **23** | Le Circle **17** |
| The Blue Elephant **9** | Leon **14** |
| The Blue Kangaroo **10** | Masala Zone **5** |
| Bluebird Restaurant **22** | Morelli's Gelato **15** |
| Boxwood Café **13** | Noura **12** |
| Buona Sera at the Jam **24** | Orangery **2** |
| Cafe Boardwalk **2** | Roussillon **21** |
| Frankie's Italian Bar & Grill **16** | Tootsies **7** |
| Gelateria Valerie **22** | Wagamama **1, 11, 20** |

## MODERATE

**Giraffe** ⊛ GLOBAL    This is the kind of restaurant every parent wishes they had at the end of their street—and with 13 branches of the "herd" (*not* chain) in London at the time of this writing, that wish might soon be a reality. For me, however, Giraffe's growth has been accompanied by a slow but sure decline in standards, in terms of both food and service—dishes tend to sound more appealing on the menu than they are on the plate, and many of the staff lack the cheeriness and patience with kids for which they were once renowned. Still, this remains a bright and stylish fallback where you'll be cheered by a mellow world-music soundtrack and an eclectic, globally inspired menu with something to suit all moods and appetites, from pancakes with blueberries and bananas to tasty Southeast Asian curries and burgers and fries. Kids get a more than adequate choice of brunch dishes (daily until 4pm). You can join them in adult versions, or let yourself be tempted by the cocktails (try the mango lime daiquiri) or good choice of wines. *Insider tip:* Weekend brunches can be hellishly busy; weekdays are quieter, and you can take advantage of special early-evening deals. Note also that Giraffe opens early, making it a good breakfast option. The most central branches are Marylebone, Bloomsbury, Islington, and the South Bank Centre.

7 Kensington High St., W8. ✆ 020/7938-1221. Highchairs. Main courses £6.95–£14 ($14–$28); kids' main courses £2.95–£3.95 ($5.90–$7.90). AE, MC, V. Mon–Fri 8am–11pm; Sat 9am–11pm; Sun 9am–10:30pm. Tube: High St. Kensington.

### INEXPENSIVE

There's a **Wagamama** (p. 123) a few steps from Giraffe on Kensington High Street.

## KNIGHTSBRIDGE, BROMPTON & BELGRAVIA

### EXPENSIVE

**Boxwood Café** ⊛ BRITISH (MODERN)    When is a cafe not a cafe?—when it's the Boxwood Café at the super-plush Berkeley hotel, with its handmade silver- and gold-leaf wallpaper, and stone floor with mother of pearl ground into it. Although overseeing celebrity chef Gordon Ramsay—he of the famously fiery temper—supposedly banned his own four kids from his eponymous restaurant at sister hotel Claridge's, because he didn't want them to grow up as food snobs, here children are welcomed with open arms. It seems a bit inconsistent, but who am I to argue? On arrival, each kid gets crayons and coloring paper. The kids' menu may not sound that exciting but, as with the standard dishes, the emphasis is on the best of seasonal British produce, prepared simply and without fanfare. Adult highlights have included a starter of baked scallops with sea urchin butter, bittercress, and apple, and a main course of pan-fried John Dory with morels, wild garlic, sea purslane and crushed Charlotte potatoes. Don't deny yourself the Valrhona hot chocolate fondue with marshmallows, banana, and biscotti for dessert, although the kids might prefer the homemade ice-cream cones, or the warm sugared doughnuts with malted milk cappuccino.

The Berkeley, Wilton Place, SW1. ✆ 020/7235-1010. Highchairs. Reservations required. Main courses £11–£28 ($22–$56); kids' main courses £7.50 ($15). AE, MC, V. Mon–Fri noon–3pm and 6pm–1am; Sat–Sun noon–4pm and 6–11pm. Tube: Hyde Park Corner.

**Le Cercle** ⊛ *Value* FRENCH    The western offshoot of Club Gascon, a famous and award-winning French restaurant in Smithfield, this is a similarly chic but simple and relaxed venue where diners also select from a menu of innovative small tapas-style dishes to share—here divided into the categories Plant, Sea, Farmyard, Regional

Dishes, Pleasures, Cheese, and Sweets. Kids up to 12 can eat for free at lunch from this menu, choosing five of the wide selection of dishes to make up their own Petit Gourmet menu. Offerings change weekly, but junior diners might enjoy the likes of tuna confit with crispy melting pork and béarnaise sauce, or stuffed rabbit with confit of red pepper and basil. The desserts will particularly fascinate them—anyone for pears with caramelized popcorn and sesame ice cream? Staff members make them feel welcome and are very happy to elaborate and advise on dishes where necessary.

1 Wilbraham Place, SW1. ℂ 020/7901-9999. Reservations recommended. Tapas-style dishes £4.50–£35 ($9–$70); kids' lunch menu free. AE, MC, V. Tues–Sat noon–3pm and 6–11pm. Tube: Sloane Sq.

## MODERATE
**Frankie's Italian Bar & Grill** ITALIAN   This is an unlikely-seeming collaboration between championship jockey Frankie Dettori and "bad boy" chef Marco Pierre White. The look is glitzy—outsize glitter balls, a leather-look ceiling, and mirrored walls—but the emphasis in on casual, Italian-style family dining, especially on Sunday lunch, when a magician does table rounds as parents tuck into either a roast or something from the standard menu of salads, burgers, fish or meat dishes, and rib-eye steaks, all at reasonable prices. Kids also get their own menu at Sunday lunch, featuring homemade burgers, fishcakes, or spaghetti, followed by chocolate cake and ice cream. They can also choose from a handful of pizzas, or any of the pasta and gnocchi dishes are available in half-price smaller portions. There are further branches in Selfridges department store (p. 224), minus the pizza menu, and Chiswick and Putney (the Criterion in Piccadilly Circus became a Frankie's but didn't work in the location and has since reverted).

3 Yeoman's Row. ℂ 020/7590-9999. Highchairs. Main courses £5.50–£14 ($11–$28); kids' menu £7.50 ($15). AE, MC, V. Mon–Fri noon–2:30pm and 6–11pm; Sat–Sun 1–4pm and 6–11pm. Tube: Knightsbridge.

## INEXPENSIVE
There's a **Wagamama** (p. 123) inside the Harvey Nichols department store.

**Leon** 🎨🎨 (Value MEDITERRANEAN/NORTH AFRICAN   It's a relief to find this little cafe and take-away—part of a small chain with other branches on Regent Street, the Strand, Carnaby Street, and in Spitalfields and the City—offering unusual and healthy treats at fair prices in this overpriced neck of the woods. It's an especially useful spot to know about for breakfast, when you can get everything from organic toast with Marmite or bacon sandwiches to organic porridge with honey, seeds, or homemade blackcurrant compote, and full English breakfasts. Put a spring in your step with a blackcurrant "power smoothie" or a carrot, orange, and ginger juice. The post-11am menu covers lunch and evening take-aways, or you can order from it in the evening with a 17.5% surcharge. It features small dishes such as Moroccan meatballs, roasted sweet potato falafels, flatbread wraps, soups, and bigger platters, including "superfood" salads and mackerel couscous. Evenings see some of the dishes reappear on a "grazing and sharing menu" of small dishes; brought out as they're ready, they include marinated ribs, patatas bravas, and chargrilled chorizo. If that's too sophisticated for your kids' tastes, there are also cakes, cookies, tarts, and indulgent old-fashioned organic shakes made with ice cream, in tempting flavors (vanilla, chocolate, banana, and cinnamon).

136 Brompton Rd., SW3. ℂ 020/7589-7330. Main courses £3.50–£5.50 ($7–$11). AE, MC, V. Mon–Fri 8am–11pm; Sat 9am–11pm; Sun 10am–10pm. Tube: Knightsbridge.

## Ice Time

The only London branch of an award-winning family firm of ice-cream makers based in Kent since the 1930s, **Morelli's Gelato** (✆ **020/7893-8959**) within the food hall of Harrods (p. 223) churns out wonderful Italian ice cream every day of the week. Super smooth and creamy because of being fresh not frozen, it comes in an extraordinary range of flavors, from traditional Italian favorites to new inventions such as green tea, French aniseed, plum cake, and even, in the festive season, Christmas pudding! However, if you're not pleased with the selection, call in your own idea for a flavor and it can be custom-made with 24 hours' notice (there's a minimum order of 1 liter for this service).

A good second is **Gelateria Valerie** (9 Duke of York Sq., SW3; ✆ **020/ 7730-7978**), an ice-cream cafe/kiosk owned by one of London's best cake houses, Patisserie Valerie (p. 234), with a huge choice of fantastic Roman-style light *gelato* (try pistachio or Nutella) and sundaes, and a terrace well placed for people-watching on the fashionable King's Road. Alternatively, try **The Fountain** restaurant in Fortnum & Mason (p. 103) for awesome sundaes, or, for something a whole lot more exotic, **Noura** (122 Jermyn St., SW1; ✆ **020/7839-2020**; plus locations in Mayfair, Belgravia, and Knightsbridge), a Lebanese brasserie serving up creamy, intensely flavored ice creams in flavors such as mango, rosewater, milk and orange blossom, and *ashta* (clotted cream).

## WESTMINSTER, VICTORIA & PIMLICO
### EXPENSIVE

**Roussillon** ☆ *Value* FRENCH    The restrained beige, cream, and chocolate decor doesn't inspire, but if you're looking to excite your kids' (and your own) taste buds, this French restaurant is a fine bet, with its seven-course Mini-Gastronome menu for under-11s, available *free of charge* on the first and third Wednesdays of the month for up to two kids accompanied by an adult. Changing seasonally as the other menus do, it offers intriguing flavor combinations such as Jerusalem artichoke soup with truffle ravioli in a warm chamomile tea, and smoked eel with scrambled eggs and almond milk—advanced stuff, then, that won't suit really young children (you'd feel out of place with them anyway, in such chic, hushed surrounds). For grownups there's a weekday set lunch that's one of London's greatest gastronomic bargains, plus vegetarian and truffle menus, and best of all a tasting menu with interesting pairings such as scallops and pear, wild duck and almond, Scottish deer and pumpkin, and chocolate and praline. All dishes are beautifully prepared and presented; the service is faultless. *Insider tip:* Visitors wishing to sample the children's menu free should come in term time, when local kids are at school.

16 St Barnabas St., SW1. ✆ **020/7730-5550**. Reservations recommended. Tasting menu £35–£70 ($70–$140); kids' menu £15 ($30), or free with adult lunch 1st and 3rd Wed of month. AE, MC, V. Mon–Fri noon–2:30pm and 6:30–10:30pm; Sat 6:30–10:30pm. Tube: Sloane Sq.

## INEXPENSIVE

**Wagamama** 🌟🌟 *(Value* JAPANESE   This phenomenally successful global stable of noodle joints based on Japanese ramen bars is always a safe bet for an inexpensive and convivial family meal—they're so noisy and hectic, nobody bats an eyelash if your kids raise the roof. Eating takes place at long communal tables with bench seating, which adds to the fun while discouraging you from lingering. (In fact, dishes arrive so quickly there's barely time for kids to make use of the crayons and paper provided.) Kids love being able to see the chefs at work and are fascinated by the electronic hand-helds with which waitstaff punch orders and zap them to the kitchen. The sides and mains (there are no starters) are brought out as they're ready, which means some members of the party get their order before others; share what's brought out and don't worry about who ordered what. The emphasis is on "positive"—healthy—fare, and the punchy noodle dishes (in soup, in sauces, or cooked on a griddle) certainly put a spring in your step, as do the zingy fresh juices. As dessert kids have a choice of vanilla ice cream or an all-natural fruit ice lolly, and they sometimes get a free "Noodle Doodle" T-shirt, too.

At the time of this writing, there were 27 branches of Wagamama in Greater London. This newish one in Victoria is pleasantly set away from the tourist hordes, meaning you avoid the queues that form at many branches, and it has the benefit of outdoor seating bordering a rooftop piazza in which kids can run off some steam; however, it does closer earlier in the evenings.

Roof Garden Level, Cardinal Place, off Victoria St., SW1. 🕐 **020/7828-0561**. Highchairs. Reservations not accepted. Main courses £5.95–£9.95 ($12–$20); kids' main courses £2.95–£4.25 ($5.90–$8.50). AE, MC, V. Mon–Sat noon–8pm; Sun noon–8pm. Tube: Victoria.

## CHELSEA

### EXPENSIVE

**Bluebird** 🌟 MODERN EUROPEAN   This vast, stylish, and convivial space has long attracted young Chelsea families in droves. It celebrated its 10th birthday with a relaunch—the look is clubbier, with books, magazines, and games encouraging you to linger, but the focus on the best of British produce remains, whether its dishes such as steak tartar and fish and chips or roast diver scallops with guacamole and poached wild halibut with asparagus and hollandaise. Crustaceans, caviar, and oysters are also a highlight. It's particularly popular on weekends, for leisurely brunches—although there's no longer a specific kids' menu, children are very welcome and their desires and appetites can be accommodated from the main menu. Come for afternoon tea or cream tea, when little ones do get their own "Tiny Tea" (£5/$10) of baby bridge rolls, fairy cakes or jelly and ice cream, and blackcurrant tisane or lemon verbena. The restaurant is part of a "gastrodome" with a large gourmet grocery and ground-floor cafe serving breakfast and lunch to a happy bunch of local mums and kids. The Bluebird is named for a brand of sports car that broke the world land speed record in the 1920s—this building, once Europe's biggest motor garage, is thought to have been where it was assembled.

350 King's Rd., SW3. 🕐 **020/7559-1000**. Highchairs. Reservations recommended. Main courses £8.50–£29 ($17–$58). AE, DC, MC, V. Mon–Sat 12:30–10:30pm; Sun noon–9:30pm. Tube: Sloane Sq.

## MODERATE

**Big Easy** AMERICAN   This "deluxe crab shack" prides itself on its down-home, genuine American cooking, which generally means lots of steak and seafood served in trencherman portions. If it works for princes William and Harry, or for Sheryl Crow, it'll probably work for you—not least because children are made welcome with an

Urchins' menu of burgers, hot dogs, chicken dippers, ribs, and fish fingers, accompanied by fries and a soft drink; alternative beverages are fresh juices, ice cream sodas or shakes, and kiddie cocktails, including a fresh-frozen lemonade. It's worth considering the Grand Appetizer Platter though, large enough for four or even six people to share—a sociable way to start a meal. Similarly, the "blowout" barbecue platter of ribs, chicken, corn on the cob, and fries is served family-style for two or more to share. Note that a good-value two-course "Lunch on the Run" is offered until 5pm during the week.

332–4 King's Rd., SW3. ℂ 020/7352-4071. www.bigeasy.uk.com. Highchairs, booster seats. Main courses £9.95–£25 ($20–$50); kids' menu £5.95 ($12). AE, MC, V. Sun–Thurs noon–11pm; Fri–Sat noon–midnight. Tube: Sloane Sq.

**Dish Dash** MIDDLE EASTERN   This is another great place for sharing food, offering a variety of Persian (Iranian) kabobs, stews, and other dishes in small and large portions, plus plenty of tempting appetizers and starters. The menu invites you to order either "the Persian way" (that is, choose three to four dishes each, plus nan bread) or "the English way" (choose one big dish with a nan and side dish), or to construct your own "Feast from the East" (two small dishes, one big dish, a side dish, and a nan). Choices range from the familiar (hummus) to the lesser-known (sarpavaran: crispy squid deep-fried in bread crumbs and sesame seeds). The menu is coded so you can easily identify hot and milder dishes, small and large dishes. Kids enjoy the exotic decor with its hanging lanterns and Persian art, and if they don't fancy sharing with you, there's a children's menu including a banana smoothie, a tomato, cucumber, and lettuce salad, a main course of balle kabob (chicken wings marinated in lemon juice, onions, and saffron), cottlet (a soft minced-lamb croquette), or koobideh kabob (ground lamb with paprika, cinnamon, or onions), all served with rice or potatoes. A selection of ice creams is included in their menu, but you might be tempted by a sharing platter of Eastern specialties. There's a branch farther south, in Balham, but it doesn't offer the kids' menu.

9 Park Walk, SW10. ℂ 020/7352-1330. Highchairs. Large dishes £7.50–£9.95 ($15–$20); kids' menu £10 ($20). AE, MC, V. Daily 11am–midnight. Tube: West Brompton.

## INEXPENSIVE

There's a **My Old Dutch Pancake House** (p. 110) on the King's Road.

**Buona Sera at the Jam** 𝕬𝕬𝕬 ITALIAN   The novelty value of this well-located and extremely friendly Italian restaurant lies in its diminutive size—that may sound like a nightmare for those with kids, but little ones just love climbing the bunk bed–style ladders up to the tables tucked under the roof (which feel both more secluded and more roomy than those at ground level), clinging onto firemen's poles as they do so. Staff have to ascend and descend the ladders several times over the course of the meal, too, including when laden with plates, which children find highly amusing. At peak times, you'll have a long wait for one of these "cabins in the sky," which have the added attraction of your own control of your lighting and music volume. Kids can have any of the authentic pizzas, risottos, pastas, and fish or meat dishes for half-price, which makes it a rare good-value spot if you're shopping on the King's Road. If the selections don't appeal to your kids, the charming, endlessly patient staff will cater to reasonable off-menu requests. Once you've been, it's hard not to go back.

289a King's Rd., SW3. ℂ 020/7352-8827. Highchairs. Main courses £7.80–£12 ($16–$24). AE, MC, V. Tues–Fri noon–3pm and 6pm–midnight; Sat–Sun noon–midnight. Tube: Sloane Sq.

## WEST BROMPTON & EARL'S COURT
### MODERATE
You'll find branches of **Pizza Express, Strada,** and **Zizzi** in this area (for all, see p. 115).

**Balans West** GLOBAL   This New York diner–style minichain (the original is in Miami Beach; the other London branches are in Soho, Kensington High St., and Chiswick) is popular with a gay clientele as well as with families, who particularly like its good breakfasts and brunches, when you can enjoy anything from porridge with plum compote or blueberry pancakes to steak and eggs or breakfast burritos. Main menus differ from venue to venue, but you'll find plenty of choice across the global spectrum: starters of Maryland crab cakes, tempura calamari, a Greek platter, or goat's cheese and spinach samosas, for instance, or a simple omelet or grill or a more complex Thai curry or fish dish as a main course. There's no kids' menu but the wide choice of large and small dishes should mean everyone comes away happy—especially if they've finished up with a slice of the banoffi pie. For parents, expert cocktails include a killer bloody mary; note the two-for-one offer weekdays from 4 to 6pm.

239 Old Brompton Rd., SW5. © 020/7244-8838. Highchairs. Main courses £7.95–£19 ($16–$38). AE, MC, V. Sun–Thurs 8am–1am; Fri–Sat 8am–2am. Tube: Earl's Court.

### INEXPENSIVE
**Masala Zone** 🎄 INDIAN   This third branch of the casual, canteen-style Asian (the others are in Soho and Islington) is a useful budget eatery in an area known for its inexpensive accommodations but not well-endowed with good restaurant options. Despite the keen prices, the food is totally authentic—much of it is the type of thing you might find at Indian street stalls. Don't miss the Bombay-style beach snacks or the brilliant *thali* plates, which combine lots of little dishes, dips, and accompaniments for an average of £9 ($18) and are perfect for sharing (note the special Ayurvedic options for diabetics). Slow-cooked curries with rice or noodles also feature on the menu, and at lunch you can order salads and sandwiches, too. Takeout is available.

147 Earl's Court Rd., SW5. © 020/7373-0220. Highchairs. No reservations. Main courses £6.50–£12 ($13–$24). MC, V. Mon–Fri 12.30–3pm and 5.30–11pm; Sat 12.30–11pm; Sun 12.30–10:30pm. Tube: Earl's Court.

## FULHAM
For a Hammersmith/Chiswick walk with eating options, see p. 199.

### EXPENSIVE
**The Blue Elephant** 🎄🎄🎄 THAI   This well-known Thai restaurant (part of a global chain with outposts in Paris, Beirut, Bangkok, and other cities) wows kids with its junglesque interior of trees, ponds, and waterfalls studded with statues and baroque ornaments. They also like the imaginative dishes and—most of all—the Sunday buffet brunches with displays of exotic fruit carved into spectacular shapes, free face-painting, and sugar-spinning demos. These cost £22 ($44) for adults, half that for kids, with no limit on the number of times you can refill your plate; last orders are taken at 3:30pm, but you're welcome to stay until 5pm. The standard menu, which includes such adventurous fare as Running Crocodile (stir-fried crocodile meat with chile, basil, and hearts of palm) and *mieng kahm* (betel leaves filled with dried shrimp, roast peanuts, lime, and ginger) is heat-coded, and there a plenty of nonspicy options suitable for kids.

Note that The Blue Elephant's Indian sibling, **La Porte des Indes** in Marylebone, hosts a similar Sunday brunch with kids' entertainment, plus live jazz, and cooking demonstrations, at the same price.

3–6 Fulham Broadway, SW6. ℂ 020/7385-6595. Reservations recommended. Main courses £11–£28 ($22–$56). AE, DC, MC, V. Mon–Thurs noon–2:30pm and 7pm–midnight; Fri–Sat noon–2:30pm and 6:30pm–midnight; Sun noon–3:30pm and 7–10:30pm. Tube: Fulham Broadway.

## MODERATE

**The Blue Kangaroo** 𝄞𝄞 GLOBAL   This venue combines full-on children's facili-ties—an entire basement area given over to softplay areas for three different age groups up to seven—with a menu of good-quality, "proper" food that won't leave grownups feeling hard up. A huge plasma screen in the ground-floor restaurant means you can keep an eye on your kids as they run riot downstairs (a 90-min. session there costs £3–£4.50/$6–$9), depending on the child's age; those under 9 months go free). If you'd rather supervise them more closely, the basement has a cafe area and a counter selling good cakes and drinks. It's all very flexible, in that kids can eat upstairs with you and then wander off when they've had enough of your company, or you can eat downstairs while they play and you chat, or browse the newspapers and magazines. The kids' menu has a wide choice of dishes: scrambled eggs with cheese and toast, penne pasta with a variety of sauces, mini-burger or fish goujons with fries, spaghetti carbonara or bolognese, pizza, salmon fishcakes, sausage and mash, or cottage pie, plus sides. Most of the meat used is organic. Alternatively, many of the dishes on the adult menu—which features the likes of mushroom tagliatelle, pumpkin risotto, and steak sandwiches—are available in half-price starter portions. Baby food jars are also sold. Note, too, that the place is open for breakfast (from toast to full English), and hosts a lively program of weekly events, including storytelling and puppetry.

555 King's Rd., SW6. ℂ 020/7371-7622. Highchairs. Reservations recommended on weekends. Main courses £6.95–£14 ($14–$28); kids' main courses plus drink £5.45 ($11). AE, MC, V. Daily 9:30am–7:30pm. Tube: Fulham Broadway.

# BAYSWATER, PADDINGTON & MAIDA VALE
## MODERATE

**Shish** 𝄞 (Value) MIDDLE EASTERN   A large, bright space with a modish canteen-like feel, Shish (which has further branches in Shoreditch in east London and Willesden Green in north London) claims to herald a "new generation in kabob culture." It's cer-tainly a far cry from most of London's cramped and greasy-looking kabob joints, and it's a fine place to introduce kids to unfamiliar flavors ranging in origin from Turkey to Indonesia, with its very good-value under-10s menu, offering chicken in pandana leaves, a cold mezze selection with pita chips, Mediterranean chicken, or falafel and hummus wrap, all served with rice, couscous, or salad, and followed by a homemade ice cream or sorbet. Adults are invited to graze on mezze and fresh breads as they choose from the shish kabobs and wrapped kabobs. These mezze include traditional Middle Eastern fare such as tabbouleh and spinach börek (pastries) but also oddities from farther afield, such as Chinese beans in sweet soy, ginger, and sesame. The weekend brunch menu (offered until 4pm) varies wildly from muesli or pancake stacks to full English or nasi goreng (stir-fried rice with honey marinated chicken skewers, topped by a fried egg).

71–5 Bishop's Bridge Rd., W2. ℂ 020/7229-7300. Highchairs. Main courses £4–£10 ($8–$20); kids' menu £4.25 ($8.50) MC, V. Mon–Fri 11am–midnight; Sat 10:30am–midnight; Sun 10:30am–11pm. Tube: Bayswater.

## INEXPENSIVE

For **Mr Fish,** see p. 140.

**Natural Cafe** 𝄞𝄞𝄞 (finds) BREAKFAST/LUNCH & SNACKS   If I lived in West-bourne Grove (or close to the other branches, in Crouch End [north London],

# Where to Dine from Bayswater to Holland Park

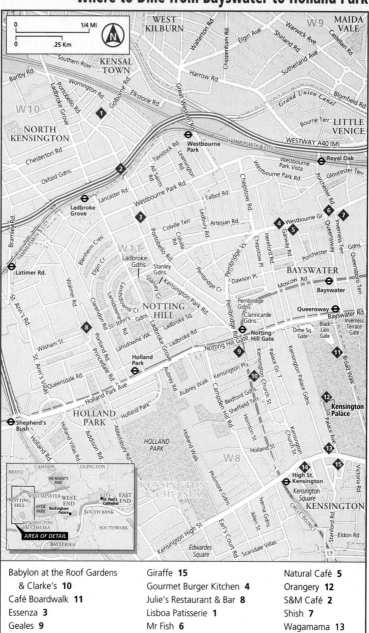

Babylon at the Roof Gardens
  & Clarke's **10**
Café Boardwalk **11**
Essenza **3**
Geales **9**

Giraffe **15**
Gourmet Burger Kitchen **4**
Julie's Restaurant & Bar **8**
Lisboa Patisserie **1**
Mr Fish **6**

Natural Café **5**
Orangery **12**
S&M Café **2**
Shish **7**
Wagamama **13**

Chiswick, Battersea, Putney, Wimbledon, or Richmond), I'd be a regular at this local cafe serving natural, often organic and/or Fair Trade, all-day breakfasts, snacks, salads, and drinks. It's a great place if your kids have wheat, gluten, soy, or dairy allergies, as it offers a fine range of breads, muffins, and cakes based on stone-ground rice flour. But it's a great place for children full stop, with masses of highchairs, and a cute port-holed nook with a screen playing cartoons, a mural, beanbags, and wooden toys. The kids' menu is vast, featuring pastas and chiles, toast and sandwiches, snacks (including items from the salad bar), and cookies, cakes, and muffins; the meal deals make it especially good value. Flexibility is also the hallmark of the main menu: As well as salad bowls from the bar, you can match mains such as sweet chile chicken or North Atlantic prawns and fromage frais with a jacket potato, sweet potato, sandwich, or wrap. There's a great choice of teas or coffees, but if you really need a pick-me-up, try a fresh juice or smoothie, from "Immune Builder" to "Detox Me," and add a natural booster shot of spirulina, wheat grass, manuka honey, or the like. Big, airy, and color-ful, this is a perfect refuge from the huff and puff of modern life.

77–9 Westbourne Grove, W2. No phone. Highchairs. Main courses £3.30–£5.10 ($6.60–$10); kids' meal deals £3.45–5.45 ($6.90–$11). MC, V. Daily 7am–8pm. Tube: Bayswater.

## NOTTING HILL & LADBROKE GROVE
### EXPENSIVE
For posh fish and chips at **Geales,** see p. 140.

**Essenza** ⊛ ITALIAN   Combining the best aspects of Italian-style dining—simple but chic decor, well-sourced ingredients, generous portions, and genuinely charming service—Essenza stands out in an area awash with places to eat. It's most popular with families at Sunday lunches, although the excellent (if pricey) children's menu is available all the time. It offers pasta (spaghetti, fettuccine, or quills) with a choice of five delicious sauces, or more ambitious fare such as Milanese deep-fried chicken breast, beef filet sautéed in extra-virgin olive oil, or deep-fried squid, accompanied by roast or mashed potatoes, mixed salad, French beans, fresh tomatoes, or deep-fried cour-gettes. Highlights for grownups range from an exemplary spaghetti with garlic, olive oil, and chile, to luscious saltimbocca (veal escalope with Parma ham, sage, and peas). If the chocolate and coffee tiramisu or chocolate soufflé with *crème anglaise* (custard) defeat you at dessert, opt for refreshing fresh pineapple.

210 Kensington Park Rd., W11. ℂ 020/7792-1066. Highchairs. Reservations recommended. Main courses £9–£18 ($18–$36); kids' main plus side dish £7.50–£12 ($15–$24). AE, MC, V. Daily 12:30–11:30pm. Tube: Ladbroke Grove.

### INEXPENSIVE
**Lisboa Patisserie** PORTUGUESE   It's almost obligatory, when shopping at Porto-bello Market (p. 233), to stop off at this authentic Portuguese patisserie for a *pastei de nata* (an Lisbon egg custard tart with a singed top). There's a wide range of other cakes if you feel like branching out, including *castanha de ovo* (a wobbly egg cake) and orange and coconut tarts. If you need something filling before progressing to the sweet stuff, sandwiches and rolls are good and cheap, or there are interesting fish and prawn pasties, salt-cod fritters, and meat croquettes. Coffee is served in glasses, in the Iberian way.

57 Golborne Rd., W11. ℂ 020/8968-5242. Cakes and pastries from about 50p ($1). No credit cards. Mon–Sat 8am–8pm; Sun 8am–7pm. Tube: Ladbroke Grove.

**S&M Café** ⊛⊛ BRITISH (TRADITIONAL)   There's no kinkiness about this small diner chain, which serves what it terms "the world's number one comfort food" (sausage and mash) in a variety of guises, even vegetarian. Depending on your mood and the daily specials, you can choose between the likes of lamb and mint, pork, lime, and sweet chile, and mushroom and tarragon sausage, and a handful of different mashes and gravies, to which you can add vegetable sides. Other mains are cottage pie, steak-and-kidney-pie, smoked haddock fishcakes, and salads. It's unlikely you'll have room for one of the old-school desserts but you may be able to force yourself to share a crumble or a dish of Eton mess. There's a small but good kids' menu with sausage or fish fingers with mash, gravy, and peas/beans, or a small version of the house salad (new potatoes, green beans, boiled egg, spring onion, and more), followed by ice cream with or without fruit salad. The great soft drinks include Victorian lemonade and smoothies. The diner is also open for all-day breakfasts, from bacon sandwiches to full English, and there's a small brunch menu at weekends. The cafe premises are pleasingly down-to-earth; the branch on Essex Road in Islington, N1, is worth visiting for its original 1920s interior. There is a further branch near Spitalfields Market.

268 Portobello Rd. (© 020/8968-8898. Highchairs. Main courses £6.25–£8.95 ($13–$18); kids' main courses £3.50–£3.95 ($7–$8). DC, MC, V. Mon–Thurs 9am–11pm; Fri–Sat 9am–11:30pm; Sun 9am–10:30pm. Tube: Ladbroke Grove.

## HOLLAND PARK TO CHISWICK
### EXPENSIVE

**Chez Kristof** ⋒ FRENCH   This younger sibling of a pair of fashionable eastern European restaurants, Chez Kristof offers a daily-changing menu of classy but comforting French regional dishes such as wild boar soup, crustaceans, and braised rabbit with beer and pears. The kids' menu also changes but features healthy and interesting dishes such as tomato and basil fusilli pasta, filet of sea bream with fries, cheese or ham omelet with mixed salad, or Toulouse sausage with lentils, followed by ice cream. It's best to bring the family at weekend lunch, when food is served until 4pm; kids' movies are also screened in the private dining room downstairs on Sundays. *Insider tip:* The adjoining deli with its long, shared dining table, around which local mums congregate with their tots, is open for more casual dining from 8am on weekdays, 8:30am weekends, including breakfasts (pastries, cereals, or full English) until 3pm, plus galettes, crepes, salads, quiches, and Moroccan-inspired dishes.

111 Hammersmith Grove, W6. (© 020/8741-1177. Highchairs. Main courses £11–£18 ($22–$36); kids' menu £7 ($14). AE, MC, V. Mon–Fri noon–3pm and 6–11:15pm; Sat noon–4pm and 6–11:15pm; Sun noon–4pm and 6–10:30pm. Tube: Hammersmith.

**Julie's Restaurant** ⋒⋒ BRITISH (MODERN)   Perennially fashionable (and famous as the venue where Charles celebrated his engagement to Diana), Julie's is the unlikely home to a Sunday-lunch crèche for children ages 2 to 12 (1–4pm), with well-trained staff occupying them with activities and games after they've eaten their lunch of roast chicken with roast potatoes and vegetables, fresh organic pasta with tomato sauce, or sausage with homemade chips and vegetables, followed by sorbet or ice cream and accompanied by juice. It's served at the same time as the parent's first course. The adult set-price menu, available as two or three courses, offers the likes of smoked mackerel and preserved lemon pâté with harissa-crushed tomatoes, a choice of roasts, or the likes of steak-and-kidney-pie braised in organic ale, asparagus, caper, and Parmesan risotto, or crispy-skinned salmon with green tomato salad and sweet chile. The sumptuous space is divided up into cozy rooms and alcoves in different styles, from Gothic to Moroccan, including a conservatory with a removable roof for summer, and a former forge with twinkling fairy lights.

135 Portland Rd., W11. © 020/7229-8331. Highchairs. Sun prix-fixe lunch menu, 2 courses £25 ($50), 3 courses £30 ($60); kids' menu £10 ($20) including nursery. AE, MC, V. Mon–Sat noon–3pm and 7–11pm; Sun 12.30–3pm and 7–10pm. Tube: Holland Park.

## MODERATE

For chain restaurants in Chiswick, see p. 115.

**Sam's Brasserie** ✩✩✩ *Value* MODERN EUROPEAN   Families flock to this outstanding (and vast) all-day neighborhood brasserie and bar—the kind of place every parent wishes was local to them—for daily brunches, snacks (including soup and a sandwich), drinks, lunch, or dinner. But they come in force at weekends, when there are toys put out for kids, plus free face-painting on some Saturday mornings (complimentary Wi-Fi access is available, too, so you could even take the opportunity to catch up on your e-mails). The head chef Rufus has two young sons and knows how to make healthy but interesting food for kids, from the best of ingredients. There's a main children's menu offering shepherd's pie with broccoli, homemade fish fingers with pea mash, pasta with homemade tomato sauce, or boiled eggs with toast soldiers, followed by either ice cream with fresh fruit, or bananas and cream. Or at Sunday lunch kids can get a half-portion of one of the roasts (which could be roast loin of pork or roast leg of lamb). As well as set Sunday lunches, the venue offers good-value set lunches and early dinners during the week, plus other special offers from time to time. Menus change twice daily and are extremely varied, but highlights have been spinach and ricotta dumplings with tomato sauce and garlic cream, and seared monkfish with parsley mash and caper butter. The blood orange and mango jelly with mint syrup shouldn't be missed when available.

Barley Mow Centre, 11 Barley Mow Passage, W4. © 020/8987-0555. Highchairs. Reservations recommended for Sun lunch. Main courses £11–£18 ($22–$36); kids' menu £5.50 ($11), kids' Sun roast £6.50 ($13). AE, MC, V. Sun–Wed 9am–midnight; Thurs–Sat 9am–1am. Tube: Chiswick Park.

## 4 South of the River

### SOUTH BANK TO ROTHERHITHE

#### EXPENSIVE

**OXO Tower Restaurant & Brasserie** ✩ MODERN EUROPEAN   This riverside venue on the top-floor of a landmark building, owned by the Harvey Nichols department store (p. 223) group, has one of London's best views (over the Thames and St. Paul's Cathedral) from both its restaurant and brasserie, plus dining on a terrace in summer. The restaurant is fiercely expensive, but neither is a bargain—think £13 ($26) for a kids' main, dessert, and juice or smoothie in the brasserie, and £20 ($40) for three courses for a child in the restaurant. Still, the food largely lives up to the views in terms of choice and quality. In the brasserie kids can count on the likes of spaghetti with meatballs in a rich tomato sauce, homemade cod fingers with creamy mash and mushy peas, and Cumberland pork sausage with creamy mash and baked beans, then chocolate-chip cookies with dark chocolate ice cream, or a banana split. The restaurant, as befits the more formal setup, offers slightly more sophisticated fare that goes down better with older kids: perhaps lentil soup, followed by Shetland organic cod with homemade chips and tartare sauce, or meatballs with penne and tomato sauce, followed by a triple chocolate-chip cookie ice-cream sandwich. Adult dishes in both the restaurant and brasserie will appeal to foodies who like to experience new combinations: Menus change constantly, but think grilled red mullet with sardine mousse and bouillabaisse as a starter, a main of black bream with oysters, champagne and asparagus, then pistachio parfait with warm cherry soup. For a more affordable experience, come for a set lunch, or, in the brasserie, a pre-theater meal. Vegetarians get their own menus, too.

OXO Tower Wharf, Barge House St., SE1. ℂ 020/7803-3888. Highchairs (brasserie). Main courses in restaurant £18–£30 ($35–$60), main courses in brasserie £16–£22 ($32–$44); kids' main courses in restaurant £8.50–£13 ($15–$26), kids' main courses in brasserie £5.50 ($11). AE, DC, MC, V. Restaurant Mon–Sat noon–2:30pm and 6–11pm, Sun noon–3pm and 6.30–10pm; brasserie Mon–Sat noon–3:15pm and 5:30–11pm; Sun noon–3:45pm and 6–10:30pm. Tube: Southwark.

## MODERATE
The revamped **South Bank Centre** (p. 246) has branches of **Giraffe** (p. 120), **Wagamama** (p. 123), **Eat** (p. 111) and more.

**fish!** ⊀⊀ SEAFOOD    This is the original restaurant and sole survivor of a chain that over-expanded and rapidly imploded, and it's all the better for being a stand-alone restaurant again. Stunningly sited beneath the railway arches of Borough Market (p. 233), it's a theatrical space in which you can sit around a central open kitchen to watch the chefs strut their stuff. (On a sunny day, though, make sure to sit out on the lovely decked terrace.) Kids love the drama, the crayons and paper provided, and the very good children's menu. This consists of strips of fish or chicken breast with fries or mash, a soft drink, and ice cream, or two kids can share a filet of tuna or certain other fish. Adults can go for classics such fish pie or more exotic dishes such as Thai crab cakes. The best option, though, is to try one of the catches of the day, steamed or grilled; your waiter will advise you on which of the sauces will do it the most justice.

Cathedral St., Borough Market, SE1. ℂ 020/7407-3803. Highchairs. Main courses £9.95–£18 ($20–$36); kids' menu £6.95 ($14). AE, MC, V. Mon–Thurs 11:30am–11pm; Fri–Sat noon–11pm; Sun noon–10:30pm. Tube: London Bridge.

## INEXPENSIVE
**The Refectory@Southwark Cathedral** ⊀ *Finds* AFTERNOON TEA/LUNCH & SNACKS    This atmospheric choice opened as part of this small Gothic cathedral's millennium celebrations, and combines a bright modern dining space with original concrete vaulting. The arches are embellished with tiles based on Roman originals in the churchyard wall, and changing artworks are displayed. It's a bit of a local secret worth knowing about for its well-priced, home-cooked snacks, lunch fare, and afternoon teas, including pastries, salads, pasta dishes, and noodles (served in kids' portions on request). The soup and cakes are particularly great—don't miss the lemon pancake torte. In fair weather there's a gorgeous cobbled courtyard just steps from the river, and occasional summer barbecues. *Insider tip:* An alternative is to shop at nearby Borough Market, a gourmet food haven (p. 233), and picnic in the lovely, lavender-scented cathedral gardens in the company of local office workers. The cathedral's worth a look, too, with its bronze of Shakespeare (whose brother Edmund was buried in an unknown grave here) and stained-glass window with scenes from some of his plays.

Montague Close, SE1. ℂ 020/7407-5740. Highchairs. No reservations. Main courses about £5.50 ($11). MC, V. Daily 10am–5pm. Tube: London Bridge.

## BATTERSEA, CLAPHAM & BALHAM
Though you're unlikely to stay in this area, there is a very child-friendly enclave around Northcote Road and Battersea Rise, with lots of family-oriented eateries—handy after a day in Battersea Park 10 minutes' walk away—including branches of **Giraffe** (p. 120) and **Gourmet Burger Kitchen** (p. 137).

## Meals in Museums

Before setting out in search of a child-friendly eatery, check what's on offer under your nose—most of London's museums and galleries have good family-oriented restaurants and cafes, many of which I've mentioned or described in the relevant reviews in chapter 7. One of my favorites is the **Café 2** ☆☆ (☎ **020/7401-5014**) on level 2 of the **Tate Modern,** the brilliant, contemporary art museum dramatically sited in a former power station on the South Bank (p. 179). You can enjoy views of the river and the modern Millennium Bridge as you plow through breakfasts, lunches, afternoon teas, and relatively light evening meals. Kids (who get crayons to create their own mini-masterpieces in homage to the artworks they've seen) get a lunchtime menu featuring such treats as spaghetti with meatballs, sundaes, and fresh juices. If they're more adventurous, they can get a smaller portion of one of the adult mains (£9.95/$20 adults; £6.95/$14 kids), which include the likes of grilled polenta with mushrooms, spinach, and Parmesan, and roasted Shetland salmon with cauliflower champ and asparagus. Don't miss the fab desserts, especially the pineapple carpaccio with lemon-grass sorbet, or the vanilla ricotta cheesecake with roasted plums.

### EXPENSIVE

**Lamberts** ☆ MODERN EUROPEAN   Foodies won't mind going a little out of their way for this neighborhood joint committed to using the finest ingredients, organic and from local suppliers where possible, in their seasonally changing menus featuring both old favorites and new interpretations of classics. Dishes often sound outlandish—beef and Guinness pudding with a poached oyster, squid stuffed with black pudding, or venison rump and haslet with red chard and clove mash to name just three—but always hit the spot. For dessert, sample a very fine selection of Neals Yard British cheeses or challenge your dentist's patience by choosing the hot chocolate pudding with milk ice cream. Sunday lunch, served until 9pm, is a popular time with families: There's a set menu for moms and dads, with plenty of variety; kids can have a mini-roast (perhaps rib of Galloway beef with creamed horseradish and Yorkshire pudding, with roast veggies and potatoes) for £4.50 ($9) or select from the standard junior menu of homemade dishes with no salt added—crunchy organic chicken, mini-fishcake, or pork sausages, with chips/mash and peas/beans, or roast cherry tomato and mozzarella pizza. Saturday set lunches are an even better value, albeit with fewer choices.

2 Station Parade, Balham High Rd., SW12. ☎ 020/8675-2233. Highchairs. Main courses £14–£32 ($28–$64); kids' main courses £3.50 ($7). AE, MC, V. Tues–Fri 7–10:30pm; Sat noon–3pm and 7–10:30pm; Sun noon–9pm. Tube: Balham.

**Le Bouchon Bordelais** ☆☆ FRENCH   This relatively long-standing neighborhood brasserie was given a shot in the arm when super-chef Michel Roux (whose dad and uncle opened the legendary Le Gavroche in Soho) became co-owner a couple of years back. But its main appeal for parents is the free nursery on Sunday lunches—a rare commodity in a restaurant of this caliber. After speeding through a fairly conventional but high-quality and very good-value menu (fish fingers, chicken breast, or Cumberland sausage with peas, fries or mash, and salad, or pasta with various sauces, plus a soft drink or fruits and an ice cream), kids ages 1 to 9 can go make mischief in a supervised play area amply stocked with games, coloring books, and videos, and refurbished in 2007. Meanwhile, adults can tuck into well-executed French classics and twists on classics, including asparagus salad with Parmesan shavings and truffle dressing, French-style gazpacho with a hint of cumin, duck leg confit with Puy lentils ragout, or just plain *steak frites*. In fine weather there are tables on a terrace. The adjoining bar is great for French and English breakfast and brunches, including *croques* (cheese on toast) and omelets; for cheapish lunches such as fish cakes, steak baguettes, and spicy merguez sausage with fries; or for lighter dinners.

5–9 Battersea Rise, SW11. ℭ 020/7738-0307. Highchairs. Reservations recommended. Main courses £12–£23 ($24–$46); kids' menu £4.95 ($9.90). AE, MC, V. Mon–Sat 10am–11:45pm; Sun 10am–10:30pm. Train: Clapham Junction.

## INEXPENSIVE

**Crumpet** ☆☆ AFTERNOON TEA/BREAKFAST/LUNCH & SNACKS    This modern tearoom was set up by locals with young kids, who wanted to create a space where people would want to hang out either with or without their children. Hence, a stroller park, a rear play area with a Wendy house and toys, and a bathroom that could accommodate a large family, not to mention a grownup front bar area where adults can sit with the paper and chill out. The specialty is "proper tea," made with tea leaves and served with scones with jam and clotted cream, but you can also come for breakfasts of muesli, porridge, crumpets, muffins, and the like, or all-day soups, sandwiches, toasties, salads (don't miss the poached salmon with yogurt and dill sauce), ploughman's platters, and cakes and brownies. The large kids' menu has a few mains (chicken or salmon fingers with mash, sausage and mash, cottage pie, or macaroni cheese, served with peas and ketchup), but also snackier fare such as toast and marmite, finger and toasted sandwiches, pots of chopped fruit or veggies, and fairy cakes. Set "picnic teas" are available for them, and there's home-cooked organic food for babies of different ages—plus little essentials such as a "messy pack" with a disposable bib and wipes, or diapers. Staff couldn't be friendlier or more patient with kids, as you'd expect.

66 Northcote Rd., SW11. ℭ 020/7924-1117. Highchairs. Main courses £3.95–£6.95 ($7.90–$14); kids' main courses £3.95 ($7.90). MC, V. Mon–Sat 9am–6pm; Sun 10am–6pm. Train: Clapham Junction.

# RICHMOND & KEW
## EXPENSIVE
For **The Victoria** in Richmond, see p. 89.

**The Naked Turtle** GLOBAL    With its singing waitresses, cartoon sketches of turtles on its vibrant red walls, and spacious front deck and rear sun-trap garden, this friendly little place feels like an offbeat neighborhood hangout. The food could almost be an afterthought, but much of it continues the zany theme—the renowned specialty, Roo Platter, comprises kangaroo and crocodile escalopes in a Thai marinade, and salads include tropical chicken skewers with pineapple, cherry tomato, and red onion in a passion-fruit dressing. There's also less outlandish fare such as fish and chips, burgers, and filet steak for the fainthearted. Adventurous families should take note of the menu of sharing dishes (five dishes for £22/$44), featuring the likes of home-smoked duck breast slices with apple compote, a mezze plate of fresh tomato salsa, homemade hummus and spiced Greek yogurt dip with marinated olives and grilled pita bread, and breaded fishcakes with a sweet chile tomato dip. The live jazz nights are great for teens, with occasional vocals by the same lovely waitresses, some of whom are trained classical singers. On Sundays, when kids ages 12 and up get free lunches, there are traditional roasts. Prices are on the high side, but remember that you're not paying extra for the entertainment. (They do appreciate tips, which supposedly go toward their singing lessons.)

505 Upper Richmond Rd. West, SW14. ℂ 020/8878-1995. Highchairs. Reservations recommended on weekends. Main courses £9.95–£19 ($20–$38); kids' menu (Sun lunch) free. AE, MC, V. Mon–Sat 7–11pm; Sun 12.30–4pm and 7–11pm. Tube: Richmond.

## MODERATE
**Stein's** GERMAN    The presence of a Bavarian beer garden in this riverside spot, where a clapped-out ice-cream parlor once stood, couldn't be more unexpected, but it's a welcome venue on a summer's day, for alfresco dining and beer (or wine) supping while the kids have fun in the play area set up for them. It's all very basic—you sit at wooden tables and benches, and order at and fetch your meals from a hut. There's no kids' menu, but portions are hefty, so two or three dishes per family of four will probably be enough, especially if you add a couple of sides. The main offerings—authentic according to the local Germanic school focused around the London German school—are pork sausages, served with sweet mustard and a variety of accompaniments, including sauerkraut and mash, pan-fried potatoes, or curry sauce. But you can also get white veal sausages with hot pretzel, *schnitzel* with potato salad, meatloaf, *Käsespätzle* (a sort of homemade pasta with cheese, onions, and salad), *Schupfnudelen* (pan-fried hand-rolled pasta dough, served with crispy *Speck* or bacon), or a jacket potato with Bavarian fromage frais, fresh herbs, and salad. Or for tiny appetites there are sausages in a white roll *(Semmel).* Top it off with a traditional dessert such as Apfelstudel with ice cream and cream, or Black Forest Gâteau. This is also a place for interesting weekend breakfasts, including the appetite-challenging Big Frühstuck with salami, ham, cheeses, yogurt, fruit, eggs, and bread.

Richmond Towpath, behind 55 Petersham Rd., TW10. ℂ 020/8948-8189. Highchairs. Main courses £3-£17 ($6–$34). MC, V. May to mid-Oct Mon–Fri noon–10pm, Sat–Sun 10am–10pm; rest of year Fri–Sun noon–10pm. Tube: Richmond (then 20-min. walk, or bus no. 65).

## INEXPENSIVE
**The Original Maids of Honour** ✿ AFTERNOON TEA/LUNCH & SNACKS
The word *traditional* takes on a whole new dimension when describing this cozy tearoom with its oak paneling and leaded-glass windows, situated across the street from the Royal Botanic Gardens (p. 191). Set up in the 18th century to sell the famous Maids of Honour cake (a sort of mini cheesecake with puff pastry thought to have been named by Henry VIII when he saw Anne Boleyn and other maids of honor eating them at his royal palace at Richmond), it's now run by the fifth generation of the same family. It's one of those places where you can find something to suit your mood or appetite at any time of day: breakfast pastries, baguettes and open-face sandwiches, full roast lunches, and—best of all—traditional afternoon teas featuring delightfully light scones with dollops of clotted cream, butter, and jam; cream cakes; and Maids of Honour. A bargain compared with the teas served at swanky London hotels, teas here can be enjoyed on the terrace in the summer.

288 Kew Rd., TW9. ℂ 020/8940-2752. Highchairs. Main courses £2.75–£11 ($5.50–$22); afternoon tea £6.55 ($13). MC, V. Mon 9am–1pm; Tues–Sat 9:30am–6pm. Tube: Kew.

## 5  East London

# BETHNAL GREEN & HACKNEY

## MODERATE

**Green & Red Cantina** MEXICAN    This is the real deal when it comes to Mexican food, or at least home-style cooking from the central state of Jalisco, home of tequila. With its fashionable basement lounge and ground-floor bar and dining area lively with the strains of funk, soul, rock 'n' roll, salsa, and Mexican hip-hop, it's not the place to bring very young kids, but older ones are made very welcome by the friendly staff members, who will guide them through the menu with a view to what may be just a touch too spicy, or what can be made less spicy (some of these chiles are *mean*). If you're a sharing kind of family, Jalisco cuisine is perfect for you—there are plenty of small dishes costing around a fiver each (try pan-fried chorizo with shallots, potatoes, and coriander, or deep-fried squid with tomatillo salsa and lime), plus a good selection of sides (£1–£3/$2–$6), including grilled sweet corn with lime and arbol chile (a hottie). Standout mains (all served with fresh corn tortillas and refried beans) are slow roast pork belly and ribs with pasilla chile and orange salt, and corn-fed chicken roast with achiote spices, with a roasted tomato salsa. Save room for a baked vanilla custard with cinnamon and orange zest, or *churros* (fried dough sticks) with thick spiced hot chocolate.

51 Bethnal Green Rd., E1. ② **020/7749-9670.** Main courses £11–£15 ($21–$40). AE, MC, V. Mon–Fri 6–11pm; Sat noon–11pm; Sun noon–10:30pm. Tube: Shoreditch.

## INEXPENSIVE

Don't forget the child-friendly cafe at the **Museum of Childhood** (p. 146).

**Frizzante@CityFarm** 𝒜𝒜𝒜 ITALIAN    A true curiosity, this genuine (and incredibly sweet) Italian cafe based on the *agriturismo* ("farm stay") concept is set slap bang in the middle of a farmyard complete with clucking chickens, with a garden with a kids' play area and handful of outdoor tables. It serves unpretentious but delicious home-made fare, including all-day breakfasts using eggs from those same chickens, good Italian daily specials (a favorite is the pasta with grilled veggies, goat's cheese, pesto, olives), plus soups, seasonal tarts, jacket potatoes, and sandwiches to eat in or take out, from sausage to grilled veggies on focaccia. Kids get simple but tasty dishes such as baked beans, mushrooms, or eggs on toast, with optional extras, pizza, or pasta with a choice of sauces. The cakes and tarts are superb, but then so is the homemade Italian gelato— I guarantee you'll be torn. Try to time your visit to coincide with some of the many children's activities run at the farm, including volunteering sessions, dance or music and movement classes, and pottery. There's stuff for parents, too, including holistic massage. Stock up on your way out with farm produce (those eggs again) or cakes; this is a handy picnic stop en route to the Museum of Childhood (p. 146).

1A Goldsmith's Row, E2. ② **020/7739-2266.** Highchairs. Main courses £5.25–£7.50 ($11–$15); kids' main courses £3–£3.75 ($6–$7.50). No credit cards. Summer Tues–Sun 10am–4:30pm; winter Tues–Sun 10:30am–4:30pm. Tube: Cambridge Heath.

**Green Papaya** VIETNAMESE    Of the numerous good Vietnamese restaurants and canteens in this area, Green Papaya stands out for its lovely garden, where you can eat in good weather (in summertime they string up fairy lanterns). It's almost impossible to choose from the large menu of modern but authentic Vietnamese dishes, but prices are so low you can afford to spring for a whole host of little starter dishes to share. (Try the green papaya or banana flower salads, with or without shredded chicken, or the *banh xeo* pancakes filled with meat or vegetables.) From the mains, rice noodle soup with fishcake, or mixed seafood hotpots with pineapple pieces and sweet basil, are sure-fire winners with most kids. Note that all dishes are prepared to order, so come for an early dinner or expect to wait a bit. Though there aren't desserts, you can stop off at one of the nearby Vietnamese supermarkets if you need a sweet fix.

191 Mare St., E8. ⓒ 020/8985-5486. Highchairs. Main courses £4.50–£8 ($9–$16). DC, MC, V. Mon–Sat 5–11:30pm. Tube: Bethnal Green.

## CLERKENWELL, SMITHFIELD & THE CITY

Restaurants in the City and neighboring areas tend to cater to expense-accounters; this is the business district, after all. However, there are good options worth seeking out if you're exploring the area, including **Bevis Marks** in the country's oldest synagogue (p. 199). Many chains are represented here too, including **Pizza Express** (p. 115), with branches close to St. Paul's Cathedral, at London Wall, and elsewhere; **Carluccio's** (p. 109), at Smithfield and Spitalfields; and **Leon** (p. 121) at Spitalfields and Ludgate Circus. Remember, though, that these will likely be packed with office workers at lunchtimes.

### MODERATE

**Acorn House** ⊛ BRITISH (MODERN)    Described by one leading critic as no less than "the most important restaurant to open in London in the past 200 years," this restaurant aims to provide adventurous but healthy food described by the head chef as "Modern London"—meaning that it takes inspiration in the capital's cultural diversity. In the evening this takes the form of such taste-bud tantalizers as beet root, cardamom, and sour cream soup; spring herb ravioli with fresh risotto; and pan-fried organic salmon filet and borlotti beans (these are all examples from a spring menu; what's on offer changes daily). But as a family you're more likely to come for the nutritious breakfasts (including power shakes and smoothies, fresh pastries, muffins, and bagels), all-day sandwiches and panini, or order from the splendid lunch buffet of fresh bread, seasonal veggies, fruits and salads, and cold meats and fish (supplemented by a menu of hot dishes made to order in the kitchen). The fabulous evening dessert menu, which might include poached rhubarb with sable stars and custard, or apple pie with cinnamon and clotted cream, is available throughout the day, too. Note, too, that this is a self-styled "eco-restaurant"—it uses organic and free-range produce where possible but also places an emphasis on animal welfare and sustainability (for instance, it serves free filtered water, and gives any profit from mineral water sold to clean-water projects). It's also a training restaurant, though, which means service can be below par.

69 Swinton St., WC1. ⓒ 020/7812-1842. Highchairs. Main courses (evening) £13–£19 ($25–$38). MC, V. Daily 8am–10:30pm. Tube: King's Cross.

**Smiths of Smithfield** ⊛ BREAKFAST/LUNCH & SNACKS    With its industrial chic (steel, concrete, and sand-blasted brickwork), the warehouselike ground-floor cafe at this four-story restaurant, bar, and club doesn't look like the most promising spot for families, but its weekend brunches draw them in from afar, to chill out on the leather armchairs and sofas, or eat at the long, bench-style tables. It's a great spot for breakfast or lunch any day of the week; in fact, big breakfasts are served all day. Otherwise, there are hot and cold sandwiches (from tuna melts on ciabatta to fish fingers with tartar sauce), salads, soups and stews (including a hearty beef stew with dumplings), pies, Welsh rarebit, comforting mains such as macaroni cheese with smoked haddock or sausage and mash, and daily pastas. The juice bar cranks out very good shakes and smoothies as well as juices. Sunday bunch is also available in the fairly expensive (and much more restrained) top-floor restaurant with its views over the City. The second-floor Dining Room is a more relaxed spot, offering woks, chargrills, and dishes cooked in a clay oven.

67–77 Charterhouse St., EC1. ℂ 020/7251-7950. Highchairs. Main courses £4–£6.50 ($8–$13). AE, DC, MC, V. Mon 7am–4:30pm; Tues–Fri 7am–5pm; Sat 10am–5pm; Sun 9:30am–5pm. Tube: Farringdon.

## INEXPENSIVE
**Gourmet Burger Kitchen** (ﾃﾃ BURGERS Part of a massively successful, fast-expanding burger chain with nearly 20 branches in London (including ones in Soho, Covent Garden, Westbourne Grove, and South Kensington), this is a very handy budget option for those exploring the City, set opposite St. Paul's Cathedral. The classic and exotic combos on offer (including simple beef burgers, a Jamaican version with mango and ginger sauce; a Kiwiburger with beet root, egg, pineapple, cheese, and relish; and a chorizo- and sweet-potato number) were designed by New Zealand chef Peter Gordon, who had already made his mark on the London dining scene with the much-missed, now-closed Sugar Club. But despite this illustrious pedigree, and although they are made from the finest, freshest ingredients (including artisan-made sourdough buns and juicy Aberdeen Angus Scotch beef), prices here are refreshingly low—partly because diners order and pay at the bar, which keeps costs down. Kids enjoy watching the chefs at work in the clearly visible kitchens. There are junior incarnations of the beef and chicken burgers, plus great fries and heavenly shakes (don't miss the lime).

Condor House, EC4. ℂ 020/7248-9199. Highchairs. Reservations not accepted. Main courses £5.45–£8 ($11–$16); kids' menu £3.95 ($7.90). MC, V. Mon–Fri 11:30am–10pm; Sat 11am–10pm; Sun 11am–8pm. Tube: St. Paul's.

**The Place Below** (ﾃﾃ (Value VEGETARIAN Heavy on atmosphere, this is set in the Norman crypt of St. Mary-le-Bow, one of Sir Christopher Wren's best churches and the one by which Cockneys are defined. (To make the cut, you need to have been born within earshot of its bells, which you can hear for 30 min. before major services or on special occasions such as the Lord Mayor's Parade; p. 23.) Kids love to watch the juicing machine whiz out a glass of beautifully scented Valencia orange juice; parents can enjoy what must be the cheapest cup of real coffee in the City—90p ($1.80) if purchased with breakfast. The highlight of the latter is toasted oat porridge with maple syrup and cream, while lunch brings a plethora of intriguing dishes on a daily-changing menu—perhaps watercress, potato, and orange soup, Thai red pumpkin curry with coconut brown rice and roast peanuts, a daily "healthbowl," sandwiches, and desserts such as chocolate and Guinness cake with chocolate sauce. *Insider tip:* you get a full £2 ($4) off the main hot dish, salad, or quiche of the day if you have an early or late lunch (11:30am–noon or 1:30–2:30pm), though they're cheap enough as they are. There's a courtyard with outdoor tables, or any dish can be sold as takeout—perhaps for a picnic in Postman's Park (p. 199).

Cheapside, EC2. ℂ 020/7329-0789. Main courses £4.50–£7.75 ($9–$15). MC, V. Mon–Fri 7:30am–2:30pm. Tube: St. Paul's.

## LIMEHOUSE & DOCKLANDS
This largely business district has a string of family-friendly restaurants along the riverside, some with attractive terraces lit up by fairy lights in the trees; they include a **Zizzi** (p. 115). There's also a **Wagamama** (p. 123) on Bank Street.

## EXPENSIVE

**Curve** ⊛ SEAFOOD    Set inside the Marriott West India Quay (p. 8), Curve has a surprisingly noncorporate feel given the number of expense-account lunches that must take place here—especially on sunny days when its French windows are thrown open onto the wharf and there are tables outside. It's also very child-friendly, with charming waitstaff and a bank of smiling chefs occupying a semi-open counter where much of the preparation goes on, happy to show kids what they're doing. Children get crayons and coloring books to occupy them as they wait for fish and chips, miniburgers, filet steak, chicken nuggets, pizza Margherita, sausages and mash, or spaghetti Napolitana, followed by a brownie, fruit salad, pancakes with chocolate sauce and banana, or ice cream sorbet. It's all well cooked and of high quality, but don't be surprised if, like my sons, they're tempted by what Mom and Dad are having—calamari tempura, for instance, or a fish from nearby Billingsgate Market, cooked in the style you want and accompanied by a choice of six sauces, from simple beurre blanc to Spanish fig with tamarind pods. If you do want to go for something exotic, many of the smiling chefs are Asian, and there's a "Palates of India" menu with lots of unusual fishy treats, including sea bass crusted with coriander seeds and pepper, with green mango, coriander, and plum tomato relish.

Marriott West India Quay, Hertsmere Rd., E14. ℭ 020/7093-1000. Highchairs. Main courses £7.50–£28 ($15–$56); kids' main courses £5–£10 ($10–$20). AE, DC, MC, V. Daily noon–2:30pm and 5–10:30pm. Tube/DLR: Canary Wharf.

## MODERATE

**The Narrow** ⊛⊛ BRITISH (TRADITIONAL)    Where the Boxwood (p. 120) is celeb chef Gordon Ramsay's chic take on a cafe, this is his upmarket version of a pub, serving traditional British grub but of a quality you're unlikely to find in any other boozer. Not long open at the time of writing, it was suffering from Ramsay's notoriety, with booking required up to 1 month in advance for dinner (though if you are prepared to eat early, you might get lucky). But you may decide it's worth the wait—the setting, within an old dockmaster's house on the Thames, is atmospheric (black-and-white photos on the wall bear witness to the area's rich history), and the food is magnificent, in a humble, unpretentious, retro way. Offerings vary seasonally, but you might expect the likes of potted Morecambe Bay shrimps with granary toast, pork pie with homemade piccalilli, or deviled lamb's kidneys for starters; or braised Gloucester pig cheeks with mashed neeps, or pea, leek, and morel flan with poached egg, as a main course. Certain dishes can be served in smaller portions for junior diners, or children can choose from the bar menu (under-14s can't go in the bar itself), which offers such simple delights as a mug of soup with crusty bread, a sausage roll with HP sauce, a pot of pickled cockles, and a traditional ploughman's platter, with prices ranging from just £1.50 to £7 ($3–$14). And everyone can enjoy the dessert menu, where you might find delicious elderflower jelly with vanilla ice cream, lemon posset with cherries, or baked egg custard with goosnargh cakes (caraway-flavored shortbread).

44 Narrow St., E14. ℭ 020/7592-7950. Highchairs. Main courses £9–£15 ($18–$30). AE, MC, V. Mon–Fri 11:30am–3pm and 6–11pm; Sat noon–11pm; Sun noon–10:30pm. Tube: Limehouse DLR.

**Royal China** ⊛⊛ CHINESE    A popular spot for dim sum, this is a serious but friendly Chinese restaurant where you can count on staff paying gracious attention to your children, no matter how young, and can usually bet on it being less busy than the more central branches (Marylebone, Queensway, St. John's Wood, and Fulham). You'll be enchanted by the stunning views up the Thames (in good weather, bag a table on the waterside terrace) and pleased by the authenticity of the food, which is testified by the percentage of Chinese who frequent the place. There's no kids' menu, so you might pick and mix a range of small dishes from across the menu—the duck is usually a very good bet, the frogspawn something for more adventurous tastes. Beware that the chefs may embellish an order of, say, plain omelets, with pork, so do say if you are vegetarian. Make sure the little ones save space for the delicious desserts, which include egg yolk buns, almond tofu with fruit cocktail, and coconut cream pudding.

30 Westferry Circus, E14. © 020/7719-0888. Highchairs. Reservations recommended. Main courses £7.50–£24 ($15–$48). AE, MC, V. Mon–Thurs noon–11pm; Fri–Sat noon–11:30pm; Sun 11am–10pm. Tube/DLR: Canary Wharf.

## 6 North London

### CAMDEN & ISLINGTON

Islington in particular has lots of child-friendly eateries, many of them branches of chains, including **Giraffe** (p. 120), **Pizza Express** (p. 115), **Wagamama** (p. 123), **Bierodrome** (a branch of Belgo; p. 113), and **S&M Café** (p. 128).

### EXPENSIVE

**Metrogusto** ★★ ITALIAN    "We are an Italian restaurant!" exclaimed the proprietor when I asked if he could provide kids' dishes, going on to explain that the lack of tablecloths in his attractive dining room with its bright modern artworks was calculated to avoid "dramas." Indeed, in spite of the brilliantly executed, generally quite progressive Italian fare served here (think duck breast with red fruit and chickpea fritters, or veal scallops with mustard seed, Marsala wine, and leeks), it's a very child-friendly spot with a real neighborhood feel. Many of the pasta and risotto dishes are more classic—*maltagliati* might come with smoked ham, sage, and Parmesan, or *tortelloni* may be filled with sweet pumpkin and accompanied by a sage and butter sauce. But in any case, parents (or kids) are encouraged to discuss their requirements with the very obliging waitstaff. A simple plate of gnocchi with tomato and mozzarella, for instance, will cost £7.50 ($15); or the kitchen can prepare a rice-based dish. Don't let them overdo it, though, as the desserts are a marvel, and most are eminently suitable for kids—thin apple tart with Parmesan ice cream, for example.

13 Theberton St., N1. © 020/7226-9400. Highchairs. Reservations recommended. Main courses £11–£17 ($22–$34). AE, MC, V. Mon–Thurs 6:30–10:30pm; Fri–Sat noon–3pm and 6:30–11pm. Tube: Angel.

### MODERATE

**The Engineer** ★ BRITISH (MODERN)    One of London's original gastropubs (old boozers converted into chic modern pub/restaurants), The Engineer remains one of its best. It offers kids a basic but good-quality menu of sausage or poached egg with chips or green beans, or penne pasta with tomato sauce, followed by organic ice cream (in fact many ingredients are organic here, or at least free-range, including all the meat). In return, The Engineer asks that young ones stay at the table, since this is quite a small, closely packed, and bustling environment. (The staff helps them keep their end of the deal by handing out crayons and coloring books.) Parents enjoy more complex dishes such as Piquillo peppers stuffed with sweet potato, with chickpea cakes and olive tapenade, though there is less challenging fare such as organic burger with baker fries and sweet tomato relish, too. Or come for a relaxed breakfast of anything from toast to baked eggs with spinach and Parmesan, toasted cornbread, and chipotle, taken in the gorgeous garden with its orange trees and lilac bushes in summer. Make sure to reserve a highchair when you book, as they can be in short supply.

## Only in London

A trip to Britain wouldn't be complete without at least one **fish-and-chip** supper, laced with salt and malt vinegar and accompanied by pickled onions, mushy peas, and/or pickled eggs (although I do contend that they're best enjoyed on the seafront, straight from the paper they were wrapped in; for Whitstable, see p. 272). Many of London's fish-and-chip shops have gone downhill over the last decade or so—if in doubt, look for ones with London taxis parked outside, as the city's cabbies have an unerring instinct for good-quality, good-value haunts. One such spot is **Fish Central** (149–52 Central St., EC1; ✆ **020/7253-4970**), with cheery staff, kids' portions, and a patio on a small square for fine weather. It's been trendified in the last few years, and offers little extras you won't see in a run-of-the-mill "chippy" (such as homemade bread, fresh vegetables, fish soup, pasta dishes, and great desserts), but you're best off sticking to the spanking-fresh traditional battered cod or haddock with lip-smacking chips and tasty mushy peas. Sometimes you'll get lucky and the owner will bring out complimentary nibbles (the likes of fish croquettes and salmon mousse).

One of the longest-standing and most famous chippies, **Geales** in Notting Hill Gate (2 Farmer St., W8; ✆ **020/7727-7528**) relaunched in 2007 after a big overhaul, with a new menu and new decor but a commitment to retaining the "great British chip shop mentality." It serves top-notch battered white fish, plus the likes of fish pie, oysters, and even lobster. Kids are welcome (and get their own menu). The place is great on a balmy summer evening, when they open the big front windows. Another good west London spot, with a bright retro feel and green and pink pastel chairs, is **Mr Fish,** just off Westbourne Grove (9 Porchester Rd., W2; ✆ **020/7229-4161**). Children's meals include fishcake or cod goujons with chips, and there's a front take-away counter, too.

A little more of an acquired taste than fish and chips, the eels sold at London's few surviving traditional **pie-and-mash shops** are eaten cold and jellied, or warm in a stew, with a splash of vinegar or parsley "liquor." Sounds hideous, doesn't it? If you can't bring yourself to try this most working-class of dishes, come anyway, for the mash, the beef and gravy pies, and—most of all—the surroundings. Dating from the 19th or early 20th century; the shops are atmospheric, family-fun places boasting their original tiled walls, wooden benches, and marble-topped tables. A meal of this kind will cost you little more than a fiver ($10). One of the best (and most central) is **M Manze** on the South Bank (87 Tower Bridge Rd., SE1; ✆ **020/7407-2985**), established in 1902 and also serving veggie pies. The nonrelated **Manze's** at 76 Walthamstow High St., E7 (✆ **020/8520-2855**), is a good place to fill up after a visit to another East End institution—the greyhound racing at Walthamstow Stadium (p. 260).

65 Gloucester Ave., NW1. (✆ **020/7722-0950**. Highchairs. Main courses £13–£17 ($26–$34); kids' main courses £5.50 ($11). MC, V. Mon–Sat 9am–11pm; Sun 9am—10:30pm. Tube: Camden Town.

# HAMPSTEAD & GOLDERS GREEN
## MODERATE
**Bloom's** ✿✿ KOSHER   You don't get much more traditional than this kosher deli-restaurant with its family atmosphere and wonderful staff, some of whom have worked here for decades (perhaps they even remember the visits by Charlie Chaplin and Frank Sinatra). The food is everything you'd expect of a place this iconic, from the faultless hors d'oeuvres of chopped liver, egg, and onion; gefilte fish; or beet-root borscht with potato; to mains such as *gedempte* (braised) meatballs. "Kiddies" are well catered to with a high-quality menu of turkey schnitzel, hot dog, burger, or pasta with tomato sauce or bolognaise, served with fries or rice and a soft drink and followed by ice cream. If you're in a hurry to get to the Heath (p. 143), stop at the deli instead, for salt beef sandwiches, potato salad, and few treats from the pickle bar, plus *lockshen* (egg noodle) pudding.

130 Golders Green Rd., NW11. (✆ **020/8455-1338**. Highchairs. Main courses £7–£24 ($14–$48); kids' menu £7.95 ($16). AE, MC, V. Mon–Thurs and Sun noon–10:30pm; Fri noon–1:30pm. Tube: Golders Green.

**Spaniard's Inn** ✿ BRITISH (TRADITIONAL)   Said to be haunted by the ghost of none other than Dick Turpin—it's claimed by some that the highwayman was born here, and there seems to be some evidence that his dad was once the landlord—this out-the-way spot was also mentioned in Dickens' *The Pickwick Papers* and Bram Stoker's *Dracula,* and has been frequented by a host of a famous artists and writers. Despite its location, it gets crowded out on summer weekends, largely with people spending the day on the Heath. Apart from its real ale and above-average pub grub, which includes ploughman's lunches, homemade pies, and sausage and mash, its Sunday lunches, and its Indian dishes (served on Sat), the big draw is its child-friendly attitude and its huge beer garden with an aviary with budgies and canaries, pergolas, a patch of lawn, a cherry tree, sculptures, and water bowls for canine customers. Turpin's Room, said to have been Dick's childhood abode, has board games, dominoes, and cards, and there's also a separate dining area.

Spaniards Rd., NW3. (✆ **020/8731 6571**. Highchairs. Main courses £5–£12 ($10–$24). MC, V. Mon–Fri noon–3pm and 5–9:30pm; Sat–Sun noon–9:30pm. Tube: Golders Green.

## INEXPENSIVE
**Kalendar** (Finds) MEDITERRANEAN   This deli, cafe, and bistro is a good place to refuel after a morning on the Heath or in Waterlow Park (p. 208), with its great all-day breakfasts featuring such treats as Neal's Yard yogurt with red fruit compote, or French toast with maple syrup. There are also Mediterranean-style sandwiches, salads, and chargrills, wonderful British cheese, homemade breads, fabulous cakes, fresh-squeezed juices, and organic shakes. The evening menu is more substantial, with pasta dishes and risottos, fishcakes, burgers, and more. The meat comes from the organic butcher next door. Try to get a table on the front terrace—inside it's a little cramped, especially on summer weekends, when competition for tables is high.

5A Swains Lane, N6. (✆ **020/8348-8300**. Highchairs. Main courses £7–£12 ($14–$24). AE, MC, V. Mon–Fri 8am–10pm; Sat–Sun 9am–10pm. Tube: Archway.

# 7

# Exploring London with Your Kids

This chapter details London's truly stellar attractions—even those who live here never get to the bottom of this inexhaustible city, and I've had to be brutal when it comes to what to list. "Top Attractions" should help you prioritize.

**Children's prices** generally apply to ages 5 to 16; under-5s usually go free. **Opening hours** can change at short notice, so call ahead if you're making a special trip to a particular attraction. All museums are closed on Good Friday, December 24 to 26, and New Year's Day. Most venues close on bank holidays, around Christmas and New Year, and in some cases on May 1.

During British **school vacations** (staggered across the country but broadly consisting of a 2-week Easter break in Apr, a 6-week summer break from late July to early Sept, and a 3-week Christmas break from mid-Dec to early Jan, plus 1-week "half-term" breaks in Feb and in Oct), major attractions get crowded and queues lengthy. On the other hand, during these periods many venues feature special **kids' activities,** so they can be good times to visit. If your trip does coincide with a British school vacation, check websites ahead of time, and pre-book activities if required.

If you plan to see lots of sights, a **London Pass** (www.londonpass.com) may be worth investing in. It offers free admission to 56 attractions in and around London, fast track tickets to some, and a pocket guidebook. The transport option offering unlimited free travel on buses, the Tube, and trains across all six zones after 9:30am (or at any time for a 6-day option) is highly recommended. One-day passes are available, as are passes for 2, 3, or 6 consecutive days, with prices varying accordingly; a 6-day pass with transport option costs £94 ($188) for adults, £53 ($106) for kids 5 to 15, and you in fact get a seventh day's free transport thrown in. Passes can be mailed to you or picked up, including the day you order them, from the Britain & London Visitor Center (p. 44). You can also buy the Pass on www.londontown.com, a site that also offers pre-booking of individual attractions.

Another website worth checking out is www.discount-london.com, which might net you reduced admission or fast track access to sightseeing attractions, plus reductions on bus tours, river cruises, and theater tickets, plus hotel rooms and restaurants.

## 1 Kids' Top 10 Attractions

**British Airways London Eye** 🦘🦘🦘 **All ages.** The world's tallest observation wheel at 135m (443-ft.) is now also the U.K.'s most popular visitor attraction: It seems no one can resist the lure of a half-hour "flight" in one of its 32 shiny glass pods, which afford stunning panoramic views stretching 40km (25 miles), taking in the Thames bridges, the Queen's garden at Buckingham Palace, Hampstead Heath to the north, and Windsor Castle to the west. The pace is slow enough to make it suitable for even the smallest kids, and if you come off-peak you may have a pod virtually to yourselves (each holds up to 25). Make sure to invest in an Essential Eye guidebook for £5 ($10) from the gift shop to help you identify landmarks, or better still stump up an extra couple of pounds for a Discovery Flight, during which an Eye guide will talk you through the city's history (available in French, German, Spanish, and Russian, as well as English). Sunset and night flights are particularly atmospheric.

Queues can be terrible during weekends and school vacations, especially on clear days, so pre-book online if possible (up to 2 hr. before your flight); this also nets you a 10% discount. You must arrive 30 minutes before your flight to collect your tickets and board; if that seems too long, more expensive fast track tickets are available. Under current anti-terrorism measures, you are expected to bring on a very minimum of hand-baggage. Strollers must be folded before boarding the Eye; there are baby-changing facilities by the customer service desks inside County Hall. After your trip, direct your kids to the website, where they can add their stories about the Eye or photos of it. The site also has joint offers with other attractions, theater shows, and restaurants, or you can book a river cruise to see the Eye from a different angle.

Millennium Jubilee Gardens, SE1; ticket office inside County Hall. $\textcircled{C}$ 0870/990-8883. www.ba-londoneye.co.uk. Admission £15 ($30) adults; £11 ($22) seniors; £7.25 ($15) children 5–15. Oct–May daily 10am–8pm (closed for maintenance 1 week in Jan); June–Sept daily 10–9pm. Tube: Westminster or Waterloo.                                        •

**Hampstead Heath** $\mathcal{R}\mathcal{R}\mathcal{R}$    **All ages.** This gloriously wild expanse of park, woods, heath, meadows, and ponds offers a taste of the countryside just 6.5km (4 miles) from Trafalgar Square, busy with breeding kingfishers and other wildlife. Londoners flock here to stroll, jog, sunbathe, fly kites, picnic, play in the eight playgrounds (the recently redesigned one on Parliament Hill has a large paddling pool), fish, and enjoy the views over the City and beyond. Sports facilities include tennis courts, a cricket pitch, and an athletics track, and you can even swim here, at the newly refurbished Parliament Hill Lido (outdoor pool) or in the Heath Ponds, which were originally brick pits; one is for both men and women, two are single-sex; children 8 and up can swim if accompanied by an adult. Golders Hill Park, part of the Heath's northern extension, has a small zoo (p. 189); the little-known Hill Garden by the West Heath is a delightfully hidden spot with a magnificent pergola, rolling lawns, and ambling ducks. Funfairs are frequently held, and walks and wildlife events are organized, some specifically for families. Summer vacations bring a full program of kids' entertainment. In fact, there's so much going on that a Heath Diary (downloadable from the website) is indispensable. Refreshment facilities include Parliament Hill Café, a great family spot with Italian food and an enclosed garden.

On the Heath's northern fringe lies **Kenwood House** ($\textcircled{C}$ **020/8348-1286;** www. english-heritage.org.uk), a country home containing period furniture and paintings by Turner, Gainsborough, and others, and hosting regular kids' activities (mainly free), including an annual Easter Egg trail, a Victorian Fairy Trail, bat- and butterfly-spotting, fungi hunts and lots of crafts workshops; again, the Heath Diary will help you to pre-plan. Kenwood's Brew House cafe is another kid-friendly spot for breakfast, lunch, or coffee and cakes, with a large garden.

You'll want to spend a half-day to a day here; the website has a downloadable map to help you plan your visit, plus transport and parking details.

# West End Attractions

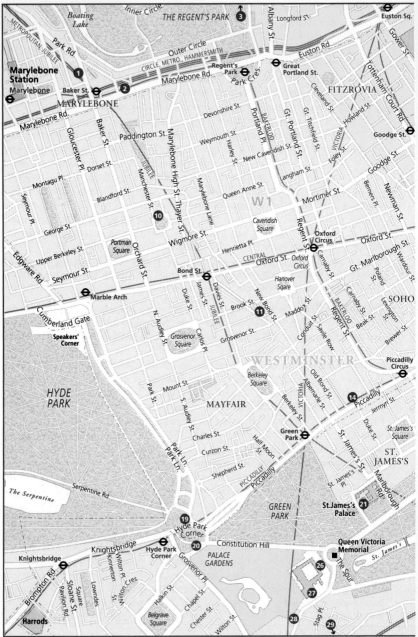

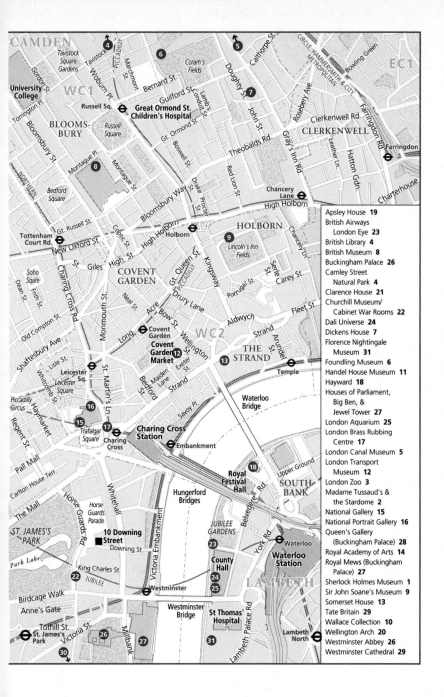

Apsley House **19**
British Airways
  London Eye **23**
British Library **4**
British Museum **8**
Buckingham Palace **26**
Camley Street
  Natural Park **4**
Clarence House **21**
Churchill Museum/
  Cabinet War Rooms **22**
Dali Universe **24**
Dickens House **7**
Florence Nightingale
  Museum **31**
Foundling Museum **6**
Handel House Museum **11**
Hayward **18**
Houses of Parliament,
  Big Ben, &
  Jewel Tower **27**
London Aquarium **25**
London Brass Rubbing
  Centre **17**
London Canal Museum **5**
London Transport
  Museum **12**
London Zoo **3**
Madame Tussaud's &
  the Stardome **2**
National Gallery **15**
National Portrait Gallery **16**
Queen's Gallery
  (Buckingham Palace) **28**
Royal Academy of Arts **14**
Royal Mews (Buckingham
  Palace) **27**
Sherlock Holmes Museum **1**
Sir John Soane's Museum **9**
Somerset House **13**
Tate Britain **29**
Wallace Collection **10**
Wellington Arch **20**
Westminster Abbey **26**
Westminster Cathedral **29**

Hampstead, NW3. ℂ 020/8348-9908. www.cityoflondon.gov.uk/corporation/living_environment/open_spaces. Free admission; fees for some events and activities. Open 24 hr. (Golders Hill Park, the Kenwood Estate, the Hill Garden, and the Pergola close before dusk.) Tube: Belsize Park, Hampstead, or Golders Green.

**Horniman Museum** 𝕜𝕜𝕜 **All ages.** As if this repository of more than 350,000 objects amassed by a Victorian tea trader wasn't quirky and eclectic enough, it recently added an award-winning aquarium to its attractions, complete with viewing dens and lots of interactive fun, as well as the Hands on Base center where you can handle nearly 4,000 items from the collections, including puppets, masks, natural history specimens, and musical instruments. The museum's "themes"—anthropology, the natural world, and musical instruments—are so broad that everyone will find something to intrigue, from torture instruments to oversize model insects, while the program of temporary exhibitions and free events and activities gives you reason to come back again and again. These include Hands-on Family Workshops every Saturday, African Storytelling, Nature Explorers, music workshops, and arts and crafts galore. Under-5s get their own story sessions at Book Zone. Some events require pre-booking; for others, always ensure you arrive early to get a place.

The cafe overlooks a lovely Victorian conservatory and 6.5 hectares (16 acres) of gardens, where you'll also find a picnic area (by the bandstand), a small animal enclosure with a nature trail, a sundial that allows you to tell the time using your own shadow, and great views over London. All exhibition spaces and facilities are stroller accessible. Allow at least a half-day to see everything.

100 London Rd., SE23. ℂ **020/8699-1872.** www.horniman.ac.uk. Free admission except for major temporary exhibitions. Daily 10:30am–5:30pm. Train: Forest Hill.

**London Transport Museum** 𝕜𝕜 **All ages.** This fascinating museum charting the evolution of the British capital's public transport systems and the way they have shaped Londoners' lives was scheduled to reopen at the time of writing, after a £20-million ($40-million), 2-year refurbishment project. It was already spiffy enough, with lots of old buses, trains, and trams to admire and often clamber aboard, and clever interactive gadgets that let you, for instance, pretend to drive a Tube train. But the overhaul of the historic old flower-market premises brings fresh sections on taxis, river travel, bicycling, and walking, and the increased overall exhibition space encompasses a new top-floor gallery, a new family learning zone, an under-5s play area, more driving simulators and other hands-on exhibits, and a state-of-the-art theater for events. Future developments in London transport will also be showcased, and placed in a contact of other major world cities. The old shop and cafe are replaced by a new two-story facility looking out over Covent Garden's famous piazza. Allow 3 hours for a visit; strollers are best checked in at the cloakroom.

39 Wellington St., WC2. ℂ **020/7565-7299.** www.ltmuseum.co.uk. Admission £8 ($16) adults, £6.50 ($13) seniors, free for children under 16. Daily 10am–6pm. Tube: Covent Garden.

**Museum of Childhood** 𝕜𝕜𝕜 **All ages.** An outpost of the mighty V&A (p. 173), this museum devoted to all things child-related reopened in a more glorious incarnation than ever in late 2006, after a multi-stage transformation lasting several years. The Victorian building that houses it is now a light and airy space configured around a three-story central atrium, with plenty of room for kids to run around and play between the glass cabinets filled with more than 6,000 items. New themes showcased since the revamp are Creativity & Imagination, and Moving & Optical Toys, but all the old favorites remain, too, from dolls in period costume, dolls' houses and puppets,

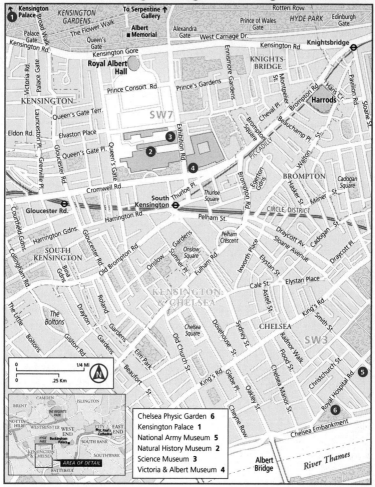

Chelsea Physic Garden **6**
Kensington Palace **1**
National Army Museum **5**
Natural History Museum **2**
Science Museum **3**
Victoria & Albert Museum **4**

to toy soldiers and trains. Video consoles allow you to see the out-of-reach objects in action, and there are dedicated areas where kids can get creative, dress up, enjoy giant board games, read books, and play with toys. The Childhood Galleries, meanwhile, explore the social history of childhood through a number of themes, including How We Learn, Children in Trouble, and World in the East End; the latter includes toys garnered from local immigrant populations, from Bangladeshis to Vietnamese.

These permanent features are backed up by a schedule of temporary exhibitions and regular events and activities for kids of all ages, including arts and crafts, weekly Wondertots sessions with art, storytelling, drama and movement for parents and toddlers. Gallery trail leaflets can be picked up at the information desk, and there are interactive tours. Most activities are free but should be pre-booked, since space is limited. There's a ground-floor cafe with lots of highchairs, serving hot dishes, salads, sandwiches and cakes, including kids' half-portions, or there are outdoor and indoor picnic areas. The gift shop is a good spot for pocket-money trinkets. The galleries are stroller accessible but there's a buggy-park if you prefer to stow them; there are also baby-feeding and -changing facilities. A visit warrants about half a day.

*Insider tip:* School trips tend to come in the mornings, so it can be better to schedule a family visit for weekday afternoons.

Cambridge Heath Rd., E2. (℗ 020/8983-5200. www.vam.ac.uk/moc. Free admission (small charge for some activities). Daily 10am–5:45pm. Tube: Bethnal Green.

**Natural History Museum** &&&    **Ages 3 and up.** Britain's mighty three-building "storehouse" of plants, minerals, and fossils can be overwhelming in its sheer scope: According to your kids' ages and interests, you might head first for Investigate, a hands-on science laboratory for 7 to 15-year-olds, with microscopes, a pond, and more, or for the Earth Lab, where visitors can handle geological specimens. Whatever you decide, make sure to pick up one of the wide range of Discovery Guides (40p–80p/ 80¢–$1.60) sold at the information desks, which will inspire kids 4 to 16 in their explorations of volcanoes and earthquakes, dinosaur teeth, and the source of the earth's energy. For under-7s, get them fab Explore Backpacks (free; £25/$50 refundable credit card deposit required) with explorer hats, binoculars, drawing material, and activities covering everything from oceans to monsters. Events and activities take place daily, whether it be dinosaur trails or fossil handling, so it's worth checking the website ahead of your visit; this also lists the regularly changing temporary exhibitions.

Truly unmissable on anyone's itinerary are the Central Hall, with its 26m (85-ft.) Diplodocus skeleton, 1,300-year-old giant sequoia tree, and primitive coelacanth fish; the Dinosaur Gallery, with its "super-sensing" animatronic Tyrannosaurus rex that detects motion and might follow your course around the room with its head; the Mammals Gallery, with its awesomely proportioned blue whale model (the length of three buses); The Power Within, where you can experience what an earthquake feels like; and the lush Wildlife Garden. But with 68 million items on everything from evolution and biology to bugs and meteorites, there's enough to keep you occupied for a day and more (touch-screen guides in the Central Hall tell you what's where).

If you have kids 8 or over, ask at the main information desk for a place on a free Explorer tour of the Darwin Centre (no pre-booking), where you can watch the museum's scientists engaged in cutting-edge research and look at some of the 22 million preserved specimens laid out along 27km (17 miles) of shelves, some of them collected by naturalist Charles Darwin himself during his famous voyage on the *Beagle*. A recent arrival is Archie the giant squid, at nearly 9m (30 ft.) in length.

Most galleries are stroller accessible, and baby-changing and -feeding facilities are available. The restaurant, cafe, sandwich bar, and coffee bar are all child-friendly, with highchairs and bottle warming; there's also a basement picnic area and snack bar, or picnics are allowed on the front lawns.

*Insider tip:* During the busy school vacations, it's usually easier to enter the museum via the Earth Galleries entrance on Exhibition Road, which is also the most stroller-friendly route.

Cromwell Rd., SW7. (℗ 020/7942-5011. www.nhm.ac.uk. Free admission (except temporary exhibitions). Daily 10am–5:50pm. Tube: S. Kensington.

**Riverboat Cruise to Greenwich** &&    **All ages.** Getting to historic Greenwich the way Henry VIII did is half the fun, if you don't mind sharing your trip with circling

# South Bank & Bankside Attractions

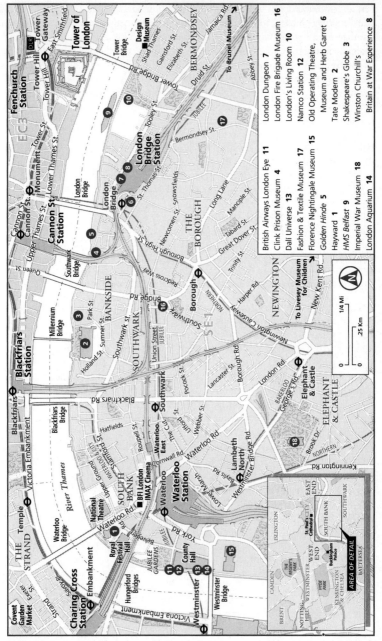

British Airways London Eye **11**
Clink Prison Museum **4**
Dali Universe **13**
Fashion & Textile Museum **17**
Florence Nightingale Museum **15**
Golden Hinde **5**
Hayward **1**
HMS Belfast **9**
Imperial War Museum **18**
London Aquarium **14**

London Dungeon **7**
London Fire Brigade Museum **16**
London's Living Room **10**
Namco Station **12**
Old Operating Theatre,
   Museum and Herb Garret **6**
Tate Modern **2**
Shakespeare's Globe **3**
Winston Churchill's
   Britain at War Experience **8**

seagulls—a reminder of how close to the ocean London is. These days, the 6.5km (4-mile) journey takes 50 to 75 minutes each way, depending on the tides and the ferry company you choose. Along the way, you pass beneath the ultra-modern Millennium Footbridge and the historic London and Tower bridges, and enjoy unparalleled views of the British Airways London Eye, the Tate Modern, St. Paul's Cathedral, the Tower of London, and much more. You'll disembark near the historical *Cutty Sark* (p. 159), beside which is the Greenwich Tourist Information Centre.

City Cruises and Thames River Services depart from Westminster Millennium Pier, Catamaran Cruisers from Embankment and Waterloo. A cheaper option (you'll save a pound or two per person) is to take a Thames Clipper commuter boat from the pier behind the Savoy Hotel. Note that Travelcard holders get a discount on all fares, that City Cruises offers a River Red Rover ticket (available in a family version) for unlimited hop-on hop-off travel, and that Thames River Services has a round-trip family ticket for two adults and two kids for £26 ($52). The latter also now runs extended trips as far as the Thames Flood Barrier (p. 155) before depositing you at Greenwich. Allow about a day for the tour and Greenwich sightseeing. You can take strollers aboard boats but may have to fold them.

Catamaran Cruises: (**C**) 020/7695-1800. www.catamarancruisers.co.uk. City Cruises: (**C**) 020/7740-0400. www.citycruises.com. Thames River Services: (**C**) 020/7930-4097. www.westminsterpier.co.uk. Thames Clippers: (**C**) 0870/781-5049. www.thamesclippers.com. Admission £7.30–£9.40 ($15–$19) round-trip for adults, £3.65–£4.70 ($7.30–$9.40) round-trip for children 5–15. Tube: Embankment, Westminster, or Waterloo.

**Science Museum** 🍀🍀🍀 **Ages 2 and up.** Like the Natural History Museum, this gargantuan five-floor museum of science and industry can be daunting to the uninitiated, so get your bearings at one of the touch-screen info terminals dotted around it, which give directions (this is not the easiest place to navigate) and suggest itineraries for families, teens, and those with special interests, such as transport or medicine. These will help you locate the hand-on galleries, which include the popular Launch Pad where visitors of all ages can push, pull, and experiment in order to experience the forces of nature, with orange-shirted Explainers on hand to fill you in on the technological background and to host the free 20-minute shows held throughout the day. Another interactive highlight is the Challenge of Materials gallery with its glass bridge spanning the main hall, responding to visitors in its changes in light and sound, plus strange items such as a steel wedding dress and cardboard chair. In Who Am I? you can morph your face to make it look older or younger and find out where your ancestors may have lived. Elsewhere, there's the SimEx Simulator, a state-of-the-art ride that lets you feel a dinosaur's breath on your neck or the impact of an explosion in space, and the Motionride Simulator that puts you in the cockpit of a Harrier Jump Jet. Specifically for tots are the futuristic Pattern Pod interactive space and The Garden, a basement section where 3- to 6-year-olds encounter simple scientific ideas through dressing up, water- and softplay, and building.

In addition to the science shows mentioned above, daily events and activities include drama performances and workshops, most of which involve making a model to take home with you. The museum also has one of only two IMAX movie theaters in London: a 450-seat venue showing spectacular nature-based 2-D and 3-D films on screens as tall as four double-decker buses. If you come for one of the blockbusting temporary exhibitions on subjects as diverse as spying and cinema animation, make sure not to overlook the permanent displays of such world-altering inventions as Stephenson's Rocket, Bell's telephone, Whittle's jet engine, the *Apollo 10* command module, and

# "The City" Attractions

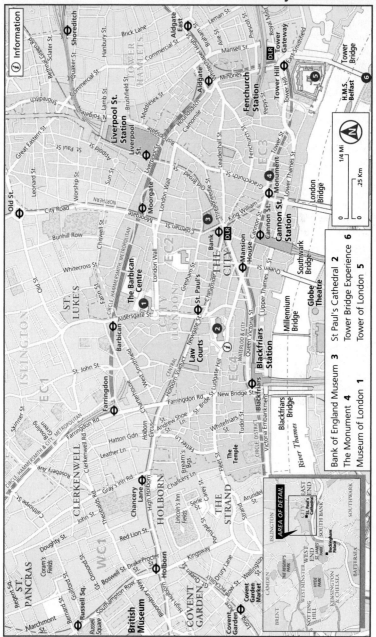

## Bedtime Fun

The fun doesn't have to stop before dinnertime on special sleepover nights for kids and accompanying adults. The **Science Museum**'s program of themed Science Nights (about once monthly) involves hands-on workshops, science shows, gallery trails, a drawing competition, and an IMAX movie viewing for 8- to 11-year-olds. You'll need to form a group of five or more kids, accompanied by at least one person over 18; prices are £30 ($60) per child or adult. Bring a sleeping bag, wash bag, evening snack, and maybe a pillow and favorite cuddly toy; breakfast is provided. For information and booking, call ℂ 020/7942-4909 or e-mail science.night@sciencemuseum.org.uk.

For themed sleepovers at the **British Museum** (p. 157), kids (8–15) must join the Young Friends (£20/$40 per year), which includes free entry to exhibitions, a thrice-yearly magazine, special events, behind-the-scenes visits, Sunday Clubs, competitions, and the use of a Friends Room. The events, during which kids and their caregivers bed down among ancient Egyptian sculptures, then cost an additional £28 ($56) per person. Call ℂ 020/7323-8566.

If the great outdoors is more your thing, **Kew Gardens** (p. 191) hosts wonderful Midnight Rambles, when 8- to 11-year-olds and caregivers can stay here overnight (in the Climber and Creepers botanical playzone), searching the 121 hectares (300 acres) for badgers, bats, and owls, learning about plantlife, playing nature-themed indoor games, and listening to stories and eating marshmallows around a campfire. Drinks and snacks are provided in the evening, as is breakfast, which is followed by an award ceremony for "Best Plant Hunter," "Best Entomologist," "Best Photographer," and more. The cost is £40 ($80) per adult or child; for dates e-mail sleepovers@kew.org.

Lastly, if you can get together a group of 15 kids ages 8 and up (by teaming up with another group if necessary), you can book a "Kip on a Ship" night (or up to 3 nights) aboard the **HMS Belfast** (p. 158). Participants sleep in real sailors' bunks in the restored 1950s mess desks, with adults in separate cabins. There must be at least one adult per 10 children. Activities are tailored toward the group. Accommodations cost £25 ($50) per person, including a buffet breakfast in the ship's Walrus Café; you need to bring a sleeping bag, pillowcase, towel, and packed evening meal unless you prefer to go to a nearby restaurant or order takeout. Call ℂ 020/7940-6327 for a booking form; be warned that for some weekends at busy times of year, dates get booked up more than a year ahead.

the computer used by Tim Berners-Lee to design the Internet. Older kids will also be fascinated by the displays on genetics, digital technology, and artificial intelligence in the Welcome Wing, and there are sleepover Science Nights (see above).

Practically speaking, there are stroller parks near the relevant exhibits, almost every floor has baby-changing facilities, and there are two cafes, a snack shop, and picnic areas on three floors. The shop is a great spot for interesting gifts.

Exhibition Rd., SW7. ℂ 0870/870-4868. www.sciencemuseum.org.uk. Free admission (except some exhibitions, rides, and IMAX cinema, with family discounts). Daily 10am–6pm. Tube: S. Kensington.

**Tower of London** 👧👧    **Ages 5 and up.** Most famous as the site of the beheadings of three queens (Anne Boleyn, Catherine Howard, and Lady Jane Grey), the murder of two little princes (the sons of Edward IV, killed by Richard III in order to remain king), and the prison of Sir Walter Raleigh, this is the best-preserved medieval castle of any European capital, and as such oozes with history and heraldry. It is also the home of the **Crown Jewels.** The oldest part, the **White Tower,** was begun by William the Conqueror in 1066–67 to keep London's native Saxons in check. Here you'll find royal armor from the reign of Henry VIII, as well as instruments of torture and execution. After William, subsequent rulers added towers, more walls, and fortified gates, and Henry III started a royal menagerie (the basis for London Zoo, housing the first elephant ever seen in the country).

Older kids won't begrudge the longish wait (reduced by moving walkways) to admire the prize exhibit, kept in the **Jewel House**—the Imperial State Crown, made for Queen Victoria in 1837 and now worn by Elizabeth II when she opens Parliament. And all children love the six **ravens** (plus two spares) registered as official residents—according to a legend, the Tower will stand as long as those ominous birds remain, so they all have their wings clipped. They're not the best-tempered critters, however, so don't let the little ones get too close.

Popular features include interactive displays in the **Bloody Tower** and **Beauchamp Tower,** which allow visitors to experience at least some of the reality of being held prisoner here, and **Bowyer Tower,** where the Duke of Clarence may have drowned in a vat of malmesley (madeira wine). There are also temporary exhibitions on aspects of the Tower's history, and regular reconstructions of historical events. If you're short on time, try a **1-hour guided tour** of the compound given by the 39 rather hammy Yeoman Warders or "Beefeaters" (Tudor-outfitted ex-servicemen) every half-hour. They also give free short talks and preside over the nightly ancient **Ceremony of the Keys,** the 9:30pm locking of the Tower. (Free tickets are available by writing to the Ceremony of the Keys Office, HM Tower of London, London EC3N 4AB, at least 2 months in advance; you must specify two possible dates, enclose a stamped, self-addressed envelope with British stamps or two International Reply Coupons and give the names of all attendees.) In summer a music event features concerts by international performers in the dry moat; visitors can bring their own picnics.

Those with kids should ask at the Welcome Centre for free family trails and Raven Watch leaflets, and look at the website for suggested itineraries of 1, 2, and 3 hours. The New Armouries **restaurant** has a kids' menu, or there's the Tower Café and Kiosk on the wharf, with alfresco seating in the shadow of Tower Bridge. Note that many parts of the Tower are far from stroller-friendly. Last admission is an hour before closing time, and all internal buildings close 30 minutes after last admission. *Insider tip:* Advance tickets can be bought by phone, online, or at the kiosks on Tower Hill, allowing you to circumvent the long queues without committing yourself to a date or time (they are valid for a week after purchase).

Tower Hill, EC3. ℂ 0870/756-7070. www.hrp.org.uk. Admission £16 ($32) adults, £13 ($26) students and seniors, £9.50 ($19) children 5–16, £45 ($90) family ticket for up to 2 adults and 3 children. Sun–Mon 10am–8pm; Tues–Sat 9am–6pm. Tube: Tower Hill.

**WWT Wetland Centre** 👧👧    **Ages 2 and up.** The world's only wetland project in a capital city, spectacularly located on the banks of the Thames in southwest London, brings you into close contact with a whole array of rare and beautiful wildlife over its 43 hectares, including kingfishers and a colony of endangered water voles. Wetland areas are second only to rainforests in the diversity of life forms they support, and are thus crucial to the world's ecology. There is a huge amount here to make it ideal for a family day out that's as fun as it is educational—a "bird airport" viewing observatory, six wildlife hides from which to spy, the Explore adventure area for kids 3 to 11 (including giant watervole tunnels to clamber through), an interactive discovery center with kids' water games, a modern visitor center with a cinema (as well as a cafe, gift shop and optics shop selling binoculars and more), free guided tours, and regular events. The latter are necessarily more frequent at weekends and in school vacations: They include birdsong identification, dawn choruses (breakfast served), bat walks (this is one of London's best bat sites), a reptiles and amphibians week with trails, guided walks, arts and crafts, and pond sessions, Father's Day barbecues, insect walks, an "animal magic" weekend with visiting animals, and perhaps best of all, Night Time Safaris for kids 8 to 14, including bat-watching and torch-lit pond-dipping (£25/$50; booking essential)—they end at 10:30pm.

All of the 14 types of wetland habitat here, which range from Asian rice paddies to Siberian tundra, are dotted with interactive displays, and the wildflower-bordered paths are wide and accessible by stroller, though there's a park where you can leave them if you prefer. The truly wild areas of the reserve can be observed via CCTV live footage. As well as the cafe, there are several picnic areas.

Queen Elizabeth's Walk, Barnes, SW13. ✆ 020/8409-4400. www.wwt.org.uk/visit/wetlandcentre. Admission £8.75 ($18) adults, £6.60 ($13) seniors, £4.95 ($9.90) children 4–16, £22 ($44) family ticket (2 adults and 2 kids). Mar 25–Oct 27 daily 9:30am–6pm (until 8pm Thurs May 31–Sept 20); Jan 1–Mar 24 daily 9:30am–5pm (until 2pm on Dec 24). Tube: Hammersmith, then "Duck Bus" (no. 283).

## 2 Best Views

Some of the best views of London can be had during a ride on the **British Airways London Eye;** see p. 142, on a **boat trip along the Thames,** see p. 181; or from parts of **Hampstead Heath** (p. 143).

**London's Living Room    Ages 2 and up.** City Hall, an egg-shaped steel-and-glass building on the south bank of the Thames, is home to the mayor of London and his local government. The public can normally access the second floor and below, where there are exhibition spaces, including the London Photomat, an impressive aerial view of the whole of London, and a cafe. But there are also special weekend openings of London's Living Room, a rooftop gallery with an external walkway affording stunning panoramic views over London, from neighboring Tower Bridge and the Tower of London to farther afield. Don't miss the ramp that winds down from the top floor to the second story—kids love it.

City Hall, The Queen's Walk, SE1. ✆ 020/7983-410. www.london.gov.uk/gla/city_hall. Free admission. Approximately 1 weekend every month, including Open House weekend, see p. 21 (other areas Mon–Fri 8am–8pm). Tube: London Bridge.

**The Monument    Ages 4 and up.** The 62m (202-ft.) height of this classical Doric column, built to commemorate the Great Fire of 1666, is no fluke—it corresponds with the distance from the structure's base to the spot where the blaze started, in a Pudding Lane bakery. The world's tallest isolated stone tower, the Monument was dreamed up by architect Sir Christopher Wren (of St. Paul's Cathedral fame). Its 311 twisting, steep stone steps can be ascended by the fairly robust and the non-claustrophobic. (A handrail can help you get up there in half an hour.) You're rewarded with a close look at the copper urn at the column's tip, fabulous 360-degree views of London, and a certificate when you make it back down. (Not everyone did—in 1842, iron railings had to be erected around the viewing platform to halt the suicides occurring here.) Note that you can purchase joint tickets with the Tower of London Exhibition (p. 156).

Monument St., EC3. © 020/7626-2717. www.cityoflondon.gov.uk. Admission £2 ($4) adults, £1 ($2) children 5–15. Daily 9:30am–5:30pm. Tube: Monument.

## St. Paul's Cathedral 𝕱𝕱    Ages 5 and up.

It's a steep 378-step climb to the **Stone Gallery** of this Christopher Wren–designed structure, and then another 152 steps to the **Golden Gallery,** but both of them amply reward you with panoramic views of the Thames and London at your feet. These amazing galleries are accessed via the disorienting gap between the outside dome and the one viewed from the interior, as is the famous interior Whispering Gallery, where an acoustic anomaly allows you to hear someone whisper at the walls way across the other side.

St. Paul's was built to replace a Norman cathedral that burned down in the Great Fire, which was itself believed to have occupied the site of two previous Saxon cathedrals and a Christian church, all of which were also destroyed by fire. Before that, a Roman temple is thought to have stood here. It's a wonder that this "new" building remains, given that it was directly hit by bombs on more than one occasion in World War II. Highlights include the crypt, with the tombs of Lord Nelson, Christopher Wren, and the Duke of Wellington; and "Great Paul," the biggest bell in England (hear it daily at 1pm). Note that a £40-million ($80-million) restoration project in honor of the cathedral's 300th birthday in October 2008 (which will result in new exhibition and interpretation galleries) means that certain areas may be temporarily off-limits.

*Insider tip:* Those visiting with kids should check out the website's "School Visits" page for downloadable self-guided tours and themed trails.

There's an atmospheric sculpture-filled cafe in the crypt, and space to picnic in the gardens, which are full of roses in the spring.

St. Paul's Churchyard, EC4. © 020/7236-4128. www.stpauls.co.uk. Cathedral and galleries £9.50 ($19) adults, £8.50 ($17) seniors and students, £3.50 ($7) children 7–16, £23 ($46) family ticket. Mon–Sat 8:30am–4pm (during restoration last admission to galleries 3:45pm). Tube: St. Paul's.

## Thames Flood Barrier    Ages 3 and up.

London's first new major public park for more than 50 years, the a 9-hectare (22-acre) **Thames Barrier Park** with its arresting modern landscaping, is on the north bank of the Thames River and affords unparalleled views of the gleaming stainless-steel **Thames Flood Barrier,** part of the flood-defense system protecting London against tidal surges and rising water levels. In addition to admiring the structure from the park, you can watch working vessels ply the waters (when they want to pass through the barrier they have to radio ahead for permission) and observe the park's birdlife—at low tide, you might see gray herons feeding and cormorants drying themselves along the shore, as well as rare wading birds such as oystercatchers. The Visitor Pavilion, with its views of the barrier, as well as wildflower meadows and manicured lawns, has a coffee shop. The park also contains picnic areas, a riverside promenade (with the best views of the barrier), a great playground, a five-a-side football/basketball court, and fountains with 32 jets that kids love to play in during hot weather, but it's not well-known so is rarely crowded.

**Thames Barrier Information & Learning Centre** on the opposite side of the river at Woolwich has a working model of the barrier, a video about its construction, functioning, and importance, colorful display boards on the Thames and its wildlife, a play area, a cafe, and a picnic area. School vacations see a variety of fun activities for 3- to 12-year-olds on ecological themes; call for information and to book places.

*Tip:* Once a month, you can see the barrier's 10 moveable gates (four of them each as tall as a five-story building when raised) in action during maintenance work; check the information center website for dates.

Park: North Woolwich Rd., E16. ℂ 020/7511-4111. www.thamesbarrierpark.org.uk. Free admission. Daily 7am–dusk. Tube: Canning Town then change to DLR to Pontoon Dock. **Information & Learning Centre:** 1 Unity Way, SE18. ℂ 020/8305-4188. www.environment-agency.gov.uk/regions/thames. Admission £2 ($4) adults, £1.50 ($3) seniors, £1 ($2) children. Apr–Sept daily 10:30am–4pm; Oct–Mar daily 11am–3:30pm. Tube: North Greenwich (then bus no. 161 or 472).

## Tower Bridge Experience    Ages 2 and up.
Pay to see the exhibition inside one of the world's greatest and most photographed landmarks, built in 1894, and you can enjoy spectacular views of St. Paul's, the Tower of London, and the Houses of Parliament from high-level enclosed walkways reaching between the bridge's north and south towers. Accessed by elevator, the walkways are fitted with special windows that allow you to take photos without being obscured by glass. Inside the bridge the exhibition features info panels and hands-on mechanisms; in the Victorian engine room you can see the boilers and steam engines that raised and lowered the bridge for passing ships. If you're here when the bridge is lifted to allow a large river craft such as a cruise or naval through (about 1,000 times a year, mostly in winter; the website has a schedule), imagine that, as late as 1952, London buses were forced to make the leap from one bascule (drawbridge) to the other when the bridge began to rise! All parts of the exhibition are stroller accessible. Last entry is an hour before closing.

Tower Bridge, SE1. ℂ 020/7403-3761. www.towerbridge.org.uk. Admission £6 ($12) adults, £4.50 ($9) students and seniors, £3 ($6) children 5–15, £14 ($28) family ticket (2 adults and 2 kids). Apr–Sept daily 10am–6:30pm; Oct–Mar daily 9:30am–6pm. Tube: Tower Hill or London Bridge.

## Wellington Arch    Ages 2 and up.
This splendid neoclassical arch built in 1830, initially to form a royal gateway to Buckingham Palace (it was moved from its original site), has wide, stroller-accessible balconies with views of the royal parks, the Houses of Parliament, and the British Airways London Eye—and, if you come at 10:40 and 11:40am Tuesday to Saturday (an hour earlier on Sun), of the mounted Horse Guards passing between the columns. For the best vista, come in wintertime; summer foliage can obscure sightlines. The statue of the angel of peace on top of the arch, which replaced a statue of the Duke of Wellington, is Europe's largest bronze sculpture. Inside the arch, exhibitions over three floors trace the arch's history. Occasional family-friendly events include the likes of talks about local highwaymen.

Joint entry (including family tickets) is possible with Apsley House across the street, once home to the Duke of Wellington and still housing some of his descendants. Visitors can admire the duke's art collection, porcelain, and silver plates: Wellington Boot activity packs will keep 5- to 11-year-olds amused, with activity sheets and puzzles.

Hyde Park Corner, W1. ℂ 020/7930-2726. www.english-heritage.org.uk. Admission £3.20 ($6.40) adults, £2.40 ($4.80) seniors and students, £1.60 ($3.20) children 5–16. Apr–Oct Wed–Sun 10am–5pm; Nov–Mar Wed–Sun 10am–4pm. Tube: Hyde Park Corner.

## Westminster Cathedral    Ages 5 and up.
The Roman Catholic Church's eccentric but lovely British headquarters, built in 1903 and based, in part, on Santa Sofia in

Istanbul and St. Mark's in Venice, has a viewing platform at the top of its 82m (269-ft.) campanile (accessible by elevator), allowing wonderful views of Buckingham Palace, Westminster Abbey, the Houses of Parliament, the British Airways London Eye, and St. Paul's Cathedral. Inside the massive structure, you'll find marble aplenty, and some fine mosaics.

Cathedral Piazza, Victoria St., SW1. ☎ 020/7798-9055. www.westminstercathedral.org.uk. Free. Mon–Fri 7am–7pm, Sat 8am–7pm, Sun 8am–7:30pm. Campanile elevator daily 9:30am–12:30pm and 1–5pm. Tube: Victoria.

## 3 More London Museums

For the **Wimbledon Lawn Tennis Museum** and **Museum of Rugby**, see p. 259.

**Bank of England Museum    Ages 5 and up.** This museum manages to make the history of the Bank of England, founded in 1694, fun—there are a reconstructed banking hall with costumed dummies, examples of bank-note forgeries, Roman and modern-day gold bars, weapons once used to defend the bank, and more. Visitors learn, for instance, that the £ sign evolved from the letter "L" (the initial letter of the Latin word *libra,* meaning a pound of money); and that the Queen's portrait did not appear on Bank of England notes until as late as 1960. You'll also find out how bank notes are made, and get the chance to lift a genuine gold bar. Activity sheets are available for under-5s (I Spy), ages 6 to 10, ages 11 to 14, and ages 15 to 17, either at the museum or in advance from the website. School-vacation events might include "Wind in the Willows" face-painting (the creator, Kenneth Grahame, was once secretary of the bank), treasure-chest making, bank-note design, and Christmas carols. Stroller access can be tricky in parts and there's no cafe, but there are baby-changing facilities and a shop with pocket-money items and Bank teddy bears.

Threadneedle St., EC2. ☎ 020/7601-5545. www.bankofengland.co.uk. Free admission. Mon–Fri 10am–5pm. Tube: Bank.

**British Library ⃰    All ages.** The world's greatest collection of books, manuscripts, newspapers, maps, music, and stamps, as well as a mighty research center and reading facility, the British Library is home to some of the world's most fabulous literary treasures, including the oldest printed book (made in China in 868). It shouldn't, by its nature, be child-friendly, but among the 18 million items in its collections are such gems as the original version of the children's classic, *Alice's Adventures in Wonderland,* handwritten and illustrated by its author Charles Dodgson (Lewis Carroll); original sheet music by John Lennon and Paul McCartney; and a Leonardo da Vinci notebook. Check the website to see if any of the temporary exhibitions might interest your kids; they sometimes focus on the likes of children's book illustrations or specific kids' authors. A program of free family events in school vacations includes storytelling, art sessions and calligraphy workshops, and occasional special activities days outside in the piazza, linked to temporary exhibitions and including performances, crafts, art installations, and food stalls.

The library has a restaurant and a cafe. Exhibition galleries are stroller accessible, and there are baby-changing facilities.

96 Euston Rd., NW1. ☎ 020/7412-7332. www.bl.uk. Free admission. Mon and Wed–Fri 9:30am–6pm; Tues 9:30am–8pm; Sat 9:30am–5pm; Sun and bank-holiday Mon 11am–5pm. Tube: King's Cross/St Pancras or Euston.

**British Museum ⃰⃰⃰    Ages 4 and up.** Originally a "cabinet of curiosities" given to the nation by a private collector in 1753, this almost absurdly huge museum now

## Travelers' Tales: London's Transport Museums

With five airports (including Heathrow, the world's busiest) and six railway stations, London is a global transport hub—a fact well illustrated in many of its museums and sights. The **London Transport Museum** and the **Science Museum** (p. 150) are good places to start; a lesser-known spot, over to the east, is the **North Woolwich Old Station Museum** (Pier Rd., E16; ℂ **020/7474-7244**; free admission; Jan–Nov Sat–Sun 1–5pm, daily 1–5pm during local school vacations), a Victorian station with a 1920s ticket office, old engines, carriages, models, posters, and memorabilia, and lots of interactive action for kids. Little ones love clambering aboard Dudley the Diesel and getting behind his controls, and there are occasional model railway days.

On the South Bank, the *Golden Hinde* ⚓ (St. Mary Overie Dock, Cathedral St., SE1; ℂ **020/7403-0123**; www.goldenhinde.org; admission £4.50/$9 adults, £3.50/$7 children, £13/$26 family ticket for two adults and three kids; Mon–Fri 11am–5:30pm, Sat–Sun 10am–5:30pm but call ahead to check) is a replica of the tiny 14-cannon ship in which Sir Francis Drake circumnavigated the globe in the 16th century. A former floating museum that has itself sailed round the world, it's a great place to learn about the Tudor age and life at sea hands-on, by turning the capstan, learning to fire a cannon, lying on Drakes's bed and more. Replica barrels, furniture, clothing, and more can be handled, and other replica items, such as sandglasses, maps, and navigational equipment, studied.

Ten minutes' walk along the riverfront, the 11,500-ton **HMS** *Belfast* (Morgan's Lane, Tooley St., SE1; ℂ **020/7949 6300**; www.iwm.org.uk; adult £9.95/$20, seniors and students £6.15/$12, under-16s free; daily Mar–Oct 1am–6pm, Nov–Feb 10am–5pm) is a World War II cruiser with an exhibition about sailors' lives in war (it played a leading role in the Normandy landings) and in peacetime, and nine decks to explore, including the engine room. The last weekend of the month sees free drop-in family events twice daily, and there are occasional creative activities. After your visit, encourage

has 4km (2½ miles) of galleries, so is best tackled over the course of 2 or even 3 days. A variety of guided and audio tours help you to break it down into bite-size chunks; the most obvious for those with kids are the Family Audio Tours £3.50 ($7), narrated by actor Stephen Fry and embracing three trails—"Bodies," "Boardgames," and "Beasts." (Note that if you print out a map for these from the website and take it along with you, you get a second audio tour for half price.) Otherwise, there are six family trail sheets to be had at the Paul Hamlyn Library, with themes such as "Dragons" or "Sailing the Nile," puzzles and games, art materials to borrow, and books to consult in the Hamlyn Children's Library. For visually impaired visitors there are special hands-on tables where objects can be touched, but all visitors can ask one of the volunteers taking groups round to handle items from the collections.

Star attractions include the **Rosetta Stone,** in the Egyptian Room, the discovery of which led to the deciphering of hieroglyphics; the **Egyptian royal tombs** (with their mummies); and **Lindow Man,** a body superbly well-preserved in peat, in the Celtic your kids to send their letters and drawings to the online Shipshape Gallery.

From London Bridge City Pier close by, hop on a ferry to Greenwich (p. 148), where another historical vessel can be found in permanent dry dock—the 1869 *Cutty Sark* (Cutty Sark Gardens, SE10; *②* 020/8858-2698; www.cuttysark. org.uk; £2/$4, under-5s free), a clipper that carried tea from China and wool from Australia and was the fastest sailing ship of its day. Tragically, this ship, the world's last surviving tea clipper, was gutted by fire in May 2007, and at the time of writing its future was uncertain. The outlook was more optimistic than it might have been, since 50% of the ship had been dismantled in the course of a huge restoration project scheduled to end in late 2008. In the meantime, a distinctive new visitors' pavilion (it looks a bit like a white hedgehog) tells you about the conservation techniques and plans for the ship. It includes a full reconstruction of the Master's Saloon and interactive displays, and a new mini-cinema and CCTV footage of the restoration work were being put into place at the time of writing. Mums and dads might like to sample a cup of the type of tea that the *Cutty Sark* used to carry.

Nearby, the vast **National Maritime Museum** *⑨⑨* (Romney Rd., SE10; *②* 020/8858-4422; www.nmm.ac.uk; free admission; daily summer 10am–6pm; rest of year 10am–5pm), which celebrated its 70th birthday in 2006, traces the history of seafaring, from early explorers to modern technology. Interactive galleries All Hands and The Bridge (open to the public Tues, weekends, and school holidays), based on the lives of seafarers, allow kids to hoist flags, steer boats, send distress signals, and more. Free activities for families include workshops based on current exhibitions, involving crafts, dressing up and performance, music sessions, storytelling, handling sessions, themed days, and planetarium shows, including ones for under-3s and ages 3 to 6. There are also babies' and toddlers' workshops. Trail guides (for ages 5 and up) are available from the info desk. The child-friendly Regatta Cafe adjoins a play area.

Europe gallery. If your heart is set on seeing a specific item, call to make sure it's on display—exhibits change throughout the year. The famous domed **Reading Room,** once part of the British Library and the place where figures as eminent as Karl Marx came to work, now houses a library and touch screens detailing the museum's collections. It's within the magnificent glass-roofed **Great Court,** an airy central plaza where you can enjoy snacks or full meals in a number of kid-friendly cafes, or in the **Children's Shop & Bookshop.** The **Ford Centre for Young Visitors** is a recent addition that forms a great spot for picnics, complete with water fountains, vending machines, highchairs, and baby-feeding and -changing facilities. It's here that most of the special **family events** take place, most of them free and drop-in; culturally themed, they may involve crafts, dancing, drawing, handling, and demonstrations.

Great Russell St., WC1. *②* 020/7323-8000. www.thebritishmuseum.ac.uk. Free admission (charge for some exhibitions and tours). Sat–Wed 10am–5:30pm; Thurs–Fri 10am–8:30pm. (Great Court Sun–Wed 9am–6pm; Thurs–Sat 9am–11pm.) Tube: Holborn, Tottenham Court Rd., or Russell Sq.

**Brunel Museum    Ages 5 and up.** This museum celebrating the world's first tunnel built under a river, the Thames Tunnel of 1843, was designed by Marc Brunel and his son Isambard Kingdom Brunel and dubbed by Victorians "The Eighth Wonder of the World." It's astonishing to think that before trains ran here, when it was still a pedestrian route, it was the site of 64 shops selling the likes of garters, silk handkerchiefs, and lovers' tokens. The museum's previous focus on the technical aspects of tunneling has now been downplayed, and there's a new gallery with memorabilia, items that used to be sold, watercolors (including one by Brunel) and an interactive Victorian peep show. Kids can also admire the bas-relief showing how the tunnel was built, created by local children.

A Fancy Fair held in the tunnel (the world's only underwater fair) saw visitors entertained by novelty acts, sword swallowers, and acrobats. Today an annual Fancy Fair held above the water includes samba and percussion. There are occasional guided tours through the floodlit tunnel by Tube train—see the website for details—and there are picturesque riverside gardens to stretch out on.

Railway Ave., SE16. © 020/7231-3840. www.brunelenginehouse.org.uk. Admission £2 ($4) adults; £1 ($2) seniors, students, and kids 5–16. Daily 1–5pm. Tube: Rotherhithe.

**Churchill Museum and Cabinet War Rooms** ✦✦  **Ages 5 and up.** Two attractions in one, this venue explores Winston Churchill's roles as a statesman, politician, and soldier, and also a husband, father, and son—exhibits include his ivory baby rattle, copies of his school reports, photos of his pets, and soft toys (pick up one to hear a recording of an animal quote by Churchill)—and contains the secret bombproof bunkers where he and his war cabinet hid during air raids on the city, maintained as they were when hostilities ended. As well as the Map Room with its huge wall maps and compasses, and the tiny Transatlantic Telephone Room housing a special scrambler phone on which Churchill conferred with President Roosevelt, you can see Churchill's bedroom-cum-office, with two BBC microphones via which he made his nation-stirring speeches, and his chamber pot (there were no flush toilets).

The whole place is surprisingly welcoming to kids, offering free audioguides for children and families, kids' trails, and a program of special events. A highlight introduced in 2007 is the Dig For Victory Week, which spills out from the museum into neighboring St. James's Park and explores what it was like to live under the constraints of food rationing, through gardening (the fruit and vegetable allotments are tended to by local kids and can be visited all summer), crafts, old-fashioned playground games, and more. Other novelties with an environmental/self-sufficiency theme are the Green City Week, Healthy Living Week, and Harvest Fair.

Strollers are manageable inside the museum, baby-changing facilities are available in male and female restrooms, and there's a cafe and a gift shop with lots of books, games, and toys.

Clive Steps, King Charles St., SW1. © 020/7930-6961. www.iwm.org.uk. Admission £11 ($22) adults, £9 ($18) seniors and students, free for children 16 and under. Daily 9:30am–6pm. Tube: Westminster or St. James's Park.

**Church Farmhouse Museum**    This old hay and dairy farm, built around 1660, is worth visiting if you're journeying to the nearby RAF Museum (p. 162). It's mounted a wide variety of different exhibitions over the years, including at least one especially for kids each year, but at the time of this writing, the museum was proposing to devote the space to a display on the history of toys and games, with lots of playthings for young visitors. There will also be a room dedicated to local life in World War II, and a gallery for temporary exhibitions. Christmas is a good time to come, with the likes of a display of traditional angels and fairies, and the 1850s dining room annually decorated as for a Victorian Christmas. Spring 2008 will see the inauguration of a new puzzle maze, with a day of themed events for kids in the garden; however, the maze was already open to the public at the time of this writing.

Call or see the website in advance or visiting, as the museum's plans were in flux as this guide went to press, as visitors' views were assessed.

Greyhound Hill, Hendon, NW4. 🕐 020/8359-3942. www.churchfarmhousemuseum.co.uk. Free admission. Mon–Thurs 10am–1pm and 2–5pm; Sat 10am–1pm and 2–5:30pm; Sun 2–5:30pm. Tube: Hendon Central.

**Clink Prison Museum    Ages 8 and up.** This is a schlocky re-creation of a medieval prison in which both adults and kids were locked up, not just for murder and theft but for "crimes" such having the wrong faith or falling into debt. Although the reconstructed cells with their shackled waxwork figures are a little threadbare, and the sound effects are overdramatic, ghoulish kids love the torture and restraining devices the same way they love the Chamber of Horrors at Madame Tussaud's (p. 167). The shop sells historical trinkets such as "lucky charms" in the form of severed heads and skeletal feet. Note that the Clink, which stood on this site, held many prostitutes (this was the city's red-light district), and exhibits on the area's colorful past include displays on the history of prostitution.

Clink St., SE1. 🕐 020/7403-0900. www.clink.co.uk. Admission £5 ($10) adults; £3.50 ($7) seniors, students, and children 5–15; £12 ($24) family ticket (2 adults and 2 children). Mon–Fri 10am–6pm; Sat–Sun 10am–9pm. Tube: London Bridge.

**Design Museum    Ages 6 and up.** This fascinating modern-design museum explains how mass-produced objects function and why they look the way they do, from chairs and telephones to cars and fashion items. All kids are given a free Design Action Pack on arrival, to help them make the best of their visit; you might want to schedule this for a Sunday, when there are creative family workshops (for kids ages 6–11) in the afternoons, on a different theme each month (£4/$8 child, £7/$14 accompanying adult; booking essential on 🕐 020/7940-8782). Or come on the Family Day in Museums & Galleries Month (p. 18), when there are exhibition trails, children's tours, drop-in design-and-make workshops, and more.

Shad Thames, SE1. 🕐 0870/833-9955. www.designmuseum.org. Admission £7 ($14) adults, £4 ($8) seniors and students, free for kids under 12. Daily 10am–5:45pm. Tube: Tower Hill or London Bridge.

**Discover** 🎃🎃 **Ages up to 8.** This wonderfully original space where younger kids come to "storybuild" through play, performances, and storytelling is well worth the schlep out of the center. Kids pick up a "storybook" bag at the door and draw and write their ideas as they follow the **Story Trail,** crossing Sparkly River on the Spider Trolley to reach Secret Cave. Along the way, they collect postcards, tickets, finger puppets, menus, and invitations to keep in their books; storybuilders are on hand to help kids get their best out of the experience. One of the highlights is the bank of TVs with cameras that let kids watch themselves "enter" stories on screen. On a sunny day, the **Story Garden,** with its spaceship, monster's-tongue slide, tunnels, weird mirrors, water features, and more is an oasis in this relatively deprived area of east London; you're free to picnic there if you don't want to use the cafe. Inside, there's stroller access, a stroller park with lockers, and baby-changing facilities.

There's an active program of events, including artist-led workshops, creative sessions involving the likes of carnival costume making and samba rhythms, and planting.

## More Travelers' Tales: London's Transport Museums

At Hendon north of the city, the superb **Royal Airforce Museum London** *(Grahame Park Way, NW9; ℂ 020/8205-2266; www.rafmuseum.com; free admission; daily 10am–6pm) displays more than 200 aircraft, half of them full-size, on the site of the original London Aerodrome, plus photos, memorabilia, and related artifacts. Platforms let you get up close to the planes, which range from classic bombers to state-of-the-art jet fighters. In addition, there are two flight simulators (£2.50/$5 per 4-min. ride), a sound-and-light show (hourly 1–5pm), and the Aeronauts Interactive Centre where kids can, for instance, take an RAF aptitude test and control a propeller rotating at 500 revolutions per minute. Special events include a Search & Rescue Weekend, with the possibility of taking the lead at the radio in mission control or being cast away in a life-size dinghy, a Pageant Weekend with living-history displays, and Wartime Christmas. There's a picnic area, or head for Wings restaurant with its new kids corner with beanbags, toys, and a PlayStation.

Also a way out of town but in the opposite direction, **Croydon Airport Visitor Centre** (Airport House, Purley Way; ℂ 020/8669-1196; www.croydon airport.org.uk; free admission; first Sun of month 11am–4pm), traces the history of the airport (London's main airport from 1920–59, and the world's first international airport) in its former control tower, with a re-creation of its radio room. Kids can inspect Amy Johnson's flight bag, dress as 1930s passengers, and use hands-on models to calculate fuel loads, identify aircraft from their silhouettes, and the like.

An impressive 19th-century pumping station by the Thames at Brentford in west London, **Kew Bridge Steam Museum** *(Green Dragon Lane; ℂ 020/8568-4757; www.kbsm.org; £5/$10 adults, £4/$8) seniors and students, free under-16s; Tues–Sun plus bank-holiday Mon 11am–5pm), houses five Cornish

*Insider tip:* Admission to the Story Trail is half price from 3 to 5pm, Tuesday to Friday during school terms.

1 Bridge Terrace, E15. ℂ 020/8536-5555. www.discover.org.uk. Admission £3.50 ($7), free for kids under 2, family £11 ($22) (4 people). Free admission to garden. Tues–Sun 10am–5pm; daily 10am–5pm during local school vacations. Tube: Stratford, then 10-min. walk.

**Fan Museum   Ages 7 and up.** The world's only museum dedicated to fans, a must for budding fashion designers of either sex, has more than 3,500 pieces on display, most of them antiques. A permanent exhibition traces their history and explains production methods, while thrice-yearly temporary displays explore a particular theme, such as ancient myths and legends. Accompanied teens can take part in the fan-making workshops (£20/$40) on the first Saturday of each month, but numbers are limited to six, so reserve ahead. The Orangery overlooking a "secret" Japanese-style garden is a civilized place for afternoon tea, served on Tuesday and Sunday. A baby-changing facility is available.

engines that pumped west London's water for more than a century. It's best to come on a Sunday between March and October, when London's only steam railway is in operation (many Victorian waterworks had their own railway); the entrance fee is £1 to £2 ($2–$4) higher at such times. Otherwise, the Water for Life gallery tells the history of water supply and use in London from Roman times to the 19th century, taking visitors through an actual section of the Thames Water Ring Main tunnel 40m (131 ft.) below ground, as well as into a mock sewer tunnel. Kids can sieve for treasure as "sewer toshers" once did, hunt for wildlife with the radio-controlled sewer robot; make a floor rubbing; be young engineers at the Meccano play bench; and more.

An intriguing little canalside museum tracing the history of the city's artificial waterways, the **London Canal Museum** in King's Cross (New Wharf Rd.; 𝄂 020/7713-0836; www.canalmuseum.org; £3/$6 adults, £2/$4 seniors and students, £1.50/$3 children 6–15; bank-holiday Mon and Tues–Sat 10am–4:30pm, to 6:30pm first Thurs of month) is set in a 19th-century ice warehouse built for renowned ice-cream maker Carlo Gatti. (The museum also tells the story of the ice and ice-cream trades.) Kids love peering down into the massive Victorian ice well used to store ice imported from Norway (for restaurants, fishmongers, and so on); on rare occasions, under controlled conditions, adults and older kids can even descend into it. Special events include towpath walks, summer boat trips through the long Islington Tunnel, summer theatrical performances, a Halloween weekend, an Ice Sunday with ice-related activities, and family activities—the latter are especially prominent in August. The museum is largely stroller accessible and has baby-changing facilities. There's no cafe, but the shop sells cold drinks and ice cream.

12 Crooms Hill, SE10. 𝄂 020/8305-1441. www.fan-museum.org. Admission £4 ($8) adults; £2.50 ($5) seniors, students, and children 7–15. Tues–Sat 11am–5pm; Sun noon–5pm. Tube: Greenwich.

**Fashion & Textile Museum** **Ages 8 and up.** Britain's first contemporary Fashion & Textile Museum, opened by posh-punk designer Zandra Rhodes in a suitably exuberant pink-and-orange former warehouse, was closed for an overhaul at the time of this writing but will continue to showcase British and global designers such as Biba, Christian Dior, and Rhodes herself, as well as hosting a couple of temporary exhibitions a year, when it reopens in February 2008. Don't miss the Fashion Cafe, where budding Carrie Bradshaws can stock up on one-off clothes, textiles, and drawings while refueling.

83 Bermondsey St., SE1. 𝄂 020/7403-0222. http://ftmlondon.org. Call for admission prices and opening times. Tube: London Bridge.

**Firepower, the Royal Artillery Museum** **Ages 7 and up.** Not for the faint of heart, this museum tracing the history of the Army's Royal Artillery within the historical

Royal Arsenal in Woolwich shakes, rattles, and hums with gunfire and other sound effects—all part of its simulations of modern warfare. Children love the military equipment and vehicles on display, including some monster tanks, but they tend, unsurprisingly, to congregate in the hands-on Real Weapon Gallery. (Don't fear—they can do little harm firing a jet of water from a small cannon.) Stroller access isn't a problem, and there are baby-changing facilities, a cafe, and a popular shop with military models and other paraphernalia.

Royal Arsenal, SE18. © 020/8855-7755. www.firepower.org.uk. £5 ($10) adults, £4.50 ($9) seniors and students, £2.50 ($5) children 5–15, £12 ($24) family ticket (2 adults and 2 children, or 1 adult and 3 children). Apr–Oct Wed–Sun 10:30am–5pm; Nov–Mar Fri–Sun 10:30am–5pm; daily bank-holiday Mon and school vacations. Train: Woolwich Arsenal.

**Florence Nightingale Museum    Ages 8 and up.** This small museum is dedicated to the life and work of Britain's most famous nurse, the "Lady with the Lamp," best known for her role in the Crimean War of 1854–57, when she won the hearts of her patients through her kindness (nursing was then considered a profession unfit for well-educated women such as her). On display are medical artifacts, battlefield relics, travel souvenirs, a snakeskin, flyswatters, personal effects, domestic objects, and even Florence's stuffed pet owl, which she used to carry in her pocket. School-vacation events (free with admission) might feature trails with prizes, costumed actors (including Florence herself, happy to chat to you about her life and work), costume-handling and dressing-up, and talks by real nurses. The shop has some great items for kids, including Victorian-style slates and pencils, and moving-picture flick books.

*Insider tip:* St. Thomas' Hospital itself has some good restaurants where you can eat very cheaply (for London), whether it be salads, pasta dishes, pizzas and burgers, or full meals. The restaurant in the North Wing has marvelous views across the river to the Houses of Parliament. The hospital also has some shops selling souvenirs that are reasonably priced compared to elsewhere.

St. Thomas' Hospital, 2 Lambeth Palace Rd., SE1. © 020/7620-0374. www.florence-nightingale.co.uk. Admission £5.80 ($12) adults; £4.80 ($10) seniors, students, and children 5–15; £16 ($32) family ticket. Mon–Fri 10am–5pm; Sat–Sun 10am–4:30pm. Tube: Westminster or Waterloo.

**Foundling Museum** ✺✺✺ **Ages 3 and up.** This touching museum tells the story of the Foundling Hospital, London's first home for abandoned children, and of its founder, philanthropic sea captain Thomas Coram. The hospital, demolished in 1926, housed some of the 1,000 babies that were abandoned every year in early-18th-century London; displays include fascinating photos and objects associated with their lives, such as poems written by the mothers, and lists of "renamed" children—at one point, a William Shakespeare and a Julius Caesar lived here. The hospital also became home to the country's first public art gallery when William Hogarth, a governor, persuaded other leading artists to donate works; you can still see paintings by Gainsborough, Reynolds, Hogarth himself, and others in the 18th-century interior. *Messiah* composer George Handel was also a governor, and you can see a collection of his manuscripts, musical scores, and more.

For kids and families there are activity packs, audioguides (with specially commissioned short stories and poems by established children's authors), storybooks, drawing activities, and special events. Annual Fun Days (in May) are the true highlight: Here you can enjoy art, music and drama, on a different theme each year, with special activities for teenagers. But all summer long, from May to August, Family Fun sessions are held on the first Saturday of the month, with crafts, trails, and drama workshops. In school vacations, Tuesdays and Thursdays also see special art, music, and storytelling sessions.

You can still see the colonnades of the original hospital building in the adjacent Coram's Fields children's park (p. 209). The museum's Clore Gallery & Walker Vaults display bright works by local children and young people. You'll find stroller access, an airy cafe, and changing facilities.

40 Brunswick Sq., WC1. ℰ 020/7841-3600. www.foundlingmuseum.org.uk. Admission £5 ($10) adults, £4 ($8) seniors and students, free for under-16s. Tues–Sat 10am–6pm; Sun noon–6pm. Tube: Russell Sq.

**Geffrye Museum** ☆  **Ages 3 and up.** This fascinating showcase of British middle-class interiors from the past 400 years, in the relative wilds of east London, hosts a lively and well-thought-out program of free family events. These include kids' arts-and-crafts workshops for different age groups, often tied in with one of the temporary exhibitions: Saturday Specials (first weekend of the month), with crafts (ages 6–15), quizzes (all ages), and more; and Summer Sunday Fun Days, with workshops, story-telling, live music, and food on a theme (from Victorian to Caribbean), plus tours of the restored almshouse (a former home for the poor and/or elderly) and picnicking. The lovely walled herb garden and period gardens are open in the warmer months, and there's an attractive restaurant, stroller access, and baby-changing facilities.

Kingsland Rd., E2. ℰ 020/7739-9893. www.geffrye-museum.org.uk. Free admission. Tues–Sat 10am–5pm; Sun and bank holiday Mon noon–5pm. Tube: Old St. (then a 15-min. walk).

**Hackney Museum** ☆ *Finds*  **All ages.** This museum, set up to preserve the history of east London and the waves of immigrants who have come to make up its population from Saxon times on, is worth traveling out of the center for its child-oriented interactive displays—kids can load a Saxon boat, dress in historical garb, make Victorian matchboxes against the clock, map their family history, and eavesdrop on the memories of local people hailing from all over the globe. Temporary exhibits touch on themes as diverse as slave trade abolition and local schooling.

The first Saturday of each month plus all school vacations see special family events, which are free, suitable for all ages, and (usually) run on a drop-in basis; each is coordinated with an aspect of the collection, a temporary exhibition, or a national event—for example, African drumming, crafts, and storytelling.

Hackney Technology Learning Centre, 1 Reading Lane, E8. ℰ 020/8356-3500. www.hackney.gov.uk. Free admission. Tues–Wed and Fri 9:30am–5:30pm; Thurs 9:30am–8pm; Sat 10am–5pm. Train: Hackney Central.

**Imperial War Museum London** ☆☆  **Ages 4 and up.** This museum of modern war—fittingly situated in the former Bethlehem Royal Hospital for the insane—isn't as bloodthirsty as you might expect. Amid the wide range of weapons and equipment on display, you'll find a huge clock hand informing visitors that the cost of warfare currently stands at more than 100 million lives. **The Trench** and **The Blitz** are vivid re-creations of life during wartime from two different perspectives, while the extraordinarily humbling **Holocaust** exhibition includes the letters of an 8-year-old French Jewish boy who hid in an orphanage before being sent to Auschwitz. Sadly, the **Children's War** exhibition, a look at life in wartime Britain through the eyes of kids, is scheduled to end March 2008 after a 3-year stint—get there if you still can.

Otherwise, be sure to check out the Battle of Britain Spitfire, a German one-man submarine, and a rifle carried by Lawrence of Arabia. James Bond buffs will love the **Secret War** exhibition exploring the worlds of espionage and clandestine warfare. Family events include drop-in art activities linked with temporary exhibitions, object-handling sessions revealing the people and stories behind the collections, and performances of wartime magic. The cafe has kids' lunchboxes and highchairs, strollers are easily maneuvered throughout most of the museum, and baby-changing facilities are available.

Lambeth Rd., SE1. ℭ 020/7416-5320. www.iwm.org.uk. Free admission except special exhibitions. Daily 10am–6pm. Tube: Lambeth N. or Elephant & Castle.

**Jewish Museum** ☆ **Ages 4 and up.** Split over two sites, the largest of them in Camden, this museum offers a vivid account of Jewish life in Britain from the Normans' arrival to the present. The centerpiece at the main site is the ceremonial art collection, which includes an astonishing 16th-century Venetian ark; arm yourself with "Doing Wonders" (£2.50/$5), written by and for children ages 6 to 12, which uses this gallery to investigate the symbols and customs of the Jewish year though facts, quizzes, and activities for both the gallery and at home. Monthly creative activities, from festival-based family workshops, puppet shows, and storytelling afternoons to craft sessions exploring Jewish life, such as mask-making for Purim, last anything from 90 minutes to whole days.

Much care is taken to involve younger visitors, with special kids' events accompanying special exhibitions and major Jewish festivals. They include calligraphy workshops and Please Do Touch! interactive family gallery tours (in Aug). But whenever you visit, the friendly volunteers are happy to answer any questions. At the front desk, ask to look at the family file of free gallery-based activities for kids 4 to 14, including animal hunts in the Ceremonial Art Gallery and a time trail of historical objects. Some of these activities even garner prizes. There's also a free children's activity for every temporary exhibition, and a "Jewish History in Britain Pack" (£2/$4) aimed at encouraging children ages 8 to 12 to discuss their own histories.

The museum's other branch in Finchley (ℭ 020/8349-1143) focuses on immigration and settlement in London, and the Holocaust. Hands-on displays such as a tailor's and a cabinet-maker's workshops allow kids to test the weight of a flat iron and find out how a suit is made. More poignant is a display of items brought by children on the Kindertransport—the rescue of 10,000 unaccompanied children before the outbreak of the World War II. This branch has a vegetarian cafe in the basement. Note that you can get joint tickets to visit both sites within 1 calendar month.

Raymond Burton House, 129–31 Albert St., NW1. ℭ 020/7284-1997. www.jewishmuseum.org.uk. Admission £3.50 ($7) adults, £2.50 ($5) seniors, £1.50 ($3) students and children 5–15, £8 ($16) family ticket. Mon–Thurs 10am–4pm; Sun 10am–5pm. Tube: Camden Town.

**Livesey Museum for Children** ☆ **Ages 2 to 12.** This stimulating, fully interactive, and free museum for younger kids hosts temporary annual exhibitions created with the help of local children, artists, and craftspeople. Past shows, all of which were aimed at children up to 12, have focused on numbers, and on maps—features have included a game room with giant dice and dominoes, and oversize board games and clocks. The emphasis is on encouraging creativity and imagination through investigating displays and objects, many of them historical items from the local museums. There's no cafe, but you will find a pleasant space for picnics in the courtyard, where you can also help to construct the "recycled greenhouse" out of old plastic bottles. There's also no elevator to the second floor, although there are plans to improve access.

682 Old Kent Rd., SE15. ℭ 020/7635-5829. www.liveseymuseum.org.uk. Free admission. Tues–Sat 10am–5pm. Tube: Elephant & Castle, then bus no. 53, 453, or 172.

**London Dungeon    Ages 7 and up.** With its genuinely chilling tableaux reproducing medieval conditions, to a soundtrack of tolling bells, this "indoor theme park of historical horror" is not for very young kids or the fainthearted (children over 3 are admitted at their guardian's discretion but it's really not suitable for under-8s). The dreadful experiences you witness include life under the bubonic plague (with real—though thankfully caged—rats); the Great Fire of London; a burning at the stake; fingernail extraction in the torture chamber; and a journey through the streets of London in the footsteps of Jack the Ripper. The £1-million ($2-million) "Boat Ride to Hell" is designed to play on many basic fears at once—of drowning, of the dark, and of death, while the "Labyrinth for the Lost" is a spooky, smoky, mirror-filled maze based on the catacombs of the church of All Hallow's by the Tower of London (p. 153). Surely most tasteless of all is the new "Extremis: Drop Ride to Hell," a ride that basically simulates a hanging (yours!) by plunging you down into darkness. The theme is taken to its logical extreme with gory gifts in the Shop of Horrors and refreshments at the Blood & Guts cafe. Note that you can get more expensive fast track tickets to circumvent the queues, or, if you're looking to save money, cheaper tickets early or late in the day. Websites such as www.lastminute.com also offer big savings.

28–34 Tooley St., SE1. ℂ 020/7403-7221. www.thedungeons.com. Admission £18 ($36) adults, £15 ($30) students and seniors, £14 ($28) children 5–15. Daily 10:30am–5pm, with some seasonal variations (see website). Tube: London Bridge.

**London Fire Brigade Museum    Ages 4 and up.** The colorful history of firefighting, from the Great Fire of London in 1666 through the Blitz to today, is recounted here via old firefighting appliances and other equipment, uniforms, and assorted memorabilia. It has one open day a year (in May), when you can meet real firefighters and experience life in a fully operational fire station, or year-round for 2-hour guided tours by prior arrangement—the latter are specially tailored to visitors' requirements. If they're lucky, your kids will glimpse recruits training next door. Ad hoc activities during the tour include drawing, coloring, and trying on uniforms. The shop sells fire-engine jigsaws, model engines, and other paraphernalia to satisfy budding firepersons.

Winchester House, 94a Southwark Bridge Rd., SE1. ℂ 020/7587-2894. www.london-fire.gov.uk. Admission £3 ($6) adults; £2 ($4) seniors, students, and children 7–14; £1 ($2) kids under 7. Pre-booked tours 10:30am and 2pm Mon–Fri. Tube: Borough.

**Madame Tussaud's & The Stardome** ⚔ **Ages 3 and up.** In an age obsessed with celebrity, it's perhaps inevitable that this world-famous attraction, set up on nearby Baker Street in 1835 and in its current location since 1884, has retained its popularity. No one can accuse it of not striving to keep up with the times—new attractions include Kate Moss, with whom you can pose for a photo shoot, and the *Black Pearl* from *Pirates of the Caribbean,* which you can clamber aboard to help Johnny Depp, Orlando Bloom, and Keira Knightley search for the Dead Man's Chest. It doesn't seem to matter to kids that it's all so cheesy and vacuous, or that the waxworks don't even resemble the celebs they're modeled on—perhaps that just enhances the experience.

The wax museum is perhaps best-known for its long-standing **Chamber of Horrors,** with re-creations of infamous murder scenes; within it you'll find **Chamber–Live!,** which features actors posing as serial killers (under-12s aren't admitted). But it's not all about cozying up to celebs, infamous or otherwise—interactive exhibits let you in on the action, dancing, singing, and collecting an award in the **Music Zone,** for instance. If you're insistent on gleaning something vaguely cultural from your visit, head for **Spirit of London,** a "time taxi" ride through 400 years of the city's history, from Shakespeare to the swinging '60s. Meanwhile, what was the London Planetarium ceded its place, in 2006, to the more celebrity-oriented **Stardome,** a 360-degree show by the Oscar-winning creators of *Wallace & Gromit*—it's still about space, but the fact-heavy presentation of yore has been replaced by a quirky take on fame through the eyes of curious aliens.

The ticket-pricing system here is complex—if you just show up and buy on the day, the fee charged depends on the date and time. Prices quoted below are the online ones that are generally in force 9am to 5pm, and do not include "Chamber–Live!" (for which, add £2/$4); you pay less if you go in the hour before closing. You can sometimes get reduced-price tickets by booking online, and you can also buy family tickets when paying in advance, plus fast track tickets that allow you to bypass the off-putting queues. Note too that joint tickets with the British Airways London Eye (p. 142) are available, saving you a few pounds.

Strollers aren't permitted (except for children with disabilities; visitors with disabilities also get in free, and have a staff escort), but there's a safe place to leave them, and carriers for babies up to 9 months are available for a small refundable deposit. A cafe and baby-changing facilities are also on site.

Marylebone Rd., NW1. ℭ **0870/999-0293.** www.madame-tussauds.co.uk. Admission £18 ($36) adults, £14 ($28) children 5–16, £54 ($108) family. Mon–Fri outside school vacations 9:30am–5pm; Sat–Sun and school vacations 9am–6pm. Tube: Baker St.

## Museum in Docklands ✶✶✶ All ages.
This museum explores 2,000 years of London's history as a river port, from Roman settlement to the modern-day regeneration of this Docklands area. It's a surprise family winner, largely because of its fabulous **Mudlarks** children's gallery, where under-12s can hoist and weigh cargoes in the Dockwork Zone, get a diver's-eye view of undersea work in the Water Zone, search for archaeological finds in the Foreshore Discovery Box, and construct scale versions of Canary Wharf buildings in the Building Zone. It also features a softplay area for tots. But be sure to make time for the rest of the building: Its **12 main galleries** have all manner of hands-on exhibits and touch screens to engage kids' interest. Particularly popular are a 1:50 scale model of the original London Bridge, the first stone structure over the Thames; and Sailortown, a re-creation of riverside streets and gas-lit alleyways, complete with the sounds of tigers and cockatoos from a wild animal emporium. Free gallery activity backpacks for 4- to 11-year-olds are available. A new gallery, **London, Sugar and Slavery,** was due to open at the time of writing, bearing witness to London's role in the transatlantic slave trade. It forms part of the bicentennial celebration of Britain's abolition of the slave trade, and related events on the theme will continue throughout 2008.

There's a remarkably diverse program of multicultural family events year-round, including drama (actors dressed as, for instance, humble dockworkers telling you their stories), Family Mystery workshops, Bollywood dance workshops, Indian storytelling and games, Diwali celebrations, and African and Caribbean dance performances and classes. Look out for Dock Life Family Days, with family portraits, drama, storytelling, and more. The museum has a cafe selling kids' lunchboxes, plus a Modern British restaurant with 10% off lunches on presentation of a museum ticket. The good lobby shop sells pirate hats, play sets, model boats, and more nautically inspired gifts and souvenirs. The galleries are accessible by stroller, and there's a baby-changing facility.

No. 1 Warehouse, W. India Quay, E14. ℂ 0870/444-3850. www.museumindocklands.org.uk. Admission £5 ($10) adults, £3 ($6) seniors and students, free for under-16s. Daily 10am–6pm (to 9pm 1st Thurs of month). Tube: Canary Wharf.

## Museum of London ⟨⟨⟨   Ages 5 and up.

This museum, which traces the compelling 250,000-year history of London since prehistoric times—in an appropriate setting overlooking the city's Roman and medieval walls—has recently begun yet another wave of expansion that is set to increase its gallery space by 25%. Until summer 2009, visitors will be unable to access the Lower Galleries while this Capital City Project is installed. New galleries will focus on London's modern history from the Great Fire to today, and a learning center will enable visitors of all ages and backgrounds to find out about their history, heritage, and community. Still accessible, however, are the London Before London, Roman London, and Medieval London galleries, and there is a special display, London's Burning (until winter 2009), on the Great Fire and related topics, with lots of interactive exhibits to bring the terrible event to life. In the Roman gallery, don't miss the "Princess of the City," the skeleton of a privileged young Roman woman found in nearby Spitalfields in 1999, with a clay facial portrait by a medical artist and her sarcophagus; in the Medieval gallery you learn that medieval London was founded twice, in different places, and that the Black Death of 1348–49 killed half its population (you can even see the excavations of a Black Death cemetery).

The year-round free activities program (Sun and school vacations) also continues apace in spite of the expansion work; family specials run the gamut, from singing or meditation workshops, candle-design sessions to explorations of firefighting, Indian cooking or puppetry, or storytelling by the likes of Roman queen Boudicca. Special events let you try out the working replica of a Roman waterlifting machine and find out what it was like to be a Roman slave. If there's nothing specific on when you visit, pick up an activity sheet, audioguide, or family activity bag. There's a cafe providing hot and cold food, family picnic areas at weekends and school vacations, a shop focusing on London, and baby-changing facility, and all galleries are stroller accessible.

London Wall, EC2. ℂ 0870/444-3852. www.museumoflondon.org.uk. Free admission. Mon–Sat 10am–5:50pm; Sun noon–5:50pm. Tube: St. Paul's or Barbican.

## Musical Museum   Ages 7 and up.

This quirky little museum, in which you can hear the workings of various automatic instruments dating from the days before electronics and microphones, was about to reopen as this guide went to press, in a new building with full stroller access. These include clockwork musical boxes; a Steinway DuoArt grand piano, reproducing the performance of pianists such as Gershwin; and a Clarabella Orchestrion, which contains all the instruments of a small dance band. There's also a new mock-up street scene with shop windows full of music, musical toys, and street instruments; and a changing program of temporary exhibitions on instruments, music in general, or local interest is lined up. The powerful Wurlitzer cinema organ, designed to accompany silent films, now takes center stage in the upstairs concert hall, where it rises up from the floor just as it did in its glory days in the 1930s.Combine a visit with a trip to the Kew Bridge Steam Museum (p. 162) just up the road.

399 High St., Brentford, Middlesex, TW8. ℂ 020/8560-8108. www.musicalmuseum.co.uk. Admission £7 ($14) adults, £5.50 ($11) seniors and students, free for children under 16. Tues–Sun 2–5pm. Tube: Gunnersbury, then 10-min. walk.

**National Army Museum** 🌟 **All ages.** The British Army's own museum, tracing history from the Battle of Agincourt in 1415 to present-day peacekeeping activities, has climbed several notches in the family-friendliness stakes since the first edition of this guide, with the introduction of its free **Kids' Zone,** an interactive play and learning space for under-10s, with a variety of areas—forest, castle, construction, reading, art, board games, and softplay for babies. The prize possession of the collections is Marengo, the skeleton of one of Napoleon's favorite horses, but older kids should also be interested by the amputation saw, the reconstructions of a World War I trench and dugout, and the modern-day Phoenix pilot-less aircraft. Hands-on fun includes trying on a Civil War helmet, assessing the weight of a contemporary cannonball, and measuring military skills through computer challenges.

Activity packs linked to the changing temporary exhibitions and suitable for older children are available in the shop (£12/$24), where you can also buy dress-up clothes and more. You can also get free activity backpacks at reception relating to the galleries as a whole, plus self-guided short tours (of an hour at most) with a particular focus, including Animals, which tell of the animals who have worked side by side with soldiers in the British Army through the centuries, from pigeons to camels and elephants. There's stroller access and a cafe, The Great Escape, with kids' meals.

Royal Hospital Rd., SW3. ℂ 020/7730-0717. www.national-army-museum.ac.uk. Free admission. Daily 10am–5:30pm. Tube: Sloane Sq., then 10-min. walk.

**The Old Operating Theatre, Museum & Herb Garret** 🌟🌟 **Ages 7 and up.** Spellbinding but little-visited, this museum is housed in the country's oldest surviving operating theater, dating to 1822—a time before anesthetics and antiseptic surgery. Long abandoned, the theater has been restored and filled with displays of old instruments (including biting gags and gigantic forceps), formaldehyde-preserved specimens, and original furniture, including a 19th-century operating table at the end of which lies a box of sawdust that was used to soak up blood. The stalls surrounding the table used to be occupied by medical students; these days they are used by those who come to watch the reconstructions of Victorian surgery (normally free on top of the ticket price), involving real amputation kits. Back then, amputations were undertaken for such minor complaints as ingrown toenails. These are part of an interesting program of gory-minded talk and events; most should be fine for older kids, but ask staff if you're not sure. A surefire alternative are the school-vacation events specially designed for visitors ages 5 to 12, including a hands-on session with the "mucky (and often yucky)" medicines of the past, including snail water, and one with old and new medical instruments, including cups and stethoscopes.

*Note:* The museum is located in the roof space of an old church and can only be accessed via a rickety spiral staircase.

9a St. Thomas St., SE1. ℂ 020/7188-2679. www.thegarret.org.uk. Admission £5.25 ($11) adults, £4.25 ($8.50) seniors and students, £3 ($6) children 5–15, £13 ($26) family (2 adults and up to 4 children from same family). Daily 10:30am–5pm. Tube: London Bridge.

**Ragged School Museum** **Ages 7 and up.** This unique little museum traces the history of London's East End, including the Copperfield Road "Ragged School," which was London's largest charity school for orphans and poverty-stricken children. In a re-created classroom, kids can learn how their Victorian counterparts were taught and can take part in workshops, treasure hunts, and canal walks designed for a variety of age groups. There are also displays on local history, industry, and culture, featuring objects as diverse as a Jewish printer's chests and a Bangladeshi flute.

46–50 Copperfield Rd., E3. ⓒ 020/8980-6405. www.raggedschoolmuseum.org.uk. Free admission. Wed–Thurs 10am–5pm; 1st Sun of month 2–5pm. Tube: Mile End, then 10-min walk.

**Royal Gunpowder Mills** 🏵🏵 **Ages 5 and up.** Kids have a blast (pardon the pun) at this attraction in Epping Forest, which illustrates the evolution of explosives and of the 17th-century Royal Gunpowder Mills. The main exhibitions, both traditional and interactive, include trying on powder-boat and mill-worker costumes; temporary displays cover a range of topics, from rockets to world wars. Outside the historic buildings are a network of canals that transported explosives around the vast site; surprisingly, you'll also see an array of wildlife here. (The mills were cut off from their surroundings by their river boundaries and the secrecy of the work, so nature took over.) You might see herons, bats, and otters from the boardwalks, bridges, and footpaths, or from the viewing tower at the woodland's edge, where there's also an animal mural. There's often a 40-minute Land Train tour (£1.50/$3 adults, £1/$2 kids 5–15) into the wildlife preserve on the north side, where you'll see Newton's Pool, 12m (39 ft.) deep and used for the testing of underwater explosives.

Wear comfy shoes, as a lot of walking is involved. On Wednesdays in summer vacations a range of free children's activities are laid on—the likes of mask-making, clay-modeling, archaeological digs, air-powered rocket-making and -firing, and orienteering. Ask, too, about free special events such as jousting tournaments, aeronautical displays, Victorian Family Days and the Guy Fawkes Experience. There's a cafe on-site, a gift shop, and a historical bookshop.

Beaulieu Dr., Waltham Abbey, Essex, EN9. ⓒ 01992/707370. www.royalgunpowdermills.com. Admission £6 ($12) adults, £5 ($10) seniors and students, £3.50 ($7) children 5–16, £19 ($38) family (2 adults and up to 3 children). May to early Oct Sat–Sun, bank-holiday Mon, and Wed during summer vacation 11am–5pm (last admission 3:30pm). Train: Waltham Cross, then 25-min. walk or short bus ride.

**Royal London Hospital Museum** **Ages 7 and up.** The star attraction at this museum in a former church crypt is Joseph Merrick—or rather a replica of a hat and veil worn by the "Elephant Man," as well as documents relating to his residence at the Royal London, once the city's largest general hospital. Visitors can also see a BBC video on Merrick. But other displays have their fascinations, particularly the 19th-century section, which looks at surgery before antiseptics; Florence Nightingale and nursing; and forensic medicine, sponsored by crime writer Patricia Cornwell and including material on Jack the Ripper and his fellow murderers Dr. Crippen and John Christie. Twentieth-century displays include X-rays, blood transfusions, and a carbon arc lamp used to give UV light treatment to King George V in 1928. If you're making a special trip, call ahead; hours can vary at short notice.

St. Augustine with St. Philip's Church, Newark St., E1. ⓒ 020/7377-7608. www.brlcf.org.uk. Free admission. Mon–Fri 10am–4:30pm. Tube: Whitechapel.

**Royal Observatory** 🏵 **Ages 4 and up.** This World Heritage Site is the original home of Greenwich Mean Time—which makes it, by international decree, the official starting point for every new day, year, and millennium. Here, you can stand in both the Eastern and Western hemispheres simultaneously, by placing your feet on either side of the prime meridian, the center of world time and space. New here in 2006 (and already award-winning) were the Time galleries, exploring the themes of Time and Longitude, Time and Greenwich, Time for the Navy, and Time and Society; these were the first stage of the vast Time and Space Project, which culminated in May 2007 in the opening of a new, state-of-the-art planetarium hosting live tours of the night sky (for ages 7 and over), a new astronomy gallery, and a horology workshop hosting sessions for the public. As before, the observatory is also home to London's only public camera obscura, which projects a live image of the city onto a viewing table. Child-friendly events (generally suitable for ages 6 and up) include performances recounting the story of the search for longitude, and sunspot-spotting. Stroller access is available.

Greenwich Park, SE10. ℂ 020/83120-6565. www.rog.nmm.ac.uk. Free admission; planetarium £6 ($12), £4 ($8) seniors, students, and children. Daily 10am–7pm; planetarium show times vary. Tube: Greenwich DLR.

**Shakespeare's Globe** ℛ **Ages 8 and up.** This faithful re-creation of Shakespeare's open-air playhouse stands close to the original site where many of his works had their debut. Inside, an exhibition features costumes, props, and models of the special effects used in the Bard's time (including how they made Ariel fly and what was used for blood and gore); sword-fighting demonstrations; and technology that allows you to add your voices to scenes played by Globe actors. Admission includes a theater tour, which runs every 15 to 30 minutes during opening hours and is suitable for adults and kids alike; combined, they will take you about 90 minutes.

Summer brings staged **performances** of plays by Shakespeare and his contemporaries, as well as modern authors. Audiences either stand or sit on hard seating as in Elizabethan times, and heckling is encouraged, so performances aren't suitable for younger kids. On certain Saturdays, those 8 to 11 can attend Childsplay workshops—while you watch the play, they enjoy drama, storytelling, and art activities, plus a 20-minute trip into the theater to see part of the production. Booking for these is essential; tickets cost £10 ($20). There is also the annual Sam's Day (early June), celebrating the birthday of Globe founder Sam Wanamaker, with free workshops, demonstrations, and platform discussions.

Note that during performances, guided tours are diverted to the nearby excavated **Rose Theater,** the first on Bankside, where Christopher Marlowe and Ben Johnson wrote their greatest plays and Shakespeare learned his trade.

The Globe has a cafe, a coffee shop, a new bar and brasserie, a shop, baby-changing facilities, and stroller access.

21 New Globe Walk, SE1. ℂ 020/7902-1400. www.shakespeares-globe.org. Admission £9 ($18) adults, £7.50 ($15) seniors and students, £6.50 ($13) children 5–15, £20 ($40) family ticket (up to 2 adults and 3 children). Oct 10–Apr 17 daily 10am–5pm; May–Sept Mon–Sat 9am–noon and 12:30–5pm, Sun 9–11:30am and noon–5pm. Tube: Mansion House or London Bridge.

**Sherlock Holmes Museum** *(Overrated* **Ages 7 and up.** Confused? You should be—Sir Arthur Conan Doyle's famous fictional sleuth is said to have lived at 221B Baker St.; this museum is at no. 239 but has a sign on the door saying 221B. Inside, the flat appears as if the detective actually existed, with his deerstalker cap, magnifying glass, and other "personal effects," including letters Holmes "wrote" to his assistant Dr. Watson. Still, if you're a fan, you'll probably be willing to swallow the charade and enjoy the waxwork tableaux of scenes from the books, as well as the re-created Victorian interiors. In the shop you can stock up on related items, from Sherlock teddy bears to Victorian top hats. Note that there's no stroller access to the museum.

In summer 2007, the museum relaunched its hansom cab rides through the London streets and royal parks, accompanied by actors dressed as Holmes and Watson; call ahead to book.

239 (221B) Baker St., NW1. ℰ **020/7935-8866**. www.sherlock-holmes.co.uk. Admission £6 ($12) adults, £4 ($8) children 5–16. Daily 9:30am–6pm. Tube: Baker St.

## Sir John Soane's Museum *✦* Ages 12 and up.

Although unsuited to younger kids, this delightful museum will appeal to older kids with artistic and/or ghoulish leanings, with its distorting mirrors, rooms within rooms, secret staircases, picture gallery filled with three times too many paintings for the space (achieved through the use of folding hidden panels); spooky crypt centered around the superbly preserved sarcophagus of Pharaoh Seti I; Gothic "monk's parlor" with a human skull; and mummified cats and fossils. Every nook and cranny of the labyrinthine building is filled with sculpture, plaster casts, or other objects amassed by Soane, an eminent 19th-century architect who lived here. *Insider tip:* Avoid Saturday mornings, when queues can be especially long. It's good to leave a donation, as the museum is restoring the neighboring house, with a dedicated Education Centre soon to open.

13 Lincoln's Inn Fields, WC2. ℰ **020/7440-4263**. www.soane.org. Free admission, except Tues candlelit evenings when £5 ($10). Tues–Sat 10am–5pm; 1st Tues of each month 6–9pm (candlelit opening). Tube: Holborn.

## Vestry House Museum    Ages 5 and up.

This local-history museum is continually striving to enhance its appeal to kids, who come mainly for its Toys and Games Gallery, full of playthings from the 19th and 20th centuries. (Replicas of some are available in the shop.) Young visitors might also like the Bremer Car, one of the oldest British-built petrol-driven cars, built in 1892; the re-constructed Victorian parlor; the Costume Gallery; and the original police cell with its bench and toilet (the building, originally a workhouse for the poor, once housed a police station). Visitors can see a tableau of a scene from 1861, and may even get locked in the cells themselves. Note that only the ground floor is stroller accessible. Surrounding the museum is the workhouse garden, with 18th-century plants, plus flower, herb, and object gardens.

Vestry Rd., E17. ℰ **020/8509-1917**. www.lbwf.gov.uk. Free admission. Mon–Fri 10am–1pm and 2–5:30pm; Sat 10am–1pm and 2–5pm. Tube: Walthamstow Central.

## Victoria and Albert Museum (V&A) *✦✦✦* Ages 3 and up.

The world's greatest decorative-arts museum is a great place to bring fashion-addict kids, to see its stunning Fashion & Jewellery galleries, full of items dating from the 17th century to today. Temporary exhibitions on the theme are strong—you've just missed one on the evolving image of pop showgirl Kylie Minogue, but until November 2008 you can catch "Fashion & Sport," with everything from a Chanel surfboard to Yohji Yamamoto/Adidas trainers. There are also textiles, art galore, furniture, product design, furniture, and musical instruments from around the word. At the time of this writing, following the sad closure of the V&A's **Theatre Museum** in Covent Garden, plans were in place for new permanent theater and performance displays here, plus a related program of exhibitions—including, in 2009, one on Diaghilev and the Ballets Russes sure to delight young ballet fans.

Most of the hands-on displays are in three "discovery areas" within the award-winning **British Galleries;** here children can try on a corset and crinoline, make a bookplate, construct a chair, guess a mystery object, design a picture frame (in the 18th-Century area), make a plaited cord, weave a tapestry, and try on an armor gauntlet (in the Tudor & Stuart Area). But there are lots of opportunities throughout these British Galleries to handle objects, draw, listen to stories, watch videos, and create designs on computers. The museum map has a hands-on symbol to guide you.

Ask at the **Free Art Fun desk** about family activities (usually drop-in). On Sunday and daily during some school holidays, these include an **Activity Cart** that helps kids 3 and up explore varying areas of the museum through getting creative with its objects: they might make a goblet, design a kimono, or create a Chinese tomb guardian's mask. Also in school vacations, and every Saturday, kids 5 to 12 can avail themselves of one of five **themed backpacks** (Emperor's Party, Chinese Treasures, Metal Detector, Magic Glass, and Fancy Furnishings; ID required), with jigsaws, stories, puzzles, construction games, and items to handle). Younger siblings are given a sheet to complement the backpack so kids of different ages can have fun together. Alternatively, there are **themed trails** for 7- to 12-year-olds, including a new "Picnic Party" whereby you plan an alfresco feast as you journey through the South Asia, Middle East, and East Asia galleries. There is also a program of drawing activities during the national **Big Draw** in October.

The museum has several interesting shops, with crafts, souvenirs, toys, gadgets, and more; two cafes (one summer-only) with half-price meals for kids under 10; and baby-changing facilities. All galleries are stroller accessible; there are steps here and there, but staff are always happy to help. Note however, that until late 2009 there's a rolling program of gallery closures as overall accessibility is improved.

Cromwell Rd., SW7. (✆) 0870/906-3883. www.vam.ac.uk. Free admission (charges for some exhibitions and events). Sat–Thurs 10am–5:45pm; Fri 10am–11pm. Tube: S. Kensington.

## Wallace Collection (★★)  Ages 5 and up.

Boasting the finest private collection of art ever assembled by one family, this national museum contains one of the world's best collections of French 18th-century pictures, porcelain, and furniture; a remarkable array of 17th-century paintings; and an armory that includes superb inlaid suits of armor and magnificent Persian scimitars. Kids can pop in to try on some armor, or to follow one of the free trails available at the information desk ("Warrior Kings" or "Looking for the Owners"). There are also children's audioguides (£1.50/$3). Special family events include The Little Draw drop-in art workshop on the first Sunday afternoon of every month; days of talks, crafts, hands-on sessions, and more during school vacations (at weekends). Among the activities you might enjoy together are clay modeling and self-portrait painting. All of these are now free.

The atmospheric glass-roofed Sculpture Garden is home to the new **Wallace Restaurant,** an all-day brasserie run by the same people as the National Dining Rooms; here, you can enjoy breakfasts (including boiled egg with toast soldiers), Parisian afternoon teas, cheese platters, and main meals. The children's menu (£7.50/$15) serves high-quality fare such as steamed lemon sole with fresh vegetables and organic beef burger with olive oil–crushed potatoes. Alternatively, picnic on the lawns fronting the elegant building. There is full stroller access, and baby-changing facilities are available.

Hertford House, Manchester Sq., W1. (✆) 020/7563-9500. www.wallacecollection.org. Free admission (charges for some exhibitions and events). Daily 10am–5pm. Tube: Bond St. or Baker St.

## Wimbledon Windmill Museum (Finds)  Ages 5 and up.

Set inside the oddly shaped but picturesque mill on Wimbledon Common, this museum about windmills contains machinery, tools, and working windmill models, including early Greek and Persian incarnations. It's a place where kids can really get involved, trying their hands at grinding wheat using a saddle stone, a pestle and mortar, or a hand mill, and even changing the cloth on the mill's sails. Push-button displays and commentaries abound;

some are about the mill after it was turned into living quarters for some local families in 1870. If you're steady on your feet, climb the ladder to the tower, where you can look up to the surviving machinery in the cap (on windy days it turns).

The shop sells the obligatory cut-out model windmills and windmills on sticks, as well as toy Womble figures and honey made by bees on the Common. There's an adjoining tearoom famous for its hearty breakfasts (apparently Mick Jagger has been known to drop by), or you can picnic on Wimbledon Common and Putney Heath, which have a stroller-friendly circular **Nature Trail** (a guidebook is available at the information center behind the mill).

Wimbledon Common (end of Windmill Rd), SW19. ℭ 020/8947-2825. www.wimbledonwindmillmuseum.org.uk. Admission £1 ($2) adults; 50p ($1) seniors, students, and children. Apr–Oct Sat 2–5pm; Sun and public holidays 11am–5pm. Tube: Wimbledon, then 10-min. walk.

**Winston Churchill's Britain at War Experience   Ages 7 and up.** There's plenty of hands-on fun at this museum of life under the London Blitz: Kids can huddle in a reconstructed London Underground air-raid shelter and hear sirens wail and bombers pass overhead; watch wartime news broadcasts in an underground cinema; and listen to messages from Churchill, Roosevelt, and others in a mock-up BBC radio studio. As well as all the interactive features, there are re-creations of a GI's club and a local street, and lots of static displays featuring real bombs, rare documents, and photos.

64–66 Tooley St., SE1. ℭ 020/7403-3171. Admission £9.95 ($20) adults, £5.75 ($12) seniors and students, £4.85 ($10) children 5–15, £25 ($50) family ticket (2 adults and 2 children). Apr–Sept daily 10am–6pm; Oct–Mar daily 10am–5pm. Tube: London Bridge.

## 4 Art Galleries

**Camden Arts Centre** ๙   This hip gallery of avant-garde art shows doesn't appear child-friendly at first sight, but closer inspection reveals an inventive program of school-vacation classes and short courses for various age groups, including infants. These include "Drawing & Making" (sculpture, painting, collage, and charcoal drawing), and creativity sessions with clay or mixed media. There are also occasional family film screenings (don't expect Disney), and special events such as Mayday Maypole, which celebrates the arrival of spring with maypole dancing, music, dressing-up, and a barbecue hosted by the very good cafe (which serves children's portions of its simple but good fare).

In terms of the displays themselves, the installation pieces often go down well with younger visitors, but be warned that some exhibitions contain risqué material. The lovely lobby bookshop has an outstanding children's section, and there's a garden with an ongoing project about sustainable city living.

Arkwright Rd., NW3. ℭ 020/7472-5500. www.camdenartscentre.org. Free admission. Tues and Thurs–Sun 10am–6pm; Wed 10am–9pm. Tube: Finchley Rd.

**Dalí Universe   Ages 7 and up.** This riverside attraction by the British Airways London Eye finds itself constrained to put up warning signs for parents, since much of the Spanish surrealist's work is erotic in nature. Steer clear of the nudes and bestiality, though, and much of Salvador Dalí's work—his lobster phones, spider-legged elephants, melting clocks, and lip-shaped sofas, for instance—is great fun for kids. For older ones, invest in a children's audioguide (£2.50/$5), with an interactive quiz to get them asking questions about the artwork.

County Hall Gallery, Riverside Building, SE1. ℭ 0870/744-7485. www.daliuniverse.com. Admission £12 ($24) adults, £10 ($20) seniors and students, £8 ($16) children 8–16, £5 ($10) children 4–7, £30 ($60) family ticket for 2 adults and 2 children. Daily 10am–6:30pm. Tube: Waterloo.

**Dulwich Picture Gallery** *(★★★ (Finds)* This little-visited gem in deepest south London boasts one of the world's most important collections of European old masters from the 17th and 18th centuries, including works by Rembrandt, Rubens, and Canaletto. Given the weightiness of its subject matter, this is a surprisingly fun place for kids, especially in summer vacations, with 6 weeks of drop-in creative workshops in the beautiful gallery gardens on Wednesdays (£2/$4 per child)—visitors are welcome to bring a picnic to enjoy on the lawns (there's also a cafe). Look out too for the summer Family Days (£2/$4 per person), with art workshops, donkey rides, Punch & Judy, storytelling, refreshments, the occasional special events where you can play croquet on the lawn, and outdoor film screenings (the likes of *Grease*).

The rest of the year, the first and last Sundays of the month see free drop-in artist-led creative workshops for kids 4-plus and their parents. On some weekends you can also hire rather nifty PDAs (£3/$6), a sort of palmtop computer that asks you questions and asks you to record your answers using the keyboard; its settings include a family fun trail, and you can even save what you do until your next visit. Drawing equipment can be borrowed at any time. If you're in the area for any duration, the museum runs evening art schools, after-school art club, holiday workshops for kids 6 and up, and summer courses for those 5-plus.

Gallery Rd., SE21. ℭ 020/8693-5254. www.dulwichpicturegallery.org.uk. Admission (permanent collection) £4 ($8) adults, £3 ($6) seniors, free for students and children. Tues–Fri 10am–5pm; Sat–Sun and bank holidays 11am–5pm. Train: W. Dulwich.

**The Hayward** **Ages 5 and up.** Part of the South Bank Centre arts complex (p. 246), The Hayward hosts an eclectic mix of changing historical and contemporary shows, with the emphasis on the latter, and a strong international flavor to the programming. The big draw for kids is not the art, however, but **Waterloo Sunset,** an elliptical glass pavilion conceived as "a drop-in center for children and old people and a space for viewing cartoons." Open for social interaction, learning, and fun (and spectacular views), Waterloo Sunset has six touch-sensitive monitors playing cartoons, artists' videos, and new media commissions. Notice how, being made of two-way mirrored glass, the pavilion is both transparent and reflective, changing as the light changes to create new optical perspectives. Kids also love checking out the landmark Neon Tower at the top of the building's elevator, with colored strips activated by changes in the strength and direction of the wind; at the time of writing, it was closed for refurbishment.

Belvedere Rd., SE1. ℭ 0871/663-2501. www.southbankcentre.co.uk. Admission varies. Sun–Thurs 10am–6pm; Fri–Sat 10am–10pm. Tube: Waterloo.

**National Gallery** *(★* **Ages 2 and up.** This majestic institution covers every great European school from the late 13th to the early 20th century, including 18th-century British masterpieces by Hogarth, Gainsborough, Reynolds, Constable, and Turner, and lots of French Impressionist and post-Impressionist works by Manet, Monet, Degas, Renoir, and Cézanne. It's strong on family events, from storytelling for under-5s to 2-day practical workshops for aspiring artists ages 15 to 17. Along the way, there are school-vacation workshops for ages 5 to 11, led by a contemporary artist; Family Drawing Events for kids of the same age the second weekend of every month; and Get

Into Art! workshops for ages 12 to 17. They're all free and non-bookable, but spaces are limited, so get here early. Look out too for the weekend family talks for those with kids 5 to 11, exploring some of the themes encountered in the Gallery's paintings.

Also here is the excellent new **National Dining Rooms & Bakery** (p. 116) and the basement Expresso Bar, which doubles up as a **multimedia room,** with 14 touch-screen ArtStart terminals providing information about the whole collection. Free family trails are also available from the information desks.

Trafalgar Sq., WC2. ✆ 020/7747-2885. www.nationalgallery.org.uk. Free admission. Thurs–Tues 10am–6pm; Wed 10am–9pm. Tube: Charing Cross.

**National Portrait Gallery    Ages 3 and up.** Next door to the National Gallery, this museum is a bit like an upmarket Madame Tussaud's, in that you come to see famous faces—in this case, portraits (including photographs) of those deemed significant to British national life over the centuries. Historical figures include Sir Walter Raleigh, Henry VIII, Shakespeare, Virginia Woolf, and Princess Di; among contemporary luminaries are the Queen (with a record 50 portraits), David Beckham, Samantha Morton, and fashion designer Alexander McQueen. The artists involved range from total unknowns to luminaries as diverse as Hans Holbein and Andy Warhol.

Rucksacks for ages 4 and up, available from the information desk, contain jigsaw puzzles, games, and activities that will help your children get a handle on the collections. Free weekend family events (some of which require a ticket, available on the day from the information desk), start with monthly drop-in storytelling sessions for kids 3 and up, called "Are You Sitting Comfortably?" For those 5 and up there's "Small Faces," an exploration of portraits followed by an artistic activity—for instance, making puppets based on Tudor paintings, clay portrait sculpting, postcard-making using digital cameras, traveling-theater making, or creating hats based on your favorite London building. In school vacations, ask about creative sessions for ages 5 and up, on themes such as London life, or travel and adventure.

*Insider tip:* The shop is a great stopping-off place for postcards. There's a cafe and restaurant, stroller-access, and a baby-changing facility.

St. Martin's Place, WC2. ✆ 020/7312-2463. www.npg.org.uk. Free admission (except special exhibitions). Sat–Wed 10am–6pm; Thurs–Fri 10am–9pm. Tube: Leicester Sq.

**Pump House Gallery** ⊛   This exciting contemporary gallery in a lovely lakeside setting in Battersea Park runs exhibitions embracing film, photography, sculpture, painting, and sound, all of them exploring big themes such as free speech and subversion. It all sounds a bit heavy for kids, but there are exciting family workshops during which artists help parents and kids 3 and up develop creative ideas inspired by works in the current exhibitions—you might make a folk costume and dress up in it, design a banner, or learn folk dancing. Events are free but you need to book ahead. Watch out for occasional special daylong events, too.

Battersea Park, SW11. ✆ 020/7350-0523. www.wandsworth.gov.uk. Free admission. Wed–Thurs, Sun, and bank-holiday Mon 11am–5pm; Fri–Sat 11am–4pm. Train: Battersea Park.

**Royal Academy of Arts    Ages 5 and up.** This venerable establishment made itself unpopular a few years back when it expelled the young son of prominent kids' travel journalist Dea Birkett for making too much noise. Much good has come out of the incident, as Birkett set up the Kids in Museums Campaign with an annual award for Britain's most family-friendly museum, encouraging institutions to take into account parents' and children's needs.

The Royal Academy, which apologized for the incident and insisted that it does "actively encourage" families to attend, holds a permanent collection built up from members' donated works and hosts popular temporary exhibitions, including a famous annual Summer Exhibition of works by its members. Its two concessions to families are free workshops (pre-booking essential), which tie in with the changing exhibition, comprising introductory slide talks, exhibition visits, and hands-on sessions; and a free worksheet for young visitors, *The Art Detective's Guide,* available at reception; this also changes according to the exhibition but usually features picture trails, fascinating facts, poem writing, and drawing. If you hand it in at the end of your visit (or post it), you stand the chance of making it onto the Royal Academy's website.

Burlington House, Piccadilly, W1. ⓒ 020/7300-8000. www.royalacademy.org.uk. Admission varies according to exhibition but averages £8 ($16) for adults and £2–£3 ($4–$6) for children 8–16, free for children under 7. Sat–Thurs 10am–6pm; Fri 10am–10pm. Tube: Green Park.

**Saatchi Gallery**   **Ages 6 and up.** As we went to press, this infamous modern gallery—the bastion of the controversial Brit art movement in the 1990s, and the home of Damien Hirst's pickled shark—was in the middle of yet another move, this time to Chelsea. Since November 2007 it has occupied the entirety of the impressive former Duke of York's headquarters, which gives it the space for a bookshop, educational facilities, and a cafe/bar. Despite its popularity, the gallery still sees itself as a spring-board to launching the career of young artists, so work tends to be provocative and suitable only for older kids. That said, it's possible to come to enjoy the galleries with younger kids (ages 6–14), whom you can deposit at a free art workshop relating to one of the temporary exhibitions (no booking required). There's also a free children's art trail with a quiz that might win you some art posters.

King's Rd., SW1. ⓒ 020/7823-2363. www.saatchi-gallery.co.uk. Admission £9 ($18) adults, £6.75 ($14) children 5–15, £25 ($50) family ticket. Sun–Thurs 10am–8pm; Fri–Sat 10am–10pm. Tube: Sloane Sq.

**Somerset House**  🅐🅐🅐  **All ages.** This wonderful place is most popular among kids for its glorious Fountain Court, which has water jets through which they love to run in hot weather; for its glittering ice rink at Christmas (p. 214); and for its annual Free Time family festival, which takes over the courtyard for 4 days each July, hosting all manner of colorful workshops and performances (as well as special treasure trails in the galleries). But the family program is full the rest of the year, too: Every Saturday and bank holiday see free family workshops (ages 6–12; tickets available on first-come, first-served basis from Seamen's Hall) that might include dreaming up a fantasy city and making architectural drawings of it, classes in quill and ink drawing, diorama making, and creating artworks inspired by the Thames (which runs alongside). There are all special art days for teens, and free school-vacation drop-in sessions.

Inside Somerset House are a trio of excellent galleries: the **Courtauld Institute of Art,** focusing on Impressionist and post-Impressionist paintings, including master-pieces by Monet, Manet, van Gogh, and Matisse; the **Gilbert Collection,** with a world-class collection of decorative arts, including snuffboxes and mosaics; and the **Hermitage Rooms,** which contain rotating exhibitions of Czarist treasures from St. Petersburg's State Hermitage Museum. There's a lovely river terrace where you can bring sandwiches and cakes from one of the cafes or the deli, a plush restaurant, and in summer a courtyard bar selling cold drinks, snacks, and ice creams.

The Strand, WC2. ⓒ 020/7845-4600. www.somersethouse.org.uk. Admission to each collection £5 ($10) adults, £4 ($8) seniors, free for students and under-18s; joint tickets and 3-day passes available. Daily 10am–6pm (courtyard 7:30am–11pm). Tube: Embankment.

**Tate Britain** 𝕬𝕬    **All ages.** Showcasing Britain's national art dating from the 16th century to the present, the Tate Britain embraces everything from old masters and pre-Raphaelites to contemporary artists of the stature of Lucian Freud, Rachel Whiteread, and Jake and Dinos Chapman, either in regularly evolving permanent galleries or temporary exhibitions. Mid-2007 saw the inauguration of a groundbreaking Turner exhibition that will continue until 2012, showing how the artist revolutionized both watercolors and print—visitors can use interactive displays to explore these methods and techniques, experience the scientific experiments with color that informed his work, and try out some of his drawing techniques for themselves, with the actual works displayed changing every 6 months.

The Tate Britain has its own Youth Forum of local people ages 14 to 25, who regularly meet to discuss how to make the Tate Britain appealing to younger visitors, and to plan events, which include graffiti master classes and fashion shows, and talks by the likes of musician Jarvis Cocker. For **families** these include weekend and school-vacation activities, both drop-in and book-ahead. A perennial favorite is the Art Trolley (all ages), with activities and materials to take into the galleries, and the possibility of having your work photographed and displayed on the new Families website, from which you can send e-postcards to your friends. Occasional family workshops (£6/$12) are designed for varying age groups (some for under-5s); themes might include food or family portraits. If you can't make it to one of these, ask for a free Spot the Circle Discovery Trail (said to be for ages 5 and over, but I've had fun with it with younger kids), which invites you to find circles not only in paintings and sculptures but also the gallery's doors, walls, floors, ceilings, and cafe (there is also a restaurant, plus stroller-access and a baby-care room).

*Insider tip:* The **Tate Boat** (£4.30/$8.60 adults, £1.45/$2.90 children 5–15, £11/$22 family) is a fun way of getting to the gallery's sister institution, the Tate Modern (18 min. away). It also stops at the British Airways London Eye (p. 142).

Millbank, SW1. ℂ 020/7887-8888. www.tate.org.uk. Free admission except special exhibitions. Daily 10am–5:50pm, plus 1st Fri of Mon 6–10pm. Tube: Pimlico.

**Tate Modern** 𝕬𝕬𝕬    **Ages 5 and up.** Britain's foremost collection of international modern art, displayed in an impressive former power station, is a superb venue for children. This is partly because it shows paintings thematically, rather than chronologically, so they can see how various themes and objects have been represented at different epochs and by different schools of art, from still lifes to sunsets. Of particular interest is its surrealist collection, one of the world's finest, full of playful curiosities that are always a hit with kids, from Man Ray's metronome to Calder's mobiles; Miró and Magritte paintings tend to go down well, too.

Two new features have been introduced to help you tackle the displays, both permanent and temporary. The first is the **Learning Zone,** which is full of hands-on games and multimedia interactives, a short film about the collection, video clips of artists working or discussing their work, and books. Then there's the **Multimedia Guide** (£1–2/$2–$4)—a hand-held computer with videos, still images, and commentaries to accompany you through the galleries. The children's version, for ages 5 and over, is colorful and fun, with music and games that direct you to some of the most family-friendly works on display and encourage you to, for example, dribble paint with Jackson Pollock or improve Matisse's snail.

As with the Tate Modern's sister, Tate Britain, both ticketed and drop-in family activities are available, plus stuff that you can do at any time you visit. Foremost among the latter is the new **Family Zone,** which is full of inspiration on ways to introduce kids 5 and up to modern art, with books, quizzes, and games. Here you can pick up a Tate Teaser activity pack to use both in the galleries and at home. Periodic workshops might involve music, giant board games, surrealist games (including "exquisite corpse"), surrealist dressing-up (think bowler hats and silly mustaches) and family portraits, and puppet-making.

The Tate Modern is stroller accessible, with a baby-care room on Level 1 and diaper-changing facilities on each floor. There's a Level 7 restaurant (also open for morning coffee and afternoon tea) with stunning views, the Expresso Bar (Level 4), which serves sandwiches and snacks, and, most family-friendly, Café 2 (p. 132). The shops are great for kids' books, art materials, and related goods.

Bankside, SE1. © 020/7887-8888. www.tate.org.uk. Free admission except special exhibitions. Sun–Thurs 10am–6pm; Fri–Sat 10am–10pm. Tube: Southwark.

## 5 Best Rides

It doesn't get any better than the British Airways London Eye (p. 142), but don't miss the **Docklands Light Railway (DLR),** a driverless overland train linking Greenwich and the Isle of Dogs with the Tube at Tower Hill and Bank stations (you can see routes on the Tube map on the back inside cover of this guide). Kids love to sit at the front and pretend to steer the train as it winds between buildings and climbs and descends like a genteel version of a roller coaster. See www.tfl.gov.uk for an interactive "Amazing Days Planner" using the DLR, including a "Kids Day Out" taking in the Museum in Docklands (p. 168), Greenwich Park and the Royal Observatory (p. 203 and p. 171), and Discover (p. 161). You can use any London Tube ticket or pass on the DLR providing it covers the correct zone (the DLR travels through Zones 1–3); alternatively, joint Rail and River Roamers allow you to combine the DLR with boat trips on the Thames, described in more detail in "River Rides" below.

But the river is not London's only waterway; you can also make very pleasant excursions on the **Regent's Canal** between Little Venice and Camden Town, sometimes stopping off at **London Zoo** (p. 190). For instance, **Jason's** (opposite 60 Blomfield Rd., W9; www.jasons.co.uk), has been giving rides on out-of-service narrow boats since 1951. Round-trips take about 90 minutes and cost £7.50 ($15) for adults, £5.50 ($11) for kids 4 to 14, or £22 ($44) for a family ticket for two adults and two kids. It also has a canal-side restaurant offering modern Mediterranean dishes and good brunches. Setting off from the other end of the route, *Jenny Wren* (Walker's Quay, 250 Camden High St., NW1; © 020/7485-4433; www.walkersquay.com) plies the waters daily from March to October, and on weekends during winter (weather permitting). Round-trips cost £7.50 ($15) for adults, £3.50 ($7) for children 3 to 15; a family ticket for two adults and two kids costs £19 ($38). This firm also has a cruising restaurant and a panoramic waterside restaurant where you can enjoy breakfast, morning coffee, or dinner. Best of all for those with kids is **London Waterbus Company** (58 Camden Lock Place, NW1; © 020/7482-2660; www.londonwaterbus. com), which allows you to stop off at London Zoo—it has its own canal gate entrance, allowing you to circumvent the queues, and offers lower-priced tickets. The narrow boats operate daily from April to September, weekends only from October to March, with round-trips costing £7.50 ($15) for adults, £5 ($10) for children 3 to 15, and a Zoo trip £15/$30 and £12/$24 respectively. Strollers can be brought aboard if small and folded. If you're feeling adventurous, ask this firm about occasional summer all-day

## River Rides

A **boat trip along the Thames** allows you to see how many of the city's landmarks turn their faces toward the water—proof that the city grew along and around its link with the sea. For a long time, this tidal river was London's chief commercial thoroughfare and royal highway—monarchs traveled along it on fairy-tale gilded barges (which you can still see at the National Maritime Museum in Greenwich; p. 159)—as well as the route via which state prisoners were delivered to the Tower of London, eliminating the chance of an ambush in one of the narrow alleys around it.

Numerous companies run trips to and from various destinations along the river, including Greenwich (p. 148). Commuter services are the cheapest; tourist-oriented cruises with live or taped commentary, refreshment services, and sometimes even live music or a cabaret are the most expensive. A laid-back if quite expensive family option is the **Sunday Lunch Jazz Cruise** (𝄐 020/7925-1800; www.bateauxlondon.com), offering a three-course set menu for 5- to 12-year-olds and for adults; its cost is £22 ($44) kids, £40 ($80) adults. The cruise leaves from Embankment and Waterloo piers and lasts about 2½ hours, passing the British Airways London Eye, Tate Modern, Millennium Bridge, St. Paul's Cathedral, and Tower Bridge.

If it's an adrenaline rush you seek, **London RIB Voyages** 𝄐𝄐𝄐 (𝄐 020/792-2350; www.londonribvoyages.com) is a newish firm offering much speedier river-based tours by Rigid Inflatable Boat—a sort of hard dinghy with motors. Skimming the surface of the water, you are shown the main riverside sights by a trained guide, and can ask questions of your own; main tours ply the waters between the British Airways London Eye (Waterloo Millennium Pier) and Canary Wharf, taking about 50 minutes; on Saturday mornings longer ones take you as far as the Thames Barrier and back in about 90 minutes. Surprisingly, there's no lower age limit for these trips—stringent safety checks are in place, with regularly tested life jackets provided for adults and children. (You are also offered loan of a warm waterproof sailing jacket.) Prices cost £29 ($58) for adults and £16 ($32) for under-12s for the main tours.

**Transport for London** publishes a comprehensive river services leaflet, available at Tube stations or online at www.tfl.gov.uk/river. (Travel information is also available 24 hr. at 𝄐 020/7222-1234.)

cruises to Limehouse to the east (a journey during which you descend through 12 locks).

If it's white-knuckle action you seek, there are two theme parks within easy reach of London. (For **Legoland**, see p. 262.)

**Chessington World of Adventures & Zoo** 𝄐    **Ages 2 and up.** Online booking or seasonal special offers can slash the cost of visiting this theme park catering to all age groups, be they mini-adventurers, junior adventurers, family adventurers (all the family, though height/size restrictions may apply), or experienced adventurers. To save yourself wandering around in a state of indecision, download one of the website's Day Guides with advice on which rides and attractions are suitable for each age range, and details of family facilities. Printing a map from the website before you go will also save you the small charge for one when you get there. Depending on the age of your kids, highlights are Land of the Dragons, with 10 rides and attractions for 2- to 8-year-olds, including a puppet theater, treetop adventure scrambles, softplay areas, and two drag-onboat rides for toddlers; Forbidden Kingdom, with its hard-core spinning Rameses Revenge ride; and Pirate's Cove, with its whirling high-seas adventure, Seastorm. Animal Land is now billed as a full-scale zoo, and the program of live shows has been accordingly stepped up (see the website for details).

Chessington is 18km (12 miles) from London, and has free parking. Trains from Waterloo take about 30 minutes, and the park is 10 minutes from the station. When you arrive, ask at admissions about child wristbands with contact details in the event that you become separated. Those with small kids should also ask at Guest Services about the Parent Swap facility, which allows you to go on rides restricted to them. The vast number of eating options run the gamut from traditional pub fare in the Greedy Goblin Family to hot dogs and nachos in the Fizz & Burp Café. Picnic areas include the new indoor Family Centre with parenting facilities and activities for young visitors. The medical center sells baby milk and food, and there are numerous nursing and baby-changing facilities where you can also buy diapers. There are even family-size toilet stalls in case a parent needs to tend to two toddlers at once.

*Insider tip:* To avoid high-season queues, pre-book an Express Pass with pre-allocated time slots on the top six rides.

Leatherhead Rd., Chessington, Surrey, KT9. ℂ 0870/444-7777. www.chessington.com. Admission £29 ($58) adults and children 12 and over, £19 ($38) children under 12, free for children under 1m (3¼ ft.) tall. Family tickets vary according to number and ages of visitors but average £74 ($148). Open hours vary throughout the year; see website for details. Train: Chessington Sq.

**Thorpe Park** ⊛ **Ages 2 and up.** While Chessington trumpets itself as a family park, Thorpe Park makes no bones about appealing to adrenaline junkies (they're both owned by the Tussaud's group, so they're not in competition). Like Chessington, however, it's much cheaper to come here if you book your tickets online in advance (at least 48 hr.), or if you snag a seasonal offer. You can also pay more to get a fast track ticket, which will catapult you to the head of the queue of your favorite rides (in high season, those queues can be huge). Hits with thrill seekers include the Slammer giant freefall ride, which catapults riders 360 degrees, and the Vortex, a giant metal structure that twists its victims around like a huge egg whisk. Concessions to younger kids include the Flying Fish first-time roller coaster (an old favorite revived in 2007), the Octopus Garden, and Neptune's Kingdom, hosting gentler rides such as "Sea Snakes & Ladders" and "Up Periscope." A Parent Swap facility enables those who want to go on rides that their kids are too young for.

Thorpe Park is 30km (20 miles) from central London, and parking is free. Direct trains run from Waterloo to Staines (taking 35 min.), from where there's a shuttle to the park. There's a fair choice of eateries, including a new Mexican diner with good meal deals for all the family.

Staines Rd., Chertsey, Surrey, KT16. ℂ 0870/444-4466. www.thorpepark.com. Admission £32 ($64) adults and children 12 and over, £20 ($40) children under 12 but above 1m (3¼ ft.) tall, £88 ($176) family of 4, £105 ($210) family of 5. Open mid-Mar to early Nov; times vary throughout the year. Strollers maximum charge of £9 ($18) with £20 ($40) refundable deposit. Train: Staines.

## 6 Royal Residences

In addition to the listings below, see **Kew Palace** (p. 192).

**Buckingham Palace, Queen's Gallery & Royal Mews** ✿ **Ages 5 and up.** One of the city's great tourist attractions and a perennial source of fascination for Brits and visitors alike, Liz and her clan are loved and hated in equal measure. Get a glimpse into their soap-opera existences with a visit to one of their not-so-humble abodes— starting, most logically, with this one-time country house, which became the official royal residence under Queen Victoria. It has 775 rooms, 19 of which you can visit during the "Annual Summer Opening," when the Royal Family has usually decamped to Scotland. (If the Queen *is* here, you'll see the Royal Standard flying from the mast outside.) These are the State Rooms, which are used by the Royals to receive and entertain guests on state, ceremonial, and official occasions, and which contain masterpieces by Rembrandt, Rubens, and others; sculpture; and fine furniture. The interactive family audiotour helps 5- to 11-year-olds explore the place. 7- to 11-year-olds can take an activity trail through the 16-hectare (39-acre) garden with a 19th-century lake and wildlife. In August, a Family Activity Room hosts creative activities for kids 5 to 11 on a drop-in basis. Note that strollers aren't allowed inside the palace but you can check them in and borrow a baby carrier.

The palace's most famous but overrated spectacle is the **Changing of the Guard** (daily 11:30am Apr–July, alternate days rest of year, but it's frequently canceled due to bad weather, state events, and so on), when the new guard, marching behind a band, takes over from the old one in the palace forecourt. Arrive up to an hour in advance to stake out a space.

Visits to the palace can be combined with tours of the adjoining **Queen's Gallery** (© **020/7766-7301;** £8/$16 adults, £4/$8 children 5–16, £20/$40 family ticket for two adults and three kids; daily 10am–5:30pm), a former chapel where Her Royal Majesty, bless her, holds a wide-ranging collection of art and treasures "in trust . . . for the Nation" (which means British citizens pay for the privilege of seeing what actually belongs to them—go figure). Free family activity trails for 7- to 11-year-olds are available, some linked with temporary exhibitions; special activities are also available at weekends and during school vacations.

From March to October, the **Royal Mews** (Buckingham Palace Rd., SW1; © **020/ 7766-7302;** admission £7/$14 adults, £4.50/$9 children 5–16, £19/$38 family of two adults and three kids; Mar–Oct Mon–Thurs, Sat, and Sun 11am–4pm, and Aug and Sept daily 10am–5pm) can be visited in conjunction with the palace and gallery. These are the Queen's working stables, where you can see carriage horses and state vehicles, including—looking like it came straight from a scene in *Cinderella*—the Gold State Coach used for coronations. Come at weekends, when families (with kids 5–11) can use the Education room with its art trolley and follow an activity trail (ages 7–11) about the coaches and carriages.

Combined tickets are available if you want to see visit more than one of these.

The Mall. © **020/7766-7300.** www.royal.gov.uk. Admission (including audioguide) £15 ($30) adults, £14 ($28) students and seniors, £8.50 ($17) children 5–16, £39 ($78) family ticket for 2 adults and 3 kids. Late July or early Aug to late Sept, daily 9:45am–6pm, with last admission at 3:45pm. Tube: St. James's Park.

**Clarence House** **Ages 10 and up.** The official London residence of the Prince of Wales, his wife the Duchess of Cornwall, and his sons William and Harry, was previously occupied by his grandmother the Queen Mother, and before that by the Queen,

Prince Philip, and Charles as a very young boy. It's open to visitors in late summer, for guided tours of five ground-floor rooms where official engagements are held and VIPs received. The rooms are filled with artworks and antiques from the Royal Collection, Charles's collection, and Camilla's family collection. Note that tickets are only available with advance booking, and that there are no restrooms—or none that you can use.

Stableyard Rd., SW1. © 020/7766-7324. www.royal.gov.uk. Admission £7.50 ($15) adults, £4 ($8) children 5–17. Aug–Sept daily 10am–5:30pm. Tube: Green Park.

**Hampton Court Palace** (★★★  **Ages 3 and up.** The most majestic palace of all (though it's no longer a royal residence), this Tudor confection is 21km (13 miles) west of London on the north side of the Thames. Given (reluctantly) to Henry VIII by Cardinal Wolsey around 1526, its subsequent royal residents included Mary I, Elizabeth I, Charles I, William III, and Mary II, and it still contains many furnishings and artifacts from their times, as well as important artworks and furnishings from the Royal Collection. Highlights are the Tudor Kitchens and the costumed guided tours of Henry VIII's apartments. Young 'uns tend to flock to the famous maze in the riverside gardens, where you can see the world's oldest vine, planted in 1768 and still going strong, and the royal tennis court. Horse-drawn carriage rides around the grounds for up to four people (£11/$22 per carriage) are also a hit. There's also a great program of free family weekend and school-vacation activities, many of them held in the Clore Learning Centre, new in 2007. You might make a king's beast mask and then wear it as you explore the palace, take a family trail, win a prize when you hand your completed quiz back in at the information center, or choose from a variety of family audio-tours best-suited to kids ages 6 and up. Those with strollers should anticipate awkward stairs and cobblestones.

A good time to come is June, when the Hampton Court Palace Festival features open-air performances by top musicians, from José Carreras to Van Morrison, plus fireworks. One of the most laid-back ways to get here from central London is by river (© 020/7930-2062; www.wpsa.co.uk; one-way £14/$28 adults, £6.75/$14 children 5–15, £34/$68 family ticket), but the 7- to 8-hour return trip, which runs between April and October, may not be suitable for restless kids, and doesn't give you much time at the palace. A better option is to sail there and return by train (half-hourly trains travel from Hampton Court to Waterloo, taking 35 min.). Along the way you see Syon House (p. 188); The London Apprentice, a famous inn where Henry VIII did some of his courting; Old Isleworth Parish Church, where victims of the Great Plague were buried; and Ham House (p. 186). Alternatively, you can stay here a few nights, at one of two Landmark Trust holiday apartments at the palace (p. 86).

E. Molesey, Surrey, KT8. © 0870/753-7777. www.hrp.org.uk. Admission £13 ($26) adults, £11 ($22) seniors and students, £6.50 ($13) children 5–15, £36 ($72) family of 2 adults and up to 3 kids. Apr–Oct daily 10am–6pm; Nov–Feb daily 10am–4:30pm. Train: Hampton Court.

**Kensington Palace**  **Ages 7 and up.** Though it hasn't been the official home of reigning kings since George II, this is a working royal residence housing the offices and apartments of various members of the Royal Family, including the Prince and Princess Michael of Kent. The birthplace and childhood home of Queen Victoria, it's furnished with items of Victoriana and paintings from the Royal Collection, which can be in its State Apartments. Although you don't get to see the apartments where Diana Princess of Wales lived with princes Harry and William until her death, the changing program of exhibitions—most of which focus on royal fashion—always includes something to do with her, from photographs to some of her priceless gowns. There's also a permanent display of royal togs in the Ceremonial Royal Dress Collection. Kids of school age are aided in their exploration by a children's trail, available from the Red Saloon. You can leave strollers by the ticket office here; it's not compulsory but there is no elevator and lots of stairs. Baby-changing is available.

For children's afternoon teas at the adjoining Orangery, see p. 186.

Kensington Gardens, W8. ✆ 0870/751-5170. www.hrp.org.uk. Admission £12 ($24) adults, £10 ($20) seniors and students, £6 ($12) children 5–15, £33 ($66) family ticket (up to 2 adults and 3 children). Mar–Oct daily 10am–6pm; Nov–Feb daily 10am–5pm. Tube: High St. Kensington.

## 7 Historic Buildings

For **Apsley House,** see the Wellington Arch, p. 156; for **Kenwood House,** see Hampstead Heath, p. 143.

**Dickens House** ⭐ **Ages 7 and up.** The only survivor of Charles Dickens's numerous London homes (he lived here 1837–39, and it was here that he wrote *Oliver Twist*) is now a museum full of manuscripts, rare editions, paintings, original furniture, and other items relating to the Victorian novelist. It all makes for an atmospheric setting for special events, including guided tours, readings from the novels, and handling sessions, during which adults and kids can write with a quill pen used by the great author and touch other objects he owned. The museum also runs various walks through Dickensian London, and temporary exhibitions, often with a lighthearted theme—Victorian beards, for instance. The very best time of all, though, is Christmas, when there are special readings (Dickens *is* the author most people associate with the festive season) and family workshops with activities around a decorated tree.

Dickens devotees should note that there's a new Dickens theme park not far from London, in Kent (p. 269).

48 Doughty St., WC1. ✆ 020/7405-2127. www.dickensmuseum.com. Admission £5 ($10) adults, £4 ($8) seniors and students, £3 ($6) children, £14 ($28) families (2 adults and up to 5 children). Mon–Sat 10am–5pm; Sun 11am–5pm. Tube: Russell Sq.

**Eltham Palace** ⭐⭐⭐ **Ages 5 and up.** Combining the remains of a medieval royal palace with Art Deco glamour, Eltham Palace was purchased by industrialist and art patron Stephen Courtauld and his wife in the 1930s, who proceeded to build their dream home from the surviving structures—the result is a real one-off. Of greatest interest to younger visitors are the centrally heated quarters belonging to Mah-Jongg, the Courtaulds' pet ring-tailed lemur, with a bamboo ladder that lets him descend to the entrance hall below. Kids also love the gadgetry that was revolutionary for the 1930s and still seems Utopian today—including sockets in every room that sucked dirt down to a central vacuum cleaner in the basement. At the other extreme, there's the impressive Tudor Great Hall, where kings and queens of England entertained as many as 2,000 people; and there are tunnels to explore (these were built as a waste system under Henry VIII). The 7.6-hectare (19-acre) gardens with their panoramic views of London are fantastic, but make sure you keep the kids away from the moat, and beware of the uneven terrain. You're welcome to picnic on the grounds, but there's also a tearoom in the former kitchen. Strollers are not allowed inside the house but can be stored, hip seats are available, and there are changing facilities.

Try to plan your visit to coincide with one of the plentiful **special events,** which range from Tudor Days and open-air performances of Shakespeare to teddy bear picnics and

1930s fashion shows. There is an information sheet to accompany families around the property (downloadable from the website, together with a history sheet to read to your kids on the journey here). Trains to Eltham from Charing Cross and London Bridge take 20 minutes or so. You might consider combining your trip with a visit to Greenwich (p. 148).

Court Yard, SE9. © 020/8294-2548. www.elthampalace.org.uk. £7.90 ($16) adults, £5.90 ($12) seniors and students, £4 ($8) children, £20 ($40) family ticket. Apr–Oct Sun–Wed 10am–5pm; Nov–Dec 23 and Feb 3–Mar 20 11am–4pm. Train: Eltham.

**Ham House** 🐸🐸 **Ages 3 and up.** This outstanding Thameside Stuart house was once home to the scheming Duchess of Lauderdale, whose ghost is said to roam the corridors (along with those of other former inhabitants, as you'll discover if you sign up for a school-vacation family ghost tour for ages 5 and up; £10/$20 adults, £8/$16 kids). The lavish original interiors embrace furniture, textiles, and paintings, but it's the lovely grounds that kids will want to roam, with their mazelike wilderness of garden rooms; walnut and chestnut trees—home to a large flock of green parakeets; water meadows; ice house (later used as an air-raid shelter); still house (where the herbalist duchess distilled potions and medicines); and dairy, with marble slabs supported by cast-iron cows' legs. Ask about the free kids' guide, quiz/trail, and activity packs. Special events include a summer Family Day with storytelling about the gardens, performances, games, and craft activities—all free for under-14s (normal admission for adults). There's also the delightful Theatre in the Garden program (£16/$32 adults, £12/$24 children), with presentations of works such as Sir Arthur Conan Doyle's *The Hound of the Baskervilles* and Robert Louis Stevenson's *Treasure Island;* bring a rug and an umbrella, as performances go ahead whatever the weather!

Note that Ham House's grounds can be visited out of season, when the house is closed up. Baby-changing facilities are available, and you can borrow baby slings and hip seats. The Orangery tearoom and terrace serves historically inspired fare made from homegrown produce, including a kids' menu.

*Insider tip:* If you and your kin are really into historic houses, there's a seasonal foot/bike ferry across the Thames close to **Marble Hill House** (p. 187).

Ham St., Ham, Richmond-upon-Thames, TW10. © 020/8940-1950. www.nationaltrust.org.uk. Admission £9 ($18) adults, £5 ($10) children, £22 ($44) family. Apr–Oct Sat–Wed 1–5pm (garden all year Sat–Wed 11am–6pm). Tube: Richmond, then 2km (1-mile) walk on towpath. Drivers take road 3km (2 miles).

**Handel House Museum** 🐸🐸 **Ages 3 and up.** Some of the world's greatest music, including *Messiah,* was composed here in the restored Georgian town house of baroque composer George Frederic Handel (who resided here from 1723 until his death in 1759). As well as prized musical artifacts such as Mozart's handwritten arrangement of a Handel fugue, you can see portraits and prints of Handel and his contemporaries, and—most importantly—hear live music, at one of a full program of concerts. If that inspires you, come and join in a singing workshop (ages 8–12). Other events might include a "Recorder Rave," beginning with instruction and composition in the museum in the morning, and culminating in an afternoon joint performance in the Wigmore Hall (p. 220). Otherwise, Saturday afternoons see free drop-in family events, with quiz trails, 18th-century activity bags, Georgian dressing-up, and baroque musicians rehearsing live. On many Sundays there are special activities, too, including workshops that explore how various composers have represented animal sounds. On certain days aspiring young musicians can also drop in with their composition for a chat with the composer-in-residence, who will dispense advice and answer questions.

25 Brook St., W1. (✆) 020/7495-1685. www.handelhouse.org. Admission £5 ($10) adults, £4.50 ($9) seniors and students, £2 ($4) children 5–15 (free on Sat). Tues–Wed and Fri–Sat 10am–6pm; Thurs 10am–8pm; Sun noon–6pm. Tube: Bond St.

**Houses of Parliament & Big Ben**    **Ages 12 and up.** The Houses of Parliament, the ultimate symbols of London and strongholds of Britain's democracy, contain more than 1,000 rooms and 3km (2 miles) of corridors. But what kids most want to see is visible only from the outside—the clock tower housing the world's most famous timepiece, **Big Ben,** though the name actually refers to the largest bell in the chime, weighing close to 14 tons. (There *are* tours of the clock tower, but they're not open to overseas visitors or kids under 11, and you have to arrange a visit in advance through your MP or a Lord; note also that there are a whopping 393 stairs to the top). This is the world's most accurate clock, so set your watch while you're here.

If your family is set on observing a debate in the House of Commons or House of Lords (which are both in the former Palace of Westminster, which was the residence of kings until Henry VIII moved to Whitehall), there's no lower age limit, but kids have to be old enough to sign the visitors' book. The best time to visit is "Prime Minister's Question Time" (Wed noon–12:30pm), when the PM has to hold his own against opposition MPs, but free tickets are only issued to U.K. residents; overseas visitors (and U.K. residents without advance tickets) can queue but are not ensured entrance. In fact, your only real option as an overseas visitor is a 75-minute guided tour during the summer recess (late July/early Aug to early Oct), when the House takes a break. It costs £12/$24 adults, £5/$10 children 5 to 15, £30/$60 family; prebooking is advised ((✆) **0870/906-3773**) and under-5s are discouraged due to the large amount of walking.

Across the street, the **Jewel Tower** ((✆) **020/7222-2219;** www.english-heritage.org. uk; daily summer 10am–5pm, winter 10am–4pm; £2.90/$5.80 adults, £1.50/$3 children) is one of two surviving buildings from the medieval palace; it's also known as "the King's Privy Wardrobe" (it was built around 1365 to house Edward III's treasures). Inside is an exhibition on the history of Parliament and a touch-screen tour of both houses of Parliament, while outside you can see the remains of a moat and medieval quay. It's a great place to come at Halloween, when there's an after-dark spooky storytelling session.

St. Margaret St., SW1. (✆) 020/7219-3000. www.parliament.uk. Free admission. Hours are complicated; see website for details. Tube: Westminster.

**Marble Hill House**    **Ages 5 and up.** Set in 27 glorious hectares (66 acres) of parkland across the river from Ham House (p. 186; ferries take you between the two), this Palladian villa was built for George II's mistress Henrietta Howard in 1724, and you can still see the restored interiors where she held court to some of the greatest wits of London society (items have been returned here from the U.S. and Australia). For parents it's a good place to steep yourself in the atmosphere of fashionable Georgian life, but there are a variety of weekend offerings for families, such as the hibernation-house building for hedgehogs in the company of the park rangers, nettle workshops (trying nettle tea and soup, and listening to talks on nettle folklore), Christmas wreath-making, and "Nature Detectives," which involves searching the grounds for evidence of animal and insect activity. Some of these are drop-in, others require pre-booking, so check in advance. There's stroller access and a cafe.

This is also the London venue for some of the southeast's famous **Picnic Concerts** (www.picnicconcerts.com), with live rock and pop (everything from Westlife to a tribute to *Dirty Dancing*), opera and classical performances, and sometimes a choreographed fireworks finale. Tickets average £20 to £25 ($40–$50); you can bring your own picnic or order one to pick up on-site.

Richmond Rd., Twickenham, TW1. ℭ 020/8892-5115. www.english-heritage.org.uk. £4.20 ($8.40) adults, £3.20 ($6.40) seniors and students, £2.10 ($4.20) children. Apr–Oct Sat 10am–2pm, Sun and bank-holiday Mon 10am–5pm, Tues–Wed for tours at noon and 3pm; Nov–Dec and Mar pre-booked tours only. Tube: Richmond/Rail: St Margaret's.

**Sutton House** This National Trust–owned Tudor residence—the oldest house in London's East End—hosts a whole raft of imaginative family-friendly events, most notably its free themed Family Days with storytelling, arts, crafts, fun, and games, held on the last Sunday of the month (Sept–Nov). School vacations also see family trails teaching you about the people who have lived here—these include, over the centuries, merchants, Huguenot silk-weavers, Victorian schoolmistresses, and Edwardian clergymen—and, every Friday in August, Art in the Courtyard, hosts outdoor arts and crafts. More earnest activities might include poetry workshops about London's role in the slave trade. On ordinary days, you can explore the oak-paneled rooms with their carved fireplaces, including the authentic Tudor kitchen with things to touch and smell. There's also a contemporary art gallery, plus a cafe, baby-changing facilities, and stroller access.

2 and 4 Homerton High St., E9. ℭ **020/8986-2264**. www.nationaltrust.org.uk. Admission £2.70 ($5.40) adults, 60p ($1.20) kids, £6 ($12) family. Thurs–Sun 12:30am–4:30pm. Train: Hackney Central.

**Syon House**  **All ages.** Sadly, one of the main attractions at this, the Duke of Northumberland's London residence way west of the city center, is no more—the **London Butterfly House** has relocated out of London to make way for a hotel in these grounds. The Tropical Forest (ℭ **020/8847-4730;** www.tropicalforest.co.uk), which displays rescued and endangered species that live in or near water, especially in rainforests, will stay until 2010. So for the moment you can still see (and in some cases handle and feed) piranhas, snakes, crocodiles, iguanas, huge marine toads, poison arrow frogs, and terrapins, in their tropical environment amid waterfalls.

There are still tours of the house's wonderful interiors (the state and private apartments), and special events such as Easter I-Spy children's trails, and historical reenactments with kids' activities. Surrounding the house are 162 hectares (400 acres) of parkland, including a great domed glass conservatory with a cactus house, formal gardens, an ornamental lake, and an ice house where ice cream and sorbets used to be made and wine cooled. There's also an **indoor adventure playground** (ℭ **020/8847-0946;** www.snakes-and-ladders.co.uk) for ages 6 months to 12 years.

Syon Park, Brentford, Middlesex, TW8. ℭ **020/8560-7272**. www.syonpark.co.uk. Admission £8 ($16) adults, £7 ($14) seniors and students, £4 ($8) children 3–16, £18 ($36) family ticket. Late Mar to Oct Wed–Thurs, Sun, and bank-holiday Mon 11am–5pm. Tube: Gunnersbury, then bus no. 237 or 267.

**Westminster Abbey**  **Ages 7 and up.** Just about every major figure in English history has left his or her mark on this remarkable place. Edward the Confessor founded the Benedictine abbey in 1065 on this spot, and in January 1066 Harold may have become the first English king crowned here. The man who defeated him at the Battle of Hastings later that year, William the Conqueror, had the first recorded coronation in the abbey, and the tradition has continued to the present day. On a darker note, the many tombs here include those of Elizabeth I, Mary Queen of Scots, Henry V, Geoffrey Chaucer, Samuel Johnson, and Charles Dickens. The latter three are in Poet's Corner, where there's a statue of Shakespeare and memorials to many other writers, including Henry Wadsworth Longfellow, T. S. Eliot, and Dylan Thomas. Various statesmen and men of science, including Sir Isaac Newton and Charles Darwin, are also interred in the abbey or honored by monuments, while the tomb of the Unknown Warrior commemorates the British dead of World War I. Bringing this up to the present day, 10 modern martyrs drawn from every continent and religious denomination are memorialized in statues above the West Front door, including Martin Luther King, Jr. If it's all a bit daunting, families can book **90-minute verger-led tours** (£5/$10 per person) that take in the shrine of Edward the Confessor, the royal tombs, Poet's Corner, the cloisters, and the nave.

The **Abbey Treasure Museum** in the crypt (admission free with abbey tickets) holds some creepy royal effigies used for lying-in-state ceremonies (because they smelled better than the corpses), plus other oddities, including Henry V's funeral armor and a corset from Elizabeth I's effigy.

Broad Sanctuary, SW1. ✆ 020/7654-4900. www.westminster-abbey.org. Admission £10 ($20) adults; £7 ($14) seniors, students, and children 11–16; £24 ($48) family ticket (2 adults, 2 children). Abbey hours: Mon–Tues and Thurs–Fri 9:30am–3:45pm; Wed 9:30am–7pm; Sat 9am–1:45pm. Museum hours: daily 10:30am–4pm. Tube: Westminster or St. James's Park.

## 8 Zoos & Aquariums

There is a small petting zoo at **Brent Lodge Park** (p. 206), and **Chessington World of Adventures** (p. 181) is partly a zoo. The **Horniman Museum** (p. 146) has an aquarium, and Syon House (p. 188) is home to the **Tropical Forest.**

**Battersea Park Children's Zoo** 🐾🐾  **All ages.** This cute zoo, in the midst of a park stretching along the Thames opposite Chelsea, is perfect for younger kids—alongside small furry creatures such as otters, owls, squirrel, and capuchin monkeys are lemurs, meerkats, wallabies, emus, and talking mynah birds; a farm area has a superb wildlife-themed outdoor playground with toddler toys for even the tiniest visitors. Other highlights include the Mouse House and the Butterfly Garden. It's all very low-key, with plenty of opportunity to get close to the animals, especially at feeding times. Weekend and school activities (some of which carry a small charge and need to be booked at the desk on arrival) include the likes of Mammal Detectives, when kids 7 and up try to solve the mystery of the stolen hazelnuts (younger siblings are welcome), Animal Camouflage print-making workshops, and quiz trails with prizes.

The Lemon Tree Cafe has indoor and outdoor tables where you can dine to the sounds of exotic birds. The zoo also has a wildlife gift shop and a baby-changing room. Note that the surrounding park is a haven for wildlife, including ducks, herons, and butterflies; see p. 207 for more info.

Chelsea Gate, Queenstown Rd. (near Peace Pagoda), SW11. ✆ 020/7924-5826. www.batterseaparkzoo.co.uk. Admission £5.95 ($12) adults, £4.50 ($9) children 2–15, £19 ($38) family ticket (2 adults, 2 kids). Daily 10am–dusk (last admission 5pm in summer, 4pm in winter). Train: Battersea Park.

**Golders Hill Park Zoo** *Finds*  This little-known mini-zoo at the northern end of Hampstead Heath (p. 143) has been developed as a breeding center for unusual species since early 2005—in 2006 it hosted the births of an alpaca and of the first South American lapwings born in a British zoo. It's impossible to say what will be here when you visit, since the young are subsequently sent to zoos across Europe, but you can generally count on seeing alpaca, muntjac deer, flamingos, cranes, wallabies, and goats—about 160 animals and birds in total. You will be in luck if you visit when the staff is hosting a Meet the Animals session, when you can learn about some of the rare breeds here and meet the babies; other summer activities might include treasure hunts and activities relating to the ducks, geese, and black and white swans that live on the ponds. You can also pick up a Hunt Pack that takes you on a nature trail around the zoo, and there are talks and walks for all ages around the zoo and park.

Golders Hill Park also has a playground, a lovely flower garden, tennis courts and golf practice nets, a bandstand, and an Italian cafe serving homemade ice cream. Its rolling lawns make for a great picnic spot.

West Heath Ave., NW11. ⓒ 020/8455-5183. Free admission. Daily 7:30am–dusk. Tube: Golders Green.

## London Aquarium    All ages.
More than a little shabby, this isn't one of the world's great aquariums by any stretch of the imagination—its strange setting within the unwieldy former County Hall building doesn't help. And prices, already high enough, have been hiked up since the last edition of this guide, and off-peak reductions are no longer available. So it will be interesting to see what happens when Biota!, a truly world-class aquarium, opens in east London in 2012.

Still, when you've got a budding marine biologist in the family like I have, you might not even be allowed to keep away, and with its location close to the boat piers and to the British Airways London Eye, this is handy if you're on a big day out and want to vary the attractions. And it *is* one of the largest aquariums in Europe, with around 350 species, including sharks, piranha, and jellyfish. The ray touchpool is one of the most popular spots, and there are daily feeds (rays and sharks), talks (including rainforests and coral reefs), and diving displays. Most weekends and daily in-school vacations, kids can get creative at a craft table on Level 2, where they can make a badge, a shark headdress, and more (from £50/$100 per item). If you don't have time to linger, you can take home a craft pack with an animal spiral mobile to create a fact sheet and leaflets on the creature you've chosen (crocodile, sea snake, or hammerhead shark). There's an Aquatic Guide for sale (£6/$12), but the 30-page *Aqua Safari* (£3.75/$7.50 with free poster) is better to help kids 7 and up navigate the aquatic habitats, with tasks and activities.

The aquarium is stroller accessible. There are various eating options in the County Hall building, **Namco Station** entertainment center (p. 260), the Dalí Universe, temporary exhibitions on the likes of *Star Wars,* and robots.

County Hall, Westminster Bridge Rd., SE1. ⓒ 020/7967-8000. www.londonaquarium.co.uk. Admission £13 ($26) adults; £12 ($24) students, seniors, and ages 15–17; £9.75 ($20) children 3–14; £44 ($88) family ticket (2 adults, 2 children). Daily 10am–6pm (until 7pm in Aug). Tube: Waterloo.

## London Zoo ⚐    All ages.
Its central location means that this zoo isn't the most spacious (hence the removal of the elephants to its sister establishment Whipsnade Wild Animal Park [p. 267] a few years ago). But it does remain one of the world's most conservation-conscious zoos, and is constantly evolving in an effort to improve conditions and reproduction rates. In 2007, for instance, it opened a new £5.3-million ($10.6-million) Gorilla Kingdom with a large island surrounded by a moat, an indoor day gym, bedrooms, and a paddling pool—a considerable step up from the creatures' previous barred accommodations, and one that, the zoo hopes, will lead to gorillas breeding here. It's proven very popular, so consider buying tickets in advance, giving you fast track admission as well as a 10% online discount. There's also the new Clore Rainforest Lookout—a transformation of the old small mammals house allowing unrestricted views of South American monkeys and birds, and well as sloths, iguanas,

agoutis, and more. An adjoining activity workshop space where younger visitors can learn about the lives of rainforest animals was in the pipeline as we went to press.

Otherwise, the giraffes, lions, tigers, a Reptile House with popular handling sessions, kids' zoo with a "touch paddock" and advice sessions on looking after small pets, and celebrated BUGS biodiversity exhibition, where you can watch white-coated men in little rooms growing trays of Polynesian snails and the like, are still here. Regular school-vacation "Animals in Action" demonstrations show different animals leaping, climbing, and flying, and there are interactive workshops and discovery sessions. Adults appreciate the shaded walkways and the zoo's famous architecture; its 12 listed buildings include the dramatic 1960s Snowdon Aviary. The main cafe, Oasis, has a buggy park, masses of highchairs, bottle-heating, and a well-considered choice of refreshments. Plenty of other pit stops are dotted around the zoo (some are closed out of season), and there are merry-go-rounds and fun rides galore and a highly rated shop without rip-off prices. Be aware that some enclosures may be locked 15 minutes or so in advance of the main zoo's closing time, so don't leave the best until last.

*Insider tip:* Combine a visit here with a canal trip via the London Waterbus Company (p. 180) to get reduced-price entry and forgo queues. You'll need a half-day to a day to see the zoo's full offerings.

Outer Circle, The Regent's Park, NW1. © 020/7722-3355. www.zsl.org. Admission £15 ($30) adults, £13 ($26) seniors and students, £11 ($22) children 3–15, £49 ($98) family ticket (2 adults and 2 children, or 1 adult and 3 children). Early Mar to late Oct daily 10am–5:30pm; late Oct to Feb daily 10am–4pm. Tube: Regent's Park or Camden Town.

## 9  Gardens & Conservatories

Lovers of green spaces should look out for the annual **Open Squares weekend** (www. opensquares.org), during which many of London's private garden squares and community gardens are open to the public. Some run family activities during the June event.

**Chelsea Physic Garden**   **Ages 4 and up.** A botanical garden set up by a king's doctor (George II's) to grow plants for medicinal study may sound tame, but not when you consider that among the 7,000 or so species residing here are numerous carnivorous specimens, including Venus flytraps. They're detailed in the "Points of Interest for Children" leaflet, which you can download in advance from the website; this also tells you about the Tropical Corridor, the smelly plants, the sensitive *Mimosa pudica,* which moves when you touch it, the deadly mandrake and its curious history, the pond with its water fleas, leeches, and more, the beehives, and the cool fernery, with plants that the dinosaurs used to eat. Make sure you impress upon your kids the importance of not touching any of the specimens, since some are poisonous.

**Family activities** in spring vacations have been extended to cater to age ranges 4 to 7 and 11 to 14 as well as 7 to 11, with under-8s requiring parental accompaniment (all ages must be accompanied while eating their packed lunch). They cost a good-value £5 ($10) and must be pre-booked. Hits have included science workshops exploring the pond and compost heap; creepy-crawly safaris; and plant-dye workshops. The teashop whips up some superior cakes.

66 Royal Hospital Rd. (entrance on Swan Walk), SW3. © 020/7352-5646. www.chelseaphysicgarden.co.uk. Admission £7 ($14) adults, £4 ($8) students and children 5–15. Apr–Oct Wed noon–dusk (or 9pm); Thurs–Fri noon–5pm; Sun 2–6pm. Tube: Sloane Sq.

**Royal Botanic Gardens, Kew** ✦✦✦   **Ages 3 and up.** The highlight, for children, of these world-famous botanical gardens is **Climbers & Creepers,** an "interactive botanical play zone" in the former cycad house, designed to teach 3- to 9-year-olds the importance of plant-animal relationships through play: They can climb into a plant to pollinate it, get "eaten" by a giant pitcher plant, and crawl through a bramble tangle. Also the venue for the Midnight Ramble sleepovers (p. 152), this play zone also has an outdoor space for fine weather, and an observation area with refreshments; the nearby White Peaks—serving organic burgers, plus children's meals and lunch boxes with their own choice of food—also has outdoor dining.

There are plenty more family-friendly eating options throughout the beautiful 120-hectare (300-acre) gardens, which actually constitute a vast scientific research center, with thousands of plant varieties, plus lakes, hothouses, walks, pavilions, museums, and an architectural heritage. Make sure you don't miss the Bamboo Garden with its bamboo musical instruments you can try out, or the Animal Farm with its cuddly rabbits, plus goats, chickens, and ducks. To get an overview or ease your way in area by area, especially with kids in tow, make use of the hop-on hop-off **Kew Explorer** bus (£3.50/$7 adults, £1/$2 under-17s). A self-guided **Habitat Trail** introduces some of the garden's amazing plants and the people involved in creating them to kids 7 to 11; it's downloadable from the Schools Education page on the website, which has other teachers' resources useful for parents. Watch out for special events, such as the Woodland Wonders May festival, a weekend of birds of prey and working horse demonstrations, puppet shows, zip-wire rides, and woodcarving sessions.

The grounds are also home to **Kew Palace** (© 0870/751-5179; www.hrp.org.uk; £5/$10 adults, £4/$8 under-17s, in addition to Gardens ticket), the smallest royal palace and George III's family home, with displays on George's boyhood and royal education as well as those of his sons. It's open in summer only.

Richmond, Surrey, TW9. © 020/8332-5655. www.rbgkew.org.uk. Admission £12 ($24) adults, £10 ($20) students and seniors, free for children 16 and under. Apr–Aug daily 9:30am–6pm; Sept–Oct daily 9:30am–5:30pm; Nov to early Feb daily 9:30am–3:45pm. Tube: Kew Gardens.

## 10 Nature Centers

For a full-on, back-to-nature experience in the city, **WWT Wetland Centre** (p. 153) is the place to head. Smaller in scale are London's many **city farms,** which were set up to offer inner-city kids the opportunity to experience a little bit of the countryside on their doorsteps. While these are not tourist attractions and are generally located in less privileged areas, they're worth visiting if you have animal-loving kids—most offer animal-petting and -feeding sessions, rare breeds, and more, and some sell their own produce. For details on locations of city farms, as well as **community gardens** (which offer handy oases in the metropolitan jungle), see www.farmgarden.org.uk or call © 0117/923-1800.

There are plenty of other natural sanctuaries if you are prepared to seek them out. One of the most atmospheric is **Abney Park Cemetery & Nature Reserve** (Stoke Newington Church St., N16; © 020/7275-7557; www.abney-park.org.uk), a 13-hectare (32-acre) Victorian burial ground and conservation area in north London, with a children's garden and a visitor center hosting events and kids' summer workshops, including woodland crafts, kite-making, and wildlife walks. (Local residents include gray squirrels, bats, and foxes.)

**London Wildlife Trust** (© 020/7261-0447; www.wildlondon.org.uk) has lots of sites in and around the city. The most central is **Camley Street Natural Park** (12 Camley St., NW1; © 020/7883-2311) on the banks of the Regent's Canal near King's Cross, with birds, bees, butterflies, and amphibians, plus a Wildlife Watch Club for

8- to 11-year-olds and other activities, such as family environmental art classes The Trust also runs the **Centre for Wildlife Gardening** (28 Marsden Rd., SE15; © **020/ 7252-9186**), which teaches kids how to attract wildlife to their own gardens.

In the East End, the dynamic **Lea Rivers Trust Discovery Team** (a waterway charity; © **020/8981-0040;** www.leariverstrust.co.uk), which administers a heritage area comprising several sites, offers a family program that includes great (free) summer Sunday craft workshops with environmental themes.

## 11 Kid-Friendly Tours

### DRIVING TOURS

**Open-top bus tours,** though touristy, are a real thrill for kids. For first-timers in the city, they're a good way to get a handle on London, allowing you to cherry-pick sights to return to at a later date. Buses depart from lots of convenient points, and you can hop on and off when the mood takes you—to see a specific sight in detail, or just for a restroom or snack break. There's usually live English commentary, or recorded commentaries in a range of languages. The following companies offer online ticket discounts, plus fast track entry to busy attractions such as Madame Tussaud's and the Tower of London.

The leader of the pack when it comes to kids is **The Original London Sightseeing Tour** ⚡ (© **020/8877-1722;** www.theoriginaltour.com), since it's the only operator offering—at least on its Red Route, which takes in all the major sights—special children's commentaries, together with a free Kids' Pack with an activity/quiz book and competitions, and a "passport" to London that gets stamped when they climb aboard. Tickets cost £19 ($38) for adults, £12 ($24) for children 5 to 15, or £72 ($144) for a family ticket for two adults and three children, and include a free river cruise; you save by buying online. The main start points are Marble Arch, Baker Street Station, Piccadilly Circus, Trafalgar Square, Embankment Station, and Victoria.

A similar option is the **Big Bus Company** (48 Buckingham Palace Rd., SW1; © **020/7233/9533;** www.bigbustours.com). In addition to another free river cruise, you get a 90-minute walking tour (themes include The Beatles, Royal London, and Ghosts by Gaslight) thrown in with your ticket, plus money off certain West End shows. Tickets cost £22 ($44) for adults, £10 ($20) for children 5 to 15. Major stops include Marble Arch, Piccadilly Circus, Trafalgar Square, and St. Paul's.

For a more personal road trip around London, you can spring for a black cab to take you to see the sights. The advantage of this is that you choose your own itinerary if you wish and can stop off whenever and for however long you like. **London Black Cabs** (© **07957/696673;** www.londonblackcabs.co.uk) offers 1-hour to 1-day tours costing from £35 to £40 ($70–$80) an hour; or try **London Taxi Tours** for kid-friendly themed tours (p. 194).

For something completely off-the-wall, **Karma Kabs** ⚡ (© **020/8964-0700;** www.karmakars.net) has a fleet of four kitschy Indian cars for hire (including the Bollywood Kar, and the bright-pink Ab Fab Kab), with prices starting at around £60 ($120) an hour. You're guaranteed to feel like royalty as people stand and gape at you in the streets, and as you set off from traffic lights you'll be treated to the sound of a horse's neigh.

### WALKING TOURS

**London Walks** ⚡⚡ (© **020/7624-3978;** www.walks.com) is London's oldest walking-tour company, with a repertory of more than 300 walks. Though the walks are pitched at adults rather than kids, some can be and are enjoyed by older kids (6 and up), including weekly costumed ghost walks, treasure hunts, and occasional Thames beachcombing walks. Another surefire hit is the costumed Mary Poppins walk ("Supercalifragilisticexpialidocious London"), with singalongs encouraged. If you want to take your kids on one of the pub walks, the company recommends "Along the Thames," which passes attractions of interest to kids, such as the *Golden Hinde* (p. 158) and Shakespeare's Globe (p. 172), and visits pubs with outdoor spaces. For older teens, the company's "Jack the Ripper" walks are far ahead of the competition (of which there is plenty).

Staff members are incredibly helpful when it comes to which walks (and which *guides*) are best for kids, so call or e-mail in advance. Walks last an average of 2 hours and cost about £6 ($12) for adults, with kids under 15 free when accompanied by an adult, which makes them an amazing value. Note that you can organize private group walks, and that the company also runs "Explorer Days outside London," including Richmond and Hampton Court (p. 184), Windsor and Eton (p. 262), and Cambridge.

## WATER TOURS

For Thames cruises and canalboat trips, see p. 181 and 148.

**London Duck Tours** ✹✹ (Chicheley St., SE1; © **020/7928-3132;** www.london ducktours.co.uk) offers a quirkier tour that children enjoy, which uses DUKWS amphibious vehicles (employed in the D-day landings) to take in various landmarks (including Big Ben and Buckingham Palace) before launching out of a slipway into the Thames for a water cruise. There is also a James Bond–themed tour. Tours begin at the British Airways London Eye, last 75 minutes, and cost £18 ($36) for adults, £14 ($28) children 13 to 15, £1 ($2) children 12 and under; a family ticket for two adults and two children under 12 is £55 ($110).

## SPECIALIST TOURS

**London Taxi Tours** ✹✹ (© **07957/272-1791;** www.londontaxitour.com) seems to have virtually given itself over to **Harry Potter–themed tours,** although a James Bond tour (which you can combine with a Potter tour) and a Monopoly Board tour are also available, as are standard London tours. Potter fans can enjoy London tours (3½ hr., £185/$370 per taxi), joint Oxford and London tours (8 hr., £330/$660 per taxi), or various other permutations, including trips as far as Stonehenge. Among the movie locations you might see are Platform 9¼ (at King's Cross), Leadenhall Market (p. 198), the outside of the Leaky Cauldron, Gringott's Bank, and Oxford University, where some Hogwarts school scenes were filmed. Guides are well versed in the books, and all are excellent with kids. Taxis can hold up to five adults and have integral child seats, with booster seats available by request.

Lovers of the small screen, meanwhile, will be pleased to hear that the popular **tours of BBC Television Centre** (Wood Lane, W12; © **0870/603-0304;** www.bbc.co.uk/ tours) include ones of the CBBC children's channel studios (ages 7 and up). They vary according to shooting schedules, but last up to 2 hours and include visits to some of the presenters' studios, the Blue Peter Garden, and an interactive studio. Standard tours, which include visits to the newsroom and sessions in an interactive newsroom, are open only to those over 9. Pre-booking is essential for both. Tickets cost £9.50 ($20) for adults, £7 ($14) for children, and £27 ($54) for a family (two adults and two children, or one adult and three children); pre-booking is essential.

# 8

# Neighborhood Strolls

London is a great city for walking—it's largely flat in the center, with stunning juxtapositions of old and new, of urban vistas and more bucolic scenes. Pay the city close enough attention, and you'll see that layers of history are just begging to unfurl around you.

The following walks are designed to provide glimpses into some of London's lesser-known and more offbeat treasures.

## 1 In the Footsteps of Peter Pan

"You must see for yourselves that it will be difficult to follow Peter Pan's adventures unless you are familiar with the Kensington Gardens," begins J. M. Barrie's little-known but magical *Peter Pan in Kensington Gardens,* published in 1906. It's in these gardens that Barrie befriended the five Llewelyn Davies boys, who dressed up and acted out stories while Barrie told them the tale that would become *Peter Pan.* The character himself was inspired in part by Barrie's brother, who died at age 13, and in part by the boys themselves.

*Peter Pan in Kensington Gardens,* originally titled *The Little White Bird,* is the first appearance of Peter, the little boy who refuses to grow up; we meet him as a baby, living a wild life with birds and fairies in the middle of London. Today, if you enter the park at Inverness Terrace Gate and turn right, you'll discover the delights of the **Diana Memorial Playground** (p. 209), which rests where an older playground funded by Barrie once stood. It has a loose Peter Pan theme—the centerpiece is a pirate ship, a stone crocodile resides here, and images from 1930s illustrations of *Peter Pan* are etched into the glass in The Home Under The Ground, named after the Lost Boys' dwelling, which houses the restrooms and playground attendant's office.

But before entering the park, go and see the house where Barrie lived, and where he wrote *Peter Pan,* not far from Queensway Tube, at **100 Bayswater Rd.**—a blue heritage plaque attests to the fact. Living so close by, Barrie walked in the park everyday.

When your kids have had your fill of the playground (there's enough to keep them happy for a whole morning and more), you can refuel at the adjoining **Cafe Broadwalk Cafe & Playcafe,** which serves flatbread pizzas and more, including a children's menu. Now stroll up **Broad Walk:** The hero of *Peter Pan,* David, imagines that the smaller paths branching off from Broad Walk are its babies and even draws it taking a little path for a walk in a pram (an old-style stroller). Before long you'll come to **Round Pond,** which David describes as "the wheel that keeps all the gardens going." Here he has a few words of warning:

"You can't be good all the time at the Round Pond, however much you try. You can be good in the Broad Walk all the time, but not at the Round Pond, and the reason is that you forget, and, when you remember, you are so wet that you may as well be wetter."

Like David, you may want to stop and sail your toy yacht here—or perhaps even better, create your own stick-boat to transport you to "buried cities" and "coral isles."

From the Round Pond you have a choice of paths, from relatively straight ones to the more higgledy-piggledy "Paths that Have Made Themselves." (David concludes that such paths must materialize at night, since he never sees them spring into life.) Take the one leading due east; at the next meeting of paths, carry on down toward the **Long Water** and turn left. Soon you'll reach the bronze **Peter Pan Statue,** decorated with fairies and woodland creatures. It was placed here in 1912; Barrie arranged for it to be installed in the middle of the night so that it retained its aura of enchantment, but he hadn't obtained permission from the authorities, and questions were asked in the House of Commons about an author's right to promote his own work in a public park. Luckily, it was allowed to stay (and was even bestowed with a plaque unveiled by Princess Margaret). Later given its own little plot in which kids are free to run riot, it's now one of the city's best-loved statues. Despite this, Peter's pipes have been stolen several times by pranksters (the pipes have always been recovered or quickly replaced).

Walking back to the Bayswater Road, past the sparkling Italian fountains on your right and the little statue of the hugging bears on your left, you may be surprised by how little has changed here in a century. Barrie once remarked on the "never-ending line of omnibuses" here, and today those buses still chug up and down; this at least makes it easy to catch a ride back into central London.

If you want to know more, read *J. M. Barrie and the Lost Boys: The Real Story behind Peter Pan* by Andrew Birkin (Yale University Press). Some scenes of the Johnny Depp movie *Finding Neverland,* which tells part of the story, were shot in Hyde Park.

## 2 A Bloomsbury Jaunt

Beneath the sedate facade of academic Bloomsbury, within the University of London, ghoulish-minded kids will find some sights that will keep them talking for the rest of their trip. Coming out of Euston Square Tube, walk down Gower Street to **University College;** visitors are free to stroll into its **South Cloister** daily between 8am and 5:30pm (except Sun) to meet **Jeremy Bentham,** the philosopher and University co-founder—or at least, his preserved body or "auto-icon," clad in his clothes and posed in a glass-fronted wooden case in the hallway. You might almost mistake it for a wax-work; except for the head (which *is* made of wax; the skull has been kept in a safe since some students stole it as a prank), this is the real McCoy, stuffed with a mixture of lavender, cotton, wool, straw, and hay. Nearby displays hold photos (not for the squeamish) documenting the preservation, plus items tracing his career. Most weirdly of all, you discover that the body sat in on University governors' meetings for years after Bentham's death in 1832, once attended a beer festival in Germany, and is still wheeled out to preside over pre-dinner drinks at the annual Bentham dinner.

Further grisly sights are on offer right next door, at the University's **Petrie Museum of Egyptian Archaeology** (© 020/7679-2884; Tues–Fri 1–5pm, Sat 10am–1pm; free admission), in the form of mummified heads, some complete with eyebrows and eyelashes. This museum displays one of the world's best collections of Egyptian and Sudanese antiquities, and contains an astonishing 80,000 objects. Among the fascinating artifacts on display here are the world's "oldest dress" (a piece of Egyptian linen dating from around 5000 B.C.), a suit of armor from the palace of Memphis, socks and sandals from the Roman period, and lots of jewelry. Note that the museum is scheduled to move in 2010, to the University's new Institute of Cultural Heritage.

A couple of blocks away is **Tavistock Square** (© **020/7974-1693;** daily 7:30am–dusk), an unofficial peace garden centered around a statue of Mahatma Gandhi, who lectured nearby. People congregate around this statue to burn incense, light candles, and practice tai chi; it's also a good picnic spot. Other peace memorials here include a cherry tree in memory of the victims of the atomic bombs dropped on Hiroshima and Nagasaki (every Aug 6, flowers are placed at the bottom of the tree, and origami birds are hung from its branches), and a 450-million-year-old slate in honor of conscientious objectors. Ironically, the street running alongside Tavistock Square was the site of the bus bombing of July 2005; there's a sundial memorial to the victims of that and to the doctors who helped them in the physic garden of the British Medical Association opposite (it's accessible to the public on the Open Squares weekend; p. 191).

From here it's a 10-minute walk via Marchmont Street (and the revamped Brunswick Centre if you're hungry; p. 110) to the very moving **Foundling Museum** (p. 164), which traces the lives of the orphaned or abandoned children taken in at the Foundling Hospital, built in 1742 on the site of **Coram's Fields**—now one of the city's best playgrounds (p. 209). After playing on the equipment and meeting the resident animals, older kids might want to make a detour to the atmospheric **Dickens House** (p. 185), home of the Victorian novelist, on nearby Doughty Street. Or wander along Great Ormond Street until you come upon the **statue of Peter Pan,** placed outside the entrance to Great Ormond Street Hospital for Sick Children in memory of J. M. Barrie, who bequeathed to the hospital the royalties from his best-known book. See p. 195 for more on the generous J. M. Barrie.

## 3 Into the City & Back through Time

It's not London's most obvious area for a family outing, but London's financial heart is where the British capital took seed, and alongside the glass-and-steel office blocks, you can see a fascinating patchwork of Roman remains, winding medieval alleys, centuries-old churches, and charming Victorian ale houses.

Approach the City from the Strand, along **Fleet Street,** famous as the erstwhile home of the British newspaper industry (now based mainly in Docklands). If you're of a literary bent, you might like to peek into the restored **Dr. Johnson's House** at 17 Gough Sq. (© **020/7353-3745;** www.drjohnsonshouse.org), where the writer compiled the first comprehensive English dictionary. Among occasional special events, you might time your visit to coincide with the masquerade family workshops, with Georgian dressing-up and makeup sessions. It's situated amid a maze of courtyards and passages just off Fleet Street, bringing to mind Johnson's own words:

"If you wish to have a just notion of the magnitude of this city, you must not be satisfied with seeing its great streets and squares, but must survey the innumerable little lanes and courts."

Leading back from Gough Square to Fleet Street, **Ye Old Cheshire Cheese** (© **020/7353-6170**) in Wine Court Lane was a favorite not only with Johnson but with his fellow writers Dickens and Thackeray. It also happens to be one of London's most child-friendly pubs, with two dining rooms where you can enjoy proper British grub such as roast beef and Yorkshire pudding, and steak-and-kidney pie. Take a look at the leather-bound visitors' books above the bar: They contain the names of prime ministers, lords, and ambassadors who supped here.

Carry on along Fleet Street, turning right after a couple of minutes down Bride Lane. Here is **St. Bride's Church** (© **020/7427-0133**), said to have been the inspiration behind the tiered wedding cake, and one of 51 city churches ravaged by the Great Fire of London but rebuilt by Sir Christopher Wren, architect of St. Paul's Cathedral (p. 155). Descend to its crypt to see some Roman and Saxon remains, including a Roman pavement dated to A.D. 180.

Back onto Fleet Street, take a left after Ludgate Circus. Here you'll find the **Old Bailey** (© 020/7248-3277), Britain's Central Criminal Court, which has seen the trials of criminals as notorious as Dr. Crippen and the Yorkshire Ripper. Kids 14 and over can watch trials from the public galleries if accompanied by an adult. The court occupies the site of Newgate Prison where, until 1868, crowds, including kids, gathered to watch public hangings. Many local children used to spend all day on these streets, enjoying the constant music and entertainment, including organ grinders, acrobats, and jugglers.

Back on Ludgate Hill, it's a short walk to Wren's masterpiece, **St. Paul's Cathedral** (p. 155), which Wren was commissioned to build after the Great Fire of London. To see where the mighty conflagration broke out, walk down Cannon Street for about 10 minutes to reach **The Monument** (p. 154), a column the height of which corresponds to the distance from its base to the king's bakery on **Pudding Lane.** This narrow street, then lined with timbered buildings, many of them housing cooking shops, was where the Great Fire took hold; it lasted 3 days and destroyed 80% of medieval London. The silver lining on this particular cloud, though, was that the fire killed off the rat population that carried the Plague (which had claimed the lives of 100,000 Londoners the previous year).

Continue east, along Eastcheap and then Great Tower Street, to visit **All Hallows by the Tower** (© 020/7481-2928), the church from which famous London diarist Samuel Pepys watched the Great Fire. The museum in its undercroft contains a perfectly preserved portion of Roman pavement (the floor of a late-2nd-c. domestic house) beneath an arch dating from an original church on the site, founded in A.D. 675. Because it is located next to the **Tower of London** (p. 153), the church has dealt with its fair share of beheaded bodies, including those of Thomas More and Archbishop Laud. William Penn, founder of Pennsylvania, was baptized here and educated in the schoolroom (now the Parish Room), while John Quincy Adams, sixth president of the U.S., was married here in 1797.

Follow the wonderfully named Seething Lane northward; more Roman walls and pavements were unearthed along here. This was also where Pepys lived—there's a bust of him in Seething Gardens. He's buried in **St. Olave Hart Street** (© 020/7488-4318), which Dickens renamed Saint Ghastly Grim because of the three skulls on its gateway. You might notice that the graveyard is nearly a meter higher than the floor of the church—this is partly a result of the number of Plague victims buried here in 1665.

In total contrast, just 5 minutes' walk northwest from here on Lime Street, you'll find the high-tech **Lloyd's Building.** Like the Pompidou Center in Paris, this building was designed by Sir Richard Roger and distinctly puts its services (elevators, power conduits, and water pipes) on the outside to leave the inside uncluttered. Though opened in 1984, it looks shockingly modern.

To go back in time again, make a detour to neighboring **Leadenhall Market,** a covered arcade dating from the 14th century and still full of traditional cheese mongers, fishmongers, and butchers, as well as restaurants and cafes. The entrance to the Leaky Cauldron in the first Harry Potter movie was filmed here. Alternatively, to stay in the hyper-modern world, continue up Lime Street and into St Mary Axe to see Sir

Norman Foster's jaw-dropping **20 St Mary Axe,** nicknamed "The Gherkin" for its peculiar shape.

Unless you refueled in Leadenhall Market, you're probably dropping with hunger by now, in which case you can combine a look around the country's oldest surviving synagogue, **Bevis Marks,** with lunch in its adjoining restaurant (© **020/7283-2220**). From the dining room you can see into the old Spanish and Portuguese house of worship with its chandeliers. The menu combines traditional Jewish fare such as chicken soup with matzo balls with inventive combos such as roast lamb with aubergine rice, Swiss chard, and red-pepper coulis. When you leave, walk along the parallel street, **Houndsditch;** once the city's eastern boundary, it got its name in the days it was a furrow into which locals tossed their dead animals.

Liverpool Street Station rises to your right. Head behind it, to a very unusual public space by the name of **Broadgate.** In pre-Roman and Roman times, this was a large marshland outside the city wall; it froze in winter, and local people skated here until the 12th century (a fact commemorated in its open-air winter ice rink; see p. 214). It's now full of sculptures that people are invited to touch and interact with, so it's a great place to bring kids. Pieces include Richard Serra's textured *Fulcrum* (which you can step into order to look up at the sky); Barry Flanagan's gravity-defying *Leaping Hare on Crescent & Bell*; Stephen Cox's *Ganapath & Devi,* stone figures based on the Hindu goddess Devi and the elephant god Ganesh; and Xavier Corbero's *The Broad Family,* consisting of three separate figures, a dog, and a ball. The space also plays host to free lunchtime entertainments and to City of London Festival events (p. 19) in summer.

Make your way down Blomfield Street to **London Wall** which, as the name implies, follows the course of the wall built nearly 20 centuries ago to enclose the Roman city. It's now a modern thoroughfare, but you can still see part of the wall, while also catching a glimpse of **St. Alphage Garden** about 5 minutes' walk away. (The gates are sometimes locked but you can see them from the street.) Adjoining **Fore Street** was the first place German bombs were dropped during World War II.

Round off your thoroughly historical day with a tour of the **Museum of London** (p. 169), built on the site of a Roman fort at the end of the London Wall; or relax in the tiny hidden gem of **Postman's Park** just south of it, with its beautiful tiled wall. The wall commemorates ordinary people who died while carrying out acts of courage in the 19th century, including children killed while trying to save their siblings or friends.

If you choose to stay in the area to dine, a branch of **Pizza Express** (© **020/7600-8880**) actually straddles London Wall (the street of that name), so that you can watch cars race by beneath you. You're also near the trendy restaurants of Smithfield Market, including **Smiths of Smithfield** (p. 136).

## 4 A Refreshing Thames Meander

Die-hard river fans might like to tackle the Thames in its entirety by walking the 350km (215-mile) Thames Path (p. 48), but mere mortals—particularly those with kids—must aim for more bite-size encounters with London's main waterway. There are few better places to do this than lovely, leafy **Chiswick,** another of London's "villages" popular with young families, not least because its historic pubs and gourmet restaurants are some of the most welcoming in the city for those with children.

Arriving in the neighborhood at Hammersmith Tube or bus station, head south along Hammersmith Bridge Road. If you turn right at the river onto the Lower Mall, you'll pass through the refurbished **Furnival Gardens,** a popular patch of green and a good spot from which to watch the annual **Oxford and Cambridge Boat Race** (p. 18). The path now becomes the Upper Mall, where you might stop at the ivy-clad **Old Ship Inn** (no. 25; 🕾 020/8748-2593) to appreciate views of the river and of the jets swooping down into Heathrow to the west. If the weather's fine, you can sit out on the spacious terrace or first-floor balcony for excellent breakfasts (daily 8am–noon) such as cinnamon French toast with fresh fruit, cream and maple syrup, or for a wide-ranging and well-priced all-day menu featuring decent kids' dishes for just £3.95 ($7.90). Barbecue buffets are hosted frequently in warmer months, and it's a great place for traditional Sunday roasts year-round (including several veggie lasagna options).

If the inn is too full, which it often is on summer weekends, a nearby child-friendly option is the colorful **Black Lion** on the site of a former piggery at South Black Lion Lane (🕾 020/8748-2639). Serving good food (including Sunday roasts) and real ales, it has a lovely big courtyard with an ancient gnarled chestnut tree, and a tragic past. An excise officer who lay in wait to shoot the resident ghost 200 years ago mistakenly killed a local bricklayer. There's a children's playground within a few steps.

When you've replenished yourselves, continue westward along the river, which has now become **Chiswick Mall,** a particularly scenic stretch with 17th- to 19th-century town houses complete with wrought-iron verandas. At the end, follow the road round into Church Street, halting perhaps at the partly 15th-century **church of St. Nicholas,** where you'll find tombstones (but not the graves) of local artistic giants J. M. Whistler and William Hogarth. **Hogarth's House** (🕾 020/8994-6757), on Hogarth's Lane, is now a gallery with some of his famous engravings and displays about his life. The wonderful walled garden surrounding it still boasts the painter's mulberry tree.

Just a few minutes' walk west again, along Burlington Lane, is **Chiswick House** (🕾 020/8994-6757; www.english-heritage.org.uk), a fine Palladian villa with amazing interiors (it was built in the 18th c. to host parties for the London elite). The beautiful old park surrounding it, with a lake, a temple, classical statues, Italianate gardens, and a water cascade, has plenty of space for kids to run around in.

From here you're spoiled for choice. One idea is to walk 20 minutes west to reach the little-visited **Kew Bridge Steam Museum** (p. 162) and nearby **Musical Museum** (p. 169). By the time you've looked around those, you'll probably be hungry again. If so, you're in luck. There' are a couple more historic riverside pubs on Thames Road: the **Bell & Crown** (🕾 020/8994-4164), an old smuggler's haunt with excellent food, a bright conservatory, and outdoor seating (children are welcome until 6pm); and the **Bull's Head** (🕾 020/8994-1204), with its creaking floorboards, worn flagstones, and leaded windows. On weekends families jostle for space at the picnic benches on the towpath. Oliver Cromwell made this inn his HQ during the Civil War, and supposedly took refuge on the island you see opposite, hence its name—**Oliver's Island.** Alternatively, Chiswick High Road looping up from Kew Bridge has branches of child-friendly chains **Carluccio's** (p. 109), **Giraffe** (p. 120), **Gourmet Burger Kitchen** (p. 137), **Pizza Express** (p. 115), and **Zizzi** (p. 115). Just off it is **Sam's Brasserie** (p. 130).

Another option is to head north from Chiswick House to shop at **Turnham Green Terrace** with kid-oriented stores, including **Tots** (🕾 020/8995-0520) for smart clothes and accessories; and **Snap Dragon** (🕾 020/8995-6618) for toys. There's also a branch of the excellent **Fishworks** seafood cafe (© **020/8994-0086;** p. 108), and **Theobroma Cacao** (© **020/8996-0431**) chocolate shop, where you can drink hot chocolate and sample truffles. To the north, on The Avenue, is the **Little Trading Company** (© **020/8742-3152**), selling kids' clothes and dress-up wardrobes, toys, books, videos, bikes, new and secondhand strollers, and secondhand furniture. A kids' hairdresser is on hand during certain days, usually Wednesday and Friday afternoons and Saturday mornings.

If shopping's not your bag, head back toward Hammersmith Tube. **Ravenscourt Park** (p. 206) has an adventure playground and a teahouse serving children's meals. Not far away, on Hammersmith Grove, you can round off your day with delicious food at the ultra-child-friendly **Chez Kristof** (p. 129).

# 9

# For the Active Family

London's parks make up one of the most advanced green-lung systems of any large urban area, so lovers of the great outdoors don't have to pine for open spaces here. Unlike the more pruned gardens of, say, Paris, London's parks are charmingly informal, though well maintained. And for the adventurous there are some pretty wild areas, too, in the form of windblown heaths and dense woods and forests.

Award-winning and innovative playgrounds also abound, both outdoor and indoor. Workshop-based activities provide a calmer alternative for those who want to get active in London.

London already has world-class sports venues, many of which will be used to host Olympic Games events in 2012—from archery at Lord's cricket ground to tennis at Wimbledon. The O2, which opened in the former Millennium Dome in 2007 (p. 258), will host Olympic gymnastics and basketball events. But most events will take place at the brand-new Olympic village being built in the lower Lee Valley, spurring regeneration of part of the city's largely deprived East End.

See www.sportengland.org for sports-related information and a searchable database of facilities.

## 1 Green London: The Top Parks

For **Hampstead Heath,** see p. 143. For **Thames Barrier Park,** see p. 155.

### ROYAL PARKS

London is blessed with eight superb royal parks totaling about 2,023 hectares (5,000 acres), all of them free for visitors. Come to stroll, jog, play sports, splash about in the water, watch open-air theater or a pop concert, romp in the playgrounds, get friendly with wildlife, admire architecture and memorials, kick back, sunbathe, or enjoy a sedate picnic. All eight parks have fascinating histories, often as royal hunting grounds. See www.royalparks.gov.uk for full information.

**Bushy Park**   It's hard to imagine that you can exhaust London's central parks, but this little-known space north of the river by Hampton Court Palace (p. 184) is worth venturing out of town for, not least for its interesting history. Its artificial waterway, the Longford River, was created by Charles I to supply the Tudor palace, and it later served as a center for planning Operation Overlord (the D-day landings) under Eisenhower. This is the second-largest royal park, providing a great spot for informal games, cycling, in-line skating, and skateboarding (allowed on all its roads—other parks are much more restrictive), as well as home for more than 300 free-roaming deer. There are also a small cafe, a playground, tennis courts, a heated open-air pool, and, on Chestnut Sunday every May, family entertainment that includes traditional fairground rides, jazz bands, and a display of classic and military vehicles. Hampton, Middlesex, TW12. © 020/8979-1586. Train: Hampton Court.

**The Green Park**   This one-time hunting and dueling ground is a short walk under the dramatic Wellington Arch (p. 156) from Hyde Park, which rather dwarfs it. Games aren't permitted here, but it's still a great place for sunbathing, picnicking, and strolling or jogging on its fine walkways. It's said that if you stand in the middle of the park on a quiet day, you can hear the gurgle of the subterranean Tyburn River that flows into the Thames. The park's main monument is the Queen Victoria Memorial, in honor of the monarch who survived three attempts on her life near this spot, in 1840, 1842, and 1849. There's also a tiny new cafe. Between Bayswater Rd., Park Lane, Knightsbridge, and West Carriage Dr., SW1. ℂ 020/7930-1793. Tube: Green Park.

**Greenwich Park** 𝕲𝕲   This oldest enclosed royal park offers impressive views over the Thames toward the City from its hilltop location. As well as the historic Royal Observatory (p. 171) and some Roman remains, it contains a large deer, fox, and bird sanctuary known as The Wilderness; a tennis center (p. 216); space for informal games; a playground and a children's boating pool; and two cafes with gardens. In summer, little ones can enjoy puppet shows and workshops. Between Crooms Hill, Romney Rd., Maze Hill, and Shooters Hill, SE10. ℂ 020/8858-2608. Tube: Greenwich DLR.

**Hyde Park** 𝕲𝕲𝕲   The city's biggest central park—once Henry VIII's deer and wild boar hunting estate, and a dueling ground in the 18th century—is focused around the Serpentine, where you can hire a paddle boat or rowboat, or even swim (or paddle in the accompanying kids' pool) in July and August. Kids' entertainment is often held by this paddling pool in summer. But all this is just scratching the surface of Hyde Park, though—you can also horseback-ride (p. 213); in-line skate (p. 214); watch the famous soapbox ranters at Speakers Corner (be aware that language can get fruity here, and hecklers aggressive); bounce around in the playgrounds (on the south side and by W. Carriage Dr.); visit the nature and wildlife education center, The Lookout, in the old police observation post; play everything from football to Frisbee on the informal sports field; enjoy a game of tennis on the "pay and play" and kids' mini course (p. 216); and take a look at the Diana, Princess of Wales Memorial Fountain—you can't paddle here but you can cool your feet in the water, or cross one of the three bridges into the center of it. Check the website for events suitable for all ages, such as guided bat walks.

You may also be lucky enough to catch a festival or concert in the park, featuring international acts such as The White Stripes or Peter Gabriel, though these often sell out well in advance (check the website before your visit). "Proms in the Park," relayed from inside Albert Hall onto giant screens, is another rousing experience (p. 249). The best dining option here is probably the newly refurbished **Dell** (ℂ **020/7706-0464**), with its large terrace overlooking the Serpentine, but you can also choose among cafes, hot dog stands, and ice-cream stands galore.

*Insider tip:* If you come in or out by Victoria Gate, sneak a peek though the railings at the curious pet cemetery, in an inner garden behind the old gatekeeper's cottage with hundreds of tiny gravestones. These date from a pet cemetery established here in 1880, after the Duke of Cambridge's pet dog was run over on the road nearby. Dogs, cats, monkeys, and birds were subsequently buried here by their upper-class owners. The cemetery was full by 1915, at which time it closed. Sadly, it can no longer be visited. Between Bayswater Rd., Park Lane, Knightsbridge, and W. Carriage Dr., W2. ℂ 020/7298-2100. www.royalparks.org.uk/parks/hyde_park. Tube: Hyde Park Corner, Lancaster Gate, or Marble Arch.

**Kensington Gardens** 𝕲𝕲𝕲   Blending in with Hyde Park (of which it used to be a part), Kensington Gardens is home to Kensington Palace (p. 184), the last home of

# Kensington Gardens to St. James's Park

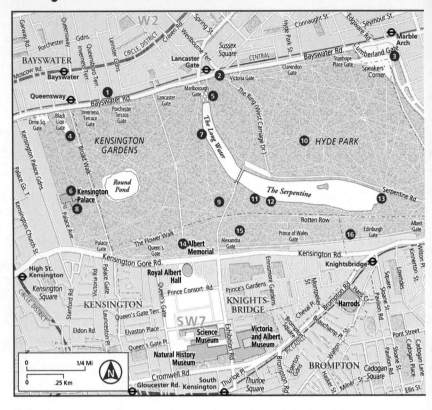

Princess Diana, who is remembered in the Diana Memorial Playground on the north side of the gardens (p. 209). Games aren't encouraged outside the playpark itself, but there's plenty else to keep Junior amused, including the Round Pond with its swooping bird life and its fish and eels (you can also bring model boats to sail); kids' entertainment three times daily in summer; and magical Elfin Oak, a gnarled tree stump brought here from Richmond Park, carved with elves, fairies, and small creatures (it's by the entrance to the Diana playground). Also worth seeking out is the bronze statue of Peter Pan, which was paid for by author J. M. Barrie, who lived nearby (see p. 195 for a Peter Pan walk). You may even strike it lucky and see a free open-air performance of the kids' classic, with dressing up optional.

Make time for afternoon tea at Kensington Palace's stunning Orangery restaurant (p. 186); or visit the Serpentine Gallery, which hosts the occasional family art workshop (p. 219). Between Bayswater Rd., W. Carriage Dr., Kensington Rd., and Palace Green, W2. ✆ 020/7298-2100. Tube: Queensway or High St. Kensington.

**The Regent's Park** ✿✿✿   This hunting ground and farming area under Henry VIII was transformed into an ornate park by 18th-century architect John Nash and is still surrounded by his glorious white-stuccoed terraces, giving it a very refined feel. Aside from the lovely formal gardens, the park contains an open-air theater (p. 248);

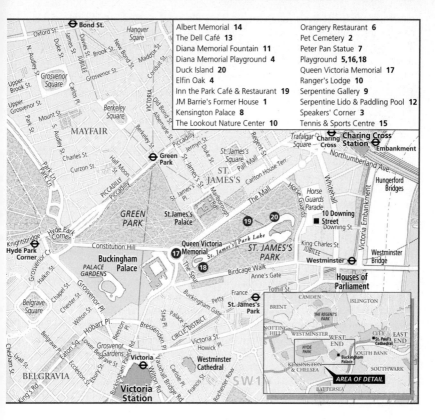

| | |
|---|---|
| Albert Memorial **14** | Orangery Restaurant **6** |
| The Dell Café **13** | Pet Cemetery **2** |
| Diana Memorial Fountain **11** | Peter Pan Statue **7** |
| Diana Memorial Playground **4** | Playground **5,16,18** |
| Duck Island **20** | Queen Victoria Memorial **17** |
| Elfin Oak **4** | Ranger's Lodge **10** |
| Inn the Park Café & Restaurant **19** | Serpentine Gallery **9** |
| JM Barrie's Former House **1** | Serpentine Lido & Paddling Pool **12** |
| Kensington Palace **8** | Speakers' Corner **3** |
| The Lookout Nature Center **10** | Tennis & Sports Centre **15** |

London Zoo (p. 190); three playgrounds; open-to-the-public tennis courts (p. 216); a huge outdoor sports facility called The Hub that includes 16 mini-football pitches for children; and large (for adults) and small (for kids) lakes for summer boating. Children flock here for summer puppet shows and other kids' entertainment—such as a Teddy Bears' Picnic with themed games, music, and drama—and there are musical concerts and community festivals galore. Cafes include The Boathouse, a family venue near the boating lakes, with a large patio, and The Garden for snacks but also "proper" meals. For wonderful views of the London skyline, head for the park's summit, **Primrose Hill.** Between Marylebone Rd., Park Rd., Prince Albert Rd., and Albany St., NW1. ℂ **020/7486-7905.** Tube: Regent's Park, Baker St., or Camden Town.

**Richmond Park** 𝄞  London's biggest open space, situated south of the river, is famous for its fallow and red deer (remnants of its history as a deer park under Charles I), its ring-necked parakeets, and its vast array of wildlife, including swans, pike, and more than 1,000 beetle species (you can even adopt an endangered stag beetle!). Because of these unique inhabitants, the park has been designated a National Nature Reserve. Locals flock here to use the playground, play informal games of football and French cricket, cycle on the designated paths (bike rentals are available in summer from the parking lot near Roehampton Gate), ride horses (from local stables), or fish on Pen Ponds (p. 212). Adventurous types use the wooded areas and hill climbs for cross-country running and orienteering, and you can learn to power kite here (p. 215). The lovely Georgian Pembroke House with its garden is a fine place for a drink or a snack. Surrey, TW10. ℂ 020/8948-3209. Train: Richmond, then bus no. 371.

**St. James's Park** ✿✿    Once a marshland near a leper hospital, before it was converted into a deer nursery by Henry VIII, this wonderful park is dramatically set at the center of three palaces: Westminster (now the Houses of Parliament), St. James's, and Buckingham. In the middle of the park is romantic Duck Island, which is also home to some pelicans (the descendants of a pair presented to Charles II by the Russian ambassador in 1662) and more than 30 other bird species. You can come and watch the pelicans being fed daily at 2:30pm, and in summer there are guided tours of the island. The Inn the Park cafe and restaurant (p. 106) is excellent. The small but imaginative playground has unusual features, including some giant wooden snails. Between Buckingham Palace, The Mall, Horse Guards Rd., and Birdcage Walk, W1. ℂ 020/7930-1793. Tube: St. James's Park.

## WEST LONDON

Lovely **Holland Park** ✿ (ℂ 020/7471-9813; www.rbkc.gov.uk) is about a 20-minute stroll west of Kensington Gardens, in the chi-chi neighborhood between Notting Hill Gate and Shepherd's Bush. This is the one-time estate of **Holland House** (ℂ 0870/770-5866), a Jacobean mansion now home to a scenic youth hostel (with a handful of rooms for two, three, and four people), a posh restaurant, and an open-air opera venue in summer. Kids love both the forested areas with their wild rabbits and the more formal Kyoto Zen garden with its koi (carp), waterfalls, and bridges. The park also features free-roaming peacocks. An ecology center in Old Stable Yard sponsors vacation activities such as pond-dipping, leaf painting, bug hunts, orienteering, and magpie walks for 5- to 10-year-olds (£3/$6); advance booking is required (ℂ 020/7471-9802). Other park amenities include an adventure playground, an under-8s sandpit play area, sports facilities (including tennis courts; p. 216), Whippersnappers music and movement classes (p. 220), and a cafe with plenty of outdoor seating.

A little farther afield but popular with kids for its summer paddling pool and its children's farm with goats, rabbits, and ducks, **Queen's Park** (ℂ 020/8969-5661; www.cityoflondon.gov.uk) is the focal point of a hip family enclave north of Notting Hill. Other attractions include a playground, a sandpit play area for under-6s, a woodland walk, a sensory garden, pitch and putt, tennis courts, and a *pétanque* rink for boules. In summer you can enjoy the paddling pool, as well as bouncing castles, performances, and an annual event featuring stalls and entertainment such as clowns and jugglers. The child-friendly cafe (p. 106) is worth the trip in itself, but try to come before the school kids flood in at 3:30pm.

A similarly family-friendly space in west London is Hammersmith's **Ravenscourt Park** (W6; ℂ 020/8748-3020), with a large paddling pool, a wooden adventure playground, an under-5s club, tennis courts, and basketball nets. It has a good event on National Playday (p. 20), or come on Bonfire Night, when there's a superb fireworks display created with kids in mind. The Tea House is a relaxing spot for breakfast, lunch, or snacks, with a children's menu.

Far to the west, just north of the National Trust's Osterley House, is **Brent Lodge Park** ✿ (W7; ℂ 020/8566-1929), which has a Millennium Maze consisting of 2,000 yew trees and an animal center, dubbed the "Bunny Park," with exotic birds and mammals such as rhea and mongooses, domestic creatures such as rabbits and sheep, and an indoor area with reptiles and spiders, plus monkeys. Next to this "zoo" is an animal-themed playground for 2- to 10-year-olds, with monkey bars, treetop huts, and crocodile benches. Nearby is the largest flight of canal locks in London, **Hanwell Locks;** you can walk up or down the flight, which is very rural in feel, and admire the Three Bridges, where a railway runs beneath a canal that runs beneath a road, built by famous railway engineer Isambard Kingdom Brunel.

## SOUTH LONDON

On the south bank of the Thames, Victorian **Battersea Park** 𝒢𝒢 (SW11; ℭ 020/8871-7530; www.wandsworth.gov.uk) is a large area of woodland, lakes, and lawns set on an old dueling ground. It underwent a huge renovation starting in 2003, so now is a great time to come. The high point for kids is the children's zoo (p. 189), but there's also a boating lake, a deer and bird enclosure, a nature reserve with trails, a riverside promenade, an adventure playground, sports fields and tennis courts, bicycle rentals (p. 211), a Japanese peace pagoda, impressive fountains with more than 50 jets performing a 15-minute crystal display on the hour every hour in summer, and the Pump House modern art gallery (p. 177). Bonfire Night sees a massive fireworks display set to music and lights—one of the best in London.

East along the river, in the area properly called the South Bank, **Jubilee Gardens** by the BA London Eye is being transformed into a world-class public park to rival those in Paris and Barcelona. Promised by autumn 2008 are a superb children's playground and a wide range of open-air entertainment and public events.

Much farther south but worth the trek, **Crystal Palace Park** 𝒢𝒢 (SE20; ℭ 020/8778-9496) is most famous for its Dinosaur Park, built in 1854 (generating its claim to be the "world's first theme park"), massively restored a couple of years back and containing 30 life-size models of prehistoric creatures, plus a geological time trail. Though some of the models have been discredited by subsequent scientific discoveries (for instance, the iguanadons are shown on all fours, rather than upright), they're still fascinating—and the attraction is free. The park was also the site of the original Crystal Palace, built for the Great Exhibition of 1851, and a few remains of the structure can be seen, including the terrace arches and the sphinx. Elsewhere, you'll find the National Sports Centre (p. 211); a concert bowl by a lily-covered pond, a maze, a boating lake and children's farm (both under renovation at the time of writing), a play area, and a family-friendly cafe. The Buzz, a program of activities for 6- to 12-year-olds, is held during Easter and summer vacations.

Farther west, **Wimbledon Common** (SW19; ℭ 020/8778-7655; www.wpcc.org.uk), best known for its fictional Womble inhabitants (from a TV show about recycling critters living on the common), is a much wilder space with woods, ponds, horse-riding tracks (p. 213), and the Windmill Museum and nature trail (p. 174). Together with adjoining **Putney Heath,** it hosts lots of events throughout the year, including funfairs, walks, and Wildlife Watch Club events such as minibeast safaris, fungi forays, and pond-dipping.

To the west of this, beside Kew Gardens, the **Old Deer Park** (ℭ 020/8831-6115) got its name from a hunting park created by James I in 1604. As well as a swimming complex called Pools on the Park (p. 216) and sports facilities, there are brilliant play areas here for tots to teens, plus circus big tops and funfairs during vacations.

## EAST LONDON

London's East End isn't best known for its green or child-friendly spaces, which makes the family-oriented **Mile End Park** ✶✶ (© 020/7364-4147; www.mileendpark.co.uk) all the more of a surprise. Subject to an ongoing multimillion-pound makeover, it now boasts an ecology park with a lake complex, a wind turbine, and wildlife habitats; an adventure park with a 21st-century metal spaceship tree house and more; a children's center with indoor and outdoor play (including under-5s drop-in sessions); an arts park with a gallery; a sports park with tennis courts and other amenities; a go-cart track; cycle tracks; a climbing wall (p. 212); tree-lined Green Bridge (with restaurants beneath it); and—new in 2006—a state-of-the art leisure center with swimming pools and more, and a skateboarding, in-line skating, and BMX facility (complete with half-pipes). A healthy program of family events includes an annual carnival parade and Halloween celebration.

A little more sedate, but worth a visit if you're in the area, is **Victoria Park** (© 020/8985-1957; www.towerhamlets.gov.uk), an appealing 19th-century canal-side park dubbed "the Regent's Park of the East End." Here you'll find deer and goats, play areas, a paddling pool, lakes, ponds, fountains, ornamental gardens, a Chinese summerhouse, tennis courts, and tearooms. Frequent festivals include fetes, circuses, and open-air concerts, and the world's oldest model boat club holds several regattas here each year. **Royal Inn on the Park** pub (© 020/8985-3321) by the main entrance has a beer garden and a good Sunday lunch.

Stretching 42km (26 miles) from the Thames at East India Dock Basin out of London into Hertfordshire, **Lee Valley Park** ✶ (© 01992/702200; www.leevalleypark.org.uk) is an astonishing 4,047-hectare (10,000-acre) network of countryside areas and parks, urban green spaces, heritage sites, nature reserves, farms, lake and riverside trails, and sports and recreation centers. A whole lot of new facilities are being added to serve as venues during the 2012 Olympics; for the meantime, the vast array of activities on offer include bird- and wildlife-watching, boating, cycling, walking, horseback riding (p. 213), and fishing. There are also an ice rink (p. 214), a swimming complex (p. 215), and a cart track. In fact, the park is so vast that you'll find it worthwhile to call in advance for advice on how to get the most out of your visit.

## NORTH LONDON

North London's most central park is Islington's **Highbury Fields** (N5; © 020/7527-4971), with its acclaimed under-12s adventure playground, tennis courts, soccer pitches, picnic area, and cafe, but there are several very good green spaces farther north. **Clissold Park** (N16; © 020/7923-3660) is a true family park, with a large animal enclosure including deer; an aviary and a butterfly tunnel; a playground and a summer paddling pool; tennis courts; and pitching grounds. The cute cafe has lawn tables overlooking a river chock-full of ducks and swans. Summer events include children's activities, circuses, and funfairs, including visits by Carters Steam Fair (p. 209). Combine a visit here with a trip to **Abney Park Cemetery & Nature Reserve** (p. 192) along the same street, then explore the quirky little shops, restaurants, and cafes of bohemian but family-friendly Stoke Newington, or "Stokey" to locals.

Over to the west, not far from Hampstead, **Waterlow Park** ✶ (N6; © 020/7974-8810; www.camden.gov.uk) is quite secluded and has remained a bit of a hidden gem. It's gorgeous, though, with its green slopes, three lakes, wonderful views of the City and south London, and tennis courts. Kids head here for its toddlers' playground, its aviary (used as a recovery center for injured birds), and most of all for Lauderdale

## Fair's Fair

Funfairs can be tacky, noisy, overbearing affairs for kids. Not so **Carters Steam Fair,** a traditional and very family-friendly event that tours various London parks (including Clissold Park and Ravenscourt Park; see p. 208 and p. 206) throughout the summer months. Here the garish rides typical of modern funfairs are replaced by lovingly restored vintage rides, including 1960s rock-'n'-roll bumper cars and the Dive Bomber, a restored 1946 thrill ride. Nearly all the side stalls, which include hooplas and a fishing game, are pre–World War II, and this is also virtually the only remaining funfair with old-style living vans (similar to caravans). Visit www.carterssteamfair.co.uk for more information, or call ℂ **01628–822221**.

House, with its enormously popular workshops and shows (p. 254), as well as its cafe terrace.

Farthest north of all is **Alexandra Park** (ℂ **020/8365-2121;** www.alexandra-palace.com), a 79-hectare (196-acre) hilltop park best known for its panoramic views over London. Surrounding the reconstructed Victorian Alexandra Palace (from which the BBC made the first public TV transmissions in 1936), the park has a boating lake, a pitch-and-putt golf course, a conservation area, an animal enclosure with deer and donkeys, a playground, a skateboarding park, and a cafe. Come for one of the vacation family funfairs, or for the superb Bonfire Night fireworks display, when there are indoor and outdoor funfairs and a food festival. There's also a year-round ice rink inside Alexandra Palace (p. 214), which is, however, scheduled for redevelopment in the coming years.

## 2 Playgrounds

Most of the parks described above have playgrounds, usually separate ones for toddlers and older children. **Highgate Wood**'s playgrounds are particularly good. For many of London's 80-plus adventure playgrounds, see **www.londonplay.org.uk**, including ones designed for children with disabilities, see **www.kidsactive.org.uk**. Also keep an eye out for notice boards near playgrounds, which often advertise children's events not publicized elsewhere.

**Coram's Fields** ★★★   This wonderful 2.8-hectare (7-acre) playground on the site of the 18th-century Foundling Hospital for abandoned children (see p. 164 for the Foundling Museum) celebrated its 60th birthday in 2006. It's a proper kids' sanctuary in a rather deprived area of Bloomsbury, with adults allowed in only if accompanied by a child—safety is paramount. There's also an overall aim to make all facilities accessible to kids with disabilities; a new sensory play area paves the way. Inside the charming space are an excellent adventure playground, an under-5s sandy play area, a toddlers' club, a summer paddling pool, a fountain, an animal-petting enclosure with goats, sheep, and ducks, all-weather sports fields, and a veggie cafe to which parents can retreat when things get too hectic (the nearby Brunswick Centre [p. 110] has also become home to several child-friendly eateries). Notice boards flag up special events. 93 Guilford St., WC1. ℂ 020/7837 6138. www.coramsfields.org. Tube: Russell Sq.

**Diana Memorial Playground** ★★★   This truly innovative playpark has a loose Peter Pan theme—a previous playground on the site was funded by the book's author,

## Going Wild in London

Halfway between Alexandra Park and Hampstead Heath, **Highgate Wood** (© 020/8444-6129; www.cityoflondon.gov.uk) was declared "an open space for ever" by London's Lord Mayor in 1886 and, astonishingly for space located in such an urban area, it has blossomed over the years into a dense, ancient forest with an array of wildlife. This is one of the best places in the city for a lung-expanding walk, even—or perhaps especially—on a downright chilling morning, when its winding, leaf-strewn pathways are at their most romantic. If you want something more structured, there are nature trails, sporting grounds, and two award-winning playgrounds, one for older kids and one for tots, with plenty of features for youngsters with disabilities. An imaginative program of events takes place year-round: readings at the Story Telling Tree, displays by a local bee-keeper, beetle safaris, and bat watches. Afterward, repair to the delightful Pavilion Cafe for a warming mug of chocolate inside or outside on its terrace. (The cafe hosts live jazz some summer evenings.) Then visit nearby Ripping Yarns bookshop for its secondhand kids' classics (p. 226).

If Highgate Wood hasn't made you feel all Blair Witch, you might venture out to **Epping Forest** (© 020/8508-0028; www.cityoflondon.gov.uk), on the far northeastern outskirts of the city. London's largest public space, this ancient woodland covers almost 2,428 hectares (6,000 acres) of grassland, heath, rivers, bogs, and ponds, and is a fantastic place to bike and horseback-ride (p. 214). It's a good idea to get your bearings at the Information Centre at High Beech, Loughton, where you can get info and advice, books, and maps.

---

J. M. Barrie. (See p. 195 for a Peter Pan walk, and p. 203 for more about Kensington Gardens, in which the playpark is set, and its Peter Pan–related events.) Designed for kids up to 12, it is based around an almost life-size pirate ship with a mast that older kids can climb, and has tepees, a beach cove with fossil imprints for paddling, "tree phones" allowing kids to communicate across the playground, a tree house encampment suitable for wheelchair users, and much, much more. On summer weekends, locals and visitors battle it out for lawn space on which to spread their picnic blankets, and the cafe becomes a scene of terrifying chaos, so try to come during the week or out of season. Kensington Gardens, W8. © 020/7298-2141. www.royalparks.gov.uk. Tube: Queensway.

## 3 Sports & Games

If you're staying at an expensive hotel or in a serviced apartment, you'll likely have access to a swimming pool (see p. 72 for hotels with pools) and health club, either directly or through temporary membership to a nearby facility, though gym equipment is usually out of bounds for under-16s. For comprehensive listings of municipal centers across the capital, as well as private health clubs, see www.health-club.net.

One of London's best general sports venues is **Westway Sports Centre** (1 Crowthorne Rd., W10; © 020/8969/0992; www.westway.org/sports/wsc), which has Britain's biggest indoor climbing center, outdoor climbing (inside a road roundabout!), eight indoor tennis courts, four public clay tennis courts, four Eton Fives (handball) courts, six football pitches, a gym accessible to those with disabilities, a basketball court and hoops, and a cafe and sports bar. Farther to the south, **Crystal Palace National Sports Centre** (Ledrington Rd., SE19; ✆ 020/8778-0131; www.bromley.gov.uk) is a world-class stadium used for national and international competitions. Facilities include four swimming pools, a diving pool with springboards and platforms, a climbing wall, a dance studio, and an indoor playground for 2- to 10-year-olds (p. 218). There are a children's activity club, a crèche, and courses in trampolining and more. The **Central YMCA** (112 Great Russell St., WC1; ✆ 020/7343-1700; www.ymcaclub.co.uk) is another option—a well-located, good-value, and well-equipped sports club with a 25m (82-ft.) pool; daily "taster" or weekly membership is available.

If you're here for a while and want to stay fit, one of the best options is to become a member of **Esporta Swiss Cottage** (O2 Centre, 255 Finchley Rd.; ✆ 020/7644-2424; www.esporta.com/swisscottage), which has children's activities and classes for various age groups, from art to swimming, plus a crèche. While the kids are otherwise detained, parents can make use of a 25m (82-ft.) swimming pool, fitness studios (one with holistic classes), saunas, steam rooms, sun beds, beauty salons and a spa, and a bar and brasserie; there's also a separate children's pool.

## BIKING

Traffic-frenzied London is not a great place for cyclists—dedicated lanes are scarce, even in many of the major parks; they allow you to cut through but not take a leisurely tour. If your heart's set on a two-wheeler tour of the capital, arm yourself with a copy of the extremely informative **Haynes' *London Cycle Guide*** (£9/$18) from www.haynes.com, which points out the best areas for cycling, from touristed sites to lesser-known areas such as waterways, many of them traffic-free. Alternatively, the **London Cycle Network** has a series of 19 free local guides with routes and useful contacts such as cycle stores—see www.tfl.gov.uk or call **0845/7305-1234** to order one. Visit www.lcc.org.uk for a list of recommended cycle-hire shops in London, details of occasional organized events, and tips for cycling with kids.

Great fun is also to be had with **London Recumbents** 🚲🚲 (✆ 020/8299-6636; www.londonrecumbents.com), which hires out all kinds of vehicles, from low-slung, horizontal bikes for adults and kids, side-by-side tandem tricycles, family tandems, and bikes with trailers that you can take for a spin around Dulwich Park in south London or Battersea Park, closer to the center. Prices start at £6 ($12) an hour. Other attractive places to cycle are tranquil **Lee Valley Park** (p. 208) and **Epping Forest** (p. 210).

## BOWLING

The most central addresses for this good, cheap, rainy-day standby are **Queens Ice Bowl,** at 17 Queensway just off Kensington Gardens (W2; ✆ 020/7229-0172; www.queensiceandbowl.co.uk), with 12 full-size bowling lanes, plus a modern ice rink, video games, and a bar/cafe with a pizza menu; **Funland** in the Trocadero Center in Piccadilly Circus (p. 260), with 10 lanes; and **Namco Station** in Country Hall on the South Bank (p. 260), with 12 ultraviolet lanes and a special floor that makes shoe hire unnecessary. Out of the center, **Tenpin** (Royal Leisure Park, Western Ave., W3; ✆ 0871/550-1010; www.megabowl.co.uk) has 28 lanes and offers "Cosmic Bowling" with fluorescent balls. It also has American pool tables and other amusements.

## CLIMBING

London is basically devoid of hills and mountains, so your best option for a spot of climbing is the fairly central **Westway Sports Centre** (p. 210), which contains one of Britain's largest climbing complexes. Facilities here include indoor bouldering, a vertigo-inducing high-ropes adventure course with rope ladders, balance beams, caving areas, and a totem pole; there are outdoor walls as well. Come Sunday, special family sessions for ages 5 and up run on a first-come, first-served basis and cost £4.50 ($9) for juniors and £8 ($16) for adults; various taster opportunities and holiday sessions are also available. Otherwise, it costs £5.75 ($12) per casual climbing session, £8.50 ($17) for adults, on top of one-off registration fees of £2.50 ($5) and £3.50 ($7) respectively.

**Castle Climbing Centre** (© 020/8211-7000; www.castle-climbing.co.uk) is another excellent facility a little farther out of town in an old pumping station in Manor House, north London. Children of any age can climb here under the supervision of a registered adult climber, and 9- to 16-year-olds can sign up for Geckos, a kids' climbing school providing supervision and instruction, including 3-day beginners' and intermediate courses. French- and Spanish-speaking instructors are available. Occasional trips are made to outdoor climbing venues, such as the Southern Sandstone in Kent and the beautiful Peak District National Park. Prices are £10 ($20) for adults after a one-time registration fee of £4 ($8), and £5.50 ($11) for under-18s.

Also a way out of town, the East End's **Mile End Climbing Wall** (© 020/8980-0289; www.mileendwall.org.uk) is an established center that has trained some of the country's top climbers and mountaineers but welcomes total novices. Its popular Kids' Club "fun-level" sessions for children 8 to 16 cost £6 ($12) and last 90 minutes. There's also a climbing wall at **Crystal Palace National Sports Centre** (p. 211).

For something a little more offbeat, visit Ellis Brigham's winter sports shop at 3–11 Southampton St. in Covent Garden, WC2, to experience the **Vertical Chill,** an 8m (26-ft.) concave real ice-climbing wall running up through its two stories. Lessons cost £40 ($80). A 1-hour Climb & Hire with equipment, for experienced climbers, is £30 ($60). There's a lower age limit of 12, but those parents with under-16s should discuss their kids' fitness, strength, and experience at the time of booking (© 020/7395-1010; www.verticalchill.com).

## DANCE

**Danceworks** ⚡ (16 Balderton St., W1; © 020/7629-6183; www.danceworks.co.uk) offers Europe's biggest selection of dance, fitness, and yoga classes (168, to be precise) in a listed Victorian building. Kids' classes include drop-in street dance for ages 10 to 15, which costs just £3/$6 for 90 minutes. You can also get one-to-one tuition in everything from ballet to Bollywood and bhangra grooves.

There are also highly popular dance and/or drama workshops at the **Tricycle** theater and cinema in Kilburn (p. 254), including the likes of a street dance day for ages 12 to 15 (£10/$20), followed by a performance.

## FISHING

London, need it be said, is not fishing central. However, attractive places at which to while away a few hours with a rod and line include **Lee Valley Park** (p. 208), **Syon Park** (p. 188), **Clapham Common,** and **Pen Ponds** in lovely Richmond Park (p. 205). The latter are open June to March by paid permit, with special rates for children. Note that anyone over 12 who fishes in fresh water in England or Wales must have an Environment Agency rod license, which is available from post offices and costs from £3.25 ($6.50) for 1 day to £67 ($134) for a season, depending on age and the type of fish caught. The fine, if you get caught without a license, is huge.

See www.londonanglers.net for a list of waters in and around London, mainly canal towpaths, that can be fished in using one of the good-value **day tickets** (£3.50/$7) for adults, £1.50/$3 for children).

## FLYING

For an uplifting experience, **Adventure Balloons** (© 01252/844222; www.adventure balloons.co.uk) offers 1-hour early-morning hot-air balloon flights from Hampshire over London and its surrounds, with a lower-age limit of 9 (their height must exceed 1.4m/55 in.). Allow 4 to 6 hours for the experience, including preparation of the balloon, deflation and packing of it, and returning to London after being dropped at the nearest Underground or rail station. (Balloons cover 3–32km/2–20 miles, with the direction determined by the wind, and spend about 1 hr. in the air). You'll fly over The O2 (p. 256), Tower Bridge (p. 156), and more. Flights cost £175 ($350) per person, include champagne for adults, and take place shortly after dawn on Tuesday to Thursday mornings from May to mid-August.

Alternatively, try a 30-minute **helicopter sightseeing tour** from Elstree Aerodrome in north London, available on Sunday and selected Saturdays (© **020/8953-4411;** www.cabairhelicopters.com/sightseeing). Flights (£149/$298 per person) follow the route of the Thames as far east as the Thames Flood Barrier, while the captain gives a full commentary.

## GOLF

Little legs tend to do better with **pitch-and-putt** short golf courses than full-size versions; two of the most convenient are at **Queen's Park** in west London (p. 206) and at **Alexandra Park** to the north of the city (p. 209). There are also putting facilities in royal **Hyde Park** and **Greenwich Park** (p. 203). For larger-scale golfing action, there's **Richmond Park** (p. 205), which has two public 18-hole courses used for pay and play, a 16-bay driving range, a large pro shop, and group lessons for kids on Saturdays starting at noon (© **020/8876-3205**).

## HORSEBACK RIDING

London may not seem like the most obvious place for horseback riding, but the sport has a long tradition in the city—all those lovely mews houses you see were originally built for horses and carriages—and there are wonderfully atmospheric places to ride here. The best riding spot of all, perhaps, and certainly the most central, is **Hyde Park** ★★★, which includes a specialist riding arena, or *maneges,* plus two designated bridleways, the North Ride and the South Ride. Trotting along the park's sandy tracks between modern and classic buildings and frolicking park-goers is a quintessential London experience, especially on a beautiful summer evening. **Hyde Park Stables** (63 Bathurst Mews, W2; © **020/7723-2813;** www.hydeparkstables.com) welcomes beginners, and its horses and ponies are extremely docile beasts. Group rides start at £49 ($98) per person, boots and hats included, and there are half-day camps for kids year-round. The minimum age for riders is 5.

Another fine royal park for equestrian excursions is **Richmond Park** (p. 205), which has several stables nearby (© **020/8948-3209** for details). One of the firms, **Wimbledon Village Stables** (24a/b High St., SW9; © **020/8946-8579;** www.wvstables. com), also offers rides on **Wimbledon Common** (p. 207). There are regular pony care sessions and 3-day children's holiday courses (£145/$290), which include a riding session, an activity, and a booklet to be filled in every day.

In a more unlikely setting beneath west London's main flyover, **Westway Stables** (© 020/8964-2140; www.westwaystables.co.uk) offers rides on the large outdoor sand area or on the nearby open space of Wormwood Scrubs, which is where folks used to come to hone their skills before exposing themselves to high society on Rotten Row in Hyde Park. Prices are keen. For really horse-mad kids, Pony Days feature grooming and other aspects of horsemanship, riding tuition, gymkhana games, quizzes, and other fun activities (half-day £28/$56, full day £50/$100).

On the other side of London, **Lee Valley Riding Centre** in Lee Valley Park (© 020/8556-2629; www.leevalleypark.org.uk) has indoor and outdoor arenas and cross-country trails. The minimum age is 5 except for private lessons, which can be arranged for younger kids. Pretty far east but specializing (not exclusively) in riding for adults and kids with disabilities is **Docklands Equestrian Centre** (2 Claps Gate Lane, Beckton, E6; © 020/7511-3917). Finally, **Epping Forest** (p. 210) is another good spot for riding.

## ICE-SKATING

London's loveliest rink, in the splendid 18th-century courtyard of **Somerset House** ✹✹✹ (p. 178), is open for a lamentably short period each year, from late November to late January. This means tickets and space are difficult to obtain, so it's often necessary to book ahead. Skating generally takes place from 10am to 10pm. It costs £10 ($20) per hour for adults, £2 ($4) for kids, and £29 ($58) for a family ticket (all including skate rental). The venue is superb whenever you come, but in the evening, flaming torches and architectural lights illuminate the building's classical facades. Don't forget a post-skate hot chocolate at the cafe overlooking the rink.

Another outdoor rink, **Broadgate Ice Arena,** is open for a longer period between November and April. It's in the City, close to Liverpool Street station (3 Broadgate, EC2; © 020-7505-4068). You might find other festive open-air rinks at the **Natural History Museum, Hampstead Heath,** the **Tower of London, Canary Wharf, Greenwich, Kew Gardens, Hampton Court Park,** and **Windsor.**

Current year-round indoor facilities include the **Queens Ice Bowl** (p. 211) near Hyde Park, which used to be huge but got scaled down to fit in the bowling lanes and gaming facilities; **Lee Valley Ice Centre** (Lee Bridge Rd., Leyton; © 020/8533-3154) in Lee Valley Park (p. 208), which offers family sessions and disco nights with a music-and-light show; **Alexandra Palace** (p. 209); and **Streatham Ice Arena** (386 Streatham High St., SW16; © 020/8769-7771; www.streathamicearena.co.uk).

## IN-LINE SKATING

There aren't many places to in-line skate in the capital, since most parks ban the sport. Your best bets are **Hyde Park** and **Kensington Gardens** (p. 203), especially alongside the Serpentine. **Citiskate** (© 07840/368712; www.citiskate.co.uk) gives group lessons here and in other London locations, including Battersea Park. Citiskate also runs Friday Night Skates (starting at 8pm from Hyde Park Corner and lasting 2 hr.; these are unsuitable for most kids), the Sunday Roller Stroll (also covering a substantial distance), and—best by far for children—the Easy Peasy Skate (every Sat from 10:30am around Battersea Park, lasting 20–30 min.). All are free. Those who want to go it alone might like to try **Bushy Park** (p. 202), where you can skate wherever you like. Citiskate's website has lists of in-line **skate retailer and/or rental firms.** It costs from £10 ($20) per day.

SkateFresh (© 0711/204-5133; www.skatefresh.com) offers tuition, including a monthly workshop for kids 6 to 10, in Hyde Park, and a "Mummy Buggy Skate" for moms with kids in strollers, near the Diana Memorial Playground. They also teach in Greenwich Park.

For the fast-growing sport of **power kiting,** head to Richmond Park (p. 205), where **Kite Vibe** 🌟🌟 (© 0207 870 7700; www.kitevibe.com) leads taster sessions and courses in it year-round. Participants age 10 and up (accompanied by an adult 18 or older) can choose from various ways to be pulled along by a kite—by sitting in a kite buggy, wearing a pair of inline skates, or riding a surf board. A class in two-line skating (the starter level) costs £30 ($60) per person, with a maximum class size of four.

## MOTOR SPORTS

Petrolheads keen to experience the thrill of driving real racing carts can head for south London's **Streatham Kart Raceway** (390 Streatham High St., SW16; © **020/8677-8677;** www.playscape.co.uk), which offers practice sessions for kids ages 8 to 16 on weekdays and "Cadet School" the first Saturday morning of the month (£35/$70). **F1 City Racing Circuit** out in the East End (Gate 119, Connaught Bridge, Royal Victoria Dock, E16; © **020/7476-5678;** www.f1city.co.uk) also offers junior racing in 72kmph (45-mph) single-engine carts on their 500m (1,640-ft.) Monaco outdoor circuit, costing £20 ($40) for 15 minutes, £30 ($60) for 30 minutes, and £45 ($90) for 45 minutes. There's also a Cadet School on Sunday mornings.

## SKATEBOARDING

With the redevelopment of the Royal Festival Hall, the **South Bank Centre** (p. 246) is no longer the city's skateboarding mecca. Another unofficial spot is under the **Westway** flyover in west London, but there's also the **Baysixty6 Skatepark** 🌟🌟 (© 020/8969-4669; www.baysixty6.co.uk), nearby at Acklam Road, W10, with a great layout and a huge variety of ramps. It's not cheap, at £6 ($12) for a 4- or 5-hour session (£3/$6 for beginners), and you should avoid Saturdays, when it's very busy.

## SWIMMING

Britain's capital is a surprisingly great place to swim, with some atmospheric venues, both indoor and out (for the latter, see "Alfresco Swimming at London's Lidos," below). One of the best is **Ironmonger Row Baths** near Old Street (1–11 Ironmonger Row, EC1; © **020/7253-4011;** www.aquaterra.org), a 1930s pool with original features and Turkish baths (steam room, massage slabs, and an icy plunge pool) where parents can take turns relaxing. At the other end of the extreme, **Crystal Palace National Sports Centre** (p. 211) is far from cozy but has world-class swimming and diving facilities.

If you're more interested in swooshing down slides than swimming laps, the following pools have extras, which may include wave machines, beach areas, rapids, and flumes: **Archway Leisure Centre,** N19 (© 020/7281-4105), **Janet Adegoke Leisure Centre,** Hammersmith, W12 (© 020/8743-3401), **Latchmere Leisure Centre,** Battersea, SW11 (© 020/7207-8004), **Leyton Leisure Lagoon,** E10 (© 020/8558-4860), **Tottenham Green Leisure Centre,** N15 (© 020/8365-0322), **Waterfront Leisure Centre,** SE18

## Alfresco Swimming at London's Lidos

Given the generally perilous state of Britain's weather, there's an amazing number of outdoor pools in London, many of them stunning reminders of architecturally more glamorous times, as well as family lifesavers on long, hot summer days. One of the best-known is the **Brockwell Lido** 🏊🏊 (Brockwell Park, Dulwich Rd., SE24; ✆ 020/7274-3088; www.brockwelllido.com), which reopened in mid-2007 in time to celebrate its 70th birthday and carry on serving as "Brixton's Beach." Whippersnappers activity sessions (music classes) for kids (p. 220) continue to run here, and a new cafe was scheduled to open at the time of writing.

Another Art Deco venue is **Charlton Lido** (Hornfair Park, SE7; ✆ 020/8317-5000; www.greenwich.gov.uk), set in a landscaped park and consisting of an unheated 50m (164-ft.) pool, a children's splash pool, sunbathing areas, and a cafe. A face-lift is in the offing. A third lido south of the river, **Tooting Bec Lido** 🏊 (Tooting Bec Rd., SW16; ✆ 020/8871-7198; www.wandsworth.gov.uk) was London's first purpose-built (1906) open-air pool, and is Britain's largest freshwater pool, at 90m (295 ft.) in length. It has a paddling pool with toy animals, and a cafe.

Richmond's **Pools on the Park** complex, now part of the Springhealth Leisure Club (Twickenham Rd., TW9; ✆ 020/8940-0561), consists of a newly refurbished 33m (108-ft.) outdoor swimming pool with a sunbathing area, plus an indoor and a learners' pool. Not too far away on the north bank of the river, **Hampton Heated Open Air Pool** 🏊 (✆ 020/8255-1116; www.hamptonpool.co.uk) on the western boundary of Bushy Park (p. 202) is an excellent lido built in 1922, with a springboard and two small slides, as well as a

(✆ 020/8317-5000), and **Lee Valley Leisure Pool** (✆ 01992/467899) in Lee Valley Park (p. 208), with a wave machine and a learner pool, as well as a softplay area.

## TENNIS

Visitors keen to get a tennis fix should consider staying at one of the moderate or inexpensive hotels in Bloomsbury's Cartwright Gardens, which offer free use of four communal tennis courts, as well as free racket and ball loan (p. 74). The Four Seasons hotel in Canary Wharf (p. 96) also allows access to a court.

Otherwise, most larger London parks have courts, with some of the best in the royal parks (p. 202), which encourage visitors to turn up and play (you can book ahead, too). Prices tend to be £10 to £12 ($20–$24) per hour; sometimes facilities are free for kids. Some offer coaching for kids and adults; among these are **Hyde Park** (✆ 020/7262-3474) and **The Regent's Park** (✆ 020/7486-4216), both of which have kids' half-size courts; **Greenwich Park** (✆ 020/8293-0276); and **Bushy Park** (✆ 020/8943-634). **Holland Park** (p. 206) also has some smart, quite central courts (✆ 020/7471-9813). **Westway Sports Centre** (p. 210) has London's only public clay courts, plus eight indoor courts; coaching is offered.

smaller teaching pool. It's open all year, with water heated to 82°F (28°C), and has a cafe.

One of London's most famous outdoor venues is in the heart of the city, in Hyde Park (p. 203), in the form of a marked-off area of the **Serpentine** 🏊🏊🏊 boating lake (© 020/7706-3422; www.serpentinelido.com). It's open May to September, but some hardy members of its swimming club take the plunge on Christmas morning. It has a paddling pool, a sandpit, swings, a slide, and children's entertainment in summer. Another central option is the outdoor pool at **Oasis Sports Centre** (32 Endell St., WC2H; © 020/7831-1804; www.camden.gov.uk), on the site of a *bagnio* (Turkish bath) used by Queen Anne and now surrounded by office blocks, making it peculiarly urban in feel. Even on a chilly winter's day, it's more popular than the center's indoor pool, though it's more of a lap pool than somewhere to splash around.

North of here, there has long been a tradition of free open-air swimming in the single-sex (nude) and mixed **ponds on Hampstead Heath** 🏊🏊, NW3 (© 020/7485-3873; www.cityoflondon.gov.uk). The men's pool is a fascinating clublike environment with a cast of chess-players, weight lifters, and readers, as well as swimmers and sunbathers. The ponds are fed by natural springs, so they're pretty clean, but they are closed for treatment if algae levels get out of control. Under-16s need to be accompanied, and under-8s are not allowed. Also on the heath, the unheated 60m (197-ft.) **Parliament Hill Lido** 🏊🏊, NW5 (© 020/7485-3873), dates back to 1938 but has recently been refurbished and has a small paddling pool.

For fascinating background on London's lidos, with lots of historical photos, see www.lidos.org.uk.

## WALKING & ORIENTEERING

London is a great city for strolling, whether through its parks, around its street markets or historic churches, or along its canal banks. See p. 195 for my top Neighborhood Strolls for those with kids.

If you're feeling more energetic, there's a **Green Chain** (www.greenchain.com) network of walks from three points along the Thames to Crystal Palace in south London, threading its way through 27km (17 miles) of open space, which takes in wildlife, ruins, farms, playgrounds, and the model dinosaurs of Crystal Palace Park (p. 207). The website has suggested children's routes, and an excellent page on walking with kids and keeping them amused along the way, from treasure hunts to sculpture-making from natural materials. You can buy an official Routes Pack (£3.50/$7 via the website) with detailed color maps.

If you're interested in orienteering in the city (orienteering is a walk—or run—during which you use a map to find your own way to checkpoints or "control sites"), there's a course of varying difficulties on **Hampstead Heath** (p. 143), with maps and compasses available from the Information Center next to the Lido.

## WATERSPORTS

There are few finer ways of spending a steamy city afternoon than taking a boat out on the lakes in **Hyde Park** 🎭🎭 (p. 203) or **Regent's Park** 🎭🎭 (p. 204). For something altogether more structured and windblown, you can try **Surrey Docks Watersports Centre** (Rope St., off Plough Way, Greenland Dock, Rotherhithe, SE16; ℂ **020/7237-4009;** www.fusion-lifestyle.com). The center offers canoeing, windsurfing, and sailing for kids, on both inland and tidal waters, plus spectator events such as regattas and dragonboat racing. Or try **Docklands Sailing & Watersports Centre** (35a Westferry Rd., Millwall Dock, E14; ℂ **020/7537-2626;** www.dswc.org), which has access to both a large sheltered dock area and the River Thames. In west London, **Canalside Activity Centre** (Canal Close, W10; ℂ **020/8968-4500;** www.rbkc.gov. uk) offers canal-based watersports such as kayaking, together with special kids' activities that include trampolining.

## YOGA

As well as teaching kids to control their emotions and relieve anxiety, yoga can increase their concentration levels and their physical strength. The enchanting **Special Yoga Centre** in Queen's Park (Tay Building, Wrentham Ave., NW1; ℂ **020/8968-1900;** www.specialyoga.org.uk) runs classes for kids ages 2 to teens. Classes cost £10 ($20) for an hour. It also offer Pilates, capoeira, and kung fu classes for all ages, pregnancy yoga, baby massage and baby yoga, and yoga for children with special needs. **Triyoga** in hip Primrose Hill (6 Erskine Rd., NW3; ℂ **020/7483-3344;** www.triyoga.co.uk) runs kids classes for various age groups, with prices averaging £11 ($22) per hour. There are also mum-and-baby sessions, and baby massage. Lastly, **Yogabugs** (ℂ **020/ 8772-1800;** www.yogabugs.com) integrates yoga postures into adventures and creative stories for kids 2½ to 7; its teachers work at health clubs and yoga centers throughout London and beyond. A sister organization, **Yoga'd Up,** has recently set up to cater to kids 8 to 12.

## 4 Indoor Playgrounds

One of the best indoor playgrounds in London is the superb plant-themed **Climbers & Creepers** area at Kew Gardens (p. 191). Syon Park also has a **Snakes & Ladders** indoor playground (p. 188), and Crystal Palace National Sports Centre (p. 211) has **Rascals.** All charge a nominal fee, and most are suitable for kids up to about 12.

Another reasonably central indoor playground is **Bramley's Big Adventure** 🎭🎭 (136 Bramley Rd., W10; ℂ **020/8960-1515;** www.bramleysbig.co.uk). Fulham is the venue for the huge new **Gambado** (www.gambado.co.uk), which has a carousel as well as softplay equipment. Farther afield, there's the excellent **Zoomaround** in Stoke Newington (46 Milton Grove, N16; ℂ **020/7254-2220;** www.zoomaround.co.uk); and **Discovery Planet** in Rotherhithe's Surrey Quays Shopping Centre (Redriff Rd., SE16; ℂ **020/7237-2388;** www.discovery-planet.co.uk).

**Gymboree Play & Music** (ℂ **020/7258-1415;** www.gymboree-uk.com) runs interactive activity sessions for babies and children up to 5. In theory, you sign up for a term's worth of classes, but you can get coupons for trial classes, and branches may allow visitors in on a one-time basis. There are relatively central branches in the O2 Centre (p. 256) and Whiteleys shopping mall (p. 240), and more in Brent Cross shopping center, Museum in Docklands (p. 168), Chelsea, Chiswick, Wandsworth, Wimbledon, Putney, and Ealing.

For a less upmarket option, where you're more likely to meet local mums with their tots rather than nannies, London has a wide network of (usually free) **One O'Clock clubs,** often in parks such as Hampstead Heath (p. 143), Holland Park (p. 206), Battersea Park (p. 207), and Coram's Fields (p. 209), generally offering painting, crafts, and softplay areas. For details on these and other parent-and-baby groups by area, see www.childcare.gov.uk.

## 5  Classes & Workshops

Most of the museums and historic houses (p. 142) listed in chapter 7 host family workshops on weekends and during school vacations, as do many theaters (p. 250).

## ART & CRAFTS

For activities at the major **art galleries,** see p. 175.

**Art 4 Fun/Colour Me Mine** ⨀    This "creative cafe" allows budding artists of all ages to come together to paint on ceramic, wood, glass, paper, silk, or fabric, or to create a mosaic. A studio session, which can last all day, costs £5.95 ($12), then from £3.50 ($7) per item. Kids can enjoy soft drinks and muffins while they work; parents can enjoy a coffee or even bring a bottle of wine. Similar activities are offered by the **Ceramics Cafe** (✆ **020/8810-4422;** www.ceramicscafe.com), with branches in Ealing and Kew, and the **Pottery Cafe** (✆ **020/7736-2157;** www.pottery-cafe.com), in Fulham and Twickenham. 172 W. End Lane, NW6. ✆ **020/7794-0800.** www.art4fun.com. Tube: W. Hampstead.

**London International Gallery of Children's Art** ⨀    A unique venue in a family-friendly entertainment mall, this center hosts a free exhibition of artworks by children from around the world. Visiting kids can use the art materials provided to produce something in response to what they have seen. See the website for Sunday workshops involving vegetable printing, doll-making, collage-creating; although these are free, donations are very much appreciated. O2 Centre, 255 Finchley Rd., NW3. ✆ **020/ 7435-0903.** www.ligca.org. Tube: Finchley Rd.

**Orleans House Gallery**    This contemporary art showcase sits in a baroque mansion to the southwest of the city near Marble Hill House (p. 187). Family-oriented events are devised to correspond with special occasions such as Easter, Museums & Galleries Month (p. 18), The Big Draw (p. 22), and Christmas; weekly after-school art workshops, school-vacation art clubs for ages 5 to 15, and family learning courses, including pottery workshops, are also available. Riverside, Twickenham, TW1. ✆ **020/8831-6000.** www.richmond.gov.uk. Train: Twickenham.

**Serpentine Gallery** ⨀⨀    A contemporary gallery beautifully set in an old tea pavilion in Kensington Gardens, the Serpentine provides an atmospheric spot for free, drop-in creative family days relating to its exhibitions: You might, for instance, create a magical installation together. Kensington Gardens, W2. ✆ **020/7402-6075.** www.serpentine gallery.org. Tube: Lancaster Gate.

## MUSIC

For family opera workshops run by the **English National Opera,** see p. 255.

**The Music House for Children** ⨀⨀    This superb west London option for aspiring musicians offers classes in music appreciation and various instruments, plus music and movement classes for babies and kids up to 3 (£6/$12), baby massage, creative dance for 2- to 4-year-olds, one-to-one tuition and more (some courses are bookable by the term, others are drop-in). An adjoining shop sells musical supplies for everyone from babies up, plus arts and crafts material and toys, and serves coffee, tea, and cakes to parents while their children enjoy their class. 306–10 Uxbridge Rd., W12. ℃ 020/8932-2652. www.musichouseforchildren.co.uk. Tube: Shepherd's Bush.

**Wigmore Hall** ★★★   The Wigmore's brilliant kids' workshops are often run in association with the Handel House Museum (p. 186). You might, for instance, attend an all-day "Recorder Rave" for kids 5 and up, during which you will learn about the history of the instrument, learn some of Handel's tunes and then make up some of your own, and put on a joint performance at the end of the day. There are also fantastic Chamber Tots music and movement sessions for 2- to 5-year-olds (£6/$12), with a short concert in the auditorium followed by workshops involving singing, percussion, and exploring rhythm and percussion. Unfortunately, all these workshops get booked up months in advance, so check them out well ahead of your visit—the website has a downloadable program of current offerings, from special family concerts exploring myths and fairy tales to jazz improvisation days for teens. 36 Wigmore St., W1. ℃ 020/7935-2141. www.wigmore-hall.org.uk. Tube: Bond St.

**Whippersnappers** ★★★   Kids get funky at these excellent drop-in workshops for 0- to 5-year-olds at Brockwell Lido open-air pool (p. 216), with African drumming, shadow puppets, and singing. The company's trademark is Pickny Beat, a mix of Jamaican and English music using reggae and dance overlaid by children's songs. Tickets cost £6.50 ($13) for the first child, £9 ($18) for two siblings. The same venue hosts an indoor and outdoor sports club offering football, acrobatics, and kung fu. Whippersnapper classes are also held in Holland Park (p. 206) and Dulwich Park in south London. Brockwell Lido, Dulwich Rd., SE24. ℃ 020/7738-6633. www.whippersnappers.org. Train: Herne Hill.

# 10

# Shopping

London can be shopping heaven or shopping hell. The range of shops and goods here is huge, but so are the crowds, and some areas that used to be fun have become touristy and overpriced—such as Covent Garden. Conversely, areas that went into decline, including Carnaby Street, have been given a new lease on life in the last decade or so.

Of course, you'll find all the multinationals here, at generally higher prices than elsewhere. Gap Kids and the Disney Store are familiar sights—you can't miss them. My advice is to investigate the best of the city's homegrown goods in London's charming, small-scale complexes and unique boutiques.

## 1 The Shopping Scene

### SHOPPING HOURS

Smaller London shops tend to open at about 9:30 or 10am and close at 5:30 or 6pm Monday to Saturday; larger shops and department stores often stay open at least an hour or two later. Thursday is the traditional time for late-night shopping, especially in the weeks leading up to Christmas. Some stores in shopping districts such as Chelsea and Covent Garden also keep slightly later hours. On Sunday, shops are generally now open for 4 or 5 hours, usually between 11am and 5pm.

### SALES TAX & SHIPPING

**Value-added tax (VAT),** British sales tax, is 17.5% on most goods (children's clothes are exempt), but it's included in the price, so what you see on the price tag is what you pay at the register. Non-E.U. residents can get back much of the tax by applying for a refund from participating retailers (who charge a small administration fee); you show them your passport to prove you are eligible, and they give you a refund form to complete. The minimum expenditure required differs from store to store. You then present your goods and form to U.K. Customs at the airport, and claim your money from the refund booth. The **National Advice Service (© 0845/010-9000)** will answer any VAT-related queries Monday to Friday 8am to 8pm.

VAT is not charged on goods shipped out of the country, and many London shops will help you beat the VAT by **shipping** for you. But watch out—this may be even more expensive than the VAT, and you might also have to pay U.S. duties when the goods reach you at home. You can ship your purchases on your flight home by paying for excess baggage (rates vary by airline), or have your packages shipped independently, which is generally less expensive—try **CargoBookers (© 0800/731-1747).** By either means, you still have to pay the VAT upfront and apply for a refund.

## SHOPPING DISTRICTS

**THE WEST END**   Central London is home to most of the city's world-class department stores; **Oxford Street,** running east-west through the heart of the capital, also has the flagship stores of most of the city's or country's high-street chain stores. It's a bit tacky these days, though, and madly busy any day of the week—if you've got little kids in tow, you might want to give it a wide berth (the Mayor's proposals to ban traffic and introduce trams within the next decade will hopefully improve matters no end). **Regent Street,** curving south from Oxford Circus to Piccadilly, is a little more upmarket; it's here that you'll find the toy-store giant Hamleys. There are some real gems to be found in smaller West End streets, including **Carnaby Street** running parallel with Regent Street through Soho; this, a key locale in the Swinging '60s, lost its cred for a while but has been revitalized and should be high on any fashion-conscious teen's "place-to-shop" list. Farther west, running north off Oxford Street up into villagey Marylebone, **Marylebone High Street** has a civilized feel, charming independent shops, lots of child-friendly eating options, and a great Sunday farmers' market.

At the eastern end of Oxford Street, **Covent Garden** is focused around the piazza, the former site of London's biggest fruit-and-vegetable market. It's scenic but touristy, and prices are hiked up accordingly. Fashion mavens, however, will find much to tempt them along **Neal Street** and the streets radiating off **Seven Dials,** with their hip boutiques and New Agey stores.

**KNIGHTSBRIDGE, CHELSEA & KENSINGTON**   Knightsbridge, home of Harrods and Harvey Nichols, is London's most luxurious shopping district—Sloane Street in particular is chockablock with designer clothing emporia. At the end of it, Sloane Square is the starting point for the **King's Road,** another spot synonymous with the Swinging '60s. These days it's far less alternative and cutting-edge, but as the number of mums and strollers testifies, it's one of the best places in town for kids' shopping. Toy stores and clothing boutiques abound, many of them unique. It's not the place for a bargain, but it's a great way to spend a day (avoid weekends if you can). Don't forget the major museums in nearby **South Kensington**—all have good gift shops. From there it's a short walk to **Kensington High Street,** a fertile hunting ground for teen-friendly street chic.

**NOTTING HILL & PORTOBELLO**   From Kensington High Street, it's a pleasant stroll up Kensington Church Street past posh antiques shops to Notting Hill, dotted with fashionable boutique stores frequented by the hippest celebs. Check out the western end of **Westbourne Grove** and intersecting **Ledbury Road** and **Portobello Road,** the latter famous for its antiques market but boasting superb clothes stores and stalls, too.

**NORTH LONDON**   There are a couple of areas farther out of the center worth a visit. **Upper Street Islington** has plenty of quirky little stores (and lots of family eating options), but as this is a main road out of London, it can feel a bit hectic. Farther afield, both **Hampstead** and **Highgate** have laid-back, villagey high streets with interesting shops in which to poke around. **Stoke Newington Church Street** is a little more bohemian, and correspondingly cheaper.

## DEPARTMENT STORES

London's wonderful array of department stores, many of them historic, provide something for all members of the family, from toy sections to superb food halls to designer clothing. On-site cafes or restaurants suit all tastes and pocketbooks, and good restroom and parenting facilities are available. You can easily lose yourself for the day in the following. Note that they are superb wet-weather standbys.

Also-rans that don't merit a review in their own right but that do have children's departments of one kind or another, parents' facilities, and in most cases, kids' menus, include: **Bhs** (252–8 Oxford St., W1; © **0845/841-0246;** www.bhs.co.uk), **House of Fraser** (318 Oxford St., W1; © **0870/160-7258;** www.houseoffraser.co.uk), **Fenwick** (63 New Bond St., W1; © **020/7629-9161;** www.fenwick.co.uk), **Harvey Nichols** (109–25 Knightsbridge, SW1; © **020/7235-5000;** www.harveynichols.com), which has a **Buckle My Shoe** concession (p. 224), and **Marks & Spencer** (458 Oxford St., W1; © **020/7935-7954;** www.marksandspencer.com). Most have branches elsewhere in London as well. The lovely and rather decadent **Liberty** (Regent St., W1; © **020/7734-1234;** www.liberty.co.uk) doesn't sell kids' stuff, but teenage girls swoon at its exquisite jewelry and accessories and love its hyper-trendy (if rather forbidding) beauty hall.

**Debenhams**    For those in the know, Debenhams, though lacking the character of the city's older department stores, is a great spot for specially commissioned fashion by international names such as Jasper Conran, Julien Macdonald, and John Rocha. And that's just the kids- and babywear! Prices, relatively speaking, aren't bad, though there's an in-house clothing line at still-keener prices. Toys run the gamut from the educational and the electronic to arts-and-crafts items and traditional board games, and this is also a good place for Early Learning Centre (p. 241) toys. There's a well-respected nursery and kids' furnishings department, and The Restaurant has a VIP Baby Service (kids' meals, low-cost jars of baby food, food- and bottlewarming facilities, highchairs, wipes, and baby-changing facilities); older kids might prefer Dee's Diner with its burgers, nachos, and shakes, and soundtrack of 1960s classics. Note that there are other branches outside the center. 334–8 Oxford St., W1. © **0844/561-6161.** www.debenhams.com. Tube: Oxford Circus.

**Fortnum & Mason**    This sumptuous St. James's store, which has been going strong since 1707, was in the final throes of a massive tercentenary overhaul as this guide went to press, emerging swankier than ever. Most people still come for the world-famous food hall, now extended over two floors, or for the food outlets—the newly refurbished Fountain is famous for its ice-cream sundaes (p. 103), and there are also a tea salon and two new restaurants and a new wine bar. However, there's still room for a select range of babywear, nursery gifts, and games on the upper floors—they're not cheap but the quality is high. 181 Piccadilly, W1. © **020/7734-8040.** www.fortnumandmason.com. Tube: Piccadilly Circus.

**Harrods** 🎇🎇    The "Palace in Knightsbridge," with its 330-plus departments over seven floors, attracts love and hate in equal measure. It doesn't come without its quota of snobbery, yet the staff are as friendly and helpful as can be. Kids will want to head straight for the fourth floor, with its vast Toy Kingdom. Here, again, you may find your head spinning at the prospect that anyone, no matter how fat his or her wallet, would contemplate spending £15,000 ($30,000) on a kids' petrol-powered off-road vehicle! Still, there are "real" toys and books here, even if the prices aren't on a par with Woolworths. It was in Harrods that writer A. A. Milne bought the original Winnie the Pooh bear for his son Christopher. There are also designer kidswear aplenty, some very chi-chi nursery furniture, a children's theater, and a kids' hair salon. If you're here during Christmas season, don't miss a visit to London's best Santa's grotto; queues can be up to 2 hours long, but it's well worth the wait, and the singing elves keep even the most fidgety kids happy with free cookies and lollipops. And a trip to London isn't complete without a visit to Harrods' breathtakingly lavish food hall.

Among the 28 food bars, cafes, and restaurants are the frenetic, family-oriented Planet Harrods with its blaring cartoons and kids' menu, and the Chocolate Bar with its gloriously thick chocolate drinks and fondues. There are baby-changing facilities throughout the building. On your way back down to reality, stop in at the second-floor pet shop, where you can buy cats and birds or order all manner of exotic beasts. (In 1967 an Albanian prince bought a baby Indian elephant here for Ronald Reagan.) For a final surreal touch, go in search of the memorial to Princess Diana and her boyfriend Dodi, who was the son of Harrods's owner Mohamed al Fayed, or of the waxwork of Al Fayed himself. 87–135 Brompton Rd., SW1. ⓒ **020/7730-1234.** www.harrods. com. Tube: Knightsbridge.

**John Lewis** ⋆⋆ (Value    John Lewis's flagship store was coming to the end of a £60-million ($120-million) modernization program as this edition went to press (with a brand-new basement food hall slated to open by Christmas 2007) but remains primarily of interest as a reliable stalwart, ranking higher than other London department stores in terms of value (the company promises that if you find the same goods cheaper within a certain radius, it'll refund the difference) and customer service. (Witness the parents' space on the fourth floor, with its comfy breast-feeding room, bottlewarming area, and baby-changing facilities.) Expectant parents flock here for nursery furniture and equipment, backed up by expert advice from staff; they come back for the practical but attractive kidswear that fits a range of budgets. The toys and books department is a little disappointing by comparison. There are other branches in the giant north London shopping center, Brent Cross, and in Sloane Square—the last, confusingly, is called **Peter Jones** and has a good restaurant with panoramic views. Oxford St., W1. ⓒ **020/7629-7711.** www.johnlewis.com. Tube: Oxford St.

**Selfridges** ⋆⋆    Stylish Selfridges excels in so many departments, you scarcely know where to begin—the great food hall with its frequent free tastings, the mouthwatering candy and chocolate department, the cutting-edge men's and women's fashions, or the unrivaled beauty hall. The small(ish) but perfectly formed Kids on the Third Floor department fuses fashion and toys in a trendy space-age setting. The clothes, by the likes of Baby Dior, Juice Couture, and Cavalli Devils and Angels, aren't cheap, but keep an eye out for periodic sales. If you hate the tyranny of blue boys' and pink girls' wear, or the predominance of pastels in many shops, this is the place to come for funkier alternatives. Toys range from the cultish (Hello Kitty) to the prosaic (Bob the Builder). Check the website for occasional children's events, such Father's Day card-making. This is also a place to come for Zoobug kids' sunglasses, Mini B'eautique swimwear, and the **Buckle My Shoe** store, purveyor of more than 250 styles (including some by Diesel, Prada, and Puma) to the offspring of, among others, Madonna and Uma Thurman. (There's another branch in Harvey Nichols; see p. 223.) And don't miss the delectable new Kas Kids range in the bedwear department.

Selfridges' 18 restaurants, bars, and cafes include the newly relaunched Food Garden Cafe, serving everything from Lebanese fare to fish and chips against views stretching from the British Airways London Eye to the Tower of London, a pretzel bar, a mozzarella bar, an Italian gelateria, and a branch of Frankie's Italian Bar & Grill (p. 121). 400 Oxford St., W1. ⓒ **0800/123-400.** www.selfridges.com. Tube: Bond St.

## 2 Shopping A to Z

# ARTS, CRAFTS & STATIONERY

There are kids' drawing and arts-based workshops at some of the art galleries mentioned on p. 175 and 219, including the National Gallery and Somerset House, and related items at many of their gift shops.

**London Graphic Centre** ☆    Central London's biggest art shop is an Aladdin's cave of supplies for everyone from industry professionals to Damien Hirsts in the making, or even younger kids just getting into crafts and drawing—for whom there are Tubtime bath crayons, Gelgems stickers, glitter face paints, Fimo animal-making sets, glass-painting kits, and much more. Of particular note is the Creativity for Kids range, which includes radios and alarm clocks you can paint and decorate (£15/$30 for a clock), kids' chairs to assemble and decorate, teddy-bear making kits, and mini windowsill gardens to grow. Older kids will be pleased with the likes of 3-D doodling kits and robotic pets to build. You'll find secondary branches in Tottenham Street, W1; and Upper Richmond Street, SW15. 16–18 Shelton St., WC2. ℂ 020/7759-4500. www.london graphics.co.uk. Tube: Covent Garden.

**Paperchase** ☆☆    With its three floors of art supplies, gorgeous handmade papers, pens and pencils, sketch- and notebooks, wrapping paper, ribbons, bows, picture frames, and storage solutions, Paperchase is irresistible. The ground floor has an outstanding choice of greeting cards and pocket-money gifts—it's worth letting the kids loose here to stock up for boring flights or car trips. On the first floor there's a cafe where you can refuel while writing home, or making an entry in your brand-new travel journal. Smaller branches include Covent Garden Piazza, WC2; and King's Road, SW3. 213–5 Tottenham Court Rd., W1. ℂ 020/7467-6200. www.paperchase.co.uk. Tube: Goodge St.

# BOOKS, COMICS & MAGAZINES

There are so many great independent kids' bookstores in London that there simply isn't enough space to list them all; noteworthy ones outside the center include the **Lion & Unicorn** in Richmond (ℂ 020/8940-0483), **The Golden Treasure** in Southfields (ℂ 020/8333-0167), and **Tales on Moon Lane** in Herne Hill (ℂ 020/7274-5759). See www.booktrusted.co.uk for a list of bookstores, as well as listings of kids' literature events, theatrical productions, and exhibitions.

**Bookworm**    A small independent kids' bookstore, Bookworm is worth a visit if you happen to be around Hampstead Heath, with regular storytelling events. It's buggy friendly, with chairs for kids to sit and read on, plus baby-changing facilities. 1177 Finchley Rd., NW11. ℂ 020/8201-9811. Tube: Golders Green.

**Daunt Books** ☆☆☆    One of the world's loveliest bookstores, with its long oak galleries, Daunt's is best known for its travel books, which are uniquely grouped with novels and nonfiction from the same country. Its kids' room is a doozy, too, containing a whole host of quirky titles that get overlooked by the more commercial stores (you won't find any movie or TV tie-ins here). The section is not huge, but there's room for junior bookworms to get down on their hands and knees and spread out their selections for further investigation. Flanked by childcare, interior design, and cookery sections for sneaky parental browsing, it's a great place to while away a couple of hours. There are other branches in Belsize Park and Hampstead in north London and Holland Park in west London. 83 Marylebone High St., W1. ℂ 020/7224-2295. www.daunt books.co.uk. Tube: Baker St. or Regent's Park.

**Forbidden Planet London Megastore**   This monster sci-fi, fantasy, and cult entertainment store has something to please both avid collectors and pocket-money browsers, whether it's a Chewbacca mask, a Buffy key ring, or a pack of *Lord of the Rings* playing cards. Come here to find a mind-boggling array of action figures, comics, graphic novels, manga, anime, cult movies, TV merchandise (from *Star Trek* to *X-Men*), books (science, fantasy, and horror), DVDs, videos, and video-game merchandise. Popular signing events allow you to get up close and personal with the likes of Christopher Lee or Leonard Nimoy. 179 Shaftesbury Ave., WC2. ✆ 020/7420-3666. www. forbiddenplanet.com. Tube: Covent Garden.

**Marchpane Children's Books** ✿✿   This lovely antiquarian specialist in rare children's and illustrated books sits in a quaint Victorian thoroughfare full of bookstores with traditional facades and signs. Stock ranges from 18th-century to modern works such as first editions of Harry Potter books, with the works of Lewis Carroll being of particular interest. Although it's not necessarily the best place to *bring* kids, this is a great place to browse for special presents. 16 Cecil Court, Charing Cross Rd., WC2. ✆ 020/7836-8661. www.marchpane.com. Tube: Leicester Sq.

**Ripping Yarns** ✿   This chaotic but charming secondhand bookstore has a large section devoted to collectible children's classics, including boys' and girls' adventure stories and annuals, and out-of-print modern kids' fiction. Staff can be a little unfocused, but otherwise this is an excellent spot for a browse on your way out of Highgate Wood (p. 210). Note that it's closed on Mondays. 355 Archway Rd., N6. ✆ 020/8341-6111. www.rippingyarns.co.uk. Tube: Highgate.

**Young Europeans Bookstore**   Although it has moved from its prime Cecil Court spot to within The European Bookshop itself, this store remains your best bet whether you are trying to teach your kids a language (despite the name, there are non-European resources, including Arabic and Japanese) or if you are a visitor from the Continent needing to stock up on reading material or audiobooks, or on related games, posters, music, videos, and software. Staff members are very helpful, and—naturally—speak a range of languages. 5 Warwick St., W1. ✆ 020/7734-5259. www.younglinguists. com. Tube: Piccadilly Circus.

## CDS, DVDS & GAMES

For small-scale **specialist music stores,** head for Soho, especially Berwick Street.

**HMV**   This music, DVD, and games megastore has two branches on Oxford Street alone (one in Selfridges; p. 224). Its clearance sales are worth looking out for, while the range of board games, perfect for chilling out in your hotel room, include *Simpsons* Monopoly and *Lord of the Rings* Risk. There are branches in the Trocadero Centre (Piccadilly Circus), in Covent Garden, and within Harrods (p. 223). 150 Oxford St., W1. ✆ 0845/602-7800. www.hmv.co.uk. Tube: Oxford Circus.

**Virgin Megastore**   Virgin is really not that distinguishable from HMV, except that its main branch occupies the coveted 1 Piccadilly Circus spot formerly held by Tower Records. You'll also find it on Oxford Street, in the newly revamped Brunswick Centre (p. 110), Camden, High Street Kensington, the King's Road, and Fulham. 1 Piccadilly, W1. ✆ 020/7439-2500. www.virginmegastores.co.uk. Tube: Piccadilly.

## DRESSING UP

**Angels** ✿   You'll pay a bit more at this glitzy six-story store in the heart of Theaterland, but the choice and quality really are inspiring—ranging from Dorothy in the

*Wizard of Oz* to the Incredible Hulk. Among the superior accessories are wigs, masks, makeup, and tiaras. 119 Shaftesbury Ave. © 020/7836-5678. www.fancydress.com. Tube: Leicester Sq.

**Escapade** 👧👧   This long-established store comes with keen prices and an impressive client list (the BBC, Disney, Nickelodeon). The thousands of costumes to hire or buy include a vast range of well-made kids' outfits, from Darth Vader to a Victorian parlor maid. Accessorize to your heart's content with masks, wigs, makeup, jewelry, and novelty products. 150 Camden High St., NW1. © 020/7485-7384. www.escapade.co.uk. Tube: Camden.

**Mystical Fairies**   In a riot of pink, this outrageous little store on a historic lane (the same one as Humla; p. 230) shimmers with anything fairy-related, whether it be sparkly tutus or bedroom accessories, ballet tights or books, luggage or collectible toys. The dressing-up gear sold is mainly of a magical or fairy-tale bent—fairies, princesses, mermaids, wizards, knights in shining armor, or pirates. And should you need a venue to host a themed party, the store is famous for hosting happenings in its delightful basement space. There's a second branch in the Bluewater mall (p. 240). 12 Flash Walk, NW3. © 020/7431-1888. www.mysticalfairies.co.uk. Tube: Hampstead.

## EQUIPMENT & NURSERY ITEMS

**John Lewis** (p. 224), **Debenhams** (p. 223), and **Daisy & Tom** (p. 241) have good nursery and stroller departments.

**Anna French**   A contemporary fabrics, lace, and wallpaper showroom, Anna French is renowned for its stunning kids' collection, which ranges from simple stripes, checks, and polka dots, to fairies, angels' wings, safari animals, boats, whales, or bees. 343 King's Rd., SW3. © 020/7351-1126. www.annafrench.co.uk. Tube: Sloane Sq.

**Blooming Marvellous**   This well-respected. competitively priced mail-order outfit has three London stores (the other two are in Richmond and Wandsworth; there's also a branch in the Bluewater mall—see p. 240) stocking most of its nursery equipment, from contemporary and travel cots to hip seats and great products for journeys and flights. It's a good place for maternity and babywear, too. 725 Fulham Rd., SW6. © 0845/458-7429. www.bloomingmarvellous.co.uk. Tube: Parsons Green.

**Designers Guild** 👧   One of the most influential names in modern interior design, Designers Guild eschews minimalism in favor of bright bursts of color that suit kids' products perfectly, from its "Bunny Hop" or "Beside the Sea" kids' bed linen to polka-dotted blankets to pretty notebooks and accessories. 267 and 277 King's Rd., SW3. © 020/7351-5775. www.designersguild.com. Tube: Sloane Sq.

**Dragons of Walton Street**   This long-standing Knightsbridge firm will hand-paint any design of your children's choice onto its traditional English handcrafted children's furniture. Favorite designs are Beatrix Potter characters and Flower Fairies, but kids can even bring in photos of pets to be copied onto items. There's also an exclusive range of kids' fabrics. 23 Walton St., SW3. © 020/7589-3795. www.dragonsofwaltonstreet.com. Tube: Knightsbridge.

**Ikea** 👧   The crowds and store layout will drive you nuts (you have to walk through the entire building to get out), but there's no arguing with Ikea's prices—where else can you get a sturdy and stylish highchair for as little as £12 ($24)? For such mass-produced stuff, this is imaginative design that sets kids aglow, especially the "play furniture," which includes funky swivel armchairs, hanging seats, rocking benches, and hedgehog cushions. You may find your kids are more than happy trying out the goods in the showroom; other distractions include a supervised play area, and school-vacation activities such as face-painting, kids' entertainers, and food tastings. The vast restaurant offers a kids' menu, baby food, food-warming facilities, and a breastfeeding area; Swedish meatballs are just one of the items on the menu. There are other suburban branches in Edmonton, north London, and Croydon, south London. 2 Drury Way, N. Circular Rd., NW10. ℭ 0845/355-1141. www.ikea.co.uk. Tube: Neasden.

**Lilliput**    This large store boasts the largest stock in London, and there certainly is an impressive range of strollers, car seats, carriers, furniture, books, toys, and accessories, backed up by excellent service and advice, and free parking (although deliveries can be made to anywhere in the country). 255 Queenstown Rd., SW8. ℭ 020/7720-5554. www. lilliput.com. Train: Battersea Park.

**The Little White Company** 🏵🏵    Lovers of The Little White Company's minimalist yet homey collections of predominantly white and gray housewares and clothing were thrilled when they opened two dedicated kids' stores (the other is at 90 Marylebone High St.) with junior versions of its chic and simple bed linen, nursery furniture, clothes, nightwear, accessories, and gifts. Pastel and even strong colors creep in here, but nothing likely to offend. 261 Pavilion Rd., SW1. ℭ 020/7881-0783. www.thewhite company.com. Tube: Sloane Sq.

**Mamas & Papas** 🏵🏵🏵    The flagship store of this designer nursery specialist has won awards both for its design and its customer service. It's basically a nursery department store, with a wealth of choices, whether it's strollers (my M&P stroller is still going strong after nearly 5 years of intensive use), car seats and travel accessories, furniture, toys, maternity- and babywear, or gifts that you are looking for. Its Cibo restaurant is a sophisticated setting for breakfast, coffee and cake, sandwiches, and Italian-inspired full meals; the good-value kids' menu is largely organic. 256–8 Regent St., W1. ℭ 0870/830-7700. www.mamasandpapas.co.uk. Tube: Oxford Circus.

**Nursery Window**    This is a dependable place for old-fashioned, expensive nursery and kids' furniture; bedding; and luxury accessories, including cashmere or lambswool throws, rabbit-eared or hooded towels, and the fluffiest of dressing gowns. 83 Walton St., SW3. ℭ 020/7581-3358. www.nurserywindow.co.uk. Tube: S. Kensington.

**Simon Horn**    This classic designer has acquired a reputation around the globe for his fine wooden beds and "metamorphic" nursery furniture, which include cots that can become beds and then sofas, and changing tables/chests of drawers. Prices are high, but these pieces are investments (and collectors' items). 117–21 Wandsworth Bridge Rd., SW6. ℭ 020/7736-1754. www.simonhorn.com. Tube: Parson's Green.

## FASHION
### CLOTHING

There are countless specialist kids' boutiques all over London. Here are some of my personal favorites, and some of the most accessible (many are in out-of-the-way neighborhoods). For **surfing-** and **skating-**inspired fashion, see p. 239. Many **department stores** (p. 222) have good designer kidswear sections. Look in designer boutiques for new kids' ranges by Chloé and Missoni.

**alsocaramel**    This hip (and pricey) boutique, with a good choice of designer casualwear, jeans, and footwear by Converse, Puma, and others, caters to kids about 6 to 12 who wouldn't be caught dead in a store selling baby items. On some afternoons they can get their hair cut (it's best to book ahead). For younger ones, **caramelbaby&child** on Brompton Road stocks clothes for kids ages 0 to 6, plus shearling baby carriers, baby oils, postcards, chocolates, and more, and there's also a plain **caramel** store on Ledbury Road in Notting Hill, with kidswear for ages 0 to 6 upstairs, and downstairs a charming tea salon with an outdoor patio, toys and crafts materials (to try out or buy), and another hair salon. Or try the concession in Selfridges (p. 224). 259 Pavilion Rd., SW1. © 020/7730-2564. Tube Knightsbridge.

**Baby Dior**  Apparently Christian Dior began designing babywear for the offspring of Princess Caroline of Monaco, and this store—fitted out like a 1950s couture salon—is a symbol, perhaps, of our era's obsession with celebrity and designer labels. Some items might well make your eyes pop out—including a silk christening gown costing almost £850 ($1,500)!—but there are less costly items such as Dior bibs and socks for that oh-so-tasteful gift. 6 Harriet St., SW1. © 020/7730-2564. Tube: Knightsbridge.

**Ben's**  Your kids might think they're too cool for a shop uniquely for teens (10- to 16-year-olds, to be precise), but chances are they'll change their minds when they see the stock at this store, which includes Armani, Prada, and Diesel. There's also a range of occasion wear, such as satin and organza dresses and Armani suits. On the same street, sister shop **Tiddlywinks** sells preteen clothes and shoes. 5 St. John's Wood High St., NW8. © 020/7722-5599. www.tiddlywinks.co.uk. Tube: St. John's Wood.

**Burberry**  Kids who want to look like grownups shop at this classic designer store: The junior section includes Burberry's trademark beige macs and pinafore dresses using the famous checked fabric (although there's also a range of more casual items). There are further branches in Knightsbridge, on New Bond Street, and at Heathrow Airport. 156–67 Regent St., W1. © 020/7968-0000. www.burberry.com. Tube: Piccadilly.

**Cath Kidston** ❀❀  These eight stores (Marylebone, Covent Garden, Holland Park, King's Rd., Chelsea Green, Fulham, Chiswick, and Wimbledon) are renowned for their floral wallpapers and fabrics with a retro feel, but also offer a delightful range of imaginative kids' items, whether it be clothing and bags, and aprons and bibs for those home baking sessions, or furniture, fabric, wallpaper, and bedding. Don't miss the outdoor range of camping, picnicking, and beach paraphernalia. 51 Marylebone High St., W1. © 020/7935-6555. www.cathkidston.co.uk. Tube: Baker St.

**Catimini**  Come here for colorful clothes, shoes, bed- and bath linen, sunglasses, cutlery, and dishes made in France but with a distinctly ethnic feel. There's another branch at 33c King's Rd. 52a S. Molton St., W1. © 020/7629-8099. www.catimini.com. Tube: Bond St.

**Chrysaliss** ❀  Bewildered by choice? This exclusive little boutique just north of Hyde Park offers 1-hour appointments with a stylist who will guide you through its stock of contemporary classics from Britain, France, Belgium, and Italy for kids up to 8. Or you can opt to have clothes tailor-made for your little boy or girl, who can play on the rugs or watch the DVD wall projection as you peruse the latest collections. 31 Connaught St., W2. © 020/7402-7109. www.chrysaliss.co.uk. Tube: Marble Arch.

**Couverture** ❀❀❀  Filled with quirky kids' gifts, housewares, and fashion, including knitwear and knitted toys, this is the type of place magazine stylists come looking for inspiration. Stock changes constantly—part of the store's charm is that you will always be surprised—but recent children's highlights have included individually customized Voyager suitcases, toy accordions, and buckled flamenco shoes, dresses, and castanets. You may also find kids' cookbooks and classic tales, and some wonderful toys amid the Vintage Collectibles range. 310 King's Rd., SW3. ℂ 020/7795-1200. www.couverture. co.uk. Tube: Sloane Sq.

**Fatface** ☆  This activewear and outdoor clothing chain has a kids' range for ages 6 months to 11 years, embracing covetable printed T-shirts and dresses, crew pants, fleeces, beachwear, and accessories, all at reasonable prices. Other London branches include Covent Garden and Brent Cross. 126 King's Rd., SW3. ℂ 020/7581-9380. www. fatface.co.uk. Tube: Sloane Sq.

**French Connection Kids**  This stylish, mid-priced casualwear company, infamous for its provocative T-shirt slogans, sells trendy kidswear in this branch and the one in the Bluewater Mall. 168–70 Kensington High St., W8. ℂ 020/7937-4665. www.frenchconnection. co.uk. Tube: High St. Kensington.

**H&M**  Hot-off-the-catwalk looks at throwaway prices translate into funky and highly desirable children's and teenagers' clothes here. The garb won't last too long, but neither will the fashions, and happy shoppers in more than 20 countries and 1,000 stores worldwide can't be wrong. This Oxford Street East branch sells the full baby and children's wear and accessories ranges, as do those in Kensington High St. and Whiteleys shopping mall in Bayswater (p. 240). 174–6 Oxford St. ℂ 020/7612-1820. www.hm.com. Tube: Oxford Circus.

**Humla Children's Shop**  This traditional affair, located on an atmospheric cobbled lane in chic Hampstead, sells well-made, colorful clothes and accessories, including lovely embroidered dresses, plus a pleasing array of wooden toys and cute furnishings. 13 Flask Walk, NW3. ℂ 020/7794-8449. Tube: Hampstead.

**Jakes** ☆☆☆  Hands-down the worthiest fashion store in town, Jakes stocks a kids' and adults' label that donates a percentage of its profits to a charity for cerebral palsy (the illness that affects the eponymous 7-year-old Jake). Items include the famous hand-printed Lucky 7 T-shirts (£10/$20 for kids) as seen on a variety of pop stars, but there are lots of other tees, short- or long-sleeved, with a retro feel, plus kids' cable knits, cargo pants, and tracksuits, and a small selection of babywear. 79 Berwick St., W1. ℂ 020/7734 0812. www.jakeskids.com. Tube: Oxford Circus.

**Jigsaw Junior** ☆  This smart, mid-price fashion chain sells almost unfeasibly cute clothes for girls up to 13 in its branch in Hampstead, and also in its New Bond Street, King's Road, Fulham Road, Westbourne Grove, and Richmond stores. Frills and flowers abound at all locations, and sparkly accessories complete the look. 83 Heath St., NW3. ℂ 020/7431-0619. www.jigsaw-online.com. Tube: Hampstead.

**JoJo Maman Bébé**  Though best known as a mail-order operation, JoJo Maman Bébé has four London stores (Battersea/Clapham, Putney, Chiswick, and Temple Fortune in north London) plus a new one in Windsor (p. 262), all selling its comprehensive range of babies' and children's wear, toys, nursery equipment, and maternity wear. Most of the child-friendly stores have play areas to keep little ones out of mischief. 68 Northcote Rd., SW11. ℂ 020/7228-0322. www.jojomamanbebe.co.uk. Tube: Clapham Junction.

**Mimmo** ☆  This exciting shop sells ultra-hip togs for kids up to 16, with designers including Nolita Pocket, Juicy Couture, and Miss Sixty, plus footwear for the most discerning young feet, from flip-flops to lime-green glitter sandals. 602 Fulham Rd., SW6. ℂ 020/7731 4706. www.mimmo.co.uk. Tube: Parson's Green.

**Monsoon Children** ⭐  Known foremost for its popular embroidered and printed dresses for women, Monsoon produces very pretty girls' clothes (ages 0–13)—at the time of writing, tropical prints and ruched summer dresses abounded. This dedicated kidswear branch is also one of the few branches to hold the boys' range (for ages up to 10), taking in attractive animal-motif T-shirts, combat trousers, waistcoats, and more. 25 Covent Garden Market, WC2. ℂ 020/7497-9325. www.monsoon.co.uk. Tube: Covent Garden.

**Oilily London** ⭐⭐  This award-winning women and children's fashion label knows its stuff when it comes to truly eye-catching babies' and kids' wear. Your wallet might not thank you for coming here, but if your kids like bright colors and fun, highly original prints, stripes, and checks, they will. And new mums might like the colorful diaper and utility bags. 9 Sloane St., SW1. ℂ 020/7823-2505. www.oilily-world.com. Tube: Knightsbridge.

**Patrizia Wigan Designs**  Strictly for traditionalists, this posh boutique places such a high value on exclusivity, it manufactures its kids' outfits in small quantities and rotates its stock every 4 to 6 weeks. Clothes are of the timeless, quintessentially English ilk, made from luxurious fabrics such as velvet, moleskin, light wools, linen, and silk, in warm countryside and seaside shades, and are apparently beloved by royals. 19 Walton St., SW3. ℂ 020/7823-7080. www.patriziawigan.com. Tube: Knightsbridge.

**Paul Smith**  Of Paul Smith's three London stores, Westbourne House near Portobello is the place to come for his gorgeous, witty babywear (think £25/$50 for a onesie), and boys' and girls' T-shirts/shirts (ages 2–12). Also sold are "classic" toys/novelties and gifts—think metal robots and classy domino sets. Westbourne House, 122 Kensington Park Rd., W11. ℂ 020/7727-3553. www.paulsmith.co.uk. Tube: Notting Hill Gate.

**Petit Bateau**  This established French name set up in 1893, with stores in Japan, Morocco, the U.S., and Brazil, has downscaled in London; its prime Regent Street flagship and its Chiswick branch have closed. But there's still this smaller outlet at South Molton Street, plus branches on the King's Road and in Notting Hill, Clapham, and Hampstead. You won't find much to surprise—this is classic, conservative stuff—but it is quality, long-lasting gear that can be boiled in the wash without losing its color (crucial for babywear), so see it as an investment. 62 South Molton St., W1. ℂ 020/7491-4498. www.petit-bateau.com. Tube: Bond St.

**Polarn O. Pyret** *Finds*  Those tired of seeing the same old styles on the high street might like to venture out to this London outpost of a Swedish chain offering fresh looks to babies and kids up to 11, plus mums-to-be. The vibe is simple and clean in a Scandinavian way, with plenty of nautical stripes in primary colors. 1F, Brent Cross Shopping Centre, NW4. ℂ 020/8203-9781. www.polarnopyret.se. Tube: Brent Cross.

**Rachel Riley**  Classic styles for children and teens, in natural fibers such as silk, wool, cashmere, and leather, can be found here. All clothes are made in workshops by the Loire, and while they might look dainty and delicate, the emphasis is on ease of laundering. Bridesmaid and pageboy outfits are a specialty. You'll find a second shop at 14 Pont St. in Knightsbridge. 82 Marylebone High St., W1. ℂ 020/7935-8345. www.rachelriley.com. Tube: Baker St.

**Ralph Lauren Children's Store** ⭐  The U.S. designer's free-standing kids' store sells classic and vintage clothes and accessories for babies, girls, and boys, plus luxury gifts and bedding. Prices are what you'd expect for its famous polos, Oxford cloth shirts, cable sweaters, and other well-made items, but there are free seasonal events such as Easter parties, with face-painting, live magic, and a lucky dip. 143 New Bond St., W1. © 020/7535-4600. http://global.polo.com. Tube: Green Park.

**Sasti** ® Come to Sasti for an injection of fun and originality at fair prices. Highlights among the playful but hard-wearing designs for ages up to 10, divided into fun categories such as Angels and Yettis, Bees 'N' Bugs, and Young Punk, are hoodies with star motifs, fleece trousers with target pockets, and zebra-stripe trousers. The store has a play area to keep junior shoppers entertained. 8 Portobello Green Arcade, 281 Portobello Rd., W10. © 020/8960-1125. www.sasti.co.uk. Tube: Ladbroke Grove.

**Their Nibs** ® This trendy neighborhood boutique focuses is on stunning original prints, including fairies, retro cars, cowboys, and pirates, which turn up on its bed-linen sets and on some of its clothes, which include tunics and tutus, and adorable long-sleeved cotton shirts for babies. 214 Kensington Park Rd., W11. © 020/7221-4263. www. theirnibs.co.uk. Tube: Ladbroke Grove.

**Top Shop** ®®® This high-street chain with its vast Oxford Circus flagship store has boomed in recent years. By offering a vast choice of the latest catwalk looks at rock-bottom prices, it's a prime hunting ground for teens, but tots aren't left out either, with the Top Shop Mini ranges for ages 3 months to 1 year (including a pair of baby skinny jeans!). Mums-to-be get their own range, too. Note the leggy beauties trying to look nonchalant outside—this is prime territory for model-agency scouts looking for the next Kate Moss, who had just released a range here at the time of writing. 36–38 Great Castle St., W1. © 020/7636-7700. www.topshop.co.uk. Tube: Oxford Circus.

**Trotters** ®®® This was London's first store dedicated to kids, and it remains a good all-rounder for quality fashion brands, backed up by an excellent choice of accessories and dressing-up items. The Trotters Express Train takes the boredom out of shoe-fitting, and there's a hair salon with an aquarium to keep kids entertained (they get a bravery certificate at the end of their first cut). The staff is clearly fond of and experienced with kids, and the atmosphere is lively. Aside from fashion, you can stock up on toys and on baby, kids', and parenting books. There are other branches on Kensington High Street and in Clapham. 34 King's Rd., SW3. © 020/7259-9620. www.trotters. co.uk. Tube: Sloane Sq.

## JEWELRY & ACCESSORIES
Many of the clothing stores reviewed above also stock jewelry and accessories.

**Accessorize** ® This treasure-trove is a few steps upmarket from Claire's (see below), but it's still good value considering how well it keeps pace with the latest trends, and wherever you are in London, you're not far from a branch. Little princesses go mad for its largely pink and sequined Girls collection, which includes everything from baseball caps and pocket bags to corsage ponies, flower gems, sparkly flip-flops, and glitter ballet pumps. 254 Regent St., W1. © 020/7287-8388. www.accessorize.co.uk. Tube: Oxford Circus.

**Claire's Accessories** This global chain's range of cheap, disposable jewelry, makeup, hair accessories, and dressing-up products is perfect for an instant glamour fix, and there are countless London branches. 108 Oxford St., W1. © 020/7580-5504. www.claires.com. Tube: Tottenham Court Rd.

**Octopus** ® It may be a chain—and a growing one at that—but walking into one of Octopus's bright little stores always feels like a discovery. Among the fun accessories, gifts, and housewares (80% of which are exclusive to Octopus), you'll find

## Market Value

Rebellious teens into body piercings, blue hair, and grungy clothing head straight for **Camden Market** (Tube: Camden Town), which is open daily but really comes to life, in its inimitably tacky way, on weekends (it's actually several markets merging into one). Another hippie paradise is **Jubilee Market** (Tube: Covert Garden) alongside Covent Garden Market, selling general goods, including cheap clothes and accessories, from Tuesday to Friday, and crafts at weekends (on Mon it's an antiques market). The world-famous **Covent Garden** hosts the daily **Apple Market** in its courtyard, selling handcrafted toys, clothes, hats, and jewelry, none of them cheap.

Perhaps London's most famous market, **Portobello Market** ✿✿ (Tube: Notting Hill Gate) is best known for its antiques stalls and shops but also sells fruit and vegetables and—best of all—some truly innovative fashion. During the week it's mostly used by locals to stock up on food and practical items, but Fridays see a secondhand market, too. (Get there bright and early in the morning to see famous fashion designers shopping for inspiration.) The best area for fashion is under the Westway, where creative young things set up their stalls, but the street is also lined with vintage clothes stores where you're guaranteed to find something original. Make sure you stop at the north end of the market, where it peters out into junk stalls, and enjoy a custard pastry at one of the Portuguese bakeries along trendy Golborne Road.

Farther afield, **Greenwich** is host to famous weekend markets with stalls selling crafts, antiques, books, clothes, and general junk.

---

animal-shaped handbags, rubber jewelry, themed watches, bright luggage, and everything from egg cups to hot water bottles. If your eco-conscience needs salving, know that lots of items are made from recycled materials. At the time of writing there were branches on Carnaby Street, in the Trocadero Centre in Piccadilly Circus, on the King's Road, and on the Portobello Road, and more in the pipeline. 54 Neal St., WC2. ✆ 020/7836-2911. Tube: Covent Garden.

## FOOD

A highlight of any trip to London is browsing some of its wonderful **food halls,** of which Harrods's and Fortnum & Mason's are delightfully over-the-top in a very uppercrust English way, and Harvey Nichols's, Selfridges's and the new one at John Lewis are more modern (and modest) in feel. (See p. 222 for full department-store listings.)

A street version of a food-hall browse involves wandering around one of London's growing number of **farmers' markets** (16 at the time of writing; see www.lfm.org.uk for the latest list and for details of all), where local food producers come to sell their (often organic) wares. There's no better experience than a stroll in the sunshine helping yourself to the free samples of breads, cheeses, jams, and other goodies as you fill your basket with top-quality produce to cook back home. The most central markets take place weekly in Marylebone, Pimlico, Notting Hill, and Islington.

In a similar vein, **Borough Market** ✿✿✿ (✆ 020/7407-1002; www.boroughmarket. org.uk) along the South Bank near Southwark Cathedral is a historic and atmospheric fruit-and-vegetable market dating back as far as Roman times. In recent years it has been transformed into a gourmet food market Thursday through Saturday, when you can taste and buy excellent meats, cheeses, breads, fruit and vegetables, coffees, patisseries, and more.

For **organic specialists,** see p. 236.

## CAKES

**The Hummingbird Bakery** 𝒦𝒦   This little oasis of American home baking has expanded into larger new premises in South Kensington, open daily and with longer hours, although the original branch on the Portobello Road remains. The specialty is cute cupcakes—little works of art, and a must-have at chic birthday parties. Adults seem to love them as much as kids: In addition to the standard flavors, there's a daily special—lavender on Tuesdays, mint chocolate on Wednesdays, carrot on Thursdays, and so on. Otherwise, there are chocolate devil's food cake, New York–style cheesecake, Key Lime pie, brownies, and cookies. 47 Old Brompton Rd., SW7. (℃ **020/7584-0055.** wwwhummingbirdbakery.com. Tube: South Kensington.

**Patisserie Valerie** 𝒦𝒦   This patisserie with further branches in Soho, Kensington Church Street, Piccadilly, Belgravia, Spitalfields, and—since summer 2007—Marble Arch, and Queensway in Bayswater, may describe itself as a "famous meeting place for starving artists and bohemians," and its decor may be charmingly shabby-chic, but its prices mean that most of its clientele is of the well-heeled variety. Queue at the counter for candies and specialty cakes, including vertiginous chocolate constructions, superb fruit tarts, handmade truffles, and the sweetest little marzipan animals (including Easter and Christmas specialties at this Marylebone branch). Or sit in for continental breakfasts, light lunches, and afternoon teas, including treats such as Belgian white hot chocolate. The owners also run the Left Wing Cafe and Gelateria Valerie (p. 122) on Duke of York's Square on the King's Road. 105 Marylebone High St., W1. (℃ **020/7935-6240.** www.patisserie-valerie.co.uk. Tube: Bond St.

## CANDY

**Charbonnel et Walker**   A long-standing favorite patronized by the royal family, this shop is famous for its hot chocolate, its seasonal chocolate-covered strawberries, and its classic rose and violet creams—go on, it would be rude not to indulge. There's a second branch in Canary Wharf, or you can also get your paws on C&W chocolates at Selfridges (p. 224), Harrods (p. 223), John Lewis (p. 224), and Harvey Nichols (p. 223), and at Heathrow and Gatwick airports. 1 The Royal Arcade, 28 Old Bond St., W1. (℃ **020/7491-0939.** www.charbonnel.co.uk. Tube: Green Park.

**CyberCandy** 𝒦𝒦 (Finds   A dentist's nightmare, this place—which has moved to a larger outlet since the first edition of this guide—is serious about its sweet stuff, whether you want American classics, British favorites, the latest Japanese crazes, limited editions, or even candy-flavored cosmetics, from Twizzlers lip balm to Gummy Bears soap. For homesick American visitors or expats, Hostess Twinkies and Ding Dongs are flown in direct from the States (they tend to sell out quickly). 3 Garrick St., WC2. (℃ **0845/838-0958.** www.cybercandy.co.uk. Tube: Leicester Sq.

**Hope & Greenwood** 𝒦𝒦   Candy stores don't get much more old-fashioned or English than this gorgeous 1955 sweet shop with an original marble counter and vintage-clad staff. Specializing in the "great and glorious confections of this land" and promising a "carnival of sugar," this place is well worth the trip out of the center (it's handy for the Dulwich Picture Gallery; see p. 176) if you hanker for such nostalgic treats as flying saucers, sherbet lemons, and cola cubes, stored in 175 glass jars. More grownup treats include handmade chocolates with such flavors as "damson in distress"

## The Sweetest Thing

If you're in town in October, you may be in luck—this month sees **Chocolate Week** (www.chocolate-week.co.uk), when chocoholics can enjoy activities in shops and venues around the city, including tastings, fruit-dipping, and displays of chocolate sculptures and fountains. Goodie bags are sometimes available, and places such as Melt may host special children's activities.

Alternatively, some of London's most interesting candies are the traditional Indian and Pakistani confections that can be sampled daily at the top of Tottenham Court Road, on Drummond Street, NW1. Try **Ambala** (no. 112–4; ℭ **020/ 7387-7886**) and **Gupta** (no. 100; ℭ **020/7380-1590**).

and "voluptuous violet." 20 N. Cross Rd., SE22. ℭ **020/8761-743**. www.hopeandgreenwood.co.uk. Train: E. Dulwich.

**Melt** 𝕣𝕣    Described by one reviewer as "the city's coolest new chocolatier," Melt fits in seamlessly in chic Notting Hill, with its all-white, laboratory-style decor. Yet there's no snobbery here—visitors are welcomed into the kitchen to see the award-winning truffles, ganaches, and other goodies being made (from organic ingredients where possible), and there's even a weekly Children's Hour (Wed, 4:15–5:15pm; booking essential; £25/$50 per child including goody bag and lolly) where kids can (6 and up) come along and learn to make their own chocolates and treats. 59 Ledbury Rod, W11. ℭ **020/ 7727-5030**. www.meltchocolates.com.

## HAIRDRESSING

In addition to the salon below, places in which kids can get shorn are **Harrods** (p. 223), **Daisy & Tom** (p. 241), **Trotters** (p. 232), and **alsocaramel** and **caramel** (p. 228).

**Junko Moriyama** 𝕣𝕣    This laid-back Japanese salon caters to a happy band of locals and their kids. The hip and youthful staff is adept at keeping children entertained, or you can book a double appointment so your offspring can be shorn at the same time as you—great if your kids aren't confident about the idea. I once even had my hair cut while breastfeeding here, without anyone batting an eyelid! Parents get free cups of green tea and an addictive 10-minute shiatsu head, neck, and shoulder massage at the end of their competitively priced treatment. There are a second branch at the other end of Marylebone, more convenient for those coming from Oxford Street, and a branch in the City. 58 Upper Montagu St., W1. ℭ **020/7724-8860**. www. jmoriyama.co.uk. Tube: Baker St.

**Zest** 𝕣 (Finds)    This family salon was opened early in 2007 by a hairdresser who used to work at Daisy & Tom (p. 241) and therefore has bags of experience cutting kids' hair. After they've been snipped, you can get yourself a cut, enjoy a brew, and peruse a magazine, while they watch videos or play on the computer or with the toys provided. There's lots of space to park strollers. 159 Battersea Park Rd., SW8. ℭ **020/7498-4688**. Train: Battersea Park Rd.

## HEALTH & BEAUTY

For eco-friendly products, see p. 236.

**Boots the Chemist**    This national chain provides life's little necessities, from medicine to mascara. All outlets stock diapers, wipes, and baby food; larger branches have kids' departments with clothes, nursery equipment, and toys. There are branches everywhere, but this one just north of Hyde Park is open until 10pm daily. 75 Queensway, W2. (C) 020/7229-9266. www.boots.com. Tube: Bayswater.

**Lush**    I defy anyone to walk past one of Lush's divine-smelling stores without being tempted in for a closer inspection of its fresh, handmade cosmetics and bath-time products, all based on essential oils and non-animal synthetics (ingredients are listed on the packaging), and some of them vegan. Choose from among slices of colorful soap, bath ballistics, massage bars, and much, much more. The 13 London branches include Regent Street, South Molton Street, Covent Garden, King's Road, and Portobello Road. 40 Carnaby St., W1. (C) 020/7287-5874. www.lush.com. Tube: Oxford Circus.

## MUSIC

**Chappell of Bond Street**    No longer, somewhat misleadingly, actually situated on Bond Street since its relocation to Soho, this music store has counted Beethoven, Richard Strauss, and Charles Dickens among its clientele since setting up in 1811. Customer service is second to none, whether your kids are budding Vanessa Maes or enthusiastic beginners who just want to mess about on an inexpensive plastic recorder (most staff have music degrees). The selection of instruments and sheet music (both classical and pop) is unparalleled, and the new three-story premises is also home to the new Yahama London store, with a wide range of Yamaha pianos, keyboards, guitars, woodwind instruments, and more. 152–60 Wardour St., W1. (C) 020/7100-6126. www.chappell ofbondstreet.co.uk. Tube: Tottenham Court Rd.

**Dot's**    This welcoming north London music store stocks a range of secondhand instruments; a good choice of chord books and playalongs, from Bob Marley to Henry Mancini; and a wide pop and classical CD selection. There's always a pot of coffee brewing, and staff members are a mine of information, particularly if you're looking for a tutor. Instruments can be hired as well as bought. 132 St Pancras, NW1. (C) 020/ 7482-5424. www.dotsonline.co.uk. Tube: Camden Town.

## ORGANIC

On Sunday, pick up organic fruits and vegetables, breads, meat, fresh tofu, chocolate, and more at **Old Spitalfields Organic Market** at 65 Brushfield St., E1 (Tube: Liverpool St.). A Hippyish treat, it also hosts craft stalls, secondhand goods, and an East Asian–style food mart.

**Green Baby** &    London's most eco-conscious kids' store sells plain, unpretentious clothes and accessories for babies and toddlers, much of it made from organic cotton by Fair Trade partners. It's also the place to come for glass and nickel- and PVC-free feeding items, wooden or cotton toys, award-winning (if pricey) bath and health products, and household products. The Canadian founder is a champion of washable nappies, but you'll find eco-friendly disposables such as Tushies or the compact Mother Earth diapers—great for those on the move. The tiny Islington branch and newer one in Greenwich stock the full product range; this two-story Notting Hill one does, or there's a bigger one still down in Richmond. 5 Elgin Crescent, W11. (C) 020/7792-8140. www.greenbaby.co.uk. Tube: Ladbroke Grove.

**Planet Organic** &    Don't come to this organic supermarket at lunchtime, when the aisles, cafe, and excellent takeout/juice bar get packed out with office workers hunting for delicious healthy fare. The rest of the day, the supermarket is a joy to wander around, with its fab cosmetics and natural remedies; a superb array of produce that buries any notion that organic fare is aesthetically inferior; and a good choice of kids' and babies' items, be it snack food or earth-friendly diapers. There are less central outlets in Fulham and Westbourne Grove. 22 Torrington Place, WC1. © 020/7436-1929. www. planetorganic.com. Tube: Goodge St.

**Whole Foods Market** *RR*    Opened in mid-2007, this U.S. "real foods" supermarket occupying a renovated department store is London's largest food retail space. Although it in some ways takes the place of the Fresh & Wild chain that WFM purchased in 2004, there remain Fresh & Wild branches in Soho, Camden, Stoke Newington, and Clapham. Baby food and products are well represented in all, and some branches have minicarts for tots to push. Most stores have in-store bakeries and cafes where you can tuck into soups, cakes, and fresh juices; the main superstore has an array of take-away counters, plus Upstairs at the Market—a dining, drinking, and meeting space with a DJ and delicacies from around the world, including smoothies, waffles, and crepes; ice creams and sorbets; pizza, tapas, Middle Eastern meze, and sushi. The basement, meanwhile, has eco-clothing, natural remedies, and treatment rooms. Don't miss a turn at the make-your-own-peanut-butter machine. The Barkers Building, 63–97 Kensington High St., W8. © 020/7368-4500. http://wholefoodsmarket.com. Tube: High St. Kensington.

## SHOES

For **Buckle My Shoe,** which was Britain's first footwear store just for kids, see Selfridges (p. 224). **Ecco,** at 445 Oxford St. (© 020/7629-8960), plus Kensington High Street and Knightsbridge, also has an excellent range of kids' sporty shoes, while some of the clothing stores reviewed above stock shoes and offer fitting services.

**Instep** *R*    At this long-established, nationwide kids' shoes chain, fashionable looks don't mean poor quality. As well as brand names such as Kickers, Nike, Start-rite, and Rhino, there's a brilliant Italian house brand, plus football boots, ballet shoes, wellies, socks, and more. The staff are more than helpful, and the fitting service is second to none. There are other London branches in Wimbledon, Wandsworth, and Harrods (p. 223). 45 St. John's Wood, High St., NW8. © 020/7722-7634. www.instepshoes.co.uk. Tube: St. John's Wood.

**Office**    Teens flock to this great chain to find up-to-the-minute fashion footwear at a fraction of what you'd pay for the designer versions. The trainers section, which includes Converse All-Stars, is particularly fine. The 15-plus London branches include the Brunswick Centre in Bloomsbury, Neal Street in Covent Garden, Carnaby Street, Oxford Street, King's Road, Portobello Road, and Camden. 55 S. Molton St., W1. © 020/7491-8027. www.office.co.uk. Tube: Bond St.

**One Small Step, One Giant Leap** *RR*    This chain's continued expansion is testament to its success in its mission to bring parents expert shoe-fitting (for which advance booking is advised), great brands, and value for money. Labels for babies through teenagers include Start-rite, Pomme d'Api, Ricosta, and Geox, and there are a great range of ballet shoes, football boots, slippers, wellington boots, umbrellas, beachwear and accessories, and girls' accessories. The bright, contemporary outlets (there are branches in Islington, Ealing, Clapham, Putney, and East Sheen) are all on the ground floor to cut the hassle for those laden with bags and strollers. There are also concessions in Harrods (p. 223) and Daisy & Tom (p. 241). 3 Blenheim Crescent, W11. © 020/7243-0535. www.onesmallsteponegiantleap.com. Tube: Ladbroke Grove.

**Russell & Bromley Kids** *R*    This long-standing, upmarket British firm offers fashionable but hard-wearing footwear and an expert fitting service, so you won't begrudge the relatively high prices. This is the dedicated kids' shop (there's another in the Bluewater Mall; see p. 240), but most branches have children's departments, stocking both the trusty stalwarts of the shoe world, Start-rite and Clarks, and big designer brands such as Diesel, D&G, and Ralph Lauren. Unit B1, Brent Cross Shopping Centre, NW4. ℂ 020/8203-4161. www.russellandbromley.co.uk. Tube: Brent Cross.

**Vincent Shoe Store** ⚘   This new store, part of an expanding Swedish chain begun by a former H&M buyer, caters to kids up to 8. Its well-priced, often witty footwear includes the green and grinning Minifrog for babies, and fabric Flagga shoes with a variety of national flags. There are funky wellies and flip-flops, too, covering the extremes of the British weather, plus smiley-faced clogs and socks. 19 Camden Passage, N1. ℂ 020/7226-3141. www.vincentshoestore.com. Tube: Camden.

## SHOWER & BABY PRESENTS
Many of the stores listed under "Clothing," "Equipment & Nursery Items," and "Toys & Games" also sell baby toys and accessories.

**Blossom Mother & Child** ⚘   This super-stylish boutique focuses on expectant moms and newborns, with maternity wear and lingerie, chic nursery furniture, plus luxury baby clothing, some of it organic, and such frivolities as a feng shui nursery kit and a leather Bill Amberg papoose (a snip at £325/$650). 164 Walton St., SW3. ℂ 020/7589-7500. www.blossommotherandchild.com. Tube: Knightsbridge.

**Brora**   This is the place to splurge on special-occasion blankets, teddies, onesies, baby booties, bonnets, and mittens in the finest cashmere, as well as adults' and kids' clothes made from the same luxurious wool. The winter sale is always a good time to snap up bargains. There are further branches on the King's Road, and in Notting Hill, Islington, and Wimbledon. 81 Marylebone High St., W1. ℂ 020/7224-5040. www.brora.co.uk. Tube: Baker St.

**Halcyon Days**   A supplier of "objets d'art" to the Queen and company, this Mayfair store is known for its enamel boxes, which include a Winnie the Pooh edition. Other special occasion gifts or future family heirlooms include *Alice in Wonderland* and *Wind in the Willows* figurines, Noah's Ark money boxes, and teddy bears' picnic *bonbonnières* (that's sweet pots to you and me). Think upwards of £100 ($200) for a gift. 14 Brook St., W1. ℂ 020/7629-8811. www.halcyon-days.co.uk. Tube: Bond St.

**Monogrammed Linen Shop**   Amid its classical and contemporary linens, laces, embroideries, cottons, and silks, this store offers exquisite christening presents that can be monogrammed to order (in about 10 working days), including pillowcases, with or without London buses or other embellishment. You can also get personalized children's bathrobes and party dresses. 168–70 Walton St., SW3. ℂ 020/7589-4033. www.monogrammedlinenshop.com. Tube: Knightsbridge.

**Peter Rabbit & Friends**   Touristy but appealing, this little shop sells all kinds of merchandise relating to the 1901 bestseller *The Tale of Peter Rabbit* by Beatrix Potter and its 22 follow-ups, from christening gifts, soft toys, and dolls, to games, clothing, books, and videos, to tableware and soft furnishings. It's a brilliant place for presents for new babies and for nursery items such as musical watering cans. The same firm runs a Paddington Bear stall in—wouldn't you know it—Paddington Station. 42 The Market, Covent Garden, WC2. ℂ 020/7497-1777. Tube: Covent Garden.

**Semmalina Starbags** ⚘   This eclectic little shop has an ever-changing range of clothes, nostalgic toys and bits and pieces of childhood kitsch, and vintage prints, and—increasingly popular, hence the name—gorgeous made-to-order party bags for both kids and adults, which are useful for baby showers, kids' birthday parties, sleep-overs, and more. A bag costs £2 ($4) per bag for the wrapping, sweets, ribbon, and cellophane; you decide on the remaining contents. 225 Ebury St., SW1. ☎ 020/7730-9333. www.starbags.info. Tube: Sloane Sq.

## SPORTS & SPORTSWEAR

**Decathlon**    It's worth the schlep out to this, the city's biggest sports store (part of a global chain). As well as selling clothing and equipment for more than 60 sports, it has repair/maintenance workshops for bikes, racquets, and skis, and a cafe. Surrey Quays Rd., SE16. ☎ 020/7394-2000. www.decathlon.co.uk. Tube: Canada Water.

**O'Neill** ☆    Budding beach bums would be mad to look elsewhere—O'Neill's range of shorts, plain or in funky prints and bright colors such as egg yolk yellow and Span-ish red, is unbeatable. For boys there are also sweats, fleeces, headgear, and warmer-weather gear such as jackets and pullovers. Girls aren't left out, with a surprisingly pretty range that includes shirts in ice-cream hues, printed dresses, and cute bags. There's another branch on Carnaby Street. 9–15 Neal St., WC2. ☎ 020/7836-7686. www. oneilleurope.com. Tube: Covent Garden.

**Quiksilver** ☆    Since the last edition of this guide, this Australian brand has added a snazzy Regent's Street flagship store to its growing empire, designed by a hip French architect and displaying its surfing and snow-boarding fashion over two floors—there's a live DJ soundtrack to accompany as you browse, and the store's own TV channel screening tricks by its riders. Two smaller branches remain, on Carnaby Street, and Neal Street in Covent Garden. The kids range includes good-quality, road-tested fleeces, snow jackets, knits, beanies, belts, underwear, snow gloves, and wallets. 229–247 Regent St., W1. ☎ 020/7493-5900. www.quiksilver.com. Tube: Oxford Circus.

**Slam City Skates**    This Covent Garden skateboarding specialist—which also sells clothing—is well known for its sales. Kids' shoes include Emerica. 16 Neal's Yard, WC2. ☎ 020/7240-0928. www.slamcity.com. Tube: Covent Garden.

**Soccer Scene**    This soccer-fan's heaven sells team replica kits, boots, trainers, and soccer memorabilia and accessories, from toddler sizes up. There are other branches on Carnaby Street and on Long Acre in Covent Garden. 156 Oxford St. ☎ 020/7436-6499. www.soccerscene.co.uk. Tube: Oxford Circus.

## TOYS & GAMES

The gift shop at the **Rainforest Café** (p. 114) is excellent for animal-themed toys. If you just want a few low-priced toys and games for your hotel room or apartment, **Argos** (150 Edgware Rd., W1, and other locations; www.argos.co.uk) and **Wool-worths** (168–76 Edgware Rd., W1, and other locations; www.woolworths.co.uk) both have lots of choices. Before you return to your home country, ask about donating them to a local community toy library (☎ 020/7255-4600; www.natll.org.uk) or take them to a thrift store. If you're heading for Bluewater Mall, there's a dedicated **Lego Store** (p. 240) there for construction junkies. Opposite Brent Cross Mall you'll find a branch of global giant **Toys R Us** (☎ 0800/038-8889; www.toysrus.co.uk).

**Benjamin Pollock's Toy Store** ☆    This old-fashioned, family-run shop still sells the cardboard toy theaters for which it was set up in the 1880s, as well as traditional toys for kids and collectors, including Czech marionettes, jack-in-the-boxes, Russian nesting dolls, and music boxes. Toy theater kits range from simple pop-ups with no cutting required, to an authentic and detailed model of Shakespeare's Globe theater

## Mall-to-Mall Shopping

London's biggest mall is way on its northwest outskirts but has its own Tube station for ease of access. **Brent Cross** (℘ 020/8202-8095; www.brentcross. co.uk) boasts 120 stores and cafes, including John Lewis, Marks & Spencer, Mothercare, Boots, H&M, Baby Gap, Gap Kids, Fatface, Monsoon, Top Shop, Claire's Accessories, Early Learning Centre, Fun Learning, and Russell & Bromley Kids. As well as special family parking spaces, it offers free stroller loan and Boobaloo toddlers' car hire—great for keeping the kids entertained and under control at the same time.

Smaller but more central (it's just north of Hyde Park at 151 Queensway), **Whiteleys** (℘ 020/7229-8844; www.whiteleys.com; Tube: Bayswater) has more than 50 outlets (including Accessorize, Gap Kids, H&M, French Connection, and Muji), plus a branch of the Gymboree kids' activity center (p. 218). There are also an eight-screen cinema and family-friendly restaurants such as Ask Pizza.

When size matters, though, you'll need to head about 24km (15 miles) out of London, to **Bluewater** in Kent (℘ 0870/777-0252; www.bluewater. co.uk; Train: Greenhithe), where you'll find more than 300 stores; 40 restaurants, cafes, and bars; and a multiscreen cinema. Kids'/parents' outlets include Petit Bateau (p. 231), H&M (p. 230), Blooming Marvellous (p. 227), the Early Learning Centre (p. 241), Mystical Fairies (p. 227), Russell & Bromley Kids (p. 237); and a **Lego Store** with construction games for babies and up (℘ 01322/427272; www.lego.com). It's also just become home to the first U.K. branch of the U.S. LittleMissMatched outlet, which encourages everyone from babies to adults to have fun mis-coordinating their footwear and accessories. If you'd rather browse for yourself or be pampered at the Molton Brown Day Spa, there's a nursery for 2- to 8-year-olds. There's also a dizzying array of nonshopping activities, including an 11m (36-ft.) climbing wall for ages 6 and up, a golf-putting course, pedaling and row-boating on the lakes, and a wildlife discovery trail through the surrounding landscaped park, around which you can also cycle (bikes, unicycles, tandems, family four-wheelers, and kids' pedal-powered go-carts are available for hire). You'll build up quite an appetite, which you can sate at the likes of Carluccio's (p. 109), Ed's Easy Diner (p. 114), or Pizza Express (p. 115).

(p. 172) for experienced modelers; none are expensive. 44 The Market, Covent Garden, WC2. ℘ 020/7379-7866. www.pollocks-coventgarden.co.uk. Tube: Covent Garden.

**Cheeky Monkeys** ⟲⟲  Distinguishable by its bright yellow frontages, this superb minichain also stands out because of its exciting stock. Four branches are located in south London (Clapham, Dulwich, Parsons Green, and Wandsworth), and one in Islington in north London. When I last visited, the flagship Notting Hill branch had just had a new lick of paint and more goodies than ever before, including a pink 1950s Murray Comet pedal car for little girls who fancy themselves '50s movie stars, a shoe-painting kit for aspiring footwear designers, and an Antquarium (developed using

NASA technology) where kids can watch ants burrow and feed. 202 Kensington Park Rd., W11. ℂ 020/7792-9022. www.cheekymonkeys.com. Tube: Ladbroke Grove.

**The Conran Shop**    This stylish housewares emporium stocks pricey but original toys that don't look out of place in the chicest of households, including a giant inflatable world globe with detachable Velcro landmarks and animals (£255/$510), a giant world map (£295/$590), and wooden playthings and dolls' houses. Look out for the funky kids' furniture and travel items, including a turtle duffle bag and a ladybird backpack. There's another branch on the Fulham Road, SW3. 55 Marylebone High St., W1. ℂ 020/7723-2223. www.conran.com. Tube: Regent's Park.

**Daisy & Tom** 🅰🅰    This is more of an experience than a store, with a traditional carousel that kids ages 2 to 10 can ride at set times of the day. There's a kids' hair salon, too, for which advance booking is required. But, you're looking for toys? Well, amid the flurry of activity, you can find everything from baby's first toys to science kits, from traditional rocking horses to Vtech electronic educational gadgets, with plenty set out for kids to try. You'll also find excellent nursery and equipment sections, a huge selection of clothing and shoes, gifts galore, and a lovely book hall with titles for both kids and parents. (You can read them together in the cozy nooks.) Prices aren't so competitive—perhaps inevitably given all the "extras." 181 King's Rd., SW3. ℂ 020/7352-5000. www.daisyandtom.com. Tube: Sloane Sq.

**Early Learning Centre** 🅰🅰    ELC's range of sturdy learning toys for kids from birth to about 4 years prove that education needn't be dull. With their great prices, you're bound to end up coming out with a few treats for your little ones. Look out for offers on seasonal products, particularly outdoor toys and equipment. Tuesday playtimes take place once a morning from 10am, offering free activities in all branches. That said, the relaxed staff seem happy to let kids play with the stock at any time, although this Chelsea branch doesn't have too much room to maneuver. There are branches in High Street Kensington, Putney, Hammersmith, Ealing, and at the Brent Cross and Bluewater malls (p. 240), and you can find ELC toys in Daisy & Tom (see above), Debenhams (p. 223), and many chains. 36 King's Rd., SW3. ℂ 020/7581-5764. www.elc.co.uk. Tube: Sloane Sq.

**The Farmyard** 🅰    This cozy outfit specializes in lovingly crafted and hand-painted toys and furniture, many of which can be personalized with a name or date. Among the tactile traditional toys on offer are wooden Noah's arks, farms, dollhouses, and London buses; there's also a selection of nursery gifts such as personalized wooden rattles and baby blankets. Items for the home include treasure and keepsake boxes, and traditional but colorful wall clocks. For exclusive hand-painted toy boxes with Groovy Cow and other vibrant designs, brightly painted chairs, and other larger items, there's a bigger branch in Richmond Hill, Surrey. 63 High St., Barnes, SW13. ℂ 020/8878-7338. www.thefarmyard.co.uk. Train: Barnes Bridge.

**Fun Learning** 🅰    The store is aimed at "graduates" of the Early Learning Centre (see above), which means that it, too, eschews movie and TV merchandise in favor of innovative and inspiring educational products—this time for kids from 5 to 13. The shop is chockablock with toys, games, books, puzzles, craft kits, posters, science kits, CD-ROMs, and software. The friendly staff encourages kids to play and will happily open boxes so they can try out the contents. *Insider tip:* This is a great place to source easily packed items for car journeys and flights, including miniature playing cards and magnetic travel games. Brent Cross Shopping Centre (opposite Waitrose), NW4. ℂ 020/8203 1473. www.funlearning.co.uk. Tube: Brent Cross.

**Hamleys** *Overrated*   This wouldn't be a London kids' guide without mention of Hamleys, but the world's most famous toy store—a tourist attraction in its own right—is a peculiarly charmless place these days, with its apathetic staff (many of whom seem barely able to speak English); and its rip-off cafe serving some of the worst food I've ever tasted. And forget English tradition; Hamleys was bought out by an Icelandic investor a few years back. That said, kids will be so in awe of the 35,000 or so toys and games arranged over its seven floors that they won't notice the cynicism behind it all. Occasional promotions are dressed up as special events, but don't go out of your way to visit Santa here at Christmas—go to Harrods instead (p. 223). Hamleys has minibranches at Heathrow and Stansted airports. 188–196 Regent St., W1. ✆ 0870/333-2455. www.hamleys.com. Tube: Oxford Circus.

**Honeyjam** ✿   This new store's main claim to fame is that it is co-owned by supermodel and brewing empire heiress Jasmine Guinness, which must make it London's trendiest toyshop. The hip Portobello Road location helps, too. But it's a good destination in its own right, with a fair selection of toys starting at pocket-money prices, attractively arranged. Many have an old-fashioned feel, and there are few concessions to TV merchandising. There are also some Fair Trade products, and other made from sustainable resources or eco-friendly in some other way—these are marked by green price tags. 267 Portobello Rd., W11. ✆ 020/7243-0449. www.honeyjam.co.uk. Tube: Ladbroke Grove.

**Igloo** ✿   Its location on the swish shopping mecca of Islington's Upper Street means prices ain't low, but then you come to this shop to seek out unique treasures that you won't find in the larger chains, whether it be toys and books, clothes for babies to 8-year-olds, bedroom and nursery furniture and homewares, or toiletries. You'll find everything from wooden fairy skipping ropes to Native American tepees for your garden and VW Beetle pedal-cars. There's a second store in St. John's Wood. 300 Upper St., N11. ✆ 020/7354-7300. www.iglookids.co.uk. Tube: Angel.

**Patrick's Toys**   This is one of London's biggest traditional toy and model shops, set up more than 50 years ago and still family run. Model makers flock here for the excellent choice of rockets, planes, cars, military vehicles, and sci-fi craft; while transport fiends come here for the Hornby and Scalextric. Also available are dolls, soft toys, traditional wooden toys, games, puzzles, outdoor equipment, and all the latest fads. 107–111 Lillie Rd., SW6. ✆ 020/7385-9864. www.patrickstoys.co.uk. Tube: Fulham Broadway.

**Puppet Planet** ✿✿✿ *Finds*   An enchanting store run by a professional lady clown, Puppet Planet is full of vintage and new puppets, from the Thunderbirds and Punch & Judy to traditional Czech marionettes and Balinese shadow puppets. There's something to please both lovers of kitsch and serious collectors, plus related toys, gifts, and books, and puppet theaters from pocket-money prices. The customized look-alike puppets (from £250/$500) make unique gifts. 787 Wandsworth Rd., SW8. ✆ 020/7627-0111. www.puppetplanet.co.uk. Tube: Parsons Green.

**Route 73 Kids**   This local shop, named for the bus that goes by it (the area is not well endowed with Tube lines), sells lovely old favorites next to the latest crazes. The focus is on stimulation, whether it be in the form of lullaby mobiles, instruments for budding Beethovens, paints and crayons, science experiments, sticky insects, fairy costumes, wands, tiaras, origami, or silk paintings. And that's just to mention a few of the goodies—it's a wonder they fit it all in the minuscule shop and still have room for a play area. 92 Church St., Stoke Newington, N16. ✆ 020/7923-7873. www.route73kids.co.uk. Bus: 73.

# 11

# Entertainment for the Whole Family

London's vast array of entertainment options is centered on the **West End,** where most of its theaters and multiplexes lie. This area is also full of great eating options (as well as its fair share of tourist traps), so you can really make an evening, or an afternoon, of it. Just across the river, the South Bank is the city's cultural hot-house, with an array of world-class performance venues that don't forget children when it comes to scheduling anything from classical music to poetry.

Don't let all this stop you from venturing farther afield, though, or you'll miss out on some offbeat jewels that only a city of London's size and ethnic diversity can spawn. Enjoy those blockbuster musicals but don't forget the countless innovative kids' companies and community centers that rely on your patronage for their survival. Similarly, catching a big Hollywood movie at a West End multiplex is all well and good, but not unique

to London. Instead, seek out atmospheric and historic little picture houses with creative kids' clubs.

**FINDING OUT WHAT'S ON** For comprehensive weekly theater, cinema, and events listings and for lively reviews of them, see *Time Out* magazine (p. 12), which has Theatre, Film, Dance, and Sports sections, as well as a dedicated Kids section. It's also well worth signing up for a free monthly e-mail newsletter from www.londonmonthly.com, which you can personalize according to your interests. For discounts on shows and the like, see www.londontown.com.

An excellent source of information for plays and shows is www.officiallondon theatre.co.uk, which has a very useful search facility allowing you to browse current shows by age suitability. You can sign up for a well-produced semimonthly e-mail bulletin on family entertainments.

## 1 The Big Venues

For theatrical performances suitable for older kids, check out **Shakespeare's Globe** (p. 172).

**Barbican Centre** 𝒜𝒜 Europe's biggest multi-arts center, with its world-class concert hall, theaters, cinemas, and art galleries, celebrated its 25th birthday in 2007. It's a wonderful space for families, hosting regular events where parents and kids can get creative together. Budding musicians ages 7 to 12 will be thrilled by the **London Symphony Orchestra's Discovery Family Concerts** (© 020/7588-1116; www.lso.co.uk), to which they can bring along instruments (you can download sheet music from the website in advance in order to practice). Screens show close-ups of the players (whom the kids can meet during the intermission) as well as short animations.

# Central London Entertainment

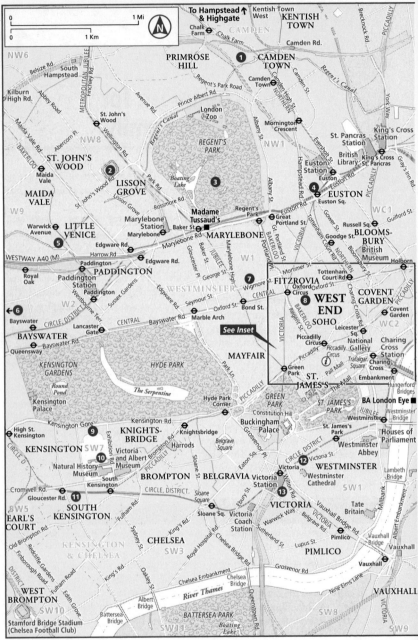

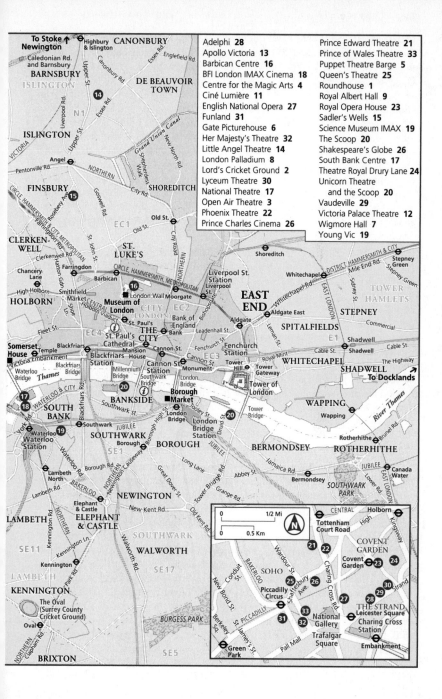

Adelphi **28**
Apollo Victoria **13**
Barbican Centre **16**
BFI London IMAX Cinema **18**
Centre for the Magic Arts **4**
Ciné Lumière **11**
English National Opera **27**
Funland **31**
Gate Picturehouse **6**
Her Majesty's Theatre **32**
Little Angel Theatre **14**
London Palladium **8**
Lord's Cricket Ground **2**
Lyceum Theatre **30**
National Theatre **17**
Open Air Theatre **3**
Phoenix Theatre **22**
Prince Charles Cinema **26**

Prince Edward Theatre **21**
Prince of Wales Theatre **33**
Puppet Theatre Barge **5**
Queen's Theatre **25**
Roundhouse **1**
Royal Albert Hall **9**
Royal Opera House **23**
Sadler's Wells **15**
Science Museum IMAX **19**
The Scoop **20**
Shakespeare's Globe **26**
South Bank Centre **17**
Theatre Royal Drury Lane **24**
Unicorn Theatre
  and the Scoop **20**
Vaudeville **29**
Victoria Palace Theatre **12**
Wigmore Hall **7**
Young Vic **19**

Tickets are £6 ($12). The concerts are preceded by free foyer events, plus Family Music & Art Workshops (£5/$10) during which you can create costumes to wear in the concert. For the LSO's Discovery Family Saturday mornings and Concerts for Under-5s, see p. 255.

Another jewel in the Barbican's crown is its Saturday-morning **Family Film Club** 𝕽𝕽𝕽, where for £4.50 ($9) each, kids 5 to 11 and their families can engage in creative activities from the Movie Trolley, based on the week's film (activities start at 10:30am, films at 11am). On the last Saturday of the month, longer themed workshops are offered by guest artists, such as nature model making; you'll need to book ahead, as these are justifiably popular. Otherwise, there's a lively program of theater, dance, music, and art for older kids to take their pick from. After your cultural fix, there's opportunity to let off steam in the massive building with its public spaces full of restaurants, bars, and cafes, and free art displays. Check out the fountain-studded courtyard lake and giant fishpond. Silk St., EC2Y. ℂ 020/7638-4141. www.barbican.org.uk. Tube: Barbican.

**National Theatre** 𝕽 Adjoining the South Bank Centre (see below), the world-class National actually houses three theaters that among them host eclectic works ranging from classics by the likes of Tennessee Williams to radical pieces from artists' collectives. You won't always find a kids' show on here, but when you do, you can guarantee it will be worth the wait—*Coram Boy,* about a foundling from Coram's Fields (p. 209), went on to Broadway and six TONY award nominations, while late 2007 saw an inspiring handsprung life-size puppet version of Michael Morpugo's *War Horse,* about a horse's experiences in World War I, for kids 12 and up. Watch out, too, for the outstanding Word Alive! storytelling sessions for 7- to 11-year-olds (£4/$8) and occasional readings by renowned children's authors and poets. Otherwise, you can always find free live music and exhibitions in the foyer spaces, including a display on the National's history, and older kids might enjoy one of the backstage tours (£5/US$10 adults; £4/$8 children under 18; £13/$26 family). There are restaurants and bars throughout the building and all over the area. South Bank, SE1. ℂ 020/7452-3000. www.nt-online.org. Tickets £17 ($34) for under-18s; adult prices vary according to show and seating. Tube: Waterloo.

**South Bank Centre** 𝕽𝕽 This series of concrete bunkers stretched along the riverbank is another outstanding venue for classical and contemporary music, dance and performance, and literary events—and, after massive renovation, including the 2-year-in-the-making transformation of **Royal Festival Hall** (one of the center's three concert halls), is now more family-friendly than ever, with a host of family-friendly restaurants and cafes with riverside terraces, including Giraffe (p. 120), Strada (p. 115), and Wagamama (p. 123). As for the culture, the Royal Festival Hall resumed, after reopening in June 2007, its series of family concerts by the resident London Philharmonic Orchestra, now renamed **FUNharmonics.** These take place on Saturday mornings once every 4 months or so, and tend to include a number of disparate pieces based around a theme: Flights of Fancy, for instance, featured music from Jonathan Dove's opera *Flight, Star Wars, The Snowman,* and the Harry Potter movies. Children's tickets cost £4 to £7 ($8–$14), adults' £8 to £9 ($16–$18), depending on seating, and concerts are preceded and followed by an hour of free fun in the foyers, including Have-a-Go instrument sessions, face-painting, and circus skills. All year, these foyers buzz with free live music and exhibitions. The excellent **Poetry Library,** with its activity trail, recordings

## Showtime: Where to Get Tickets

With kids in tow, you're not going to be able to and/or be willing to book seats far in advance, so you may want to go to the opposite extreme and snap up last-minute bargains (usually half-price tickets, with a £2.50/$5 service charge) for top West End shows at the two official discount **TKTS** ticket booths in Leicester Square (Mon–Sat 10am–7pm; Sun noon–3pm) and at Canary Wharf DLR Station (Mon–Sat 10am–3:30pm; note that cash is not accepted at this branch). Notice boards detail what's available in front of the booths; or check the daily listings on www.officiallondontheatre.co.uk (which also sells advance tickets).

If tickets for the show you want to see are not available at **TKTS,** try the theater directly; some release limited numbers of tickets for same-day performances at noon, but they can only be purchased in person at the box office and may be limited to two per person—so a family of four may end up sitting in two separate groups. You can also buy advance full-price tickets from a theater's box office by phone or via its website, though the latter will actually link through to **See** (© **0870/264-3333;** www.seetickets.com), **Ticketmaster** (© **0870/154-4040;** www.ticketmaster.co.uk), or **www.londontheatredirect.com,** which also offers theater-dinner deals and discounted hotel rooms. Ticketmaster also has ticket centers, at Camden Tourist Information Center at 173 Arlington Rd., and at the Greenwich Tourist Information Center beside the *Cutty Sark,* or you can get tickets at the Britain & London Visitor Center (p. 44). Wherever you get your tickets, you'll be subject to a booking fee of about £1.50 ($3) per ticket.

archive, and selections of poems by or for children, hosts readings as part of the Imagine Children's Literature Festival. **Queen Elizabeth Hall,** meanwhile, hosts chamber music, opera, dance, and occasional appearances by famous kids' authors. For **The Hayward Gallery** and **Waterloo Sunset Pavilion,** see p. 176. Belvedere Rd., SE1. © 0871/663-2501. www.sbc.org.uk. Tickets vary according to show. Tube: Waterloo.

**Royal Albert Hall**   This world-famous circular building of gargantuan proportions (it seats 5,200) is a versatile space hosting a variety of performances, from ballet and the Cirque du Soleil (a circus with acrobatics and aerial displays) to Brazilian funk. It's best known, though, for its summer **Proms** concerts, which it's hosted since 1941. Incorporating a medley of rousing, mostly British orchestral music, this is great fun for older kids, especially if you buy standing-room tickets in the orchestra pit and get a peek at the musicians on stage. Don't despair if you can't get tickets for the spectacular Last Night: The event is relayed on big screens in Hyde Park (p. 203). There are also lots of very popular pre- and post-Prom events including a program for families to come and make music together, no matter what instrument they play or the level they play at (these are held at the Royal College of Art), introductory workshops (ages 7 and up; at least one member of the attending family must be under 16), and a Brass

## Out in the Open

There's no finer way to appreciate a long summer evening in the City than to take the family to one of its magical outdoor events. Right in the heart of London, in lovely Regent's Park, the **Open Air Theatre** 🎭🎭 (Inner Circle, NW1; 🕿 08700/601811; www.openairtheatre.org) hosts Shakespeare, light opera/musicals, and a kids' show suitable for all ages—perhaps Roald Dahl's *Fantastic Mr. Fox*. Tickets are £12 ($24) for all tickets for kids' shows, but you can save £3 ($6) on each if you buy well in advance. The grounds open early so you can enjoy a buffet and barbecue amid the fairy lights, or you can bring your own picnic (see p. 106 for tips on where to buy great picnic fare). The season lasts from early July to mid-September.

Another delightful way to spend a balmy evening is at an **English Heritage Picnic Concert** 🎭🎭 (🕿 0870/890-0146; www.picnicconcerts.com) at Marble Hill House (p. 187). Performances range from soul and Motown, and 1980s revivals, to Vivaldi's The Four Seasons, with classical concerts culminating in a fireworks display. Gates open early, so bring a picnic and a rug (you can also hire deck chairs). Be warned that these events are wildly popular, so book well in advance. Ticket prices average £25 ($50), with only tiny concessions for kids, so it's an expensive night out—but one they won't forget in a hurry. Similar concert, fireworks, and picnic extravaganzas are held at the 1-week **Summer Swing** at Kew's Royal Botanic Gardens (p. 191), with kids under 5 attending free of charge (otherwise tickets average £30/$60). Crystal Palace Bowl in Crystal Palace Park (p. 207) has just relaunched its **Pops in the Park** season of concerts by the Royal Philharmonic Orchestra, with performances ranging from opera and classical to James Bond. They take place every weekend in August, with premium tickets (including a deck chair) costing £25

Day with preliminary workshops and the chance to take part in a performance. Alternatively, there's the Blue Peter Proms in association with the kids' show *Blue Peter;* tickets for the latter are £10 ($20), half that for under-16s. The hall now runs backstage tours that grant you a glimpse into the Queen's Box and the Royal Retiring Room (£7.50/$15 adults, £6.50/$13 children 5–18, £25/$50 family of five). Kensington Gore, SW7. 🕿 020/7589-8212. www.royalalberthall.com. Tickets vary according to performance. Tube: S. Kensington.

**Young Vic** Occupying an award-winning new building constructed around an old butcher's shop now serving as the foyer, this groundbreaking theater—set up in the 1970s to bring audiences of all ages the classics and new plays by younger writers, directors, actors, musicians, and technicians at low prices—has three small auditoriums, in none of which you sit more than seven rows from the action (tickets don't reserve specific seats, but there are no obstructions). Offerings range from community opera to the likes of a South African musical version of Dickens's *A Christmas Carol;* the website gives age indications, with about half of shows suitable for kids 8 and up. 66 The Cut, SE1. 🕿 020/792-2922. www.youngvic.org. Tickets £16 ($32) or £22 ($44) adults; £9.50 ($19) under-6s.

($50), those for the grassed area costing £20 ($40), and family tickets for up to five at £60 ($120). On one weekend there's a Noisy Kids concert when kids 5 to 12 can help to create a new piece of music—this is free but you must book in advance (© 020/7608-8813; www.popsinthepark.co.uk).

Few people haven't heard of the Last Night of the Proms, the rabble-rousing climax of the summer season at Royal Albert Hall (p. 247). But many don't know that the event has spilled over into adjacent Hyde Park to become **Proms in the Park** ☆☆ (www.bbc.co.uk/proms/pitp). The highlight of the night is the relaying of the concert inside Royal Albert Hall onto giant screens watched by an audience sitting outdoors beneath the stars. Events actually begin late in the afternoon with concerts by other performers. Tickets, available from the Royal Albert Hall, cost £23 ($46); under-3s go free.

Something a little more offbeat is in store for you if you book one of the enchanting "promenade performances" by the **London Bubble Theatre Company** ☆☆ (© 020/7237-1663; www.londonbubble.org.uk), during which the audience follows actors around one of a variety of London parks (including Waterlow Park; p. 208) as they perform works such as The Dong with a Luminous Nose, generally suitable for kids ages 7 and up. Performances are particularly atmospheric because they begin at 8pm, as the light begins to fall; tickets cost £15 ($30) for adults, £8 ($16) for kids, and are refunded or replaced in cases of bad weather.

Lastly, funfairs and circuses such as Carters Steam Fair (p. 209) and Zippos and the Chinese State Circus pitch their tents on London's green spaces throughout the summer season; for information, see *Time Out* magazine.

## 2 Seasonal Events

One of the best times to visit London if you have theatrically minded kids is **Kids' Week** ☆☆☆ (www.kidsweek.co.uk), during which you can get free tickets for 5- to 19-year-olds to top West End shows throughout the second half of August—so for 2 weeks, not 1. There are also exclusive shows and activities for under-5s. Booking opens in July; you get one free ticket with every adult full-price ticket, plus the option of a further two kids' tickets at half price. Related events include backstage visits, dance workshops, and stage-fighting, although there's a one-activity-per-child rule because they're so popular. Many restaurants let kids eat for free, and travel and accommodations are available, too—see the website for details.

As winter begins to bite, along come Christmas **pantomimes** ☆ (or "pantos") to cheer you up. A British institution based on popular kids' stories and fairy tales such as *Cinderella,* these demand plenty of audience participation. A recent highlight has been *Dick Whittington* by young British playwright Mark Ravenhill at the Barbican (p. 243). Other venues for Christmas specials are the Young Vic (p. 248), Sadler's Wells (p. 256), and the Lyric Hammersmith (p. 254). Details are released on **www.thisistheatre.com/panto.html** throughout the year.

## 3 Theater

A seemingly unstoppable trend among younger kids is touring shows based on some of the most popular British, U.S., and Australian children's TV shows and characters, such as *The Wiggles*, *Scooby Doo*, and *Noddy*. Such events run for a night or two at large venues such as The O2 (the former Millennium Dome; p. 258), the new Wembley Arena (p. 259), or the Hammersmith Apollo. To keep up-to-date, watch your chosen show's website, or log on to www.ticketmaster.co.uk and check forthcoming family events.

### CHILDREN'S THEATER COMPANIES

**artsdepot** This dynamic arts venue in north London, open since 2004, is worth going out of your way for because of its exciting kids' programming, featuring shows by a wide range of innovative theater companies in its Studio Theatre. Specific shows vary, but the venue generally caters to kids 4 and up, and there are dance classes (the likes of street and Bollywood) for older children. 5 Nether St., N12. (C) 020/8369-5454. www.artsdepot.co.uk. Tickets £7 ($14) adults, kids £5 ($10). Tube: West Finchley.

**Chickenshed Theatre** ⨀ A delightfully named company (its original home was indeed an old chicken shed), this theater comes with a long-standing reputation for imaginative new works and creative adaptations using ingenious staging. It's a fair schlep out of central London, in the northern suburb of Southgate, but you won't regret the trip. Much of the freshness comes from the fact that its youth theater has an all-inclusive policy, allowing anyone ages 5 to 24 to join without audition (although a huge waiting list has now built up). The main offering for kids is *Tales from the Shed* every Friday and Saturday—a critically acclaimed interactive production designed to encourage numeracy, literacy, and communication skills in under-7s. Chase Side, N14. (C) 020/8351-6161. www.chickenshed.org.uk. Ticket prices vary. *Tales from the Shed* is £5 ($10) adults, £3.50 ($7) kids over 6 months. Tube: Oakwood.

**Half Moon Young People's Theatre** An exciting East London venue for shows for kids from birth to age 17, Half Moon produces and tours two shows of its own each year. (Venues include Jackson's Lane; p. 254). From September to April, it also hosts performances by outstanding visiting companies, such as Little Angel Theatre, with a particularly good choice for kids ages 2 to 6. 43 White Horse Rd., E1. (C) 020/7265-8138. www.halfmoon.org.uk. Tickets £4 ($8). Tube: Stepney Green.

**Little Angel Theatre** ⨀⨀ A magical little marionette theater, Little Angel devises shows that go on to tour nationally and internationally, and hosts performances by visiting companies. All types of puppets are used, and themes and stories are drawn from a variety of cultural traditions. A recent highlight was the interactive "Claytime," during which kids 3 to 6 suggested a story, setting, and characters to be modeled from clay. Age ranges are normally 2 to 5, and 5 and up, with strict rules about taking in kids younger than that so as not to disrupt performances. Look out for family interactive workshops (£25/$50 for one adult and one child, including show tickets), in which you and Junior can create puppets and play with them together, using the performance you've just seen as inspiration. Watch out, too, for PWYC (Pay What You Can) performances, where tickets are offered at whatever price you can afford upwards of £1 ($2). 14 Dagmar Passage, N1. (C) 020/7226-1787. www.littleangeltheatre.com. Tickets £8 ($16) adults, £6 ($12) children. Tube: Angel.

**Polka Theatre** 🎭🎭   This inspiring space manages to be both a beloved local venue and a world-renowned center of young people's theater. Events range from teen dramas to modern-day literary adaptations; certain productions include "Watch with Baby" performances so parents with older kids can see shows without worrying about childcare for the youngest (if your baby gets restless, you can take him or her into the foyer and carry on watching the show on the monitor). Performances are split between the Main Auditorium for ages 4 and up, and the Adventure Theatre for younger kids. Most performances in the Adventure Theatre are aimed at those 3 and up, but it's hosted a number of developments in theater for babies (6 months plus), and all ages are welcome, with babies under 1 year free.

A full program of extras includes summer courses and workshops (drama, songs, storytelling, puppet-making), and interactive performances by spoken-word artists (with complimentary ice cream) on Saturdays at 10:30am (free, but pre-booking required). There are great facilities, too, including a welcoming cafe with a kids' menu (staff members are happy to warm up baby food), a baby-changing room, and a stroller park. 240 The Broadway, SW19. ℂ 020/8543-4888. www.polkatheatre.com. Tickets £6.20–£9 ($12–$18). Tube: Wimbledon.

**Puppet Theatre Barge** 🎭   This unique and atmospheric 50-seat floating theater presents marionette and rod puppet shows. In winter the vessel is moored in the lovely Little Venice neighborhood of west London (p. 52), in summer (July–Oct) it plies the Thames, giving performances at Henley, Marlow, Cliveden, and Richmond. Shows are firmly divided into family performances (the likes of *Brer Rabbit Goes to Africa*) and more adult fare such as adaptations of Joseph Conrad stories. Blomfield Rd., W9. ℂ 020/7249-6876. www.puppetbarge.com. Tickets £8.50 ($17) adults, £8 ($16) kids. Tube: Warwick Ave.

**Unicorn Theatre** 🎭🎭   This award-winning theater company is now firmly ensconced in its new £13-million ($26-million) building close to Tower Bridge—the U.K.'s first purpose-designed professional theater for children. Its self-stated aim is to produce works that challenge kids 4 to 12, but you'll also find occasional special shows for kids 6 months to 2 years, shows for children 3 and up, and even for those up to 19 with complex disabilities such as autism, in its two auditoriums. Touring companies hosted here include Oily Cart (see below), and there's dance as well as plays. It's best to come on a Family Day (£ 24/$48 per person; booking required), which combine workshops with performances followed by the chance to meet the cast, and include refreshments. The theater has a branch of Frizzante (p. 135), offering kids' pasta dishes and omelets, and you can hang out in the foyer with its changing exhibitions of artwork oriented at children. 147 Tooley St., SE1. ℂ 08700/534534. www.unicorn theatre.com. Tube: London Bridge.

## TOURING THEATERS

**Oily Cart** 🎭🎭 (ℂ 020/8672-6329; www.oilycart.org.uk) is a national touring company offering hip-hop musicals and other groundbreaking and highly interactive and multi-sensory performances for under-5s, plus kids with severe disabilities. London venues include the Lyric Hammersmith (p. 254) and Unicorn Theatre (see above). Keep an eye on the tour schedules of **Pop-Up** (ℂ 020/7609-3339; www.pop-up.net), an innovative company producing thought-provoking work for over-3s by outstanding kids' authors such as David Almond. **Quicksilver Theatre** 🎭 (ℂ 020/7241-2942; www.quicksilvertheatre.org) has won awards for its boldly visual new plays for

3- to 7-year-olds and older kids, performed at the artsdepot (p. 250) and other venues. The long-standing **Theatre Centre** (© 020/7729-3066; www.theatre-centre.co.uk) presents specially commissioned works on three broad themes ("Rites of Passage," "Contemporary Culture," and "The Releasing of the Authentic Voice") to kids 7 and up, at venues such as the Unicorn. Pioneering **Theater-Rites** *R̄R̄* (© 020/7953-7102; www.theatre-rites.co.uk), presents richly poetic works for kids an adults to enjoy together, such as an installation piece performed in a disused ward of a real hospital. It also visits venues such as the Unicorn.

## LONG-RUNNING SHOWS

At press time, the West End shows listed below indicated they would continue indefinitely. Because some last nearly 3 hours (including an intermission), families with kids ought to consider a midweek or weekend matinee performance. Count on spending between £10 ($20) and £65 ($130) per person. For advice on booking, see p. 247.

As well as the shows specifically oriented toward kids reviewed below, older children enjoy the following long-runners: **Stomp**, a wordless, plotless, highly choreographed piece using found objects such as brooms, garbage cans, and oil drums to make uplifting rhythms inspired by **street theater** (Vaudeville Theatre; www.vaudeville-theatre.co.uk/www.stomponline.com); the worldwide Andrew Lloyd Webber smash **Phantom of the Opera** (Her Majesty's Theatre; © 0870/040-0046; www.her majestys.co.uk), about a beautiful opera singer who falls in love with a deformed young composer living a shadowy existence beneath the Paris Opera; the melodrama **Blood Brothers** (Phoenix Theatre; www.phoenix-theatre.co.uk), about twin brothers separated at birth whose lives become unavoidably linked; and **Mamma Mia!** (Prince of Wales Theatre; www.mamma-mia.com), about a holidaying single mom and her daughter, who pepper their lives and fantasies with renditions of their favorite ABBA songs, which often gets the audience singing and dancing in the aisles. The number to call for all is © **0870/040-0046.**

**Billy Elliot** *R̄R̄*    This feel-good musical trades on the Oscar-nominated movie of the same name, set in a mining town in northeast England and following a young boy's realization of his dream to become a ballet dancer in spite of his father's wish that he become a boxer. The tunes are by Elton John. Victoria Palace Theatre, 8 Victoria St., SW1. © 0870/040-0046. www.victoria-palace-theatre.co.uk. Tickets £18–£60 ($36–$120). Tube: Victoria.

**Joseph and the Amazing Technicolor Dreamcoat** *R̄*    This family crowd pleaser returned to the London stage in mid-2007 for a lively retelling of the biblical tale of Joseph, sold by his jealous brothers for being his father's favorite, as symbolized by his colorful coat. The relaunch was given momentum by a TV series based on auditions for a new leading man. Singalong hits include *Any Dream Will Do* and *Close Every Door.* Adelphi Theatre, The Strand, WC2. © 0870/040-0046. ww.adelphitheatre.co.uk. Tickets £18–£60 ($36–$120). Tube: Charing Cross.

**Les Misérables** *R̄R̄*    This adaptation of the Victor Hugo novel of 1862, one of the world's most popular musicals, has been around for more than 20 years in London. It's melodramatic stuff, but the plot—about social justice—can be a little dark for kids, and the music isn't best suited to singalongs. You can now get them better involved by signing up for one of the thrice-monthly **Les Miz Kids Club workshops** for children ages 8 to 11 and 12 to 15 (© 0870/850-9171), which last 2½ hours and include a behind-the-scenes tour, the chance to try on costumes, a drama workshop with improvisation games, a snack-pack lunch, a meeting with a cast member, and a certificate of attendance. Prices vary according to whether the seat you choose at the attendant matinee, but start at £30 ($60), plus £10 ($20) for an adult seat at the show. Queen's Theatre, 51 Shaftesbury Ave. ✆ 0870/950-0930. www.lesmis.com. Tickets £17–£53 ($34–$106). Tube: Piccadilly Circus.

**The Lion King** 👧👧    An award-winning Disney blockbuster musical about life, love, and rivalry on the savanna, *The Lion King* uses puppetry and masks to magical visual effect. A limited number of seats for the day's performance are released at the box office at noon, but you can only buy two per person, so a whole family may end up not sitting together. Lyceum Theatre, 21 Wellington St., WC2. ✆ 0870/040-0046. www.lyceumthe-atre.co.uk. Tickets £23–£65 ($46–$130). Tube: Covent Garden.

**Lord of the Rings**    A new production in 2007, this is a stage adaptation of Tolkien's 200-million-selling book trilogy, combined into one event with a spectacular set design and cast of more than 70 actors, singers, and musicians. Be aware that it's on the long side—3 hours, in fact. It's believed to be the world's most expensive musical ever. Theatre Royal Drury Lane, Catherine St., WC2. ✆ 0870/040-0046. www.theatreroyaldrurylane.co.uk. Tickets £15–£60 ($30–$120). Tube: Covent Garden.

**The Sound of Music** 👧👧    A surefire new hit for West End supremo Andrew Lloyd Webber, this much-loved musical was the last Rodgers & Hammerstein collaboration before becoming the Oscar-winning movie. Based on the true story of the Von Trapp family's escape from the Nazis, it's full of all the favorite singalongs, including *The Hills are Alive, My Favourite Things, Do-Re-Mi, Edelweiss,* and *Climb Ev'ry Mountain,* and the child performers are delightful. London Palladium, Argyll St., W1. ✆ 0870/040-0046. www.london-palladium.co.uk. Tube: Oxford Circus.

**Wicked**    This popular new show recounting the "untold story" of the witches from The Wizard of Oz, based on Gregory Maguire's 1995 novel, *Wicked: The Life & Times of the Wicked Witch of the West,* appeals best to teenage girls. Apollo Victoria Theatre, 17 Wilton Rd., SW1. ✆ 0870/040-0046. www.apollovictoria.co.uk. Tickets £15–£60 ($30–$120). Tube: Victoria.

## WEEKEND SHOWS

**Chats Palace**    This gritty East End community arts center hosts top professional children's entertainment on Saturday at 2pm, involving puppets, music, clowns, magic, and more, most aimed at 3-year-olds and up. Tickets are a steal, and there's lots of free entertainment, including games and face-painting, from noon until 4pm. You can get the kids fired up for the performance with dance and drama workshops for ages 2 to 5, or bring them down gently with post-show arts-and-crafts workshops for ages 4 to 8. 42–44 Brooksby's Walk, E9. ✆ 020/8533-0227. www.chatspalace.com. Tickets £2 ($4). Train: Homerton.

**Comedy Club 4 Kids** 👧    Britain's first stand-up comedy club for children ages 7 ("alternative comedy without the swearing") tends to move venue, so check the web-site for the latest information. Generally held on the first Sunday of every month, it's usually hosted by well-known comedian James Campbell, who has toured his non-condescending, surreally silly kids' show around the world, and features regular guest comics. Shows tend to be free-form, with Campbell running with feedback from kids in the audience, but topics might include dead hamsters, boring relatives, or the dan-ger of being hit by flying cows while walking home from school. Kids with comedic aspirations get a 5-minute shot at the mic. (They have to attend a course at the "acad-emy" first—see the website for classes and workshops.) ✆ 07891/125652. www.fatcat products.co.uk. Tickets £6 ($12).

**Jackson's Lane**    A 30-year-old north London community center in a converted church, Jackson's Lane was closed for widespread repairs as we went to press, after suffering severe storm damage, but hoped to reopen in the near future. The standard bill includes weekend shows for various age groups by companies such as Quicksilver Theatre (p. 251) and Half Moon Young People's Theatre. Visits for an excellent interlude between a romp in Highgate Wood (p. 209) and a browse in Ripping Yarns (p. 226). 269a Archway Rd., N6. ℭ 020/8341-4421. www.jacksonslane.org.uk. Tickets: ask for details. Tube: Highgate.

**Lauderdale House** ℛℛ    This outstanding cultural center in a lovely 16th-century house built for London's lord mayor, set in secluded Waterlow Park in north London (p. 208), is heaven for kids. Saturday mornings see two performances (10 and 11:30am) of a show that may involve puppetry, singing, storytelling, or a musical session, or a combination of those, for ages 3 to 8. In mid-May the shows are part of the Hampstead & Highgate Festival, which features family workshops. School vacations are filled with kids' creative activities, including painting, crafts, movement, and storymaking. Tots aren't forgotten: They get their own music, dance, and drama session. Refuel in the cafe-restaurant before enjoying the rest of the park. Highgate Hill, Waterlow Park, N6 5HG. ℭ 020/8348-8716. www.lauderdalehouse.co.uk. Tickets £4.50 ($9) adults, £3 ($6) kids. Tube: Archway.

**Lyric Hammersmith** ℛℛ    This Victorian theater enclosed within a modern shell in west London hosts Saturday kids' shows by the likes of Oily Cart (p. 251), most lasting just less than an hour, plus special shows in the school vacations. The age range for each varies, but ages 3 months to 13 years are catered for at some time (babies are welcome to all performances but must be taken out if they cry). The majority of performances encourage little ones to jump out of their seats and get involved (one even featured lots of water, and required the audience to bring a towel and a change of clothes!). Look out for annual events, which might include an Easter Parade or a Summer Party with interactive shows and events for all the family. The theater's Cafe Brora has kids' lunchboxes. Lyric Sq., King St., W6. ℭ 08700/500511. www.lyric.co.uk. Tickets Saturday shows £8 ($16) adults, £6 ($12) kids, £24 ($48) family of 4. Tube: Hammersmith.

**Tricycle** ℛℛ    This lively little north London theater, cinema, and gallery is well worth going out of your way for, especially for its Saturday children's theater. Each show tends to differ in its age range, but something suitable for kids ages 2 to 12 is regularly featured. It may be a traditional Hans Christian Andersen tale or a magic and juggling show with lots of audience participation. If you're in London a while, your kids might like to sign up for the popular term-time dance, drama, and/or music workshops for those from 18 months to 16 years old. Similar half-term workshops, usually lasting 1 to 2 hours and focused on the likes of mask-making, mini-garden creating, and street dance, get booked up long in advance. Saturdays see family films, and there's a vibrant cafe/bar. 269 Kilburn High Rd., NW6. ℭ 020/7328-1000. www.tricycle.co.uk. Tickets £5 ($10). Tube: Kilburn.

## MAGIC
### Centre for the Magic Arts ℛ (Finds)    The Magic Circle's HQ is open to visitors 14 and over (sometimes younger kids are allowed in by arrangement) for regular special evenings (usually Tues twice a month) called "Meet The Magic Circle," where you can see tricks close up, listen to a talk on the history of mystery from 4000 B.C. onward, and watch a stage show in the theater. You'll hear all about the famous bullet-catching

trick that has killed several magicians, and about the exploits of Houdini. While you're here, you get access to the Magic Circle Museum (normally open only to members), which has exhibits on great musicians of the past, posters, and other memorabilia. Aspiring young talents should inquire about the Young Magicians Club for 10- to 18-year-olds. 12 Stephenson Way, NW1. © 020/7387-2222. www.themagiccircle.co.uk. Tickets £26 ($52). Tube: Euston.

## 4 Classical Music, Dance & Opera

For the **Wigmore Hall** classical venue, see p. 220. For the large multi-arts venues, see p. 243.

**English National Opera** 🎟 Your best bet for opera-going in London with kids, especially if you're new to the art form, is the London Coliseum, home to the ENO, which performs all works in English, making it far easier for novices to follow the story. Works range from crowd-pleasing classics such as *Carmen* and Gilbert and Sullivan operettas to more experimental modern opera. Regular ENO Baylis family events (£3/$6; attendance sometimes gets you reduced-price opera tickets) allow kids 7 and up to study the themes of an opera currently being performed. London Coliseum, St. Martin's Lane, WC2. © 020/7632-8300. www.eno.org. Tickets £5–£30 ($10–$60). Tube: Leicester Sq.

**LSO St Luke's** 🎟🎟 As well as its Family Discovery concerts at the Barbican (p. 243), the London Symphony Orchestra hosts more special concerts, this time for under-5s, here in its restored East London church complete with concert hall. Held on Saturdays at 1pm, and dirt-cheap (free to under-1s), they retell well-known children's stories through a mixture of traditional and new music. Beforehand, you might like to attend a Discovery Family Saturday Morning (£2.50/$5; under-1s free) for those with kids under 8, featuring musical activities (music technology, gamelan, toddler workshops, and informal concerts). There's a cafe on-site. UBS and LSO Music Education Centre, 161 Old St., EC1. © 020/7490-3939. www.lso.co.uk. Tickets for under-5s concerts £1 ($2). Tube: Old St.

**Royal Opera House** 🎟🎟 The city's more grownup option, the Royal Opera House is home to both the Royal Opera and the Royal Ballet, as well as hosting international companies such as La Scala. Operas are usually sung in the original language, with

---

### London Beats

Nightclubbing and rock gigs might be strictly for parents (if you have the energy . . .), but there are options for children who want to dance themselves dizzy or catch some up-and-coming London bands. The fashionable Roundhouse in Camden hosts Saturday-afternoon **Artrocker All Ages Gigs** in its FREEDM Studio (Chalk Farm Rd., NW1; © 020/7424-9991; www.roundhouse.org.uk), with bands and supporting DJs. Entry is free, and there's a record stall. Especially for tots, meanwhile, **Babygroove** 🎟🎟 (www.babygroove.co.uk) was *the* hit of 2007, with plans to relaunch after a summer break as this guide went to press. A relaxed monthly event for children and their parents, it presents an afternoon of funky house music plus a chill-out area, a buggy park, free snacks, and a bar. Entry is £7 ($14) adults, £5 ($10) children over 1. Venues in 2007 included the White House in Clapham and High Road House in Chiswick (p. 53).

supertitles projected. School vacations often see Creative Families musical weeks inspired by a current opera: They include workshops on vocals/composing, sound exploration, storyboarding, and dance and drama. Prices are £5 ($10) per workshop for adults, £3 ($6) for children 7 to 15, and everyone is expected to participate! You need to book well ahead, too. Daily backstage tours for those 8 and over (£9/$18 adults; £7/$14 children) vary according to what's going on, but may include a glimpse of the Royal Ballet in class, or of the impressive behind-the-scenes technology in action. Bow St., WC2. ℭ 020/7304-4000. www.royalopera.org. Tickets £8–£185 ($16–$370). Tube: Covent Garden.

**Sadler's Wells** 👧👧  This is a top-ranking venue for mainstream and cutting-edge contemporary dance (including tango, tap, and flamenco), opera, and family shows, such as Christmas ballets and adaptations of works by kids' authors. (Some perform-ances are at the sister Peacock Theatre, WC2). Occasional family workshops that take place prior to a matinee performance involve trying out some of the dances and moves from the performance you are about to see, plus another activity. The minimum age for these is 6, and pre-booking is a must. Younger kids can come along to drop-in Babygroovers music and movement sessions, for ages 4 weeks to 1 year and 1 to 3 years, costing £3 ($6) per session. Rosebery Ave., EC1. ℭ 0844/41-4300. www.sadlers-wells.com. Ticket prices vary by show. Tube: Angel.

## 5 Movies

London has more than its fair share of multiplex cinemas offering the latest Holly-wood blockbusters for consumption with monster buckets of popcorn. For reviews and detailed weekly listings, see *Time Out* magazine, published each Tuesday and available from all newsagents. Most of the big-hitters (Empire, vue, Odeon) are in Leicester Square and adjoining West End streets.

Be aware that cinema-going in the center can empty your wallet in no time, with adult tickets averaging £12 ($24), and kids about £8 ($16), and that's before you've factored in the rip-off drinks and popcorn. By contrast, some farther-flung venues offer good family deals, such as **Odeon Swiss Cottage** in north London (ℭ 0871/2224-4007; www.odeon.co.uk) with its £21 ($42) ticket for two adults and two kids (or one adult and three kids). The chains also offer Saturday- and Sunday-morning **Odeon Kids Clubs** with screening at pocket-money prices and a free adult ticket for each kids' one; branches at which this is available include Swiss Cottage and White-leys (p. 240; same phone number as Swiss Cottage). The program also runs through school vacations.

Another option a little farther north is **O2 Centre** (Finchley Rd., NW3; ℭ 020/794-7716; www.o2centre.co.uk), mall with an eight-screen **vue cinema** (ℭ 0871/240240; www.myvue.com), plus a bookstore, a branch of Gymboree (p. 218), the London International Gallery of Children's Art (p. 219), various eating options, the Esporta health club (p. 211), a big supermarket, and holiday events such as egg hunts and balloon modeling, so you can make a day of it. The mall has a nature theme, with weird rock-formation walls and fish tanks dotted about.

London's smaller independent picture-houses are more congenial than the City's blockbuster cinemas and often run special family screenings or film clubs. For Barbi-can's Family Film Club, see p. 246; for the Tricycle, see p. 254. Note that by British law, kids under 8 must be accompanied by an adult in a cinema.

**Ciné-Lumière** 🎬🎬  The Ciné-Teens & Kids program of screenings at the cinema inside the Institut Français language and cultural center has a bias toward French-language movies but also shows films in other languages, including English, German, and Russian. These (shown with English subtitles when necessary) range from classics of French cinema, including the Jacques Tati "Monsieur Hulot" farces, to nature documentaries and animation. Age ranges vary but overall there's something for ages 4 and up. A children's library in the building offers books, comics, magazines, videos, DVDs, and more for kids up to 12, and there's also a "médiathèque" for old children and adults. A bistro offers regional Gallic dishes and snacks. 17 Queensberry Place, SW7. ℂ 020/7073-1350. www.institut-francais.org.uk/cineteensandkids. Tickets £5 ($10) adults, £3 ($6) under-18s. Tube: S. Kensington.

**Clapham Picture House** 🎬  This eclectic local cinema showing both mainstream and art-house films caters to parents in two ways: with its Saturday-morning Kids Club for 3- to 10-year-olds, preceded by creative activities and games; and with its Big Scream Parents and Babies Club every Thursday morning, which allows moms or dads to enjoy one of two full-length features, including current blockbusters, classics, and foreign-language films, with babes on their laps (£6/$12 including tea/coffee and a pastry). The Clapham has baby-changing, a stroller park, and a good cafe/bar, and hosts bimonthly film quizzes. 76 Venn St., SW4. ℂ 08707/550061. www.picturehouses.co.uk. Tickets Kid's Club [bp]3 ($6). Tube: Brixton.

**Electric Cinema** 🎬  This achingly trendy Notting Hill cinema stands out for its comfy and roomy leather seating (including sofas, footstools, and tables for food and drink). It hosts a Kids' Club on Saturdays, showing new releases suitable for different ages, and "Electric Scream!" parents'/caregivers' and under-1s' screenings on Monday afternoons; tickets for the latter cost £7.50 ($15) with a footstool and £5 ($10) without. The bar at the back eschews popcorn in favor of calamari-in-a-cup, rice crackers, brownies, and cappuccino. 191 Portobello Rd., W11. ℂ 020/7908-9696. www.electriccinema.co.uk. Tickets Kid's Club £4.50 ($9). Tube: Ladbroke Grove.

**Everyman Cinema Club**  Here's another chi-chi local cinema with handcrafted leather sofas and armchairs, primarily of interest to parents because of its "Everyman Baby Scream" parents'/caretakers' and babies' showings (£7.50/$15 per adult; advance booking required) in its luxurious second screening lounge every Wednesday and Thursday. You can bring older kids along to these, too, providing the film's rating allows it; alternatively, some of the films showing in the regular program are suitable for older kids Afterward, there's a cafe for cakes and excellent coffee. Note that the venue also hosts Culture Kids music sessions for preschoolers. 5 Holly Bush Vale, NW3. ℂ 08700/664777. www.everymancinema.com. Tickets for standard seats on regular films £6 ($12). Tube: Hampstead.

**Gate Picturehouse**  This is one of London's most atmospheric cinemas, set in a converted coffee palace boasting Edwardian plasterwork and red velvet armchair seating. Part of the same chain as the Clapham Picture House (see above), it hosts a similar Saturday-morning Kids' Club, with activities and a screening. 87 Notting Hill Gate, W11. ℂ 08707/550063. www.picturehouses.co.uk. Tickets Kid's Club £3 ($6). Tube: Notting Hill Gate.

**Ritzy**  This restored five-screen Edwardian cinema, another of the Picturehouse chain (see the Clapham and Gate, above), also offers a Saturday-morning Kids' Club for 3 to 12-year-olds, but there are no accompanying activities, so it's cheaper than at the other venues. There's also another popular weekly "Big Scream!" on Friday mornings; tickets (£6/$12) include tea or coffee in the funky cafe/bar. Ask, too, about the good-value family tickets for four or five on regular screenings. Coldharbour Lane, Brixton, SW2. (C) 08707/550060. www.picturehouses.co.uk. Tickets Kids' Club £1/$2. Tube: Brixton.

**Sing-a-Long-a-Sound-of-Music (Prince Charles Cinema)**   This well-known cheapie cinema just off Leicester Square was the original venue for the Sing-a-Long international phenomenon that allows audiences to burst into song in accompaniment to some of their favorite movies. *The Sound of Music,* which shows approximately twice a month, is screened with subtitles, and audience members are encouraged to come dressed as nuns. It's worth stressing that this is an option for older kids, as the screenings are at 7:30pm on weekends and can get a little rowdy. It's not cheap, either. 7 Leicester Place, WC2. (C) 0870/811-559. www.princecharlescinema.com. Tickets £14 ($28). Tube: Leicester Sq.

## IMAX CINEMAS

London has two "image maximum" cinemas that create the illusion, through huge screens and huge sound systems, that the film you're watching is happening all around the audience. On the South Bank, the dramatic circular **BFI London Imax Cinema** (1 Charlie Chaplin Walk, SE1; (C) 0870/787-2525; www.bfi.org.uk/showing/imax) houses Britain's biggest cinema screen (the height of five double-decker buses), viewed from 14 tiered rows of seats that allow everyone—kids included—to enjoy unobstructed views. Screenings range between specially made 3-D shows, about wildlife, the deep sea, or outer space, and new releases—some, such as *Harry Potter and the Order of the Phoenix,* shown with a 3-D finale. Tickets are £8 to £12 ($16–$24) for adults, £5 to £9.75 ($10–$20) for kids 4 to 14, free to under-3s.

The second IMAX is at the **Science Museum** (p. 150); it shows the same specially commissioned nature- and space-based shows but in greater variety, including, new in 2007, *Dinosaurs Alive! 3D.* Prices are £7.50 ($15) adults, £6 ($12) children, £4 ($8) for a family of four.

## 6 Spectator Sports

In 2007 the Millennium Dome in east London reopened as **The O2** (www.theo2.co.uk) an entertainment destination that hosts sports events such as National Basketball Association matches and ice hockey. It's scheduled to host certain events in the 2012 London Olympics, including the gymnastics and basketball finals.

**Football** (soccer for Brits) has almost assumed the status of a national religion, but it's neither a cheap interest to take up, nor is it easy to get into a top match. The English football season runs from August to May. Within that time span there are a number of major tournaments, including the Football Association Cup. Premiership (top-division) matches (which involved London teams Arsenal, Tottenham Hotspur, Fulham, Chelsea, Charlton Athletic, and Crystal Palace at press time, though the latter was looking likely to drop off the list) last 90 minutes, not including an interval of about 15 minutes. Saturday at 3pm is the best time to catch a game at all stadiums, which thankfully now have special family enclosures. Tickets cost £40 ($80) and upwards (about half that for kids), but most matches are heavily oversubscribed (club members get priority on tickets). If your heart's really set on a match, try west London's Queen's Park Rangers ((C) 0870/112-1967; www.qpr.co.uk), who are in the less-prestigious Nationwide League. Also check out www.4thegame.com for team and match details and general soccer news.

The stunning new national stadium, **Wembley** (www.wembleystadium.com), hosts major football matches during the World Cup and other tournaments, plus rugby and athletics (to include Olympic events in 2012). See the website for news about stadium tours, scheduled to launch as this guide went to press. You can sign up for the **Chelsea Football Club Stadium Tour** (✆ **0870/603-0005;** www.chelseafc.com), a 75-minute behind-the-scenes look at London's biggest football stadium. Visitors see the changing rooms and can have their photo taken next to their favorite player's shirt, and have access to the new Centenary Museum, with old photos and paraphernalia, a Champions' Room dedicated to the title-winning side of 2004–05, and videos. There are three tours daily Monday to Friday and two daily on the weekends; they cost £14 ($28) for adults, £8 ($16) for children, with a 10% discount if booked online.

For another great London sporting institution—Rugby Union—your best bet is to travel a little south out of the capital to **Twickenham Stadium** (✆ **0870/405-2000;** www.rfu.com), where you might be lucky enough to catch an England international match, or at least a club or county game. On nonmatch days, fans can take a guided tour of the stadium and visit its **Museum of Rugby.** (Combined tickets cost £10/$20 adults; £7/$14 kids; £34/$68 family of two adults and three kids.)

Watching **cricket** is a leisurely summer pastime best enjoyed at the world-famous **Lord's** (St. John's Wood Rd., NW8; ✆ 020/7616-8595; www.lords.org), which hosts international test matches between Britain and Australia, the West Indies, India, or New Zealand. Daily 1-hour, 40-minute tours (£10/$20 adults, £6/$12, £27/$54 family) of the ground include the players' dressing room, the indoor school with its 160kmph (100-mph) bowling machines, and the MCC Museum with paintings, photos, and artifacts tracing the history of the sport. Kids always seem to be most fascinated by the stuffed sparrow here, which was killed by a shot in 1936 (the ball is displayed, too).

Undoubtedly, though, the quintessential sporting event of the British summer is **Wimbledon** ⟨⟨⟨ (✆ 020/8946-6131; www.wimbledon.com), where some of the world's best tennis players battle it out at the All England Lawn Tennis & Croquet Club from roughly the last week in June to the first week in July, with matches lasting from about 2pm until dark. With unpredictable kids in tow, you probably won't want to bother with applying to enter the public ballot for tickets the previous year; nor will you want to queue for several hours on the day (gates open at 10:30am); instead, make do with standing room, and just enjoy the strawberries and cream on sale and the sense of occasion. If you're not in town at the right time of year, the **Wimbledon Lawn Tennis Museum** has garnered awards since reopening after a multimillion-pound transformation in 2006. A Reaction Zone challenges you to turn off as many illuminated balls as possible in 30 seconds, a 200-degree 3-D cinema screen allows you to experience the feeling of playing on Centre Court, and a walk-through of the men's dressing room shows how it looked in the 1980s, with commentary by John McEnroe. Entry costs £7.50 ($15) adults, £4.75 ($9.50) kids, or it's included in the price of a behind-the-scenes tour (£15/$30 adults, £11/$22 kids).

Those with equestrian kids will be glad to learn that all a **day at the races** is an affordable treat, with all British racecourses offering free admission for accompanied children under 16 or 17 (adults pay an average of £12/$24). Kempton Park, Sandown Park, Epsom Downs (home of the world-famous Derby), Windsor, and Ascot (best known for the exuberant headgear worn at its royal meet, and its superb thoroughbreds) are all within 50km (31 miles) of London. Older kids will love seeing racehorses and jockeys close up and watching the bookies in action, while younger children will be greeted with nurseries at some courses and bouncy castles and the like on weekends and holidays. The comprehensive website www.britishracecourses.org has details on family evenings and family fun days with free kids' entertainment such as face-painting, traveling farms, soccer coaching, and competitions.

For an altogether different kind of day at the races, and a real London institution, head east to **Walthamstow Stadium** (☎ **020/8498-3300;** www.wsgreyhound. co.uk), a world-famous **greyhound racing** track. The atmosphere is always electric, and you can usually spot some real old East Enders dressed up in all their finery. Children under 15 are admitted free, and all visitors get in free Monday and Friday for the lunchtime races. (It's £3–£6/$6–$12 to get into the evening meetings, depending on which enclosure you choose.)

## 7 Story Hours

For **bookstores** with regular storytelling slots, see p. 225. Many of the **museums** (p. 157) and **galleries** (p. 175) listed in chapter 7 have story hours as part of their kids' activities programs.

All **libraries** in the central Westminster area (which includes Charing Cross, Marylebone, Mayfair, and Mayfair) offer under-5s story times based around storytelling, singing, and rhymes, and ending in a craft activity that can be taken home or displayed in the library. There are also toys to play with, and refreshments are available. One of the best programs is at Pimlico library, where there are also "Wiggle and Jiggle" movement session, a "Baby Bounce and Rhyme Time," under-5s sessions in Spanish, and a "Just for Dads" session. Days and times vary from venue to venue and are subject to change; see www.westminster.gov.uk for the latest information. The venerable British Library (p. 157) also has storytelling sessions during summer vacations.

**The Crocodile Club**     This weekly 90-minute storytelling, puppetry, singing session, and role-playing session for kids ages 2 to 5 is held in a charming antiques shop in the family-friendly enclave of Muswell Hill in north London. Tots get to create their own adventure, whether it be a voyage to the bottom of the sea or a journey into space. The shop also has a cafe popular for its chocolate cake. It's handy for a visit to Alexandra Park (p. 209) or Highgate Wood (p. 210). Crocodile Antiques. 120–2 Muswell Hill Broadway, N10. ☎ 020/8444-0273. Tube: East Finchley. Tues 10–11:45am.

## 8 Arcades

If the rain won't let up, and all else really has failed (I can scarcely believe it will, but I know what kids can be like), your most central arcade is **Funland** (www.funland.co.uk) in the Trocadero Mall at Piccadilly Circus. One of the world's biggest indoor entertainment centers, it features state-of-the-art simulator rides, more than 400 of the latest high-tech video games, bumper cars, and a 10-lane bowling alley (p. 211). Parents can flee the mayhem for a few beers in the American pool hall or Sports Bar. Entry is free: You pay as you play, using cash or tokens. **Namco Station** (☎ **020/7967-1066;** www.namcoexperience.com), in the same building as the London Aquarium on the South Bank, is a similarly dark and noisy prospect, also with bumper cars, "techno" bowling with ultraviolet lanes (p. 211), and the latest simulators and video games.

If all this sounds a bit brash, make the effort to get to **Oriental City** in north London (399 Edgware Rd., NW9; © **020/8200-0009;** Tube: Colindale), which has the makings of a really great, off-the-wall family day out. In addition to its futuristic **Sega Dome** arcade, it has a vast Asian food mall with goodies from Japan, China, Vietnam, and Indonesia—at cheap stalls and in stores and supermarkets—to take home. Plus check out the Asian bookstores, housewares stores, salon, and indefinable shops selling Hello Kitty items and such. Hurry though—as this guide went to press, the center was under threat from developers (check the current situation at www.saveorientalcity.co.uk).

# 12

# Side Trips from London

There's so much to do in London, you'd be forgiven for not wanting to venture outside its boundaries. If you have time, however, some of the following attractions (many of them off the tourist trail) may tempt you away from the bright lights.

This is when having a car is a bonus: www.easycar.com offers competitive hire prices, but whoever you rent from, think about investing in an excess liability waiver or you'll only be covered for a fraction of what you will have to pay if the car is stolen or seriously damaged. Check that 24-hour breakdown assistance is included, too.

If you're using Britain's woefully inadequate and overpriced railway network, the **National Rail** number is ℂ **08457/ 484950;** or check www.nationalrail.co.uk.

## 1 Windsor Castle, Eton College & Legoland ⊛

30km (19 miles) W of London

The Thames-side town of Windsor packs a triple punch: It's the site of England's greatest castle, of its most famous boys' school (Eton College), and of Legoland theme park. You're unlikely to fit all the fun into 1 day, so my advice is to stay over rather than travel in and out of the City. Note also that Thorpe Park theme park (p. 182) is not far from Windsor.

It takes from 34 minutes to travel from London's Paddington Station to Windsor & Eton Central station, sometimes with a change at Slough; for times and fares see www.firstgreatwesternlink.co.uk. From a bus stop close to the station, a service runs direct to Legoland 3km (2 miles) from the town center. If you're traveling by car, Windsor is a straightforward journey west along the M4 from London, then south along the A332.

### EXPLORING WINDSOR

With 1,000 rooms, **Windsor Castle** (Castle Hill; ℂ **020/7766-7304;** www.royal residences.com) was built on the orders of William the Conqueror. Admission is £14 ($28) adults, £8 ($16) children 5 to 16, £37 ($74) family of five; hours are March to October daily 9:45am to 5:15pm; November to February daily 9:45am to 4:15pm. Windsor is the world's largest inhabited castle. It's been a working palace for more than 900 years, and when the Queen and Royal Family are in residence (a few days in mid-June), the State Apartments, furnished with treasures from the Royal Collection that include paintings by Rembrandt and Rubens as well as sculpture and armor, are off-limits. (Admission prices to the rest of the castle are reduced.) *Note:* The castle is often used by the Queen for state ceremonies and official entertaining, so you must check opening arrangements before setting out (call ℂ **01753/831118**).

The highlight for kids is undoubtedly **Queen Mary's Doll's House.** This palace in perfect miniature (on a 1-in. to 1-ft. scale) was designed by the architect Sir Edwin Lutyens and took 1,500 tradesmen and artists 3 years to complete. Each room is exquisitely furnished, and every item is made exactly to scale. There's even electric lighting, working elevators that stop at every floor, and five bathrooms with running water. From October to March visitors can enjoy George IV's private apartments (**"Semi-State Rooms"**) with their richly decorated interiors. Older kids will appreciate the drawings by Leonardo da Vinci in the **Drawings Gallery.** To make the most of a visit, ask at the desk for family **audiotours** and **activity trails** (available in English only), and find out about family activities and workshops hosted at weekends and in school vacations.

Parents should be aware that only bottled water and ice cream are available within the castle perimeter; if you need further refreshments, the town's many restaurants, cafes, and pubs (see "Where to Dine," below) are within a few minutes' walk—ask for free reentry bands at the Middle Ward or Lower Ward Shop. The town itself is charming, with several 17th-century buildings set along its narrow cobbled streets. **Windsor Great Park** (www.theroyallandscape.co.uk), where the Queen sometimes rides and Prince Charles plays polo, consists of a 405-hectare (1,000-acre) patch of woodland, streams, and ponds where you can blow away the cobwebs. It contains a deer park and the charming Savill Garden (open Mar–Oct; £6.50/$13 adult, child 6–16 £3.25/$6.50, family of 4 £17/$34), with its hidden, interlocking gardens; the latter's new visitor center has a restaurant.

**Eton College** (© **01753/671000;** www.etoncollege.com) is an easy stroll across the Thames Bridge. Founded in 1440 by Henry VI, this boarding school has educated 20 British prime ministers, as well as such diverse literary figures as Percy Shelley, Aldous Huxley, George Orwell, and Ian Fleming. Inside its vaulted undercroft, the **Museum of Eton Life** traces its history, with displays including a turn-of-the-19th-century boy's room, canes used by senior boys to apply punishment to their juniors (and birch sticks used by masters for the same purpose), and letters written home by students describing day-to-day life at the school. Casual admission (to the School Yard, College Chapel, Cloisters, and Museum) costs £4 ($8) for adults, £3.25 (U$6.50) for children. There are also 1-hour guided tours daily at 2:15 and 3:15pm, costing £5 ($10) for adults, £4.20 ($8.40) for children 9–15; no booking is required but call (© **01753/671177**) if you're making a special trip. The hours are roughly late March to mid-April and July to early Sept 10:30am to 4:30pm, mid-April to the end of June and last 3 weeks of September, from 2 to 4:30pm, but it's imperative to call in advance, as dates vary from year to year, and the college closes on special occasions.

There are various appealing ways to explore the environs. **Boat trips** of 35 minutes will take you to Boveney Lock and back, passing the castle and college, Windsor racecourse, and more (© **01753/851900;** www.boat-trips.co.uk) for £4.80 ($9.60) adult, £2.40 ($4.80) child, £12 ($6) family of four. Among other cruises run by the same firm are a 45-minute jaunt past historic Runnymede (where King John signed the Magna Carta, now home to memorials to JFK and Air Force personnel who died in World War II) aboard the *Lucy Fisher,* a replica of a Victorian paddle-wheeler built in 1982 for the Tarzan film *Greystoke* and also used in *Chaplin.* It makes a very short stop at **Runnymede Pleasure Grounds;** you might like to return separately to this popular riverbank picnicking spot with its children's paddling pool.

Fifty-minute open-top **bus tours** of Windsor, Old Windsor, and Eton (✆ **01708/ 866000;** www.city-sightseeing.com) start from Castle Hill. They take place daily from mid-March to mid-November, weekends only the rest of the year. The cost is £7 ($14) for adults, £3.50 ($7) for kids 5 to 15 (who get a free kids' passport with puzzles, games and a drawing competition to enter, and felt-tip pens), £18 ($36) for a family of four. Somewhat more elegant tours are available in horse-drawn Victorian carriages that travel from outside the castle (opposite the Queen Victoria Statue) down the Long Walk into Windsor Great Park. Trips can last 30 minutes or an hour, and run all year, weather permitting. The cost is £19 ($38) per 30 minutes for up to four (✆ **01784/435983;** www.orchardpoyle.co.uk). Lastly, the **Royal Windsor Information Centre** in the old Royal Station sells leaflets for two **self-guided walking tours** around Windsor (50p/$1), one 45 minutes, the other about 2 hours.

## VISITING LEGOLAND

This unlikely theme park, based loosely around the famous building bricks, has more than 50 rides and attractions, ranging from water slides and a Whirly Birds helicopter ride to carousels and themed mazes. Most rides are designed for the 3- to 12-year-old range; older kids might find it tame, but younger ones will find much to amuse them (there's a downloadable sheet on the website with recommendations for kids under 4). A key addition in mid-2007 was the Vikings' River Splash water ride through a fantasy Viking world created from Lego bricks. The park is open mid-March to early November from 10am to 5, 6, or 7pm, depending both on the season and on special events (including a fireworks extravaganza over several nights in late Oct and early Nov); check ahead (✆ **08705/040404;** www.legoland.co.uk) as there are sporadic closure days.

*Insider tip:* The already expensive entry fees have been hiked up—a 1-day pass is now £33 ($66) for adults, £24 ($48) for kids 3 to 15; a 2-day pass is £61 ($122) for adults, £47 ($94) for kids 3 to 15. So it's worth asking about money-saving packages, including rail travel, shuttle bus, and park admission, sold at most major stations in Britain. Alternatively, find out about nearby hotels offering Legoland packages (see below). If you buy tickets online and print out at home, you'll save a healthy £5 ($10) per person, and it will allow you to jump the main queue.

## WHERE TO STAY

Just 8km (5 miles) southeast of Windsor on the banks of the Thames at Egham, **Runnymede Hotel & Spa** (✆ **01784/220980;** www.runnymedehotel.com), sister to the Athenaeum in central London (p. 67) and The Grove near the Chilterns (p. 268), is a quite luxurious option with both classic- and contemporary-styled guest rooms—including family rooms with ingenious sofas that convert into a single or bunk bed as required, plus space for a cot (£5/$10)—and three lovely riverside apartments. The apartments, each comprising a double bedroom, living/dining space with sofa bed, fully equipped kitchen, and private terrace, are good for families, though you can't have a cot—for that you need one of the larger hotel rooms, which can alternatively fit an extra bed at a cost of £10 ($20). The apartments (about £250/$500 a night) also require a minimum 7-night stay.

The hotel offers a kids' pack (complimentary soft toys, coloring books, and pencils) and a kids' catalog full of toys and books for various age ranges, which you can have brought up to your room for a small deposit. The health spa boasts an 18m (59-ft.)

pool, a wonderful toddlers' pool, a gym, and a dance studio. Of the eating options, Charlie Bell's has a kids' menu with the likes of chargrilled chicken breast or Caesar salad with a choice of accompaniments (£11/$22 for two courses); a play area is near its attractive summer riverside terrace, and on the lawns are amusements such as giant chess. Legoland packages can be arranged by the hotel (with 1- or 2-day passes), starting at £249 ($498) per night for a family of four (with children under 12).

For those on a tighter budget, **Clarence Hotel** (© 01753/864436; www.clarence-hotel.co.uk) in Windsor offers en suite family rooms (three or four people) in an attractive building with a garden for £60 to £99 ($120–$198). Its Legoland package gives you a free second consecutive day at the park. The Legoland website (p. 264) also has a hotel-booking facility with park tickets.

## WHERE TO DINE
In Windsor, **Browns Restaurant & Bar** on The Promenade, Barry Avenue (© 01753-831976; www.browns-restaurants.com) is part of a countrywide chain with distinctive, colonial-style venues. The good kids' menu (£4.95/$9.90) basically consists of downsized versions of some of the regular dishes, including salmon and spring onion fishcake, and grilled chicken topped with proscuitto and taleggio cheese, followed by ice cream or fresh melon and pineapple with yogurt and blueberries. The mezzanine terrace with its Thames view is a buzzing area.

For what may be the gastronomic treat of a lifetime, travel a few kilometers to the picturesque 16th-century village of Bray, where chef Heston Blumenthal owns the legendary **Fat Duck** (© 01628/580333; www.fatduck.co.uk), holder of three Michelin stars and voted the best restaurant in the world, no less, by an international panel of experts in 2005. (Blumenthal, famous for his groundbreaking scientific gastronomy, has written an award-winning book, *Family Food,* about involving kids in the kitchen.) Though the restaurant welcomes kids, you may prefer the more informal (and cheaper) **Riverside Brasserie** (© 01628/780553; www.riversidebrasseries.co.uk) nearby, on Monkey Island Lane at Bray Marina. This used to be owned by Blumenthal; its current patrons believe that kids enjoy the same food as their parents if it's presented in the right way, so the children's menu features the same ingredients as the main menu arranged slightly differently, in half-size portions with prices to match. Adult mains, such as confit of seabass with crushed potatoes and fennel purée, cost about £15 ($30).

## 2 Roald Dahl Country & Beyond ✶✶✶
33km (20 miles) NW of London

Unlike Windsor, the Chiltern Hills an hour or so northwest of London are firmly not on the tourist track. Yet with the opening of the Roald Dahl Museum & Story Centre in Great Missenden in mid-2005 (supplementing the Roald Dahl Children's Gallery in Aylesbury, Whipsnade Wild Animal Park, the little-known outpost of the Natural History Museum in Tring, and the working steam rail museum at Quainton), this region now offers a vast number of kid-pleasing outings. And that's not to mention the fab discount shopping at Bicester village.

## ESSENTIALS
Great Missenden, Aylesbury, and Bicester are on a train route from London's Marylebone Station (www.chilternrailways.co.uk), with the journey taking about 40 minutes, an hour, and 90 minutes respectively, sometimes with a change for Aylesbury. Silverlink

(www.silverlink-trains.com) trains between London Euston station and Birmingham city serve Tring Station about 40 minutes away, though not all their trains stop there. Buses run between the main towns in the area. For local taxis, call ⓒ **01494/868699.** Driving from London is relatively straightforward—take the A40 out to Gerrards Cross, then follow the A413.

Whipsnade is about a 30-minute drive north of central London. You can catch a First Capital Connect (www.firstcapitalconnect.co.uk) train from St Pancras or King's Cross to Luton (from 22 min.); or a Silverlink train (www.silverlink-trains.com) from Euston to Hemel Hempstead Boxmoor (from 24 min.), then a 10-ride on Centrebus X31 (ⓒ **08707/444746;** www.centrebus.co.uk) from either station.

## ON THE TRAIL OF ROALD DAHL

The Buckinghamshire town of Great Missenden celebrates its most illustrious son, one of the greatest children's authors of all time, in the form of the **Roald Dahl Museum & Story Centre** ⓇⓇⓇ (81–83 High St.; ⓒ **01494/892192;** www.roald dahlmuseum.org). Hours are Tuesday to Sunday, plus bank-holiday Mondays, 10am to 5pm; admission is £4.95 ($9.90) adults, £3.50 ($7) kids 5 to 18, £16 ($32) family ticket for up to five. Visitors step through doors fashioned as huge chocolate bars and emblazoned with the name "Wonka" into two galleries filled with displays that range from the studious (handwritten research material and early drafts) to the playful (interactive bookcases and an exact replica of the garden shed in which Dahl wrote, famously banning disturbances by real children). It's suitable for kids about 6 and up. Cafe Twit serves coffee, organic juices and smoothies, sandwiches, daily specials, cakes and cookies, and more, and there's a deli counter and seating outdoors in the court-yard on nice days. The courtyard also hosts, again when the weather allows, free daily craft activities, and storytelling sessions at weekends in the school vacations (otherwise they're held indoors). There are also regular workshops along the lines of chocolate bar decorating or comic-strip making (about £3/$6 on top of museum entry; advance booking needed).

The museum has a self-guided trail of the surrounding village to discover the places that inspired the author, who lived at Gipsy House. You can't go inside (his widow still resides there), but you can visit his grave in the churchyard of **St. Peter & St. Paul,** which is often decorated with chocolate bars left by fans.

It's about a 10-minute drive along the A43 to Aylesbury, home to the magical **Roald Dahl Children's Gallery** at the Buckinghamshire County Museum (Church St.; ⓒ **01296/331441;** www.buckscc.gov.uk/museum/dahl), suitable for younger kids. Admission is £4 ($8) for anyone over 3. See the website for the highly variable hours; visits are by timed ticket and last 1 hour; booking is advised. This is one of a network of community-based Centers for Discovery & Imagination providing younger kids with imaginative hands-on play facilities. (Others include Discover [p. 161], the Livesey Museum for Children [p. 166], Hands on Base at the Horniman [p. 146], and Pattern Pod and The Garden at the Science Museum [p. 150].) Inside, kids can study minibeasts with a video microscope in the Giant Peach; send themselves into TV like Mike in *Charlie and the Chocolate Factory;* walk through an enormous book into Matilda's Library, full of books where they can discover more about Dahl's life and works; and ride in the Great Glass Elevator up to the Imagination Gallery with its Magic Mirrors, eyeball maze, magic writing wall, and Twits's upside-down room.

## ANIMAL MAGIC

The area's best-known attraction is **Whipsnade Wild Animal Park** (© **01582/ 872171;** www.zsl.org/whipsnade). Admission (including a £1.50/$3 optional dona-tion) is £16 ($32) adults; £13 ($26) kids 3 to 15; £1.50 ($3) for saver tickets for two adults and two kids, or one adult and three kids. You get 10% off admission with online booking except on family tickets. Hours are March to early October daily 10am to 6pm; last 3 weeks October, daily 10am–5pm; rest of year daily 10am to 4pm. The park lies at the northern end of the Chilterns near Dunstable, about 45km (28 miles) from its sister establishment London Zoo (p. 190), and is one of Europe's biggest wildlife conservation parks. It's home to larger animals such as elephants and rhinos, who appreciate its wider spaces, as well as bears, giraffes, Siberian tigers, hip-pos, camels, and pandas—around 150 species, in fact, spread over a 243-hectare (600-acre) site. The Jumbo Express steam train is a good way to see many of them without tiring little legs; kids ride free, and commentary is provided. If you've come by car, you can cruise the "Passage Through Asia" area. Car admission to the park costs an extra £13 ($26); if you leave your car in the external parking lot, the fee is £3.50 ($7). Espe-cially popular with kids are the Discovery Center, with sea horses, dwarf crocodiles, giant centipedes, Egyptian tortoises, and more; and for tots, the kids' farm with its shire horses, pygmy goats, and alpaca. Regular events include daily sea lion feeding and themed animal weeks, and there's a good playpark.

A more obscure attraction just a few minutes' drive away is the little-known **Nat-ural History Museum at Tring,** an outpost of London's mighty Natural History Museum (p. 148) until recently known as the Walter Rothschild Zoological Museum. Set in the town of Tring 53km (33 miles) north of London (on Akeman St.; © **020/ 7942-6171;** www.nhm.ac.uk/tring), it's open Monday to Saturday 10am to 5pm, Sunday 2 to 5pm; admission is free. Among the 4,000 preserved animals on perma-nent display are a giant salamander, an Indian pangolin, and a 2m-long (6½-ft.) tur-tle. The temporary exhibitions embrace such themes as local butterflies, and the folklore and myths behind fossils; some of the family events and activities (for many of which there's a small charge) tie in with them—the likes of butterfly mobile mak-ing, butterfly walks, and card-making inspired by fossils. Activity sheets and gallery trails are always available for 50p ($1) each; pencils, paper, and clipboards are loaned. The interactive Discovery Room features a Find Out About Yourself activity sheet, magnifying glasses to look at fossils, natural history–related jigsaws, and children's books. The Zebra Café has bottlewarming facilities and highchairs, or you can picnic outdoors or in the wildlife meadow across the street.

## WEST OF AYLESBURY

Train enthusiasts might like to stop off at Quainton, home to the **Buckinghamshire Steam Centre** (© **01296/655720;** www.bucksrailcentre.org). Admission is £7 ($14) adults, £4.50 ($9) children 5 to 15, £21 ($42) family of two adults and up to four chil-dren on "Special Steaming Days," when a full-size engine offers unlimited free rides, and miniature train rides can be enjoyed, too (at a small extra cost). It's less expensive to visit on "Static Viewing Days," when you can visit the steam museum displaying, among other items, a carriage in which Winston Churchill and General Eisenhower devised war strategies. Best, and costliest, are the "Special Events," which combine the attractions of the Steaming Days with activities and visiting attractions, such as a pets corner for children or appearances by Thomas the Tank engine or Father Christmas.

Nearby **Bicester Village** (℃ **01869/323200;** www.bicestervillage.com) is open Monday to Friday 10am to 7pm; Saturday from 9:30am to 7pm; Sunday from 10am to 6pm. It holds pleasures of an altogether different order, in the form of discount designer clothes and housewares outlets, including Petit Bateau and Ralph Lauren Boys & Girls for fashion-conscious kids.

## WHERE TO STAY

The top place to stay in the area is **The Grove** 🎔🎔, an award-winning country estate hotel with one of the country's most highly regarded spas and a golf course just east of the Chilterns inside the M25 (Chandler's Cross; ℃ **01923/296010;** www.the-grove.co.uk). Anouska's, its club for kids from 3 months to 10 (daily 9am–5pm; £6/$12 per hour) has an adventure playground, indoor activities such as crafts and storytelling, and a kids' indoor pool (parental supervision required)—although young guests can also swim in the large outdoor pool in the Walled Garden in summer, and over-8s can use the indoor pool in the spa between 9 and 11am and 3 and 5pm. Children's golf clubs, instruction, and tennis racquets can be provided; croquet equipment is available; and nature trails, treasure hunts, and cycling are arranged around the vast estate. Anouska's also arranges extra activities on weekends and during school vacations. In 2007, The Grove launched a summer "urban beach" in the Walled Garden, with an international standard beach volleyball court, a designated kids' play area, a beach bar, spa treatments, a concierge to attend to your requirements for sunglass cleaning and rosewater spritzing, and six beach huts with their own sand gardens, which hotel guests can hire for £95 ($190) a day (they're kitted out with plasma TVs, iPods, and Xboxes; one specially for kids is stuffed with toys). If you want to venture outside, the amenable staff can arrange family day trips in the vicinity.

Good kids' menus (plus coloring books and crayons) are available in The Stables and Glasshouse restaurants, as well as on room service (£6.50/$13 for two courses), and there's a special children's breakfast menu. Organic baby food is available, too. Older kids who prefer to order from the main menu are given a 50% discount in the Glasshouse. Colette's is a more grownup option if you arrange a sitter and feel decadent. Accommodations-wise, one child up to 12 can sleep in a parent's deluxe-category room, in a travel cot or a sofa bed, at no extra charge. Those families with two or more children can book interconnecting rooms in the contemporary-styled West Wing, with the children's twin room going for 25% the price of the parent's room. All rooms boast a fun, contemporary decor, and prices (doubles start at £280/$560) get you milk and cookies, mini bathrobes, and age-specific toy boxes in the rooms, and access to a basement game room with video and arcade games. Every room also has a TV with giant plasma screen, and there's a DVD library with movies for all ages. All in all, it's heaven.

A much less glamorous but great-value, family-friendly option is **Holiday Inn** in Hemel Hempstead (Breakspear Way; ℃ **0870/400-9041;** www.ichotelgroup.com), where, with at least 7 days' advance booking, it's possible to net a room with a double bed and a sofa bed that converts into two single beds for just £85 ($170), depending on the time of year and day of the week. On-site are an outdoor children's play area with a slide, swings, and rockers, an indoor swimming pool, and board game loan.

## WHERE TO DINE

One of the area's loveliest places to eat is the Cock & Rabbit by the village green at Great Missenden, a traditional pub housing a great Italian restaurant, **Cafe Graziemille**

(The Lee; ℂ 01494/837540; www.graziemille.co.uk). The house pasta (penne with a dressing of yogurt, thyme, olive oil, and wild garlic gathered in nearby woods) stands out, but there are lots of meat, fish, and vegetarian choices, plus a good range of daily pasta dishes chalked up on the board. Mains average £10 ($20). Food is served in the garden in summer.

Not far from Aylesbury, in the village of Shabbington near Thames, the **Old Fisherman** (Mill Rd.; ℂ 01844/201247; www.theoldfisherman.com) has a large riverside garden with play equipment. Outside you can enjoy quite good meals-in-a-basket, including an under-11s menu (£5/$10) of salmon fishcakes, scampi, and more (served with chips). The menus served inside are a touch more expensive, and in addition to the same basic mains (not served in a basket) give a choice of mash as an alternative to chips, plus fresh vegetables, peas, or beans. The adult menu is more wide-ranging. Don't miss the specialty local ice creams, such as blackberry or hive honeycomb, available in adult and children's portions.

## 3 Chatham, Leeds Castle & Whitstable (★(★(★

30km (19 miles) E of London

This is another offbeat tour, this time to the east of London as far as the Thames estuary. Its beauty is that it combines five very different attractions—two very eccentrically English little theme parks (one of which was brand-new in 2007), a maritime heritage site, a fairy-tale castle, and an atmospheric seaside town.

### ESSENTIALS

Diggerland, Dickens World, Chatham's Historic Dockyard, and Leeds Castle are best reached by car, especially if you are combining visits to all three on a trip out of London. (For train options to Rochester or Chatham, see www.nationalrail.co.uk.) The first is off the A228 (up from the M2) toward Rochester; the second two are just past Rochester and through the Medway Tunnel; the drive from London to all takes about an hour. Leeds Castle lies just off the M20 leading from Maidstone to the Channel Tunnel.

Whitstable is a half-hour farther along the M2; then you take the A299. Direct Southeastern trains (www.setrains.co.uk) run to Whitstable from London Victoria station, taking about 1 hour, 20 minutes.

### VISITING DIGGERLAND & DICKENS WORLD

The unique adventure park known as Diggerland (one of four around the country), set up to tap into kids' attraction to mechanical diggers, is set in Strood near Rochester (Roman Way, Medway Valley Leisure Park; ℂ 08700/344437; www.diggerland.com). Opening times are basically 10am to 5pm weekends, bank holidays, and daily in school vacations. Under strict supervision, kids (and adults if they like) can take a ride in, and perhaps even drive, various kinds of construction machinery, including dump trucks and mini diggers. Staff members are on hand to instruct and explain the machines' workings. For kids too young to ride, there are special play areas. The Dig Inn serves burgers, snacks, and so on. Entry is £13 ($26) for anyone age 3 and up, with unlimited rides and drivers except on the coin-operated attractions. Pre-booking isn't required but does afford you small discounts: It's £34 ($68) for a ticket for three people, then £11 ($22) per person, purchased online.

A whole different kettle of fish is **Dickens World** (ℂ 08702/411415; www.dickens world.com) a few minutes away at Chatham, which opened in mid-2007. Surreally set within a modern hangar the size of four soccer fields in the town where Dickens's dad used to work (in the naval dockyard), this "theme park" aims to bring to life 13 novels by Victorian novelist Charles Dickens, as well as the overall times in which he lived. Although the emphasis is squarely on fun, rather than the bleak world of poverty and urban squalor depicted in novels such as *Oliver Twist* and *Great Expectations,* the amusement is of a dark kind—the longest water ride in Europe, for instance, takes you through a Victorian sewer complete with animatronic rats and past a graveyard, and there's also Ebenezer Scrooge's Haunted House, a Victorian schoolroom, cobbled streets, and mock period buildings populated by costumed actors and entertainers. For tots there's a softplay space, rather tastelessly named Fagin's Den. Look out for snow and carol-singing at Christmas, a time of year oft associated with Dickens. Entry is £13 ($26) for adults, £7.50 ($15) for kids; hours are 10am to 7pm daily.

Chatham is also home to **The Historic Dockyard** (© **01634/823807;** www.chdt.org.uk), a maritime heritage site where Dickens's dad once worked. It's home to three historic warships, a Cold War submarine, and more than 100 historic buildings, populated by costumed actors. Galleries with historic displays include the old Ropery, where you can still join in with rope-making, and there's a Family Fun Trail and indoor and outdoor play areas. Some weekends a steam locomotive does the rounds. Prices (which allow repeated visits over a full year) are £13 ($26) for adults, £7.50 ($15) kids 5 to 15, and £33 ($66) for a family of 4; opening hours are mid-February to late March, daily 10am to 4pm; late March to late October, daily 10am to 6pm; and November, Saturday and Sunday 10am to 4pm.

## EXPLORING LEEDS CASTLE ✹✹✹

This ravishing, romantic fortress (© **01622/765400;** www.leeds-castle.com) is open daily from April to September 10:30am to 6pm and October to late March 10:15am to 3:30pm, although check the website for a handful of closure days. The grounds have longer opening hours. It was built by the Normans on two little islands in a lake and transformed into a palace by Henry VIII. Retaining its medieval and cobbled causeways, it is full of charming—and often slightly eccentric—attractions: a maze decorated with mythical beasts, with a secret underground grotto at its core; a moat with black swans; a Duckery with ducks, wild geese, and waterfowl; an aviary housing more than 100 species of endangered exotic birds (some of whom talk); a museum of dog collars dating back to the 15th century (some made of iron and bearing fearsome spikes); and a land train that motors visitors up and down the main drive. In 2007 the toddlers' play area and turf maze was complemented by the addition of the Knight's Realm playground, a huge adventure play space built entirely of wood, with a scale model of the castle itself, for ages 5 and up. The castle also has a hot-air balloon, but if a trip in that is too daunting or too expensive, you can enjoy a view of the castle and surrounds from a static tethered helium balloon that rises to a height of 120m (400 ft.)—rides last 15 minutes and cost £15 ($30) for adults, £8 ($16) for under-16s (combined tickets with the castle are available).

Inside the castle you can see some stunning interiors, including a medieval queen's room, Henry VIII's banqueting hall, and the 1920s drawing rooms of Lady Baillie, the castle's last private owner. Guides in all the rooms are happy to elaborate on its history. Tickets cost £14 ($28) for adults or £8.50 ($17) for kids 4 to 15. Especially good times to visit are during the summer open-air classical or pop concerts; for the Wildlife Weekends with their pantomimes; on the summer Family Fun Weekend; for the

Mythical Firework Spectaculars, complete with lasers, projected images, sword fighting, juggling, and fire-eating; and at Christmas, when there's an ice rink and other festive happenings. (See the website for a full list of what's on offer.)

## EXPLORING WHITSTABLE

Situated on the north Kent coast just to the north of Canterbury, Whitstable has been famous since Roman times for its Royal Native oysters. It still hosts a summer festival devoted to the slippery sea creatures every July, which includes a regatta, an oyster-eating competition, Punch & Judy shows, crab catching, and street entertainment. Whitstable is a great, low-key place to visit if your experience of Britain's often-tawdry seaside has been limited to amusement arcades and cotton candy. The seafront, littered with oyster shells, is lined with cute weatherboard cottages and fishermen's huts and boats. Streets bear such intriguing names as "Squeeze Gut Alley," home to art galleries and craft shops.

Horror movie fans will be interested to learn that actor Peter Cushing (the star of late-1950s horror films) lived here: He gave the town a viewing platform with a bench, and there's a display on him in **Whitstable Museum** (5a Oxford St.; ✆ **01227 /276998;** www.whitstable-museum.co.uk). Hours are Monday to Saturday, from 10am to 4pm, plus Sunday 1 to 4pm in July and August; entrance is free. You can view Cushing's makeup, props, artwork, and some film stills. The museum also has an exhibition on oysters, shipping, and diving—kids love the fossils, shells, and seaside wildlife; the model ships; and the life-size diver; as well as the full-size horse-drawn fire engine. The staff hands out drawing materials and clipboards so junior visitors can record their impressions, and some of the results are displayed in the museum. You can also attend frequent free family events—the likes of sock-animal making, minibeast microscope sessions, and photo safari trails.

From Herne Bay just up the road, you can embark on a variety of open-yacht trips from April to November (✆ **01227/366712;** www.wildlifesailing.com). A yacht trip out to the Thames Estuary includes a 5-hour seal watch (during which you can sometimes swim with seals), costing roughly £20 to £23 ($40–$46) each, or a more manageable 45-minute bird-watch, which costs £6 ($12) per adult, £5 ($10) for kids under 14.

## WHERE TO STAY

*The* place to stay in this neck of the woods is Whitstable's **Hotel Continental** (29 Beach Walk; ✆ **01227/280280;** www.hotelcontinental.co.uk), which has eight guest accommodations in old fishermen's cockle-storing huts on the shore. Six are for families—they have a double bed on the first floor and two twins on the ground floor, plus a bathroom, TV, beverage-maker, and private parking. For more space, ask for the Anderson Shed, a boat builders' shed overhanging the sea wall, with a sea-facing lounge, two double rooms and a twin room, and a fully outfitted kitchen. Family huts start at £115 ($230) per night, while the Anderson Shed costs from £150 ($300). On Friday and Saturday, a 2-night stay is required.

If you want to stay close to Diggerland, Dickens World, or The Historic Dockyard, **Holiday Inn Rochester-Chatham** (Maidstone Rd., Chatham; ✆ **0870/400-9069;** www.ichotelsgroup.com) has an indoor pool and toddler's pool, plus an outdoor play area, and kids eat free in its restaurant. A 10-day advance booking could net you a rate as low as £84 ($168) for a room with a double bed and sofa bed. Family packages can include entry to The Historic Dockyard.

## WHERE TO DINE

The attractions in and around Chatham have eateries and refreshment outlets of varying standards. For good food it's worth heading to Whitstable and the **Crab and Winkle** at the harbor (South Quay; ℰ **0845/2571587;** www.crab-winkle.co.uk), where you can linger over a meal—of lobster, local sea bass, or fish pie—because there's so much activity for the kids to watch on the quayside. Staff members are extremely friendly, and the kids' menu features ingredients that are wild, foraged, or organic where possible. Open throughout the day, it's situated on the site of the world's oldest railway passenger service, built in 1830 and named the Crab & Winkle line after some of the cargo it transported. Alternatively, get takeout from one of the many fish-and-chips shops and eat on the beach.

# Index

See also Accommodations and Restaurant indexes, below.